Education

Contending Ideas and Opinions

Stand!

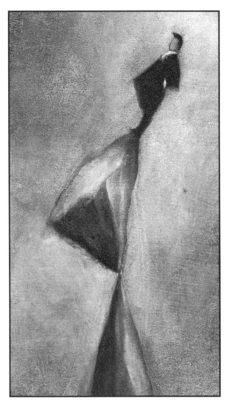

Education

Contending Ideas and Opinions

Academic Editors

Margaret A. Laughlin and Sandra M. Stokes

University of Wisconsin–Green Bay

coursewise
publishing
inc.

Bellevue • Boulder • Dubuque • Madison • St. Paul

Our mission at **Coursewise** is to help students make connections—linking theory to practice and the classroom to the outside world. Learners are motivated to synthesize ideas when course materials are placed in a context they recognize. By providing gateways to contemporary and enduring issues, **Coursewise** publications will expand students' awareness of and context for the course subject.

For more information on **Coursewise,** visit us at our web site: http://www.coursewise.com

To order an examination copy, contact Houghton Mifflin Sixth Floor Media: 800–565–6247 (voice); 800–565–6236 (fax).

Coursewise Publishing Editorial Staff

Thomas Doran, ceo/publisher: Environmental Science/Geography/Journalism/Marketing/Speech
Edgar Laube, publisher: Geography/Political Science/Psychology/Sociology
Linda Meehan Avenarius, publisher: **Courselinks**™
Sue Pulvermacher-Alt, publisher: Education/Health/Gender Studies
Victoria Putman, publisher: Anthropology/Philosophy/Religion
Tom Romaniak, publisher: Business/Criminal Justice/Economics
Kathleen Schmitt, publishing assistant
Gail Hodge, executive producer

Coursewise Publishing Production Staff

Lori A. Blosch, permissions coordinator
Mary Monner, production coordinator
Victoria Putman, production manager

Note: Readings in this book appear exactly as they were published. Thus, inconsistencies in style and usage among the different readings are likely.

Cover photo: Ian Lawrence/1998/Nonstock

Interior design and cover design by Jeff Storm

Library of Congress Catalog Card Number: 99-65615

ISBN 0-395-97370-8

Printed in the United States of America by Coursewise Publishing, Inc.
7 North Pinckney Street, Suite 346, Madison, WI 53703

10 9 8 7 6 5 4 3 2 1

from the Publisher

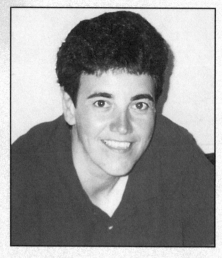

Sue Pulvermacher-Alt
Coursewise Publishing

Courage is what it takes to stand up and speak; courage is also what it takes to sit down and listen. —*Winston Churchill*

You've cracked the front cover on *Stand! Education,* and you're reading this opening note. Now I invite you to be courageous.

What you're exploring here are complex issues surrounding education. What is the role of the school in developing a child's character? Will national standards and board certification make teaching a true profession? Does assessment really promote learning? How has recognition of multicultural and gender issues had an impact on the curriculum and on classroom instruction? To what extent do educational alternatives answer the criticisms of public education?

As you examine these and other issues both in this book and online at our **Courselinks**™ site for Education, please show some courage. Sit down and listen to your instructor and your fellow students, and hear their positions on each issue. Consider the alternative positions carefully; then make up your own mind about each issue. Finally, stand up and state your personal position forcefully.

As publisher for this volume, I had the good fortune to work with Margaret Laughlin and Sandra Stokes as the Academic Editors. Winston Churchill would be proud of them both because of the courage they exhibited throughout this process. They sat back and listened to my ideas, but when I started pretending I knew the content too well (or made too many demands on their busy schedules), they were quick to stand up and speak. It has been a good collaboration, and I'm pleased with the end result.

The Academic Editors and I were helped by a top-notch Editorial Board. At **Coursewise,** we're working hard to publish "connected learning" tools—connecting theory to practice and the college classroom to the outside world. Readings and web sites are selected with this goal in mind. Members of the Editorial Board offered some critical feedback and posed some interesting challenges. My thanks to Sandy, Margaret, and the entire Editorial Board.

As you use our print and online resources and continue to build your understanding of issues surrounding education, let me know what you think. How'd we do in representing these issues? What worked and what didn't work in this *Stand! Education* volume and the accompanying **Courselinks** site? I have the courage to sit down and listen; do you have the courage to stand up and speak?

Sue Pulvermacher-Alt, Publisher
suepa@coursewise.com

from the # Academic Editors

Margaret A. Laughlin

Sandra M. Stokes

Margaret A. Laughlin
University of Wisconsin–Green Bay

Sandra M. Stokes
University of Wisconsin–Green Bay

As students begin their teacher education program, they are excited, pleased to be accepted into the teacher preparation program, filled with numerous questions, eager to be in a classroom in the "real world," and ready to interact with young learners who have a range of abilities and interests. They are also assessing their own abilities to teach, organize instruction, meet the needs of the students, work effectively with colleagues and parents, ensure that students achieve academic content standards, be professional, and still have time for a personal life.

There are no simple suggestions for helping teacher education students grapple with each of these topics and other similar concerns. Our advice is to encourage teacher candidates to read widely; to reflect on their personal and professional experiences; to engage in thoughtful conversations with peers, professors, experienced educators, and others who are knowledgeable of the content and concepts in education about issues; to learn about the context of educational decisions, which will help them recognize that many educational decisions are, in reality, political decisions; and to use their common sense.

This *Stand! Education* volume is designed to bring to your attention five educational strands as major current topics that address eleven issues through thirty-six readings. The issues identified are of current concern to teachers and are likely to be subjects of discussion in the coming years. Many of these issues are controversial, and there are no correct answers to the questions posed. Rather, we challenge you, the reader, to discuss the issues, think critically about your responses (however tentative) to the issues, and share your thinking with others. In addition, you should pose your own questions and extend your professional reading beyond the assigned textbook and selection of readings in this volume. It is important for you to consider alternative perspectives from other sources. No single book or article is ever complete, due at least in part to new research findings related to the teaching and learning process, student growth and development, and ongoing changes in society.

In this volume, each section is introduced by the WiseGuide Intro and learning objectives; each issue has a brief overview and illustrative questions. These features should help you as you consider the issues presented by various perspectives. A WiseGuide Wrap-Up at the end of each section summarizes the issues being discussed. We recommend that you check out the R.E.A.L. (Relevant, Enhanced, Approved, and Linked) web sites that are current at the time of this writing (and always up-to-date at the **Courselinks**™ site for Education). These web sites provide information sources to increase your understanding of the issues. At the end of the book is a "Frame the Debate" review form to help you organize your thoughts about each reading.

We would be pleased to receive your comments about the issues and readings selected.

Margaret A. Laughlin is a professor of education at the University of Wisconsin–Green Bay. Her interests and expertise are in the areas of social studies education, curriculum, foundations, and research. She has prior public school teaching experience and over 20 years experience in higher education in California and Wisconsin. Currently, she serves on the board of directors of the National Council for the Social Studies and is a member of the executive board of the Wisconsin Council for the Social Studies. She has authored and edited several articles and publications, and has made presentations at international conferences.

Sandra Marie Stokes is an associate professor of education and women's studies at the University of Wisconsin–Green Bay. She has been published in numerous journals, including The Reading Teacher, Multicultural Education, The Reading Professor, *and* Remedial and Special Education. *She has also contributed to monographs from the Council for Exceptional Children and an edited book,* Practical Applications of Language Experience. *She serves on the Research Committee of the Wisconsin State Reading Association, the Teacher Education Committee of the College Reading Association, and the Small Program Caucus of the Council for Exceptional Children's Teacher Education Division.*

Editorial Board

We wish to thank the following instructors for their assistance. Their many suggestions not only contributed to the construction of this volume, but also to the ongoing development of our Education web site.

WiseGuide Introduction

Critical Thinking and Bumper Stickers

Question Authority

The bumper sticker said: Question Authority. This is a simple directive that goes straight to the heart of critical thinking. The issue is not whether the authority is right or wrong; it's the questioning process that's important. Questioning helps you develop awareness and a clearer sense of what you think. That's critical thinking.

Critical thinking is a new label for an old approach to learning—that of challenging all ideas, hypotheses, and assumptions. In the physical and life sciences, systematic questioning and testing methods (known as the scientific method) help verify information, and objectivity is the benchmark on which all knowledge is pursued. In the social sciences, however, where the goal is to study people and their behavior, things get fuzzy. It's one thing for the chemistry experiment to work out as predicted, or for the petri dish to yield a certain result. It's quite another matter, however, in the social sciences, where the subject is ourselves. Objectivity is harder to achieve.

Although you'll hear critical thinking defined in many different ways, it really boils down to analyzing the ideas and messages that you receive. What are you being asked to think or believe? Does it make sense, objectively? Using the same facts and considerations, could you reasonably come up with a different conclusion? And, why does this matter in the first place? As the bumper sticker urged, question authority. Authority can be a textbook, a politician, a boss, a big sister, or an ad on television. Whatever the message, learning to question it appropriately is a habit that will serve you well for a lifetime. And in the meantime, thinking critically will certainly help you be course wise.

Getting Connected

This reader is a tool for connected learning. This means that the readings and other learning aids explained here will help you to link classroom theory to real-world issues. They will help you to think critically and to make long-lasting learning connections. Feedback from both instructors and students has helped us to develop some suggestions on how you can wisely use this connected learning tool.

WiseGuide Pedagogy

A wise reader is better able to be a critical reader. Therefore, we want to help you get wise about the articles in this reader. Each section of a *Stand!* reader has three tools to help you: the WiseGuide Intro, the WiseGuide Wrap-Up, and the Frame the Debate review form.

WiseGuide Intro

In the WiseGuide Intro, the Academic Editors give you an overview of the issues covered in that section. At the beginning of each issue, the Academic Editors explain why particular articles were selected and what's important about them. You'll also find questions designed to stimulate critical thinking. Wise students will keep these questions in mind as they read the articles for each issue. When you finish reading the articles for an issue, check your understanding. Can you answer the questions? If not, go back and reread the articles. The Academic Editors have written sample responses for many of the questions, and you'll find these online at the **Courselinks**™ site for this book. More about **Courselinks** in a minute. . . .

WiseGuide Wrap-Up

Be course wise and develop a thorough understanding of the topics covered in this course. The WiseGuide Wrap-Up at the end of each issue will help you do just that with concluding comments or summary points that repeat what's most important to understand from the articles you just read.

In addition, we try to get you wired up by providing a list of select Internet resources—what we call R.E.A.L. web sites because they're **R**elevant, **E**nhanced, **A**pproved, and **L**inked. The information at R.E.A.L. sites will enhance your understanding of a topic. (Remember to use your Passport and start at http://www.courselinks.com so that if any of these sites have changed, you'll have the latest link.)

Frame the Debate Review Form

At the end of the book is the Frame the Debate review form. Your instructor may ask you to complete this form as an assignment or for extra credit. If nothing else, consider doing it on your own to help you critically think about the readings for each issue.

Prompts at the end of each article encourage you to complete this review form. Feel free to copy the form and use it as needed.

The Courselinks™ Site

The **Courselinks** Passport is your ticket to a wonderful world of integrated web resources designed to help you with your course work. These resources are found at the **Courselinks** site for your course area. This is where the readings in this book and the key topics of your course are linked to an exciting array of online learning tools. Here you will find carefully selected readings, web links, quizzes, worksheets, and more, tailored to your course and approved as connected learning tools. The ever-changing, always interesting **Courselinks** site features a number of carefully integrated resources designed to help you be course wise. These include:

http://www.courselinks.com

- **R.E.A.L. Sites** At the core of a **Courselinks** site is the list of R.E.A.L. sites. This is a select group of web sites for studying, not surfing. Like the readings in this book, these sites have been selected, reviewed, and approved by the Academic Editor and the Editorial Board. The R.E.A.L. sites are arranged by topic and are annotated with short descriptions and key words to make them easier for you to use for reference or research. With R.E.A.L. sites, you're studying approved resources within seconds—and not wasting precious time surfing unproven sites.

- **Editor's Choice** Here you'll find updates on news related to your course, with links to the actual online sources. This is also where we'll tell you about changes to the site and about online events.

- **Course Overview** This is a general description of the typical course in this area of study. While your instructor will provide specific course objectives, this overview helps you place the course in a generic context and offers you an additional reference point.

- **Take a Stand!** Register your opinion about the issues presented in your *Stand!* reader online. You can see what students and faculty members across the country are thinking about the controversial issues presented in your text. Then add your own vote.

- **www.orksheet** Focus your trip to a R.E.A.L. site with the www.orksheet. Each of the 10 to 15 questions will prompt you to take in the best that site has to offer. Use this tool for self-study, or if required, email it to your instructor.

- **Course Quiz** The questions on this self-scoring quiz are related to articles in the reader, information at R.E.A.L. sites, and other course topics, and will help you pinpoint areas you need to study. Only you will know your score—it's an easy, risk-free way to keep pace!

- **Topic Key** The online Topic Key is a listing of the main topics in your course, and it correlates with the Topic Key that appears in this reader. This handy reference tool also links directly to those R.E.A.L. sites that are especially appropriate to each topic, bringing you integrated online resources within seconds!

- **Message Center** Share your ideas with fellow students and instructors, in your class or in classes around the world, by using the Message Center. There are links to both a real-time chat room and a message forum, which are accessible all day, every day. Watch for scheduled CourseChat events throughout the semester.

- **Student Lounge** Drop by the Student Lounge, a virtual "hangout" with links to professional associations in your course area, online article review forms, and site feedback forms. Take a look around and give us your feedback. We're open to remodeling the Lounge per your suggestions.

Building Better Stand! Readers

Please tell us what you think of this *Stand!* volume so we can improve the next one. Here's how you can help:

1. Visit our **Coursewise** site at: http://www.coursewise.com
2. Click on *Stand!* Then select the Building Better *Stand!* Readers Form for your book.
3. Forms and instructions for submission are available online.

Tell us what you think—did the readings and online materials help you make some learning connections? Were some materials more helpful than others? Thanks in advance for helping us build better *Stand!* readers.

Student Internships

If you enjoy evaluating these articles or would like to help us evaluate the **Courselinks** site for this course, check out the **Coursewise** Student Internship Program. For more information, visit: http://www.coursewise.com/intern.html

Brief Contents

Contents

At **Coursewise,** we're publishing connected learning tools. That means that the book you are holding is only a part of this publication. You'll also want to harness the integrated resources that **Coursewise** has developed at the fun and highly useful **Courselinks**™ web site for *Stand! Education.* If you purchased this book new, use the Passport that was shrink-wrapped to this volume to obtain site access. If you purchased a used copy of this book, then you need to buy a stand-alone Passport. If your bookstore doesn't stock Passports to **Courselinks** sites, visit http://www.courselinks.com for ordering information.

section 1
Democracy and Education

section 2
Teaching
As a Profession

section 3
Academic Standards and Assessment

section 4

Curricular Issues

section 5

Meeting the Needs of Students

Topic Key

This Topic Key is an important tool for learning. It will help you integrate this reader into your course studies. Listed below, in alphabetical order, are important topics covered in this volume. Below each topic you'll find the reading numbers and titles, and R.E.A.L. web sites addresses, relating to that topic. Note that the Topic Key might not include every topic your instructor chooses to emphasize. If you don't find the topic you're looking for in the Topic Key, check the index or the online topic key at the **Courselinks**™ site.

Academic Standards for Content Areas

17 Where in the World Are World-Class Standards?
18 The Standards Movement and the Emperor's New Clothes
19 National and State Standards: The Problems and the Promise

Mid-Continent Regional Education Laboratory
http://www.mcrel.org/resources/plus/index.asp?option=404

State Curriculum Frameworks and Contents Standards
http://www.ed.gov/offices/OERI/statecur/

U.S. Department of Education
http://www.ed.gov/

Assessing Student Knowledge

20 The Trouble with Testing
21 Portfolios in the Classroom: A Vehicle for Developing Reflective Thinking
22 Semantics, Psychometrics, and Assessment Reform: A Close Look at "Authentic" Assessments

National Assessment of Educational Progress
http://nces.ed.gov/naep/

FairTest: The National Center for Fair and Open Testing
http://fairtest.org/

Brain Research and Teaching

23 Cognitive Science and Its Implications for Education
24 Brain Research Can Help Principals Reform Secondary Schools

The James S. McDonnell Foundation
http://www.jsmf.org/articles&papers/EDWEEK1-96.html

The Brainstore
http://www.thebrainstore.com/

Character Education

7 Education and Character: A Conservative View
8 How Not to Teach Values: A Critical Look at Character Education
9 Becoming a School of Character: What It Takes

The Character Education Partnership
http://www.character.org/

Education and Democracy

1 A Public Educational System for the New Metropolis
2 The Educational Requirement for Democracy
3 Democracy and Education: Who Gets to Speak and Who Is Listened To?

Sudbury Valley School
http://www.sudval.org/

Gender and Multicultural Issues

33 Culture Defined: A Twenty-First Century Perspective
34 Focus on Research: A Conversation with Gloria Ladson-Billings
35 Multiple Literacies and Critical Pedagogy in a Multicultural Society
36 A Longitudinal Study of Gender Differences in Young Children's Mathematical Thinking

The American Association of University Women
http://www.aauw.org/

Individualizing Instruction to Maximize Learning

28 Parents', Teachers' and Administrators' Perceptions of the Process of Inclusion
29 The Deception of Inclusion
30 Bilingual Education: The Controversy

31 Programs for the Gifted Few or Talent Development for the Many
32 The Development of Academic Talent: A Mandate for Educational Best Practice

IDEA Partnership Projects
http://www.idea.practices.org

Renaissance Group
http://www.uni.edu/coe/inclusion/index.html

Special Education Inclusion
http://www.weac.org/resource/june96/speced.htm

Lemoore High School and Inclusive Education
http://www.caltash.gen.ca.us/lhsinc.html

The Council for Exceptional Children
http://www.cec.sped.org

Attention Deficit Disorder: Solutions for Teachers and Parents of ADD/ADHD Kids
http://www.addhelp.com

Bilingual Education: Focusing Policy on Student Achievement
http://www.ascd.org/issues/language.html

Multiple Intelligences

25 The First Seven...and the Eighth: A Conversation with Howard Gardner
26 Variations on a Theme: How Teachers Interpret MI Theory
27 Integrating Learning Styles and Multiple Intelligences

Multiple Intelligence Development Assessment Scales
http://www.angelfire.com/oh/themidas/index.html

Project Zero at Harvard University
http://www.pz.harvard.edu/Research/MISchool.htm

section | Democracy and Education

1

Learning Objectives

By studying the issues related to democracy and education, students will:

- Examine school reform designed to meet the ongoing needs of learners in a rapidly changing society.

- Reflect on societal conditions that help or hinder the creation of truly democratic educational experiences for young learners.

- Discuss who should control student learning in public and private schools today.

Education must be defined within the context of a particular society because education is responsible for passing on the cultural heritage and for improving individuals and society. In a democratic society, education is vital because the society is based on the concept of "enlightened citizens." As Thomas Jefferson (1820) wrote:

I know of no safer depository of the ultimate powers of the society but with the people themselves; and if we think them not enlightened enough to exercise their control with a wholesome discretion, the remedy is not to take power from them, but to inform their discretion through instruction.

Individuals must understand their cultural heritage; possess a working knowledge of the political, social, and economic factors that constitute human ecosystems; understand the rule of law, legal limits to freedom, and majority rule with minority rights; possess the attitudes of fair play and cooperation; demand quality in character; and work for themselves and others. And so our first priority and public policy goal is to ensure our survival as a democratic nation through the development of enlightened citizens. Within this context, education plays a dominant role at all grade levels. Education must be concerned with the development of reflective, democratic citizens within a rapidly changing technologically oriented global context.

Education includes learning from both single discipline and multidisciplinary perspectives and should address the following educational goals:

- Develop enlightened democratic citizens who are capable of participating effectively at local, state, national, and international levels of involvement.

- Appreciate and understand our cultural heritage, that of others, and the roles of cultural heritage in contemporary society.

- Acquire knowledge and apply skills that study the motives, actions, and consequences of human beings as they live as individuals and within groups and institutions in varied places and time settings.

- Experience the joy of learning about self and others throughout one's lifetime.

- "Learn to learn" so as to grasp complex ideas and how to create new ideas.

While these are ideals to which many have subscribed in the past, and which many still seek today, education has not always allowed individuals and groups to achieve them. Currently, education is directed to make schools more challenging, to raise academic standards even higher, and to provide young learners with the necessary skills for competing successfully in the global marketplace. Persons who teach in the twenty-first century will need to be well prepared academically in both content and pedagogy. Those who can will teach, while others will elect to prepare for a different career.

Education
for Democracy

Questions

Reading 1. To what extent is it likely that the proposed decentralization model of educational responsibilities will more effectively enable schools to meet the needs of learners? Is such decentralization limited primarily to large school districts, or is it possible for smaller districts to decentralize as well? Why or why not?

Reading 2. How would you describe the ideal democratic school? How much democracy is desirable? What role(s) might you have in such a school? What role(s) should students have in shaping their educational and learning experiences?

Reading 3. To promote education for a democracy, how much power, authority, or control should parents and the community have over schools and education? What role(s) should students have in making decisions about their own education?

To what extent do schools in the United States transmit democratic values and practices?

Today, various groups believe that education in the United States is not adequately preparing young people to enter and compete in the workforce. Suggestions for school reform are many and varied.

In Reading 1, Paul T. Hill argues for a decentralization of education decision making from bureaucratic centralized offices to that of the individual school levels as a way to meet more effectively the needs of diverse learners. For such a change to be effective, new roles for administrators, teachers, and parents would need to be defined, implemented, and evaluated. Several aspects of school decentralization have been put into place, but Hill suggests a new vision with both attractive and unattractive features.

Living in a democratic society requires people to participate in community decision making and to take civic actions based on informed decision making. These responsibilities extend to school decisions. In Reading 2, Benjamin Levin argues that schools should embody principles of democracy because it is right and proper and because students should have a voice in these decisions.

In Reading 3, Joseph P. Farrell discusses who has power and control of schools. He asks readers to reflect on this question and to consider alternative perspectives.

A Public Educational System for the New Metropolis

Paul T. Hill

University of Washington

In the decade since the publication of *A Nation at Risk* (National Commission on Excellence in Education, 1983), educators and policy makers have tried many different approaches to improving the performance of urban public school systems. The first efforts focused on raising course-taking requirements to ensure that more high school students received instruction in algebra, English, laboratory science, and foreign languages. These initiatives have not had the pervasive effects on K–12 education that their originators had hoped. Elementary and middle schools, expected to work at preparing students for more rigorous high school curricula, changed little, and many high schools relabeled courses rather than changing them.

Subsequent reforms have been similarly disappointing. High-stakes testing has improved scores on the specific examinations on which students and teachers were rewarded and punished, but it has not affected other measures of educational performance. Efforts by Ted Sizer and others to create new curricula, improve school staff commitment and morale, and introduce new instructional methods have led to the creation of small numbers of excellent schools,

but these have not been widely imitated or reproduced.

Urban public education has proven extremely resistant to change. Although there are and always have been good urban public schools, the disappointing results of recent reforms have brought public faith in educators and the educational system to new lows. John Chubb and Terry Moe (1990) have argued that the public school system is fundamentally unreformable. They claim that the trappings of public control—legislative rule making, daily governance of schools by political boards, civil service employment of teachers, and accountability based on processes and inputs—are fundamentally incompatible with effective schooling. Their chosen agents of change are antigovernment forces—aroused citizens voting in referenda or Thatcher-style state and national leaders—that will disestablish public education as an institution and replace it with a market based on publicly funded vouchers.

As the articles in this issue by Guilbert C. Hentschke and David Menefee-Libey (with colleagues) show,* professionals are generally willing to contemplate far less radical reforms of public education than are outsiders. Local central office administrators and teachers union leaders understand that vouchers and privati-

*These articles do not appear in this publication.

Paul T. Hill, EDUCATION AND URBAN SOCIETY, Vol. 29, No. 4, pp. 490–508, copyright © 1997 by Sage Publications. Reprinted by permission of Sage Publications, Inc.

zation would eliminate much of their power and many of their jobs. The public support necessary for such an upheaval is also lacking: To this point, voucher advocates have not been able to overcome voters' uncertainty about how vouchers would affect schooling.

There is a growing consensus in favor of greater school-level responsibility for instructional decision making and student performance. Support for school-level initiative might simply represent a swing of the centralization-decentralization pendulum. But it also reflects the results of serious research showing that many different curricula and instructional approaches can work, if they are thoughtfully implemented by teachers and principals who accept responsibility for the results. For over 20 years, research on school effectiveness has shown the importance of clear goals for what students are to learn, concentration of staff and student effort on learning, principal leadership focused on student learning, and habits of collaboration and sharing among teachers.

There is, however, great uncertainty about how to promote school-level initiative. Many site-based management plans leave intact the mandates, civil service system, and labor contracts that constrain schools. Superintendents have proven unable to keep their own assistant and associate superintendents from imposing new restrictions on schools; school boards have been unable to resist solving problems with new mandates; school district financial officers cannot find ways to create school-site lump-sum budgets; and teachers unions cannot agree to site-level teacher evaluation, salary determination, or firing (see Hill & Bonan, 1992; Malen & Ogawa, 1988; Murphy & Beck, 1995). Even in Chicago, where site-based management is backed up by locally elected school-site councils with the authority to fire the principal and request regulatory waivers, far less than half the schools have been able to make significant changes in staffing, staff training, or instructional methods (Bryk & Sebring, 1993).

To this point, decentralization has been an idea that makes sense in theory but has never been fully put into practice. Bimber (1994) shows that relaxation of a few regulations and mandates is seldom enough to change the way a school operates. He argues that the various elements of school policy—funds allocation, staffing, staff assessment, curriculum, and staff development—are highly interdependent and that none can change significantly if all the others are held constant. His conclusion, that school staffs can gain the initiative only if they are given control over all aspects of the school, indicates the need for far more sweeping changes in school district governance than most school boards, teachers unions, and superintendents have been willing to contemplate.[1]

Can Decentralization Lead to School Improvement?

What, if anything, can now be said about whether decentralization of public school systems is possible and, if so, under what conditions is it likely to lead to changes in instruction and improvements in student outcomes? In particular, how do central offices and school boards need to change, and what other sources of extra-school support are necessary if decentralization is to lead to widespread school improvement? This article makes a first attempt to answer these questions. It reviews the degree to which school systems' reform efforts have in fact created decentralization, and it identifies changes in the missions and capabilities of public school boards, superintendents, and central offices that must be made before decentralization can have the desired effects on the performance of public schools.

There are examples of individual schools improving after their staffs have been given new freedom, and a subdistrict of a large metropolitan school system (East Harlem) apparently won freedom from regulation and created many distinctive and effective schools (Fliegel, 1993). Some schools have improved after their instructional programs have been reorganized in ways that fit the special needs of students (Orfield, 1992). There are, furthermore, many examples of magnet and alternative public schools built successfully from scratch to serve academically elite or disadvantaged populations or to provide distinctive academic programs.

There are, however, only a few documented cases of existing schools that improved dramatically in response to a districtwide decentralization policy. Perhaps the best evidence for such changes in existing schools comes from Charlotte-Mecklenburg, where Superintendent John Murphy has rigorously pursued a standards and accountability approach: Many schools report rapidly increased student test scores, especially for minority students (see Bryk, Shipps, Hill, & Lake, 1997). Additional confirming evidence is provided by Bryk and Sebring's (1993) studies of Chicago school reform. They show that dozens of Chicago schools have adopted serious and plausible reform strategies and increased staff collaboration, actions that are logical preconditions for enhanced student performance but do not in themselves prove that instructional improvement has taken place. The same studies also show that a majority of schools have not changed in these ways.

Experience to date suggests that reduction of external controls on schools does not in itself lead to serious self-analysis or search for instructional improvements.

Specific external pressures and assistance, such as offered under Charlotte's CEO-driven decentralization plan and contemplated by Los Angeles' LEARN and LAMP initiatives, are apparently necessary. Without strong external pressures, few school staffs make even those changes that their local decentralization plans would permit. Bryk and Sebring's (1993) Chicago studies estimate that some number between one fourth and one third of the city's elementary schools have taken the opportunity offered by decentralization to make changes in curriculum and instruction. In other cities, only a tiny minority of schools have seriously reviewed their own performance in light of student needs or initiated changes in instructional practices. In Cincinnati, for example, schools took few if any initiatives during a nearly 2-year period when the central office was barely functioning because of vast personnel cuts. There, as in Chicago, many school staffs continue as before, some awaiting central office permission for any change and others operating as they did before the changes in the central office happened.

Such inaction may be due to many things. Teachers and principals may suspect that removal of external controls is a temporary phase, after which central office control will be restored with a vengeance. In focus groups of urban teachers and principals conducted for an unpublished study by the Education Commission of the States, many respondents expressed the belief that decentralization was a trick to get school staff to make decisions during a period of budget cuts and that centralization would be back as soon as the school budget increased. Decentralization, some said, is just another in an endless series of new initiatives adopted in order to create a sense of hope and momentum, and it will soon be succeeded by something else; anyone who makes dramatic changes now will have to unmake them soon. As the present author's earlier study of site-based management showed, most school boards reinforce this belief by enacting new constraints on schools shortly after proclaiming a strategy of deregulation (Hill & Bonan, 1992).

Within schools, the most senior teachers often resist changes in instructional methods and work routines. In anthropological studies of schools working with the Coalition of Essential Schools, Muncey and McQuillan (1996) found that most schools contained a core of older, tenured teachers who resisted review and revision of school missions and instructional methods. Richard Elmore (1996) identified an additional reason for staff inaction, that many of the new instructional methods advanced by reform advocates are so difficult to implement that only the most adventuresome school staffs would ever attempt them. As he observes,

Models of good practice we have developed . . . require deep and complex knowledge and understanding, . . . they are developed in hot-house settings by people with a high degree of commitment, and they don't travel well—when other people try to do what the models require they somehow don't get it right. Quality . . . tends to be synonymous with connoisseurship. . . . Most people don't share the rarefied sensibilities required. (p. 2)

Decentralization initiatives create the opportunity for school communities to assess their own performance and adopt serious improvement strategies, but they do not guarantee that school staffs will take the initiative. Few of the local, decentralization plans studied to date include the incentives and assistance necessary to guarantee that teachers, principals, and parents focus their attention on the quality of instruction and other services to children.

For Decentralization to Work, What Needs to Change Outside the School?

The expectation of spontaneous improvement is inconsistent with the experience of business, where decentralization is often driven by chief executive officers and involves dramatic and painful disruptions at every level of the organization. The decentralization movement in business has decimated central office staffs and relieved local operating units of many routine controls, but it has not eliminated chief executive officers or reduced their ability to set goals for the corporation as a whole or for individual units, make investments that upgrade staff and equipment, or take strong actions to close, restaff, recommission, or replace local units.

In education, as in business, change requires efforts to extinguish some behaviors and reward others. If school staffs are supposed to take initiative and responsibility, there must be indicator systems so everyone knows how they are doing and strong rewards for those who change and penalties for those who do not. This is as true for central office administrators, who must be faced with the choice between helping and getting out of the way, as it is for principals and teachers. Central office units whose very purpose is contrary to the reform will inevitably interfere with it.

Some school communities are complacent and need help recognizing the need for improvement (or, as some have characterized it, reaching the threshold of disgust with their own performance). Empowering school communities is the first step in decentralization, but public officials can give only a few extra chances to teachers and principals who have accepted mediocrity for themselves and their students. A reform must give public officials a repertoire of actions, to allow them to deal aggressively with schools that will not or cannot seize opportunities.

The results of a study of a dramatically transformed business organization bear directly on this problem. As Wilms, Hardcastle, and Zell (1994) conclude from their study of NUMMI, a formerly low-performing Chevrolet factory that is now one of the most productive and high-quality automobile assembly plants in the world, a dramatic turnaround requires three changes: first, a sharp discontinuity with the past, such as replacement of key staff, or, as in the case of the NUMMI plant, a close brush with unemployment that puts staff members in touch with the vagaries of the labor market and weakens their connection to the old ways of doing things; second, strong new ideas about how work can be done, such as Toyota's production method, around which the NUMMI plant was rebuilt; and third, forums for open discussion among staff and between staff and management about how the new method can be made to work in the current situation.

This formula drawn from Wilms et al.'s (1994) work on industrial restructuring is far more sophisticated than any of the theories of school system decentralization. It relies on staff initiative, but within well-established parameters. Professionals, managers, and blue-collar workers alike understand that their employment is not unconditional; they are hired on the condition that they work according to a basic philosophy of production; they are free to work together to adapt the philosophy to current conditions, but first principles are established a priori.

What does this imply for reform of public schools? Schools are not auto plants, but they are supposed to be productive organizations, not opportunities for staff to express their values or become more fulfilled persons. Staff and parent satisfaction is a means, not an end. And from the experience of other kinds of organizations, both productivity and staff satisfaction can come about through means other than full staff-level control of the production process.

As decentralization is put into practice, school-level reform must be supported by some systemwide leadership and quality control functions. The existing central office structure must be profoundly changed, and units dedicated to central control of schools must be replaced by organizations that set basic goals for students and schools and create opportunities, incentives, and assistance for schools trying to meet the goals. The next major section sketches how such changes can be made.

Redefining Systemwide Missions and Capabilities

Like most organizations, public school systems do pretty much what they are designed to do, and they are not much good at doing anything else. Local school boards were created to make policies of general applicability affecting all schools. And that is what they do, typically responding to problems that might occur in one or a few schools with a new policy or regulation that constrains all schools. The roles of the superintendent and central office bureaucracy complement that of the board: The superintendent advises on and implements policies that affect all schools, and the central office staff administers state and federal categorical programs, procures and maintains buildings and real estate, and manages districtwide programs, including curriculum, program evaluation, staff development, and curriculum improvement. None of these traditional roles inclines the board, central office, or superintendent to regard an individual school as a distinct entity with its own needs, problems, and strategies for improvement.

A system of empowered and initiative-taking schools will need to provide for monitoring of individual schools' performance, equitable admissions and treatment of minority and disadvantaged children, and intervention to change or improve schools that are performing badly. Because existing boards and central offices are not designed to perform these functions, what other arrangements are necessary? This section makes a start at identifying the kinds of external support and oversight that public schools need under decentralization. It suggests a far more radical upheaval in the roles and missions of school boards and central offices than is contemplated by initiatives such as LEARN and LAMP, which were designed within the education profession. The system suggested is, however, compatible with the vision of the local public school system as a basic urban industry, which is structured to respond to the ever-changing needs of a diverse population and a varied and unpredictable economy.

Public Accountability and School-Level Entrepreneurship

A public education system designed to meet the needs of the new urban economy will mix public accountability with school-level entrepreneurship. The school board and central office will not run or control schools; they will perform irreducibly public functions, that is, authorizing schools to receive public funds, assessing the productivity of individual schools and the district as a whole, ensuring that there is a large enough supply of effective schools to permit every student to attend one, and helping students whose schools have failed them find better alternatives. All schools will continue to need assistance, but those forms of help that are most useful if they are tailored to meet the needs of individual schools—technical advice, staff training, and business-oriented services such as accounting, building maintenance, insurance, and legal representation —will be provided by networks formed by the schools themselves, organizations funded by businesses and foundations, and by fee-for-service vendors (including, in some cases, school system central offices).

This vision is presented in detail in a new book by Paul T. Hill, Lawrence Pierce, and James Guthrie (1997). It proposes a radical alternative form of governance for public education, under which every school would operate according to a unique agreement that defines its mission, guarantees public funding, and provides grounds for accountability. These agreements, which would be similar to the warrants under which existing magnet and special-program schools now gain freedom to control their own programs and select only those staff members who fit the school's instructional strategy, could, if made explicit and formal, be called contracts.[2] Such agreements would have two parties—the local school board, which would waive most current rules to allow a school to provide a focused and distinctive instructional program, and the school itself, which would be contractually obligated to provide the agreed-on services, use public funds and assets responsibly, and produce student outcomes linked to state and district goals.

Under a fully decentralized system, a local school board would be party to many different agreements, one with each school. Every school's agreement would specify the amount of public funds it would receive, the type of instructional program it would provide, and types and levels of student outcomes it expects to produce. The board's agreements with failing schools or schools that did not attract students could be terminated. New agreements would be offered to groups or organizations that have run successful schools or that propose programs deemed likely to succeed.

Such school-specific agreements can clarify the relationships between individual schools and public authorities. They can allow schools to pursue their instructional missions free from the continual changes in policy and mandates that political school boards inevitably create. A system based on school-specific agreements can also lead to the creation of a diverse public educational system, one that takes account of differences in student needs and parent preferences and provides a variety of schools in order to hedge against uncertainties about what works best and what an unknown future economy will require.

The idea of school-specific agreements is not new. Public school boards have purchased private contract services for many years, and some privately owned schools now derive all their income from contracts with public education authorities. These schools usually serve other than mainstream students, for example, the severely handicapped or students who have dropped out of regular schools. What is new about the idea of decentralization via school-specific agreement is that all schools, including those that serve students without special needs, would have them.

The proposal for decentralization via school-specific agreements is based on a simple insight about effective schools. Schools whose students learn steadily and deeply are not uniform products of a bureaucratic culture. They have something that sets them apart: a warrant to be different. This warrant supersedes many of the rules that govern the public education system as a whole. Effective schools often select, train, and evaluate staff differently than other schools, and they make rigorous academic and behavioral demands on students. The warrants for being different in these ways are sometimes written down and explicit and sometimes based only on tacit agreements among the local superintendent, school board, the school staff, and outside financial supporters. But in any case, the agreements on which such schools are based are essentially contracts, specifying what mission the school will perform, whom it will serve and how, and on what grounds the school's special status will be continued or revoked.

Under this vision of decentralization, each school would become a real organization with its own staff, mission, approach to instruction, budget, and spending authority. In contrast, traditional public schools are bureaus in a larger bureaucracy. Today's public schools do not receive real-dollar budgets: Funds are spent on their behalf by the central office, and assets purchased (teachers, administrators, books, equipment, staff development programs) are allocated according to processes established by board policies, state and federal regulations, and civil service procedures. The result is that few schools can control staff hiring, promotion, duties, or evaluation. Within districts, schools in poorer neighborhoods often get junior teachers who have no other choices; because these are also the lowest-paid teachers, the real-dollar per pupil expenditures in these schools can be less than half what supports schools in better-off areas of the same school district. (See Hill et al., 1997, chaps. 2 and 6.)

Functions of School Boards, Central Offices, and Teachers Unions

In a system that operated via school-specific agreements, the local public school board and central office would be, in effect, investors and portfolio managers, causing new schools to be organized in place of failed ones, supporting expansion or imitation of successful schools, and terminating spending on failed schools. Under this vision, the central office would lack the power or administrative capacity to micromanage schools or compete with school staff members for control of curriculum, instructional methods, in-service training, or teacher selection and evaluation. What would such a central office look like? It is best explained in terms of the new roles for key actors.

School boards would no longer have responsibility for directly hiring, evaluating, paying, or dismissing teachers, administrators, or other employees for individual schools. In essence, neither school boards nor central office administrative staff would be responsible for managing day-to-day practical operations of the schools within their jurisdiction.

The two main functions of the board would be first, to enter into a set of agreements that would, in the aggregate, offer a range of programs and services that meet the diverse needs of the local student population; and second, to ensure that all children receive a quality education. To meet these objectives, the board would determine the needs of the district, create and maintain a portfolio of diverse schools to meet those needs, evaluate schools and provide information about all schools' performance, and close and replace schools that consistently fail their students. The board would identify the need for particular schools: For example, a district with a significant population of Spanish-speaking children might decide to run a bilingual elementary school, or a district containing a new software industry might want to provide a school whose curriculum was built around schools and software development. The board would then seek providers for the schools by offering seed money to a qualified group that wanted to start such a school, by negotiating directly with a proven provider of such schools, or by issuing a request for proposals. The board would monitor schools to determine that all admit students fairly (in particular that no school discourages applications from poor or minority families or selects students by any method other than random selection among applicants), that no child is obliged to attend a bad school, and that students attending failing schools are provided with viable alternatives.

A school board could also maintain quality by pruning its portfolio of schools, meaning the lowest-performing schools routinely could be closed and replaced. School boards would have to live in the real world, and they could not close or replace a school unless there were some more promising alternative available (See Hill et al., 1997, chaps. 4 and 5 for a discussion of state and local governments' needs to invest in formation of new school-provider organizations.)

With the school board functioning as a portfolio manager, the superintendent would become the chief executive officer of a highly diversified organization. Plans for individual schools would have to be evaluated in terms of their match to the needs of a particular neighborhood or group (e.g., immigrant settlement areas; students with special interests in art or technology), and performance would have to be assessed in light of the special needs and prior academic preparation of students. Although school boards would have ultimate authority, superintendents would probably be their main advisers in suggesting the need for particular schools, identifying appropriate performance measures for particular schools, supervising their evaluation, interpreting evaluation results for the board, and recommending whether the board should continue to fund a particular school or encourage formation of an alternative.[3]

Playing this role, the superintendent would be heavily engaged in long-range planning and analysis of the match between the community's needs and the mixture of schools it provides. Superintendents would no longer have direct responsibility for the day-to-day management of schools or for the management of a functionally organized central office that has the status of a monopoly provider of such services as personnel recruitment and selection, teacher evaluation, curriculum advice, transportation, food service, and warehousing. A superintendent would supervise a small central-office staff responsible for such functions as: writing RFPs for schools of types needed to meet emerging needs or fill holes in the district's portfolio, negotiating draft agreements with existing schools and new school providers, writing checks to schools on the basis of their enrollments, keeping school-based financial accounts, helping schools identify and select providers of staff development and other services related to instructional improvement, selecting contractors to evaluate individual schools according to general districtwide standards and additional criteria specified in their agreement with the board, managing a lottery-based student admissions process for schools that were oversubscribed, and publishing unbiased information about all schools' programs and performance.

Central administrative offices would lose many of their current functions but gain others. They would not employ large numbers of staff development, curriculum, or compliance specialists. They would, however, employ people capable of helping schools gain access to independent sources of help in such areas.

Under its agreement with the school board, an individual school could choose to take responsibility for structuring its own staff, educational programming, and school day. General district policy would no longer dictate such things as the number of administrators or teaching aides in a school, the titles of books in its library, or the discipline policy enforced by its staff. These decisions would be left up to the school. The central administration would provide basic accounting and funds allocation services for schools, and it would maintain a small staff to help schools find sources of assistance. The central office could also offer some services, such as building maintenance, food service, payroll, and negotiation with insurance and annuity providers, on a fee basis and at the discretion of individual schools.

Although school systems can decentralize to some degree under existing law, the full vision presented here requires changes in federal categorical program rules and state laws affecting the composition and powers of local school boards, the staffing and yearly calendar of schools, and teacher collective bargaining. These are discussed in Hill et al. (1997) and, in greater detail, in Millot (1996). Some of the necessary changes are already being contemplated by Congress and by state legislatures enacting systemic reform or charter schools laws.

Although several districts have cut their central offices as part of a decentralization effort (e.g., Seattle, Chicago, Cincinnati, Charlotte), none has developed a positive new central office model. In the absence of a specific exemplar, it is difficult to estimate the cost savings exactly. If, as Cooper (1993) and others estimate, central office costs represent 20% of all spending by school districts, a 25% reduction in those costs should result in a 5% increase in spending at the school level.

Schools would choose their own teachers. They might seek assistance in the hiring process from the central office or teachers union; they might also simply consult a registry of certified teachers or advertise job vacancies on the open market.

These changes would create a true labor market for instructional and administrative staff. Schools would make decisions about hiring, evaluating, and terminating their own staff members. On the other hand, teachers and administrators would be free to assess and select their workplaces. Schools might accept a district-set salary schedule, or some might prefer to let salaries be set by the market. In any case, schools could compete for good staff by providing incentives to prospective teachers, such as a good benefits package or training programs. Teachers could demand higher pay for difficult situations or heavy responsibilities, and schools could offer bonuses for high performance.

Teachers unions' roles would change, but unions would not disappear. They might still bargain with the school district over benefits, but pay scales and working conditions would be set by schools, constrained only by the terms of their individual agreements with the school board. Teachers in different schools could have different employment contracts; thus, unions would represent teachers in their relationships with schools.

Teachers would still need a professional association. Teachers unions would continue to engage in activities such as arranging insurance and other fringe benefits for teachers. They might also offer training for current and prospective teachers and act as hiring halls or guilds to help schools find teaching talent. Unions might even enter agreements to manage certain schools. If they ran some schools, teacher unions would no longer simply be labor;

they would also become entrepreneurs or providers, like professionals in other fields, such as law, medicine, and accounting. (This analysis parallels that of Kerchner & Koppich, 1993.)

Consequences for Schools and Neighborhoods

Schools would become independent organizations and legal persons, with the power to raise, spend, and invest funds, enter contracts for goods and services, hire staff, develop and administer their own services, enter leases, and expand or shrink their operations. Although most school operators would probably be community agencies and group of educators organized into nonprofit corporations or cooperatives, all would have to create businesslike structures for policy making and fiscal control. Some organizations might run more than one school, and even run schools in more than one locality. Most schools would be overseen by private boards of trustees that would be legally responsible to fulfill the school's contract with the local public school board. In most cases, the chief executive officer of the school would be responsible to the board of trustees for the school's educational performance and financial soundness.

Opportunities for profit-making organizations interested in operating whole schools would be limited, both by the finite amounts of public funds available and by competition from (theoretically) more efficient nonprofits. Whether they were profit making or nonprofit, all schools would have the same need to attract students and stay within their budgets. Schools would presumably follow a range of different strategies to attract and keep parents and teachers. Some would strive to attract the most advanced students, but only a few could succeed that way. Like private schools, most would need to present themselves as places where a student of average ability could do well. Also like private schools and charter schools, many are likely to try to provide safe, orderly, studious environments for economically and ethnically diverse groups of students. Most are likely to be conventional, but a few might follow niche strategies, offering especially innovative or unusual academic programs.

School operators would have strong incentives to offer high-quality services and to operate efficiently, but some will fail. As in all other areas of human endeavor (including traditional public education), a few school operators will indulge in nepotism, fraud in selecting students or handling money, or inefficient management. Schools that violate their contracts, discriminate against minority students, mismanage their funds, drive away good teachers, or lose parent support would go out of business, and local public school boards would need to make sure there were places for their students, either in existing or newly contracted schools.

A whole industry of small providers is likely to grow up around a truly decentralized school system. Schools would have broad discretion about what goods and services to buy and from whom. This would create a new demand for vendors of all sorts of goods and services to schools—accounting and payroll, buildings and grounds maintenance, supplies, food service, and transportation. Many of these vendors could be small and neighborhood based. As Ted Kolderie, University of Minnesota researcher, suggests, the form of decentralization sketched here would also create opportunities for small new private providers of professional development programs and specialized instruction (e.g., tutoring for slow-learning students; whole courses in foreign languages, sciences, and mathematics; and special enrichment courses). Although some large vendors might prosper by building strong local reputations and exploiting economies of scale, small neighborhood-based vendors might compete successfully, especially where schools adopt a "buy locally" policy.

Central offices and state-funded regional service districts might also compete for schools' business, but they should not be able to anoint themselves sole providers. A system in which schools control funds and can choose among independent vendors has a great advantage over a service monopoly by the central office bureaucracy: A school can fire and replace an ineffective provider.

Need for New Assistance Organizations Funded by Business and Foundations

Although decentralization should increase the amount of money that is spent at the school level, it is unlikely to change the imperative for schools to spend every penny they can get their hands on for direct services to students. Under decentralization, the shortage of funding for program development, evaluation, dissemination, staff training, and assistance to whole schools will continue.

If neither schools nor school districts can fully finance needed investments in quality improvement, from where can the new intellectual resources come? Some forms of high-quality assistance may ultimately be available only from the state education agency, colleges and universities, and independent organizations funded by businesses and foundations. Schools that want to incorporate well-developed approaches to instruction (e.g., those developed by Montessori or by Robert Slavin's Success for All design team) will need to affiliate with regional or national organizations. Schools will be able to pay some fees, but most high-quality assistance organizations will continue to rely on business or foundation grants to pay for their basic research, development, and self-evaluation, as

well as for many of the services they provide schools. Under the decentralized public education system sketched here, the need for such organizations funded by charitable contributions is likely to grow.

These needs put new demands on private sector donors. They might not require a higher level of giving than businesses and foundations now sustain, but they do require that contributions he guided by a clear vision of a decentralized school system. Some public school districts may offer these forms of support from public funds, and all should help schools find and assess the relevance of privately provided services. But a mixture of private and public assistance to schools is more compatible with decentralization than is a public monopoly. If school districts can fund their own operations by taxing school budgets or skimming dollars off the top, they can quickly upset the fine balance of school autonomy and accountability that decentralization is intended to create. In education, as in all other areas, the power to tax is the power to destroy. A rich variety of private providers of instructional improvement and business services is necessary for successful and stable decentralization.

Conclusion

The foregoing is a completely new vision of public school governance and management, but it is perfectly straightforward and commonplace in most other contexts. It assumes, as do the systems of contracts that define productive collaborations in the private sector, that clear goals and flexible resources lead to efficient arrangements. It rejects the governmentalist assumption that an enterprise seeking a public good must be overseen in detail by large numbers of civil servants. It embraces the idea that schools should be controlled to the greatest degree possible by professionals and the families they serve; yet, it provides for a new form of public authority that can adjust its portfolio of schools in response to new needs and that can take action to replace unproductive schools with better ones. This vision of decentralization also includes clear and permanent assistance and quality control functions for local business and charitable organizations.

In addition to these managerial requirements, it is clear that a decentralized school system must value ideas and embody them in schools. Better instruction is not just a question of teacher morale and technique. It requires each school to be built, like the NUMMI plant, on a definite philosophy of instruction. A school that is able to develop its own distinctive mission and instructional philosophy should be free to do so. But groups of parents, teachers, and administrators who have worked together for years in a regulated public school system may not be able to define or agree on a single educational mission or approach to instruction. If decentralization is to produce effective instruction, most schools must accept outside help, in the form of a mission and philosophy based on the experience of others. Groups of teachers, parents, and administrators that want to invent their own philosophy and methods would have the opportunity to do so. But locally invented schools would get no special consideration if they failed their students.

Two beliefs widely held in the education profession interfere with effective public action in support of a decentralized public school system. The first is the belief that the essence of public education is equity, defined as uniformity of practice based on the requirement that all schools must meet the needs of all children. No school so constrained can have a clear mission and a definite instructional approach, and although few existing public schools actually operate as this belief implies, it interferes with any deliberate effort to create a system of decentralized, diverse, and focused public schools. This new system is strongly dedicated to equity, in the sense of providing equal opportunity for all children to attend effective schools that meet their needs. It does not require all schools to be alike, and it holds public school boards, not individual schools, accountable for meeting all the needs and aspirations present in a metropolitan area.

The second belief that gets in the way of a decentralized public school system is that ideas about education can only be developed at the school level, through extended discourse among teachers. As great innovators like Deborah Meier have demonstrated, ideas about instruction can be developed in that way. But as Deborah Meier has also demonstrated by opening new schools based on her original model, a powerful instructional philosophy can be used elsewhere. The schools she has built on the philosophy developed at Central Park East Elementary School are all staff run but based on an idea that teachers and parents can readily understand and can be adapted to meet specific local needs. Many of the teachers and administrators in those schools might someday choose to invest the immense effort required to develop their own new approaches to schooling. But for now they are productively using an idea developed elsewhere.

In summary, creation of a decentralized system of schools for a diverse urban community requires many things in addition to increasing initiative at the school site level. It requires new public management capacities that let public officials, particularly school superintendents, oversee portfolios of distinctive schools, take aggressive action to close and recommission schools that fail, and recommission new ones. It takes acceptance among educators and parents that good public schools can and should be different from one another. And it requires organizations capable of helping schools choose and put into practice well-developed educational philosophies.

Notes

1. Anita Summers (1994) and other authors of chapters in a recent book by Hannaway and Carnoy (1993) question the ultimate promise of decentralization, on grounds similar to those covered by Bimber.
2. Hill et al. (1997) propose a fully developed contracting system in which schools would be fully independent legal persons and contracts would be enforceable in court. The discussion in this article takes a softer line, assuming that decentralization might also be founded on explicit agreements within a publicly owned school system.
3. Current evaluation practice focuses on programs that are either parts of schools or include all schools. Because individual schools are not now held responsible for student performance, little has been done to develop evaluation methods for whole schools. The Chicago Consortium for School Research has begun developing an evaluation framework for the increasingly independent schools participating in the Chicago school reform. The need to maintain universal standards of performance yet take account of the circumstances of individual schools has led the Consortium to propose a two-track evaluation system. It uses objective measures, including student test scores, to identify schools whose performance is low or falling and then follows up with detailed school inspections that lead to remedial plans, including school restaffing and closing (see Bryk, 1997). This two-step method, using objective data as a trigger for closer inspection rather than as the sole grounds for remedial action, parallels the practice of many businesses that manage diverse local operations.

References

Bimber, B. (1994). *The decentralization mirage.* Santa Monica, CA: RAND.

Bryk, A. (1997). *Democratic localism: A lever for institutional renewal.* Los Angeles: Westview.

Bryk, A., & Sebring, P. (1993). *A view from the elementary schools: The state of reform in Chicago.* Chicago: The Consortium in Chicago School Research.

Bryk, A, Shipps, D., Hill, P., & Lake, R. (1997). *Decentralization in practice: Toward a system of schools.* Paper prepared for the 1997 Annual Meeting of the American Educational Research Association, Chicago.

Chubb, J. E., & Moe, T. E. (1990). *Politics, markets, and America's schools.* Washington, DC: Brookings Institution.

Cooper, B. S. (1993). *School-site cost allocations.* Paper presented at the general meeting of the American Educational Finance Association, Chicago.

Elmore, R. F. (1996). Getting to scale with good educational practice. *Harvard Educational Review, 66*(1), 1–26.

Fliegel, S. (1993). *Miracle in East Harlem.* New York: Manhattan Institute.

Hannaway, J., & Carnoy, M. (Eds.). (1993). *Decentralization and school improvement: Can we fulfill the promise?* San Francisco: Jossey-Bass.

Hill, P. T., & Bonan, J. (1992). *Decentralization and accountability in public education.* Santa Monica, CA: RAND.

Hill, P. T., Pierce, L., & Guthrie, J. (1997). *Reinventing public education: How contact schools can transform American education.* Chicago: University of Chicago Press.

Kerchner, C. T., & Koppich, J. E. (1993). *A union of professionals: Labor relations and educational reform.* New York: Teachers College.

Malen, B., & Ogawa, R. T. (1988). Professional-patron influence on site-based governance councils: A confounding case study. *Educational Evaluation and Policy Analysis, 10*(4), 251–270.

Millot, M. D. (1996). *Autonomy, accountability and the values of public education: A comparative assessment of charter school statutes leading to model legislation.* Seattle: University of Washington–RAND Center on Reinventing Public Education.

Muncey, D. E., & McQuillan, P. J. (1996). *Reform and resistance in schools and classrooms: An ethnographic view of the coalition of essential schools.* New Haven, CT: Yale University Press.

Murphy, J., & Beck, L. G. (1995). *School-based management as school reform: Taking stock.* Thousand Oaks, CA: Corwin.

National Commission on Excellence in Education. (1983). *A nation at risk: The imperative for educational reform.* Washington, DC: Government Printing Office.

Orfield, G. (1992, July). *Desegregation and educational change in San Francisco: Findings and recommendations on consent decree implementation.* Submitted to Judge William Orrick, U.S. District Court, San Francisco.

Summers, A. A. (1994). Review of Hannaway and Carnoy. *Journal of Policy Analysis and Management, 13*(3), 608–609.

Wilms, W. W., Hardcastle, A. J., & Zell, D. M. (1994, Fall). Cultural transformation at NUMMI. *Sloan Management Review,* pp. 99–113.

Form at end of book

The Educational Requirement for Democracy

Benjamin Levin

University of Manitoba
Winnipeg, Manitoba

Abstract

The ideals underlying education are essentially similar to those underlying democracy, suggesting that schools should embody principles of democracy for students as part of a sound education. Changes in social conditions make this requirement even more important today. School practices, however, are far from democratic in most cases, even though the arguments against democratic practices are not strong. The article concludes with suggestions for democratic practices in working with students.

"*I know, but I do not accept. And I am not resigned.*"
—Edna St. Vincent Millay, "Dirge without Music"

Introduction

This article probes the relationship between democracy and education.[1] I will ask what arrangements for schooling are consistent both with ideals of democracy and with ideals of education, especially in the context of changing social conditions. These words "democracy" and "education" are among the most highly charged in our language. In addition to their de-notative meanings, they each carry a considerable weight of emotional content. They are value-laden words. When thinking about the values that inform these two concepts, what may we say about their linkage in the institution of schooling? In particular, I will focus on the appropriate role and treatment of students in a school that seeks to embody democratic ideals. I will not approach this problem from the point of view of rights, but instead from the standpoint of the values of both democracy and education, and what they require of us.

Ideas are shaped by our individual and collective biographies. My own ideas about democracy were affected strongly by growing up in a household where politics was a daily feature at the dinner table, and where children were treated as people whose ideas and opinions mattered. As a high school student I was heavily involved in efforts to organize a students' union among high schools in my community. That experience, in which I discovered that school administrators were at best nervous about and at worst totally opposed to granting students a greater role in the schools, has also had a powerful impact on my thinking about schools and democracy.

My experience was far from unique. The late 1960s were the heyday of youth protest, of the questioning of all kinds of institutions and

---

Questions

How would you describe the ideal democratic school?

How much democracy is desirable?

What role(s) might you have in such a school?

What role(s) should students have in shaping their educational and learning experiences?

their rules. In the 1960s, Edgar Friedenberg, Paul Goodman, and others wrote about the ways in which schools demeaned students, and made it clear that they—the students—were of little account. Students' ideas, beliefs, and thoughts didn't matter. We were simply to do what we were told, and if what we were told did not make sense to us, that was our problem.

The Idea of Democracy

Many concepts of democracy can be found in the literature, although it is surprising how often one encounters a piece on democracy in which the term is not defined. One common view of democracy is to see it as formal politics: voting, elections, political parties, and so on. This tendency may be especially strong today, when everything is being compared to a market, and democracy is seen as another market choice—in this case one involving the supply of and demand for policies or politicians. There is a school of thought in political theory that takes political activity to be a form of consumer preference. Canadian political theorist C. B. Macpherson, who does not endorse this view, describes it this way: "The purpose of democracy is to register the desires of people as they are, not to contribute to what they might be or might wish to be. Democracy is simply a market mechanism: the voters are the consumers; the politicians are the entrepreneurs" (1977, p. 79).

Another sense of democracy, one much more common in education, involves participative processes at the action level. The central idea here is that people should be closely and extensively involved in making decisions that affect them. Pearson, borrowing from Gutmann, described it as follows: "A democratic society, or a participatory democracy . . . is one in which its members are empowered to make decisions and policies concerning themselves and their society but where such decisions are constrained by the principles of nonrepression and nondiscrimination" (1992, p. 84).

Haller and Strike (1986) offer a third definition. They describe democracy as a process for making collective decisions in which the wants of each individual are fairly considered and each individual has a fair influence on the choice (p. 230).

These simple definitions hid tremendous complexity around matters such as majority and minority rights (Plank and Boyd 1994). For the purposes of this article, I note that in most definitions of democracy the key element is people's right or ability to participate in some meaningful way in the making of public decisions. Neither participation nor decision are easy concepts to pin down. Without providing an in-depth discussion of these concepts, we can note some of the problems. Does participa-

tion mean having the opportunity to voice an opinion? Or does it mean an opinion that carries influence on a decision? And what would "influence" on a decision mean? The problem of which decisions can legitimately be considered public ones is also troublesome. The language of "decisions that affect us" is not very helpful, since in some sense almost every decision affects many of us, or even all of us; surely we have learned that truth from the environmental movement. The boundary between public and private is a difficult one to draw, which is why the question has been of interest to so many philosophers, perhaps especially so to those with an interest in feminism (Greene 1988; Held 1984; Stone 1988).

Past Efforts to Extend Democracy in Schools

In schools, advocacy of democracy has usually had one or both of two senses. Some have asserted that educational democracy requires a much greater role for teachers in school decision making. This idea, quite common twenty years ago, has recently made a resurgence under the heading of "teacher empowerment" (Fullan 1991; Lieberman and Miller 1990; Rice and Schneider 1992). A second version of school democracy, also strongly advocated in the 1960s and 1970s, focused on what was then called "community involvement" or "community control." In practice this has often meant the creation of some kind of school council with parent representatives who have an advisory or a decision-making role in some school matters. A greater role for parents in school governance has also reemerged as an issue recently (Epstein 1995).

Efforts have been made to put both these conceptions into practice. A number of U.S. jurisdictions have taken steps toward teacher empowerment through various versions of what is called "school-based" or "site-based management," or through other, similar vehicles. Parental involvement, too, has seen a resurgence in recent years, and has been the focus of some remarkable experiments in England, in New Zealand, and in parts of the United States such as Chicago.

Without reviewing these efforts in any detail here, I draw the conclusion that neither practice has resulted so far in much significant change in the educational experiences of students. For example, in regard to teacher empowerment, Weiss (1992) studied twelve U.S. high schools, and came to the conclusion that a greater role for teachers in decision making did not lead to very much change in school practices. Murray (1992) found that the move to greater teacher involvement in Rochester had some positive impacts, but that these were quite modest. White (1992) came to a similar conclusion after interviewing one hundred teachers in three school districts, although she supports increased teacher involvement for other reasons.

In regard to parents, the literature suggests that meaningful involvement in governance is difficult to create and not necessarily very significant when it is put into place. Instead, we find that few parents get involved, that involvement may drop off after the first few years, that councils are often dominated by school administrators, and so on (see, e.g., Coe, Kannapel, Aagaard, and Moore 1995; Deem 1994; Furtwengler, Furtwengler, Hokomb, and Hurst 1995; Levacic 1995). In Britain, although budget authority officially belongs to school governors, financial decisions are being made predominantly by heads (principals) (Maychell 1994; Thomas and Martin 1996). In Quebec, a decade after legislation required the creation of local school councils, two researchers concluded that the effort "to grant more authority to the local school can only be described as a failure" (Henchey and Burgess 1987, p. 56). Most importantly, there is no reason to suppose that simply changing governance structures will refocus people's attention onto the important educational issues (H. Levin 1992).

Much of the literature on teacher and parent involvement, including that already cited, also points out the problems associated with changing traditional governance arrangements. These include the time required, the conflicts that arise, and the political issues that are often difficult to handle. In short, the creation of democracy is not a simple matter.

Particularly interesting has been the absence of attention in the reform literature on changing the role of students, who continue to be substantially excluded from the discussion about democratizing schools and empowering teachers. There was a movement toward increased student involvement in governance in the 1960s and early 1970s (B. Levin 1977), but it had little lasting impact. Some efforts have since been made to create school settings that do give students a major role in governance (Evans, Corsini, and Gazda 1990; Wood 1990). For example, Lawrence Kohlberg's concept of the "just community" has been taken up in a few schools (Murphy 1988). But these ideas have been more advocated than practiced; the ERIC system shows more entries for the creation of just communities in prisons than in schools (Carter 1986)! A few noble experiments may have been made, but lasting effects on the shape of schooling are hard to discern (Watts 1989). Moreover, most of these proposals do not make an explicit tie between changes in governance and the educational mission of the school; governance is seen merely as being related to, rather than as an essential part of, education itself.

There is considerable irony in a reform movement that advocates one kind of practice for its staff, and a very different practice for its clientele (if one can use that term to describe students who, after all, are *compelled* to attend school) (B. Levin 1994a). Yet the test of democratic practice in any institution should rest at least in part on the treatment of the least powerful. In schools, these are the students. I will return to this point later in this article.

An Alternative Perspective

That past efforts to extend democracy in schools have not been unambiguously successful is not necessarily a basis for pessimism about future prospects. Perhaps we have simply been looking for something in the wrong places. We have been focusing on issues of politics and governance rather than on questions of morality and education. Seeing democracy as essentially a matter of who is involved in which decisions is insufficient, especially in education. In the rest of this article, I want to lay out the alternative view that the very idea of education requires a stringent sense of and commitment to democracy. The requirements of democratic life and the nature of education provide mutually reinforcing rationales for this position.

To begin with, we need to add elements to the formulations of democracy discussed earlier. First, democracy is a characteristic of communities or societies, not of individuals. In understanding democracy, we must stress not just individuals and their actions, but communities or social wholes (Greene 1988; Stone 1988). An individual cannot have democracy all by himself or herself. Societies are, it is true, made up of individuals, but those individuals' own identities, senses of meaning, understandings of life—in fact, almost everything about them—are just as much shaped by the collective lives (for everyone belongs to more than one community) they take part in as by any effort of individual will. There are many excellent philosophical treatments of this issue of individuality in a social context in addition to those already cited (see Giddens 1976; Natanson 1970; Schutz 1967, 1970). Here I will simply assert it.

Also, democracy should be something more than just arrangements for choosing governments and making rules. At its best it is a way of life. As Macpherson put it (here stating his own view of the matter), democracy is "a quality pervading the whole life and operation of a national or smaller community, or if you like as a kind of society, a whole set of reciprocal relations between the people who make up the nation or other unit" (1977, p. 5).

In this extended view, democracy still involves individuals and their participation in decisions, but places them within a larger and fuller concept of a community life and a set of cultural practices. The literature on participation in education, which tends to be concerned with pragmatic or political questions, has generally not given sufficient attention to either point. Yet keeping them in mind, it is possible to see strong connections between democracy and education as ideal practices.

The Growing Importance of Democratic Practice

One can also make a strong argument that macrolevel changes occurring in societies give increasing importance to attributes of democratic living. Anthony Giddens suggests that we are developing a kind of "generative politics" that will require "dialogic democracy" (1994, p. 16). Deliberation in various forms will become—is becoming—much more important than political actions such as voting. Increasing diversity coupled with greater and quicker communication and higher levels of education will necessitate much more problem solving through discussion and mutual accommodation. Similarly, as scientific and other expert knowledge become more and more important, people will need the ability to work out the implications of such knowledge. Even relationships between parents and children are much more a matter of negotiation today than was the case fifty or a hundred years ago (Giddens 1994, p. 199). The skills of discussion, negotiation, and understanding each other—the ability to develop "active trust"—will be critical. "Dialogic democracy presumes only that dialogue in a public space provides a means of living along with the others in a relation of mutual *tolerance*—whether that 'other' be an individual or a global community of religious believers" (Giddens 1994, p. 115).

The Connection between Democracy and Education

The connections between democracy and education have to do with a common interest in a particular moral view of human life and human agency. The purposes of education are essentially moral, for they are based on attempts to realize certain ideals about human beings. Insofar as schools are places of education, they need to be centrally concerned with what humans should know, do, and be. Gary Fenstermacher (1990) has been among the most eloquent proponents of this view. There are, of course, important skills involved in education, such as reading. But all technical considerations fall within an overarching moral viewpoint. We do not simply want students to be good readers, competent writers, and able calculators.

Much more importantly, we want them to have these skills in order to contribute to the betterment of human life. Most teachers understand this truth even if only intuitively, which is why they give more weight in their evaluations of students to effort and behavior than they do to test results and other academic measures (Canadian Teachers' Federation 1992).

Schools also embody a particular point of view as to how the capacity to live a worthwhile life is to be acquired: through learning about ideas and skills. Other routes are clearly possible, but they are not a major part of Western schooling. Our schools do not attempt to embody the idea of coming to terms with life through meditation, or through contemplation of the great mysteries, or through physical experience and a great quest, or even, except to a very limited extent, through the arts. All of these are ways of living that have their own legitimacy, and their own impressive pedigree, but they are something different from schooling. Instead, schools are concerned with the habits of reason and rationality, with the acquisition of information, with the empirical world.

The idea of democracy has the same characteristics. It is a moral conception of how people ought to live together, driven not by considerations of efficiency, but by a powerful vision of what is right and proper. Although arguments of efficiency can be made (and have been made) in defense of democracy, in the end the idea that people should all have a share in political power has to stand on its own merit as an idea—because it appeals to a deep sense of what is right as shown by intense striving in many places around the world to create democratic institutions (Plank and Boyd 1994). Churchill's too-famous quote about democracy expresses the deep moral yearning that lies behind the idea of equal participation in political life.

Too, democracy as an ideal rests on a concept of people as reasonable, sufficiently so if not ideally so. If everyone has an entitlement to take part in political life, then it can only be because everyone has the capacity to come to informed and reasonable judgments about what a society ought to do. If we believed that people were essentially unreasonable, and that appeals to evidence or to reasons for actions were largely useless, then we could not defend democracy. Precisely the same comment could be made about education, which is a sensible undertaking only if one presumes that people have the capacity to grow in understanding through the exercise of reason.

To empower people to make decisions requires that they learn to become reflective thinkers who utilize moral principles to prevent repression and discrimination. It would seem to be a central task of education in a society that claims to be democratic in this sense to provide this learning for its members. (Pearson 1992, p. 87)

The ideas of democracy and of education are inextricably connected, and should be thought of as parts of the same vision. It is no accident that mass education developed at about the same time as the mass electoral franchise. One cannot imagine one without the other.

Combining Democratic and Educational Values

If this argument is accepted, it follows that schools as organizations should embody norms of democratic practice. To do otherwise would be to contradict the very idea of public education. But to make this assertion is not to say that schools have been organized to fulfill this requirement. A well-developed critique of schooling asserts that schools are more concerned with inculcating in students the requirements of a capitalist economy and hierarchical workplace than they are with developing the skills of democratic living (see, e.g., Apple 1990; Connell, Ashendon, Kessler, and Dowsett 1982; Carnoy and Levin 1986). It seems reasonably certain that schools do serve, at least as one of their purposes, to perpetuate existing social and economic practices. Wentzel cites evidence that "teachers were more appreciative and positive towards students who were cooperative and persistent . . . than [towards] students who were less responsible but displayed high levels of creativity and achievement" (1991, p. 9).

But such a conceptualization, while important, is not the entire truth. A complex institution such as schooling inevitably includes many different ideas about what can and should be done (Silver 1990). For the purposes of this article, I will simply assert that education is an enterprise that must have some link to the realization of ideals. Teachers are idealistic because the whole idea of education implies the possibility of improvement. So even if schools do serve other, less noble purposes, as educators we must be trying to realize the ideals about participation and community that are essential to the idea of education.

Even granted this proposition, we are faced with important questions. What would it mean to embody democratic ideals in schools? Who are the participants in the democracy of the school? Is it staff? Parents? The general community? And what should the role of students be in a democratic school? How do we combine the idea of schools as democratic institutions with the idea of schools as places of development? If we begin to examine these questions, we immediately run into difficult and controversial questions concerning organization and practice.

I prefer to start from another direction. Instead of beginning with organizational arrangements, let us step back to regard values, and ask what values should be embodied in a school that would be consistent with democracy and with education.

Here is my list. A democratic school would be characterized by the following:

- It would focus on moral principles and questions as being primary over technical ones. This means that those in the school, or involved with the school, would always be asking questions such as "Is this right?" "Is this connected with making the world a better place?" "Is this consistent with principles of justice, caring, and equity?"

- Reason and knowledge would be paramount over rank and authority. We could not use authority as the sole justification for action except under the most dire circumstances, where it is clear that safety or social order are threatened, and even then the authority would have to have been granted in a reasonable way.

- The school and everyone in it would be concerned with creating the conditions for dialogue about practices. Everything in or about the school would be open to question and change if convincing reasons could be given for such change. Processes for such debate would themselves be democratically established.

- There would be respect and tolerance for divergent views, and a willingness to understand the views of others and to consider seriously the possibility that others are right while we are mistaken.

- Everyone in the organization would not only tolerate but work actively to create participation in the school by all, which means moving away from a passive notion of citizenship, just as we want to move away from a passive model of learning.

- The school would strive to build community and solidarity while also respecting diversity and divergence. These can be seen as mutually reinforcing rather than antithetical. The model is not simply one of constant debate, but also, and equally, as the feminist philosophers have shown us, about caring for each other even as we disagree (Gilligan 1982; Martin 1985; Noddings 1984).

- The school would recognize and encourage alternative sources of authority and power. People who are good at things would be recognized for their abilities and contributions, regardless of their position or status in the organization.

Strike has a similar view, though phrased somewhat differently.

[T]he central requirement is that we develop institutions that attempt to make decisions by argumentative discourse as much as is practical and that invoke claims of sovereignty as rarely as possible. The principal aims are three: (a) to assert the merits of the better argument against power; (b) to assert the merits of equality and reciprocity against bureaucratic hierarchy; and (c) to assert the merits of autonomy and solidarity against domination and coercion. (1993, p. 266)

Neither list brings to mind an institution that looks much like most present-day schools, especially secondary schools. There are undoubtedly people in our schools who believe in values much like these, and who strive to practice them. Education includes some of the most committed democrats anywhere and some schools go a considerable way toward meeting at least some of these principles.

Individual efforts, however, are not enough. The general institutional form of our schools, and the general way power is organized in them, makes it very difficult to operate classrooms or individual schools in accord with these principles. Indeed, many of the standard practices of schools are quite inconsistent with principles of democracy.

It may be helpful to cite some evidence that schools presently often fail to embody principles of democracy. Cullingford (1991) interviewed 110 English students who were at the end of primary or the beginning of secondary school. A major theme of his book is the exclusion of students from discussion about what school is for and about. He concludes that students are not informed, let alone consulted, about what is being done to them and why.

Children go to school because they have to. It is part of the preordained experience. . . . Very rarely, if ever, is the purpose of school discussed with children. They go to school without deeply questioning why they should. . . . Teachers simply do not spend time engaged in delineating why things need to be learned. (p. 159)

Nor does the situation improve much as students get older and, presumably, more mature. Ironically, in many ways elementary students, and particularly those in primary years, have more control over what they do and how they do it than at any other time in their school careers. Fine's (1991) study of dropouts in a New York high school documented the extent to which critique and dissent were stifled in that setting. A study of twenty-one Canadian secondary schools nominated as "exemplary" shows that traditional patterns of order and hierarchy were overwhelmingly dominant (Canadian Education Association 1995). Many other qualitative or ethnographic studies of schools have had similar findings (e.g., Fullan 1991; Rudduck, Chaplain, and Wallace 1996; Wilson and Corcoran 1988). On a larger scale, John Goodlad's (1984) huge study of U.S. schools in the early 1980s came to these conclusions about secondary schools.

The picture that emerges from the data is one of students increasingly conforming, not assuming an increasingly independent decision-making role in their own education.

On one hand, many teachers verbalize the importance of students increasingly becoming independent learners; on the other, most view themselves as needing to be in control of the decision-making process. (p. 109)

Students in the classes we observed made scarcely any decisions about their learning. (p. 229)

The current status and treatment of students in our schools has particularly important implications for students' political education, for the way they come to understand the nature of politics, whether at the national level or at the microlevel of the classroom or the family. At precisely the age when young people are formulating their political views, they are in an institution in which they have few political rights and no real political role. It is bad enough that so little effort is given to having students deal with real world issues of power, politics, or poverty in ways that actually raise what is controversial in our public life. It is even worse that what is done is almost entirely an exercise divorced from any practical consequences other than students' grades. Students simply do not get a chance to learn the skills of democratic living. Cullingford (1991), although his book is not primarily about politics, has this to say:

Although children are deemed to have little interest in politics, they all express political views, and learn their political attitudes just at a time when little ostensible attention is given to them. . . . They learn about power and authority and the ways in which human beings organize themselves, which is the stuff of politics. No one can escape the consequences of the need for the translation of social action into a means of control and organization. Children are as capable as the indifferent voter of having political insights. (p. 176)

Moving from this state of affairs toward the principles outlined earlier would require very significant changes in the way schools operate. Democracy in schools, in this view, is far more than school-based management, or school councils, or teacher empowerment. The political role of teachers would certainly be expanded considerably under a set of values such as those described. The change in authority patterns would mean that principals and school district administrators could no longer simply *give* instructions; rather, issues in the school would have to be settled by educational means: through discussion and dialogue.

Curriculum could not only be something determined by experts—whether teachers or others—and passed on to students as something they should learn without question. Relationships among all parties in the school would need to be much more respectful. Just as administrators would need to be willing to engage in discussion with staff about policies and practices, so would teachers and administrators need to have the same sort of openness to students. A school could no longer be a place in which a few made up the rules that governed the many without any consent from the latter. Students would need to be active creators of the school rather than its passive beneficiaries, not simply within the curriculum framework, but in the total life of the school. They would have to take on the real challenges of living, not the artificial ones of textbooks.

Implications of the Democratic School

Well, one might say, how much can we expect? Do other institutions do better? Aren't these expectations unreasonable?

In one sense, they probably are. After all, the world is a pretty imperfect place. Our existing political institutions, most of us would agree, are far from ideal, either in conception or in practice. Why should we expect schools to be better political institutions than are our overtly political institutions, such as political parties? Yet in another, more important way, we are right to hold schools up to expectations that are especially high and especially difficult to meet. Precisely because schools have charge of young people, and precisely because schools play an important role in the formation of young people (the French word *formation* has no precise English translation but embodies something much more akin to the shaping of character than do the English words "education" or "training"), they have to meet obligations beyond those pertaining to institutions dealing only or mostly with adults.

If we think of democracy as a way of life in which communities make choices through processes involving all their members, we can see that in schools students are not thought of in this way. They are not considered to be partners in a community. Instead, our dominant metaphor for schooling is that of the factory, with students usually cast as the raw materials to be processed. Schooling is organized to have things *done* to students according to somebody else's plan of what will produce the desired results. Such a view is incompatible with notions of democracy, and also incompatible with the concept of education, which is surely not something that can be done to people, but something they must do for themselves (B. Levin 1994b).

Are Students Capable?

A change in the status of students to full partners in their own education will not come easily. Several objections may be raised. Some authors talk about democracy in schools entirely instrumentally, to be justified only if it serves to prepare the young for living in a democratic society.

The question of how much democracy within schools is desirable remains doubly difficult to answer, therefore, because we have incomplete data on the educative effects of more democratic methods and because we rightly value the disciplinary as well as the participatory purposes of primary education.

Without more empirical evidence, we cannot say precisely how much democracy in schools is desirable. (Gutmann 1987, p. 91)

This position treats democracy as a matter of effective technique, and is inconsistent with the idea of democracy, which is not about preparation for living, but about living itself. We make a mistake when we think of school as simply instrumental—a place in which to learn how to live through some sort of technical process of being taught (Dewey 1968, p. 49). It's not as if students spend ten or twelve years preparing for life while doing something else. Instead, we should see students as being at all times active constructors of their own worlds, and in this case how they live is a critical feature of any curriculum.

To be sure, learning about democracy is an important aspect of schooling. But democracy in schools is not only a matter of how best to train people in some sort of skill, with the decision as to how much democracy to have resting on empirical evidence. What kind of empirical evidence would we gather, after all? Are we to assess whether students make good decisions when given the chance? But how would we know? Are we to assess whether they learn more geography or read more books when in a democratic setting? Indeed, it seems highly doubtful to say that democracy is justified at all on the basis of empirical examination of its outcomes. Would we say that the decision about how much democracy to have in our society is empirical? If it turned out that better outcomes—whatever that might mean—occurred when only the elite made decisions, would we discontinue democracy as a political practice and embrace absolutism?

There is a strong case to be made for students of all ages having the same rights, political and otherwise, as adults (see Cohen [1980] for an extended and careful argument along these lines, and Callan [1988] for a somewhat more conventional position). But here I am not going to make that case. Nor will I argue for democracy because of its economic importance (Carnoy and Levin 1985). Rather, I believe in democracy in schools, especially for students, from the point of view of what is required for educational reasons. Schools, because they are educational institutions, have particular obligations in regard to their political arrangements, requirements that go beyond those of other institutions. Gutmann has suggested that we ought to direct our attention away from whether high schools prepare students for jobs, and pay more attention to whether they prepare students to participate in the decisions that determine the future of high schools, of the labor market, and of our social arrangements (1987, p. 148).

The objection will also be made that students are incapable of playing a more important part in the operation of schools. It has often been argued (see White 1983; Wringe 1984; Callan 1988) that an institution centrally concerned with children must have an essentially paternalistic orientation. Since children are immature, and do not know what is good for them, adults must make these determinations whatever the children may think. After all, we wouldn't let children eat as much candy as they wanted, or run out into the road as ways of demonstrating their equality as persons, would we? Isn't it farcical to give students the authority to make decisions which they clearly aren't ready to make? As Gutmann, who is generally favorable toward student participation in schools, put it, "Students lack the competence necessary to share equally in making many decisions" (1987, p. 88). Zeichner (1991), although a strong advocate of greater democracy in schools, includes students rather as an afterthought, and then only at the secondary level. Strike (1993, p. 267) acknowledges them as "in some sense junior members" of the deliberative communities he supports. Even John Dewey's model schools left many of the key decisions to teachers with no student role (Gutmann 1987, p. 93).

Certainly we need to take into account in organizing schooling the nature and needs of children. Yes, we do have legal responsibilities, and, even more importantly, ethical ones toward students: the obligation to help students make good decisions, and the obligation to intervene when danger exists. Teachers do have knowledge and skills that put them on a different footing from students. But we can doubt whether these considerations require such a thorough-going authoritarianism as characterizes our schools.

It is not clear why competence is a criterion at all for students' participation in schools. In our political system competence is not required as a condition of participation. We are entitled to vote at a certain age whether or not we know anything about politics. We have legal rights regardless of our knowledge and worth as persons. Indeed, that is a key part of what it means to have a right. It is, then, not evident why students should have to demonstrate competence to merit political participation when adults do not.

Are students ready to play an active role in determining the nature of schooling? The danger of abuse does exist. It is possible that students would massively opt for less demanding programs, although this is a pessimistic assumption without much evidence to support it. Where students in secondary schools do have some choice they often want to take the more demanding programs and have to be dissuaded by staff who feel they aren't able to handle them. Indeed, it may be that students are more conservative about many school practices than are many teachers (Townsend and Bedard 1994). This hardly suggests that students will usually take the easy way out. Polan (1989) thinks that the real problem is not one of avoiding chaos, but of how seldom institutional arrangements are altered significantly, and of how often "potentially radical reorganizations and restructuring of institutions results in relatively conservative outcomes" (p. 43).

We can also look at nonschool situations in which students do get to participate more actively, such as youth organizations. Would not experience with these organizations indicate that young people do have, and can further develop, reasonable decision-making skills? Some so-called developing countries have organized schools that attempt to assign students a more important role (see Farrell 1993).

What does it mean to be ready to exercise authority? The argument about lack of readiness or lack of maturity has been used historically to oppose every proposal to extend political rights. It has been used to justify and support colonialism, the dismal treatment of aboriginal peoples, the denial of voting and property rights to women, and, until the last couple of centuries, political democracy itself. Every group that now has a political role was at one time excluded on the grounds of lack of capacity. Looking at the North American political culture, we might well wonder whether we as adults are ready for democracy. Are we mature enough? Are we too ready to opt for the easy choice? Is it reasonable to think that young people will be significantly worse at it?

We should also recognize that interest "grows by what it feeds on." Callan points out that it is hardly surprising that students will not devote time and effort to becoming skilled at something that they aren't allowed to do in any case (1988, p. 141). A meaningful political role is likely to be a considerable spur both to political interest and to political skill. It isn't only that practice is required to develop certain skills and dispositions, but also that the absence of opportunity to use such capacities will likely lead to a disinterest in them.

In education the argument about readiness is particularly double-edged. If students, after eight or ten years of school, have not yet learned to take part in political debate, to justify a point of view, to hear and understand the views of others, and to recognize reasonable and unreasonable choices, is that not a failure of schooling? After all, these skills—critical thinking, making choices, tolerance for diversity—are among the most important goals of school. If we haven't been able to develop them in students over these years, what does that say about our educational practices (Callan 1988)?

We cannot have it both ways. If schooling is important because of its role in developing skills, then it should be evident that those skills are developing, and the means of seeing this is to allow students to use the skills in ways that really matter. If, on the other hand, we claim that skills such as critical thinking are largely a function of age—that one simply doesn't develop them until eighteen or twenty-one of whatever age—then we cannot use the importance of these skills as a grounds for defending schooling. Why should people invest in schools if such key abilities are not, in fact, learned there?

No doubt, some of the views expressed or decisions made by students will not be, in the eyes of some adults, good ones. Young people will make mistakes, just as we do—probably in about the same proportions. Here the idea of education is important, since educational values require that people have the opportunity to learn from their actions, which will inevitably include their mistakes. Although much lip-service is given to the value of mistakes in education, schools seem generally concerned with preventing mistakes, not using them as opportunities to learn.

What to Do with Authority?

If sharing authority has problems, so does paternalism. All political systems and human institutions involve an unavoidable problem of power. Tinder (1991) framed the problem when he wrote that "[a] political system is essentially a set of arrangements by which some people dominate others. How can this be made morally tolerable? Civilization is carried on under a great moral shadow" (p. 162). Berger described the problem even more starkly:

At the foundations of every historical society there are vast piles of corpses. . . . There is no getting away from this fact, and there is nothing to be done about it. It is an inevitable burden of the human condition. (1974, p. 150)

We cannot wish the problem of authority away. And we certainly cannot depend, as history shows only too clearly, on the goodwill of those in authority to exhibit characteristics of care and concern for those in their charge. Whether one considers the historic behavior of monarchs or dictators, or the widespread existence of violence and abuse in present-day families, Lord Acton's dictum about the corruptions of power remains forceful. Nor are these problems unique to politics or the family. Similar evidence can be adduced in regard to schools. We have only to look at the literature on tracking, on placement in special education, and on disciplinary practices to see that adults in schools do, disturbingly frequently, make decisions about students that are not in the students' best interests. Even if we assumed that every educator was solely driven by a perception of students' best interests, it would be surprising if their (our) understandings of those inter-

ests were always more accurate than the understandings of the students themselves. Think of how we react when others presume to tell us what is best for us. Even where there are clear technical grounds for expertise, such as medical diagnosis, we are frequently distrustful, and always reserve the right to a second opinion. Moreover, in most circumstances a doctor cannot undertake a procedure without our explicit consent, even though the doctor has expertise that we lack. Yet schools are authorized to, and frequently do, take actions that students see as wrong for them.

There may be problems with the wider distribution of authority to students, although I believe that these problems are overstated, but there are obviously enormous problems with the concentration of authority, also. If we are to give attention to the problems of wider democracy, we must also be open about the dangers of concentrated power.

Restrictions on students in school should therefore be such as are consistent with the ideals listed earlier, which apply both to democracy and to education. They should be consistent with evidence and careful argument as to why students are being treated differently from adults. It is not at all evident that students are as incompetent as is claimed, nor that their political rights should be affected even if they are.

Let us note as well that nothing said so far suggests that schooling should be turned over to students. The principles listed earlier do not assign primacy to any particular group in the school; they only suggest that *every* group and *every* person has a right to participate in the work of the institution. I do not advocate giving students all the authority over schooling any more than I advocate giving all the authority to teachers, administrators, parents, elected officials, or any other group. The teacher, as someone with more knowledge and skill, will always stand in an unequal, but mutually respectful, relationship with students—what Strike (1993, p. 268) refers to as "first among equals." Teachers need to play a particularly important role—more important than is currently the case in many schools—in influencing and shaping what happens in schools. Parents and other community members also have a right and an obligation to participate. Each group, each individual, must take into account the views and desires of others. We cannot always have our own way, whether in political life or anywhere else. That is a fact that children learn very early.

Education is not about giving authority to any particular group to make decisions. Education has to do with the creation of situations in which there is debate and discussion, in which people learn about what to do, and in which decisions are subject to challenge, and to the requirement to give good reasons, taking into account others as full, human persons who deserve respect (Greene 1988).

Democracy in schools must itself be educational, having to do with learning more, gathering and weighing evidence, working through what might constitute good reasons for believing something, coming to understand and appreciate why others might hold a different view—in short, all those things that we rightfully expect an educated person to do. It involves learning to put aside for the moment one's own views and interests to think seriously about those of others (Wringe 1984, p. 62). This applies to students no more and no less than to teachers, administrators, parents, or other community members. The concept of the reflective thinker in a reflective community is both democratic and educational, and accords with the changing needs of human society.

We should also note that students do not participate as free-form individuals, but in a social context that has powerful influences on their thinking. We shouldn't make the mistake of thinking that individual desires precede society. The two are part of the same whole. The way in which school as an organization is shaped will therefore influence how people participate, what they see as desirable, and what views they express.

We cannot abolish authority, or give it away, but we can and should create in our institutions the conditions that allow authority to be challenged, and to be taken over by others who are ready to use it well, because this is what is required for a democratic society to operate. The analogy holds very well in education. Good teachers have natural authority, just as good administrators do (by "good" I mean people acting from deeply moral convictions with regard for the other as a full human being). Where authority is exercised in this way, with concern and care for others, there is rarely a challenge to it. Indeed, acting from moral conviction and personal concern is a source of authority. The massive obedience of students in our schools shows clearly that students are disposed to accept the authority of adults as reasonable and legitimate. Cullingford (1991) points out that children do accept the need for rules and authority in the school. Nor do we find in settings where children do have more autonomy, such as private lessons or social activities, that they engage any more than do adults in widespread disobedience or efforts to render the activity meaningless in the service of some immediate pleasure.

The process of education itself carries implications for authority. Wringe has pointed out that

education is democratic to the extent that both teachers and pupil are subject to the canons of whatever discipline is being explored. A good argument or a relevant piece of evidence is still as good or relevant when brought forward by a mediocre student as when the same argument or evidence is produced by an outstandingly well qualified teacher. (1984, p. 83)

Fenstermacher (1990) has made the point that teachers must seek to make their students authoritative in their place. Teaching consists of giving knowledge away such that the student becomes as knowledgeable and as competent, and preferably even more knowledgeable and competent, as the teacher. Teachers begin from a superior status in terms of knowledge (though not a superior status as a person), but seek deliberately to make the students their equals. In this important sense, teachers should always be seeking to give authority away, and it is difficult to see how this can be done if the students do not play an active role in all phases of their education.

What Might Be Done?

Just how this altered view of the role of students would take shape in practice is not simple. Education has such wide implications and so many people have a stake in it. There are limits to democracy in education, as there are in every other area of political life. The limits are those imposed by our sense of what education is and requires. Because everyone has an interest in education, decisions cannot simply be made by teachers, or teachers and students, or even teachers, students, and parents, let alone by administrators, who have a very shaky claim to decision-making power except insofar as it is delegated by public bodies such as school boards (Haller and Stiker 1986). The reconciliation of education and democracy rests not on an organization chart that shows who is superior to whom, but on a vision of a society in which reflection, dialogue, critical thinking, and mutual care are central. Within this framework, people can and do come to decisions that recognize the authority of expertise, or that empower certain roles or persons with particular authority, because that is seen as being desirable in the interests of all. There is no requirement that a democratic organization be one in which every decision is debated endlessly, and in which everyone plays an identical role, as long as other arrangements are themselves the result of democratic processes (Wringe 1984, p. 65). Whatever form we adopt will have problems, and will need review and change from time to time. The key is less the organizational form than the ideals it embodies.

It is clear from the historical evidence (Watts 1989) that schools that have attempted to alter their political nature in important ways have faced enormous obstacles. The apparently small impact of the student power movement of the 1960s, or of the Kohlberg "just community" concept, illustrates the same dynamic. Some of the problems are internal, as those involved try to come to terms with arrangements quite different from those they may be used to. The literature on change cited earlier makes frequent mention of the difficulties involved: not enough time, insufficient skills, inability to cope with conflict. When success proves elusive, people may become disenchanted and lessen their effort. But the obstacles are not only internal. The external pressures to conform to the existing image of schooling are even more powerful; many schools that set out on an independent course were eventually forced back to doing more or less the same thing as everybody else. So we don't necessarily know how to create a democratic school, and it is not at all certain that such a creation would be allowed to continue even if it could be brought about. There should be no naïveté that a simple call for democracy will actually bring results in practice; the history of education is littered with injunctions to schools that were never fulfilled (and sometimes just as well).

Nonetheless, there are some steps that could be taken by individual teachers or administrators that would not likely produce great resistance, and that would do much to move schools in the directions outlined here. Many of these things can be done quite readily, in a single class or an entire school. All of them proceed from a dual commitment: to make education an important part of democracy and to make democracy an important part of education.

Probably the most important step is to make a practice of raising with students, in classes and other settings, the central issues of schooling as propositions to be discussed seriously, but without evident right answers. We can start to treat students as community members with a stake in what happens, and as people who can and will learn as they deliberate and act. We could encourage discussion within the school community about all those educational matters that require thought and are open to different points of view, such as curriculum content and organization, grading and student evaluation practices, the merits and place of critical thinking, the role of political education, how best to handle controversial issues, and so on. All of these, subjects of debate for educators and informed parents, could and should be made problematic for students as well, so that they, too, can confront the question of what education is. Taking this approach would tell students that what they think matters and that the quality of their thought is important, thereby encouraging active learning. Students would also learn that answers to important questions are always provisional, subject to changes in our knowledge, purposes, circumstances, and values.

The literature contains descriptions of many ways to organize such practices of inquiry (see Duke and Jones 1985). At the simplest level, it is always possible to begin in a classroom by asking students to talk about what their interests and concerns are. What bothers them about the school? What would they like to change if they could? What ideas do they have for making schools more educational? Listening with real attention, asking questions, and asking students to develop their ideas is a start that can be made by any teacher or administrator. These activities require key educational skills: reading, writing, discussing, thinking. One might find as a side benefit that beginning this kind of dialogue gave students a different perspective on their role with fewer disciplinary problems resulting.

A student voice in selecting topics for study, textbooks and readings, and evaluation practices could be part of every classroom. Any issue that is important enough to refer to a parent-teacher meeting or to a school board is also likely to be an issue on which students could be consulted. Schoolwide fora, systems of elected representatives, or referenda (preceded by debate) on important questions are all means of creating and legitimizing discussion on issues that matter. One only needs to look at the political vehicles available in society generally to get ideas about how these can be used in the microcommunity of the school. Development jointly with students and parents of school or district policies on homework or discipline or tracking or textbooks has been done in many schools, and could be extended to become a normal practice rather than something exceptional. The key is to make it normal, even expected, that students would have a reasoned, informed, and respected voice in school decisions.

We need also to give real tasks to student organizations. Student councils in secondary schools are seldom involved in the important questions facing the school (Schmuck and Schmuck 1990), or welcomed if they try to involve themselves. In elementary schools student organizations are altogether rare (Robinson and Koehn 1992). Work done in both alternative and mainstream secondary schools in Canada and the United States around the development of codes of students' rights and responsibilities exemplifies one kind of meaningful political activity that could be replicated in elementary schools too. Student councils could see and comment on agenda items for staff or school board meetings. They could be expected, after a process of involving other students, to make an annual presentation to the school board on educational issues. Students can be given observer status at school or district activities concerned with budgeting, staff development, or curriculum development. Student organizations can have a role in setting disciplinary and other policies in the school.

The practice of democracy should be tied clearly to the school's educational program. Issues of education can become part of the curriculum itself. Almost every social studies guide advocates teaching students about democracy, but usually the means suggested involve simulations or role plays rather than real and meaningful involvement in school decisions. The concept of reflective practice (Schon 1983) that is so frequently mentioned as important for teachers can equally be a key part of students' learning.

Students can be involved in designing courses and learning activities, something that can be done with students of all ages. A colleague who is a school principal recently experimented with having her grade four health class students take over responsibility for the conduct of the course. Within a few classes students were asking to take home the provincial curriculum guide so that they could determine what content needed to be stressed, and how they could best organize the classes! Surely asking students to think about what should be learned, how it should be learned, and how learning should be assessed is part of the creation of reflective learners. Student involvement in developing evaluation activities is particularly relevant, since evaluation has such a powerful impact on the way students think about school. A larger student role in setting assessment practices is quite consistent with emerging ideas about alternative forms of assessment, such as portfolios. Attention to all of these issues could be part of the curriculum of a classroom or school. In preschool and primary school settings, "school" could become a theme along with "seasons," "families," "transportation," or the others currently used. Older students, too, can be asked—indeed, should be expected—to research, discuss, study, and write about their experience of schooling, alternative school practices, and other aspects of education.

These ideas sound simpler in a few phrases than they would be in practice; it is much easier to formulate a perfect world on paper than it is to work in a quite imperfect reality. There are real problems of time, energy, skill, and knowledge. Yet, though it is essential to recognize the limits of the possible, it is equally important to hold onto our ideals despite all the problems and imperfections.

> For a democracy, a soberly realistic stance towards the world paradoxically requires high ideals. . . . But it is part of the human condition that high ideals are often undercut by the means required to pursue them. Our ideals must be deeply enough grounded and richly enough formulated to sustain the arduous debates necessary to determine means acceptable to pursue them, and resilient enough to undergo renewal after their inevitable corruption. (Bellah, Madsen, Sullivan, Swidler, and Tipton 1991, p. 224)

Will this make our work as educators harder? Absolutely. Will it cause anguish as we try to decide what is right? Yes. There are no simple answers to be given. We will simply have to work hard at it. There are always possibilities if we are serious about wanting them. William Yeats wrote in one of his last poems, "The Circus Animals' Desertion,"

Now that my ladder's gone
I must lie down where all the ladders start
In the foul rag and bone shop of the heart.

The problems, although daunting, are also exciting. A changed view of democracy in schools would make them more interesting, powerful, meaningful places for everyone. We would truly have an opportunity to try to make our ideals real, and this is what we have to do if we want democracy, and education, to flourish.

Notes

I wish to acknowledge the helpful comments of two anonymous reviewers and my colleagues J. A. Riffel, Romulo Magsino, and Jon Young in preparing this article,, and to thank the Seven Oaks School Division for giving me the opportunity to begin exploring these ideas.

This article is dedicated to Thomas B. Greenfield (1928–1992), of the Ontario Institute for Studies in Education, whose work has been so important in leading me and many others to think about the central role of values in educational administration.

References

Apple, M. 1990. *Ideology and curriculum* 2nd ed. New York: Routledge.

Bellah, R., R. Madsen, W. Sullivan, A. Swidler, and S. Tipton. 1971. *The good society.* New York: Vintage.

Berger, P. 1976. *Pyramids of sacrifice.* New York: Vintage.

Callan, E. 1988. *Autonomy and schooling.* Montreal, Quebec: McGill-Queen's University Press.

Canadian Education Association. 1995. *Secondary schools in Canada: The National Report of the Exemplary Schools Project.* Toronto: Canadian Education Association.

Canadian Teachers' Federation. 1992. *Teaches in Canada: Their work and quality of life.* Ottawa: Canadian Teachers' Federation.

Carnoy, M., and H. Levin. 1985. *Schooling and work in the democratic state.* Stanford, CA: Stanford University Press.

Carter, D. 1986. Review of research applications: Kohlberg's theories in correctional settings. *Journal of Correctional Settings* 37: 79–83.

Coe, P., P. Kannapel, L. Aagaard, and B. Moore. 1995. Non-linear evolution of school-based decision-making in Kentucky. Paper presented to the annual meeting of the American Educational Research Association, San Francisco.

Cohen, H. 1980. *Equal rights for children.* Totowa, NJ: Littlefield, Adams.

Connell, R. W., D. J. Ashendon, S. Kessler, and G. Dowsett. 1982. *Making the difference.* Sydney, Australia: George Allen & Unwin.

Cullingford, C. 1991. *The inner world of the school: Children's ideas about schools.* London: Cassell.

Deem, R. 1994. The school, the parent, the banker, and the local politician: What can we learn from the English experience of involving lay people in the site based management of schools? Paper presented to the annual meeting of the American Educational Research Association, New Orleans.

Dewey, J. 1968. *Experience and education.* New York: Collier. (Originally published 1938)

Duke, D., and V. Jones. 1985. What can schools do to foster student responsibility? *Theory into Practice* 24: 277–285.

Epstein, J. 1995. School/family/community partnerships: Caring for the children we share. *Phi Delta Kappan* 76(9): 701–712.

Evans, T., R. Corsini, and G. Gazda. 1990. Individual education and the 4Rs. *Educational Leadership* 48: 52–56.

Farrell, J. 1993. Planning education: An overview. In *International encyclopedia of education,* 2nd ed., ed. T. Husen and N. Postlethwaite, 499–510. Oxford: Pergamon Press.

Fenstermacher, G. 1990. Some considerations on teaching as a moral profession. In *The moral dimensions of teaching,* ed. J. Goodlad, R. Soder, and K. Sirotnik, 130–151. San Francisco: Jossey-Bass.

Fullan, M. 1991. *The new meaning of educational change.* New York: Teachers College Press/OISE Press.

Furtwengler, C., W. Furtwengler, E. Holcomb, and D. Hurst. 1995. An assessment of shared decision-making and school site councils. Paper presented to the annual meeting of the American Educational Research Association, San Francisco.

Giddens, A. 1976. *New rules of sociological method.* London: Hutchinson.

Giddens, A. 1994. *Beyond left and right.* Cambridge, UK: Polity Press.

Gilligan, C. 1982. *In a different voice: Psychological theories and women's development.* Cambridge, MA: Harvard University Press.

Goodlad, J. 1984. *A place called school.* New York: McGraw-Hill.

Greene, M. 1988. *The dialectic of freedom.* New York: Teachers College Press.

Gutmann, A. 1987. *Democratic education.* Princeton, NJ: Princeton University Press.

Haller, E. and K. Strike. 1986. *An introduction to educational administration.* New York: Longman.

Held, V. 1984. *Rights and goods.* New York: Free Press.

Henchey, N., and D. Burgess. 1987. *Between past and future: Quebec education in transition.* Calgary: Detselig Press.

Levacic, R. 1995. *Local management of schools: Analysis and practice.* Buckingham, UK: Open University Press.

Levin, B. 1977. The silent partner: Student participation in school decision-making. In *The politics of Canadian education,* ed. S. Wallin, 109–114. Ottawa: Canadian Society for the Study of Education.

Levin, B. 1992. School-based management. *Canadian School Executive* 11 (9): 30–32.

Levin, B. 1994a. Education reform and the treatment of students in schools. *Journal of Educational Thought* 28: 88–101.

Levin, B. 1994b. Students and educational productivity. *Phi Delta Kappan* 75(10): 758–760.

Levin, H. 1992. Expanding democracy through schooling. Paper presented to the Seven Oaks School Division Symposium Series, Winnipeg, Canada.

Lieberman, A., and L. Miller. 1990. Teacher development in professional practice schools. *Teachers College Record* 92: 106–122.

Macpherson, C. B. 1977. *The life and times of liberal democracy.* Oxford: Oxford University Press.

Martin, J. R. 1985. *Reclaiming a conversation: The idea of the educated woman.* New Haven, CT: Yale University Press.

Maychell, K. 1994. *Counting the cost: The impact of LMS on schools' patterns of spending.* Slough, UK: National Foundation for Educational Research.

Murphy, D. 1988. The just community at Birch Meadow Elementary School. *Phi Delta Kappan* 69: 427–428.

Murray, C. 1992. Rochester's reforms: The teachers' perspective. *Educational Policy* 6: 55–71.

Natanson, M. 1970. *The journeying self.* Reading, MA: Addison-Wesley.

Noddings, N. 1984. *Caring: A feminine approach to ethics and moral education.* Berkeley and Los Angeles: University of California Press.

Pearson, A. 1992. Teacher education in a democracy. *Educational Philosophy and Theory* 24: 83–92.

Plank, D., and W. L. Boyd. 1994. Antipolitics, education, and institutional choice: The flight from democracy. *American Educational Research Journal* 31: 263–281.

Polan, A. 1989. School: The inevitable democracy. In *The democratic school,* ed. C. Harber and R. Meighan, 28–47. Ticknall, UK: Education Now Cooperative.

Rice, E., and G. Schneider. 1992. A decade of teacher empowerment: An empirical analysis of teacher involvement in decision-making. Paper presented to the annual meeting of the American Educational Research Association, San Francisco.

Rudduck, J., R. Chaplain, and G. Wallace, eds. 1996. *School improvement: What can pupils tell us?* London: David Fulton.

Schmuck, P., and R. Schmuck. 1990. Democratic participation in small-town schools. *Educational Researcher* 19: 14–19.

Schon, D. 1983. *The reflective practitioner.* New York: Basic Books.

Schutz, A. 1967. *The phenomenology of the social world.* Chicago: Northwestern University Press.

Schutz, A. 1970. *Reflections on the problem of relevance.* New Haven, CT: Yale University Press.

Silver, H. 1990. *Education, change, and the policy process.* London: Falmer Press.

Stone, D. 1988. *Policy paradox and political reason.* New York: HarperCollins.

Strike, K. 1993. Professionalism, democracy, and discursive communities: Normative reflections on restructuring. *American Educational Research Journal* 30(2): 255–275.

Thomas, H., and J. Martin. 1996. *Managing resources for school improvement.* London: Routledge.

Tinder, G. 1991. *Political thinking.* 5th ed. New York: HarperCollins.

Townsend, R., and G. Bedard. 1994. Students and academics look at school improvement. In *Education and community: The collaborative solution,* ed. S. Lawton, E. Tanenzapf, and R. Townsend, 41–60. Toronto: Ontario Institute for Studies in Education.

Watts, J. 1989. Up to a point. In *The democratic school,* ed. C. Harber and R. Meighan, 17–27. Ticknall, UK: Education Now Cooperative.

Weiss, C. 1992. Shared decision making about what? Paper presented to the annual meeting of the American Educational Research Association, San Francisco.

Wentzel, K. 1991. Social competence at school: Relation between social responsibility and academic achievement. *Review of Educational Research* 61: 25–70.

White, P. 1983. *Beyond domination: An essay in the political philosophy of education.* London: Routledge and Kegan Paul.

White, P. A. 1992. Teacher empowerment under "ideal" school-site autonomy. *Educational Evaluation and Policy Analysis* 14: 69–82.

Wilson, B., and T. Corcoran. 1988. *Successful secondary schools.* London: Falmer Press.

Wood, G. 1990. Teaching for democracy. *Educational Leadership* 48: 32–37.

Wringe, C. 1984. *Democracy, schooling, and political education.* London: George Allen & Unwin.

Zeichner, K. 1991. Contradictions and tensions in the professionalization of teaching and the democratization of schools. *Teachers College Record* 92: 363–378.

Form at end of book

Democracy and Education:
Who Gets to Speak and Who Is Listened To?

Joseph P. Farrell

*Ontario Institute for Studies in Education
of the University of Toronto
Toronto, Ontario*

I am writing these words at the end of a massive province-wide teacher strike in the Province of Ontario. For two weeks there were approximately 126,000 teachers on the picket lines, and about 2.1 million primary and secondary students out of school. It was the largest teacher strike in Canadian history. Public opinion was passionately split. Before the strike began public opinion appeared from the polls to be running strongly in favor of the government; by the end of the strike it was strongly in favor of the teachers. (The final opinion polls indicated that about 60 percent of the general public and, quite surprisingly to many, about 70 percent of the parents of schoolchildren, who were being inconvenienced by having their youngsters out of school, supported the teachers.) The teachers called their action a "political protest." The government labeled it an "illegal strike" and tried to obtain a legal injunction forcing the teachers back to work. The presiding judge rejected the government's case, siding quite strongly with the teachers, which caused considerable embarrassment to the government. Emotions within the government, within the schools, and in the society at large, were and are running very high. There is a complex welter of questions involved,

but the two fundamental issues are educational *expenditure* and *control* of education. The government (a strongly neo-conservative sort of the Thatcherite variety) proposes, using its substantial and completely controlled legislative majority, to enact a massive reform that will, among many other things, dramatically centralize control over public education in the hands of the cabinet, with no judicial appeal of cabinet or ministry decisions possible, so as to reduce substantially educational expenditures. The teachers, and by polling results most of the public, oppose. The teachers are now back in their classrooms. Only time will tell who "won" or "lost" what. What is important for present purposes is that *control* has been the central issue, and that deep passions came very quickly to view.

This should not have been terribly surprising. Comparative evidence indicates that extremely and necessarily political matters surround the world's educational policy and practice and its change, much as some educators and educational bureaucrats might wish it otherwise, and these educational politics can, and frequently do, become very passionate very quickly. It could hardly be otherwise. The people most directly implicated, the students, are those about whom most of us care most deeply—our own children, or grandchildren, or other young kin, or other people's children of whom we are fond. The issues involved typically implicate

Questions

To promote education for a democracy, how much power, authority, or control should parents and the community have over schools and education?

What role(s) should students have in making decisions about their own education?

some of our most deeply and fervently held beliefs and values about what constitutes the "good human being we wish these young people to become, what constitutes the "good" society in which we wish them to live their adult lives, and how what happens in the schools affects both their individual development and the development of the society. Given all of this it would be quite astonishing if public discussion of such matters remained cool, abstracted, and dispassionate (except perhaps in some classes in faculties of education!). The larger and more dramatic the change, the more volatile the politics. Even in relatively homogeneous societies views on these matters differ widely—hence the often passionate conflict. The more heterogeneous a society, the more widely the opinions will vary—hence the more likely it is that such passionate political conflict will erupt. In most such conflicts the question of control of education is central, sometimes implicitly, often, as in Ontario, quite explicitly. Which individuals and groups do and should have access, how, and to what degree to influence decisions regarding public schooling? The issue then is *power* over public education, its degree of centralization or dispersion, and the breadth of the range of stakeholders within the system and external to it who have some legitimate degree of influence upon and participation in educational decisions. These matters are central to two of the articles in this issue, and the book review dialogue, and provide a set of questions to be addressed to the other two articles.

Benjamin Levin builds an argument for significantly deepening and broadening our understanding of the relationships between "education" and "democracy." His argument, while easy to follow is complex and multilayered, and I could not fairly and accurately recapitulate it here in detail. At base, Levin argues that democracy is not just a set of mechanisms for making decisions; it is a way of life based upon a set of moral principles or ideals about how life, individually and collectively, should be lived. Arguments for democracy in education should not, he claims, be grounded solely on "practical" outcomes (e.g., it will produce "better" decisions, or young people need to learn democratic decision-making in school if they are to practice it effectively as adults). While sound as far as they go, there is a deeper argument to be made. The "ideals," the values and moral principles, undergirding democracy as a way of life are the same as those undergirding education. Schools then should embody the principles of democracy not simply for practical reasons but because they are a necessary part of a "sound education."

He proceeds to discuss a list of factors that in his vision would characterize a democratic school, and develops an explanation of why schools are generally found wanting in this area. Although he refers to the fact that teachers are often excluded from meaningful involvement in a range of educational decisions, and that parents are even more rarely involved or included only through rather clumsy and ineffective mechanisms, he focuses mainly on including students more fully in school decision-making.

Students would need to be active creators of the school rather than its passive beneficiaries, not simply within the curriculum framework, but in the total life of the school. They would have to take on the real challenge of living, not the artificial ones of textbooks. . . . Schooling is organized to have things done to students according to somebody else's plan of what will produce the desired results. Such a view is incompatible with notions of democracy, and is also incompatible with the concept of education, which is surely not something that can be done to people, but something they must do for themselves.

I sympathize with this viewpoint. About twenty years ago a colleague and I wrote a small book advocating much the same thing, based upon a broad study of student participation in decision-making in the secondary schools of Ontario. We found that such participation generally ranged between minimal and nil. Moreover, among the very few who were involved, generally through some form of "student council," the learning outcomes were strongly negative. Their beliefs about democratic institutions in the broader society were much more cynical than those of students generally. And the deeper their involvement, and the longer they stayed involved, the more cynical they became. They were learning that democratic institutions were a sham, manipulated by those few with "real" power, and not permitted or capable to deal with issues of any serious concern to their constituents. Surely not the intended outcome (Farrell and Alexander 1975)!

By Levin's reckoning, things haven't changed in these past twenty years. One of the reasons Levin notes for this continuing condition is a pervasive belief that students do not have the knowledge and maturity to make wise decisions. He wryly (but I think accurately) observes that if the criteria of sufficient knowledge and maturity were applied to participation in democratic institutions more generally, a large portion of the adult population would have to be politically disenfranchised. More importantly, he asserts that young people are generally much more capable of practicing wise and sensible democracy than we give them credit for. As part of the support for this view he notes the following: "We can also look at non-school situations in which students do get to participate more actively, such as youth organizations. Would not experience with these organizations indicate that young people do have, and can further develop, reasonable decision-making skills?"

I can affirm that claim from personal experience. As I have noted in previous editorials in these pages, I have been a scout troop leader for many years, since 1958. A properly run scout troop is a small self-organizing democracy. A "troop" is a collection of small groups (called "patrols," usually 4 to 6 kids) of eleven- to fifteen-year-old youngsters (the age range varies somewhat from nation to nation) who collectively make most of the important decisions about what they will learn and do, how they will go about it, what kind of "expert assistance/teaching" (sometimes from adult leaders, more often from older scouts) they need, all within a general set of moral/ethical principles and "curriculum" guidelines. As adult leaders (as with teachers, as Levin notes) we *do have* more knowledge and expertise in some areas (although far fewer than you might imagine if you haven't worked with kids in this kind of learning program), and we do have legal and ethical responsibilities for their welfare while under our tutelage, but the general pedagogical approach is: give them the general guidelines and constraints, let them decide, show them how to go about it if they need to learn, and then get out of their way and let them get on with it, stepping in again only when and if something starts to go seriously awry. And through it all enjoy their company and have fun with them, building up a relationship of trust that may permit them to talk about "serious personal problems" as and when the need arises.

Almost always, when kids come into this program around eleven years of age, they have had no experience in collective decision-making. (That is in itself a reinforcement of Levin's argument and an indictment of how we arrange the "formation"—that wonderful French word that has no simple English translation—of our young.) But, and this is the most important point, they generally learn very quickly, as kids usually do when they are engaged in something important to them and are given space to "learn" rather than to be "taught." Within a year or two at the most, they commonly become very good at democratic behavior, and quite adept at such democratic arts as negotiation, accommodation of differing interests and preferences, and compromise. And the decisions they come to are generally very sensible and wise (and in the few cases where not, they usually welcome some gentle adult guidance about how to get off the rock they are stuck on). Indeed, and I do not say this facetiously, if I compare the democratic decision-making behavior of the scouts I work with to that of your typical university faculty meeting, or other adult groups in which I participate, the scouts win hands down. My personal experience with this is not atypical or idiosyncratic, and it is not social class or wealth-bound. In my "paid university role" I travel around the world a great deal. Almost everywhere I go, in nations rich and poor and neighborhoods rich and poor, I end up hooked into local scouting groups—it is a world-wide brotherhood/sisterhood. Almost everywhere it is fundamentally the same. There are currently well over 25 mil-

lion young people, in almost every nation/culture in the world (the majority in nations that we in rich nations would arrogantly call "developing"), successfully carrying out the scouting program. It is the largest youth movement in the world. And almost everywhere it works very easily in enacting routinely what Levin calls "the educational requirements for democracy." This is one of the reasons the World Organization of the Scouting Movement was the first organizational recipient of the International Prize for Peace Education initiated by UNESCO in the early 1980s. This experience clearly gives lie to the notion that kids are not capable of, and therefore cannot be trusted with, democracy. If those of us who are supposedly "experienced," "knowledgeable," and "mature" adults can't figure out how to unleash that learning potential of young people within the formal school system, then it is not the kids' problem; it is *ours*.

Levin's basic claim, to return to the original theme, is that *students* should have more power and control over their own learning, and that they are capable of wisely and responsibly exercising that authority, under a much looser form of adult guidance and supervision than is typical in our schools. In the book review argument between Mark Holmes and Thomas Kellaghan a different claim to power over education is debated. At issue in this quite heated debate, which comes close to the limits of what is generally acceptable in academic discourse, is the power of *parents* with respect to the education of their children. Levin claims, correctly in my view, that students can reasonably easily, with appropriate educational guidance, learn how to sort out differences among themselves democratically. But what then of the parents' claim to authority and power over the education of their children? Here we have a tripartite authority/control conundrum: the school, students, and parents. Holmes claims that the Kellaghan et al. book sets up the "school," through "parent education" or "parent involvement" programs, as a teacher not only of *students,* but of their *parents,* in how to "parent" their children well so as to prepare them and support them for the purposes of the school. Besides claiming based on empirical evidence that the school cannot in reality much affect "parenting" among families whose lifestyles do not happen to match the expectations of the school, Holmes argues that the power relationship should be the other way around—parents upon school rather than school upon parents: "It would be salutory for educators to begin to think in terms of how parents may involve schools (and educational experts in the universities) in the education of their children" (rather than the other way around). In arguing for parental power on the education of the parents' children, Holmes constructs a now rather familiar argument for allowing/developing/encouraging different sorts of schools among which parents can choose according to their own lights about how they want their children to grow and learn.

One quite fascinating thing here is that while Levin pays scant attention to the importance of the power of *parents,* Holmes and Kellaghan pay no attention at all to the potential power of *students* in the complex tripartite educational equation. Each argument effectively leaves out of consideration one key stakeholder group. It all becomes either students vs. the school, and forget the parents, or school vs. the parents, and forget the students. Surely we can, if we wanted to, do better than that in the complex business of sorting out who should have what kind and degree of authority on educational decision-making, and responsibility for its consequences.

Holmes notes that the "parental power" or "parental choice" view of things can only work well if the parents (again, no mention of the possibility of the children having a different point of view—as a parent, an educator, and a scout leader this seems to me an odd stance implicitly to take) are part of a value community such that they can search out a school or school system that matches and reinforces for their children the value stances they as a community of parents have. He notes that such "communities" are rare, and increasingly so, in North America. (This is also an increasingly uncommon condition throughout the world.) Fagan's article about a small community in Newfoundland illustrates just how complex and multifaceted the idea of "community" is even in a very small place. This is a fascinating and very instructive account of life in a small place that geographically is in North America but is about as far removed in terms of lifestyle, culture, and history from the standard (mostly urban) North American experience as can be imagined by most of us. This account is not, however, just a bit of interesting exotica for those of us who live our lives in the big cities. What Fagan finds is that even in this very small and seemingly homogeneous community, with strong and very old traditions and many ways of culturally reinforcing them, there are still important differences in how "education" and "literacy" are understood and valued. "The study points up the importance of identifying the many stakeholders in education [even in a very small and homogeneous community—my observation] and in making provision for them to influence school policy and curriculum decision." A very important differentiator of opinion and value stance is *age* (hence the words "Cross-Generational Perspectives on Educational Issues" in the title of the article). Of particular importance here is that the views of young people (students) about education differ markedly from those of people in the age range of their parents. This should hardly surprise us—even in a small and homogeneous community. But given this, how then do we reconcile the argument for more student power

over educational decisions with the argument for more parent power over educational decisions? Perhaps by bringing both groups more fully into educational decision-making, all involved, including the school-people, will have to learn better the arts of democracy for which Levin argues—but it will surely not be a simple task. The issues raised here are fundamental to thinking about the other two articles in this issue, although they seem, at first glance, unrelated.

Both argue, based upon detailed analysis of a few students and/or school classes, for the fundamental importance of increasing the importance of, indeed, infusing the curriculum with, "the arts." Gabella provides a detailed and thoughtful account of how "the arts" are included in the teaching of history in one secondary school. While arguing strongly and evocatively for this, and more generally for using "the arts" as a point from which to view curriculum building and educational inquiry, she also carefully analyzes a variety of significant and complex epistemological, curricular, and moral questions which arise from her study of student reactions to and comments upon their "arts-infused" history course. Roosevelt uses a very detailed analysis of the growth of one nine-year-old boy as a writer in a "writing workshop" program (this article can usefully be read in conjunction with the dialogue between Lensmire and Lin on writing workshops in the previous issue of this journal) to argue that we should examine children's writing not as necessarily autobiographical (as such writing is usually understood), but within the concepts of and literary analysis of *fiction* writing.

Questions arise here with reference to the issue of power and control over educational decision-making. Both authors present us with compelling and complex tales of student growth and questioning within these "arts-based" curricular approaches. But what, one may well wonder, did their *parents,* taking Holmes' point of view, and the point of view of the older (parental) generation in Fagan's account of a small village in Newfoundland, think of all this? Why did neither Gabella nor Roosevelt include the parents' points of view in their research? And what if the parents did not feel comfortable with what the educators (both teachers and university professors) were doing with their children? We don't know. It is a question not dealt with, yet from the standpoint of the passionate politics of education it may be the most important question. Brendan, the boy in Roosevelt's tale, indicates in his end-of-year self-evaluation a "sense of accomplishment and growth, as a writer and a student . . . it is evident that he is thinking of himself *as* a writer of fiction, that is, as a person—an author, a *maker*—who shapes events and language in purposeful narratives . . ." In his self-evaluation report Brendan seems to agree. "I think i am a good writer. I really want to write like Stephan King when i grow up. I think Writing Work Shop has helped me with my working abilities and has kind of been icouriging me to do better in school." Brendan also reports the following: ". . . I need to work on my punchuaction. . . . punchuaction and people not under standing my writings get in my way." So Roosevelt and Brendan agree that some powerful learning has been going on here. On the evidence given this seems a reasonable conclusion to me. I wonder, however, what Brendan's parents thought of all of this. Did they appreciate his growth as an authentic author? Or did they worry (as many of the "back to basics" parents do) about the fact that by the end of grade four he still had serious problems with "punchuaction" (and, obviously, spelling)? I expect, from my experience of school communities in various places, that opinion on the question would vary dramatically. The dilemma here is that to argue for democracy in education is to invite a wide variety of different and strongly held views into the discourse. How do we reconcile them? Whether we can invite those differing views into our inquiry and our practice, or simply exclude them because we know that we know best, may be the ultimate test of whether we are willing to and capable of working toward the vision of education and democracy that Levin proposes.

Reference

Farrell, J. P., and W. P. Alexander. 1975. *The Individualized System: Student Participation in Decision-making.* Toronto: OISE Press.

Form at end of book

Schools As Social Institutions

Questions

Reading 4. In your present community and during your teaching career, investigate the changes in the social services provided to families and children. What services are currently available? When and why were they initiated? Who do these programs serve? Are these programs effective in meeting the needs of the community? What changes, if any, would you propose?

Reading 5. What types of day- and child-care facilities exist in your local community? Are they public or private? What sites are used? To what extent are parents and the larger community involved in these programs? Who are the students served? How are the programs funded? How do the local programs compare with the twenty-first century, School Development Program (SDP), or Comer-Zigler programs? Are there data to indicate the impact of the local programs on those enrolled? Share your findings about various programs with classmates.

Reading 6. Beginning with the Comer process for extending the role of the school beyond educating students, there have recently been efforts to add services for families at neighborhood schools. A study by Hardiman, Curcio, and Fortune, however, reveals that a large percentage of board of education members do not believe that schools should go beyond educating the students who attend those schools. As a prospective teacher, what role(s) might you play in educating all members of the community about the new services that schools are being called on to provide?

How can schools as social institutions meet the needs of society?

With the changing nature of society, virtually all social institutions, including schools, must change to successfully accommodate changing demographics, workforce demands, family expectations, and political, social, economic, and cultural needs. Over the years, schools have assumed a variety of tasks assigned by political, economic, and social interests. Among these tasks are providing free or low-cost meals (breakfast, snacks, and/or lunch), promoting racial and ethnic integration of society, providing some health-care services (medical and dental), developing before- and after-school activities, and offering preschool programs to prepare young children for kindergarten. At least to some extent, such programs have been helpful to the target audiences. These and other challenges remain even as new support services are established.

In Reading 4, Sharon L. Kagan is concerned specifically with the needed support systems for families (both adults and children) residing in urban inner-city situations. Various social institutions, such as schools, religious organizations, and human service institutions, are working together to foster learning and to create a new social fabric of society. Kagan suggests that school-linked/service integration may well be a means of supporting families in their quest to function successfully in the coming years.

In Reading 5, Matia Finn-Stevenson and Barbara M. Stern describe a school for the twenty-first century that links child-care opportunities with public schools, whereby parents and other adults work together to plan and implement learning experiences that promote optimal child development. The authors describe the experiences of three model programs using the Comer-Zigler Initiative and the plans for evaluations and a wider dissemination of data related to the program.

Despite the research cited by the authors of Readings 4 and 5, the authors of Reading 6 (Priscilla Hardiman, Joan Curcio, and Jim Fortune) report that a national survey of school board members revealed that a majority of those board members disagree with the notion of schools meeting any needs beyond those of schooling for the students in their districts.

Support Systems for Children, Youths, Families, and Schools in Inner-City Situations

Sharon L. Kagan

Yale University

This article is about rights, learning, and the need for support systems that foster both. It begins with the premise that we have been attitudinally misguided in our understanding of the truly important learnings for life and structurally misdirected in where and how such learnings take place. This article suggests that only when America realigns its attitudes about, and structures for, learning will all children— and inner-city children in particular —have the means and intents to thrive in an American democracy appropriate for the 21st century.

The Current Context

Access to knowledge and the pursuit of equal rights and social justice have long been laudable goals—goals that Americans like to think distinguish this nation from all others on earth. Given this historic commitment, why are so many currently concerned that inner-city children are being short-changed on both accounts? And why is there such urgency to reexamine these issues? Such concerns emerge, in no small measure, because so many of our nation's social institutions are simultaneously in flux.

The Family

Contemporary families look and behave differently than those of eras past. This is not a small change; Mintz (1991) noted that over the past three decades, "American family life has undergone a historical transformation as radical as any that has taken place in the last 150 years" (p. 184). Soaring numbers of divorced adults, nontraditional families, single-parent households, and working mothers frame the social landscape. It is axiomatic to note that the prototypical family arrangement of breadwinner father, housewife mother, and two children now constitutes less than 15% of American households (Mintz & Kellogg, 1988), with that number steadily decreasing.

Fueled, in part, by personal preference, such changes have been exacerbated by structural changes in the American economy. Gordon (1995) noted that it is the political economy of the nation, along with the priorities it sets, that influences family functioning. Exportation of jobs offshore and the growth of nontaxable multinationals create an economic climate that prohibits many individuals from adequately supporting a family. A reality for all, the ravages of the changing political economy are

Questions

In your present community and during your teaching career, investigate the changes in the social services provided to families and children. What services are currently available?

When and why were they initiated?

Who do these programs serve?

What evidence suggests that these programs are effective in meeting the needs of the community?

What changes, if any, would you propose?

Sharon L. Kagan, EDUCATION AND URBAN SOCIETY, Vol. 29, No. 3, pp. 277–295, copyright © 1997 by Sage Publications. Reprinted by permission of Sage Publications, Inc.

particularly devastating for low-income minority families. Wilson (1987) suggested that declining economic and employment opportunities for African American men have reduced the desirable marriage pool, contributing to the number of single-parent, female-headed African American households. Galston (1993) noted that the "causal arrow" could point in the opposite direction, that is, changes in family structure could precipitate poverty. Ellwood (1988), for example, indicated that 73% of children from one-parent families experience poverty at some point in their childhood, compared with only 20% of children from two-parent families.

Whatever the cause of these changes, the effect is huge. The well-being of children has declined, and the percentage of children in poverty is soaring. In 1993, for example, 15.7 million U.S. children were poor, the highest number in 30 years. In addition, low-income children are "two times more likely than other children to die of birth defects and three times more likely to die from all causes combined" (Children's Defense Fund, 1995, p. 19). Demographics for subgroups of children are noteworthy: 4.1 million American children are growing up in neighborhoods where at least 40% of the population is poor (Children's Defense Fund, 1995). Further, among children younger than age 6, one in four lives in poverty; among African American children, the ratio rises to one in two (Galston, 1993).

Human Service Institutions

If such dramatic changes in the nation's familial institutions were matched by human service institutions that could suitably respond, the impact could probably be mitigated. Social service institutions, however, are faced with their own problems: inadequate funding, personnel shortages, service delivery fragmentation, and overly burdened, dysfunctional, and costly bureaucracies, to mention just a few. Morrill (1992) noted that the human services system (in which he includes education) is a system of significant size and expense. In 1989, for example, "countable human service expenditures on behalf of children totaled $239.8 billion in federal, state, and local funds, plus another $38.6 billion in tax expenditures—a total of $278.4 billion" (p. 36).

Perhaps fueled by such large public expenditures, human services have been a focus of criticism and cries for reform. As one target for a "reinvented government," social services institutions are examining not only operational efficiencies but also the very orientation of their work. Richman (1995) considered this the monetary and functional bankruptcy of the social services. Chaskin and Richman (1992) posited that a predominant emphasis on the casework approach to social services rather than on

community development and individual opportunity (as in the settlement houses) has created a social service void where little attention is accorded to the intersection of individual, familial, and community interests. Embedded in a deficit orientation in which individualized services were designed to ameliorate individual failings (mental health, health, juvenile delinquency, child abuse), current social service reform is undergoing an inside-out/outside-in reconstruction. Many practitioners and theorists are calling for vast reform in the human services, with emphasis on outcomes, collaboration, systemic linkages, community embeddedness, cultural sensitivity, nondeficit orientation, prevention, and new roles for families and human service providers (Bruner, 1991; Kagan & Weissbourd, 1994; Richman, 1995; Tyack, 1992). In short, like the institutions of families that they were designed to serve, human service agencies are undergoing massive changes, attempting to adjust to a new social fabric and to incorporate new learnings in the pursuit of institutional improvement and service justice.

Educational Institutions

Not immune to public pleas for reform, formal and informal educational institutions are also undergoing massive efforts to realign approaches to learning and equity. Like their counterparts in the human services, educational institutions have received their fair share of criticism, the recent wave dating from *A Nation at Risk* (National Commission on Excellence in Education, 1983). Americans, although often satisfied with their own local schools, are frequently dissatisfied with schooling in general. Although the literature does not always support this broad-based dissatisfaction (National Center for Education Statistics, 1994), the American public expresses concern about increases in drop-out rates, the readiness of American students for employment in a global economy, and growing disparities between the accomplishments of the rich and those of the poor. More than 60% of those polled in a recent study say academic standards are too low; more than two thirds want to raise standards for promotion from grade school to junior high school (Johnson & Immerwahr, 1994). Further, grave concern exists for the safety of youngsters in American schools—and for good reason. About 16,000 thefts and violent crimes occur on or near school grounds every day (Children's Defense Fund, 1995).

To address these concerns and the many pressing educational problems, politicians, the business and philanthropic communities, and educators have enacted scores of reforms: site-based management, service integration, reformed curriculums, outcomes orientation, professional development, charter schools, and new technology.

Additional efforts include the countless "name-brand" programs being developed and implemented by educational innovators, along with various state policy reforms originating with legislation. Federal initiatives—including Title I, Goals 2000, and the School to Work Opportunities Act—all seek to improve the structure and practice of the nation's educational and social service enterprise.

Other Community-Based Organizations

Aside from the public bureaucracies that support children and families, a brigade of highly effective community institutions also warrants attention, as they, too, are engaged in promoting learning and social equity. Among them are a class of services for children and youths, known as youth-serving organizations, including clubs, service organizations, and mediating facilities. Although different from schools and other formal institutions in character and culture, these youth-serving organizations have been, and continue to be, extremely successful in attracting and maintaining the interests of young people by providing opportunities for authentic, ongoing learning (Heath & McLaughlin, 1994). Even though they have been long underrecognized for their educative value, youth-serving organizations have provided many youths with a kind of education and support not available through schools.

Such organizations are also being asked to make changes to accommodate new social needs. They are being encouraged to work with schools, because schools can offer a number of unique contributions and resources, including staff who are committed to children and their learning, space set up for learning, and resources such as computers to extend learning opportunities. Moreover, youth-serving organizations are increasingly seen as making unique contributions through environments that stress all domains of learning. Other types of community-based organizations that support learning are the growing numbers of private, nonprofit organizations that support families. Salamon (1992) defined these organizations as privately incorporated entities that serve a public purpose such as the "advancement of health, education, scientific progress, social welfare, or pluralism" (p. 5). Composed of hundreds of thousands of organizations including social clubs, member cooperatives, business groups, and services providers, these private nonprofit organizations form a significant component of the community service structure, augmenting the work of formal institutions.

Among these institutions are more than 350,000 religious organizations—churches, mosques, synagogues, and other places of worship—that primarily exist to meet the educational and spiritual needs of their members. Enjoying a favored position in American law (via their tax exempt status), churches make a substantial contribution to the social fabric of the community. Their focus on learning and on fostering social justice has historically placed many such institutions at the cusp of reform. This continues to hold true, with many religious institutions offering services such as child care (Lindner, Mattis, & Rogers, 1983) and family support.

Churches that serve minority communities historically have been meccas for support, learning, and personal expression, and have therefore been revered. For example, Caldwell, Greene, and Billingsley (1994) noted that "no other institution in the history of the African-American community has garnered more respect and devotion than the Black church" (p. 138). In contemporary society, an estimated 75,000 Black churches serve more than 24 million churchgoers (Lincoln & Mamiya, 1990). Today, Black churches, many of them in inner cities, are providing educational services, support services, and counseling and intervention. And in some communities, the church is the primary core of support for children and youths—a spiritual, emotional, and physical safe haven.

Seeing the Context Whole

As the conditions of families and children become increasingly stressed and complex, social institutions are constantly asked to respond to these stressors. Indeed, such institutions are not immune from the responsibility to be adaptive, to consider new roles, and to capitalize on new opportunities (Crowson & Boyd, 1993). Moreover, few human service institutions are immune from fostering human learning—for their workers and for the public. Learning is not the private purview of schools; all institutions are in the learning business. To verify this, we simply need to observe social institutions as they come to grips with new learnings about changing social needs and about their capacities as individual institutions and as institutions seeking to reform themselves. We see institutions and organizations grappling with revamped structures, policies, and practices as they seek to accommodate the contemporary needs of children and families. It is to these structural changes, changes that seek to incorporate new learnings, that we now turn.

Redirecting Structures for Learning

The Schools

Cremin (1977), in his Pulitzer prize-winning trilogy on American education, noted that when the Colonists arrived, they transported an educational configuration known to them, one that included the household, the church, and the school. Each stood in time-honored relation to the others, with the household carrying by far the greatest burden for education. As the society changed and immigrant children—fresh from school with lessons of a new culture—became interpreters of change for their families, schools became more important as institutions of learning. Abetted by the swelling numbers of professional educators, organized professional organizations, unions, and curriculum theorists and developers, schools soon became the center of the learning industry.

In so doing, schools specialized in a brand of learning that focused on cognitive attainment. Schools also promoted processes and places for learning. Mechanisms of drill, repetition, and adherence to quiet and order obtained in special rooms and buildings were established especially to promote this brand of instruction. Except for notable interludes, lost in the process was a commitment to, and understanding of, learning that transcended the school. What happened after school or on weekends in homes, boys' and girls' clubs, and religious settings was considered optional. Indeed, the importance of formal schooling was sealed when compulsory attendance was mandated, with a bevy of truant officers to enforce the mandate.

Despite this emphasis on formal learning, schools have been asked repeatedly to become instruments of social change by taking on more and different responsibilities (Cremin, 1976). Faced with the economic depression of 1893 and fueled by the social reformers of the times, schools were asked to take on services such as providing school lunches, kindergartens, medical and dental inspections, home visiting efforts, vocational guidance and counseling programs, services for wayward youths, and summer programs, to name a few (Tyack, 1992). By the 1930s, community schools had taken root, rising to full prominence in the 1950s. In its 1952–1953 annual yearbook devoted to community education, the National Society for the Study of Education (1953) reported that schools had two emphases: to serve the entire community (not merely the school-age population) and to develop the resources of the community as a part of the educational enterprise. This commitment to expanding the definition and services associated with schools was reaffirmed in the 1960s, when educational reformers focused on supporting families, not simply the children in them.

Recent analyses optimistically suggest that despite some resistance to change, headway has been made in fostering structural reform and in augmenting the nature of schools' "self-conception." Tyack (1992) noted that despite intentions to return to an emphasis on academic rigor, schools actually have opened their doors to a broadened agenda. According to Tyack, administrators have become managers of schools that deliver social and health services as well as instruction, evidenced in the fact that teachers constituted only 52% of all school employees in 1986—compared with 70% in 1950. Moreover, in that same period, the ratio of individual pupils to support staff fell from 83 to 30. Graham (1993) concurred that American schools have long been involved in carrying out a social agenda, noting that education delivered what society wanted. When the nation wanted greater access for all students and more sustained attendance, we got it. Thus, rather than being chided for failing or disappointing the populace, American education should be (and once was) accoladed for its abilities and accomplishments. In short, as they do now, schools have historically altered their structures to accommodate new learnings about the comprehensive needs of children and families.

The Schools and Other Community-Based Institutions

Closely aligned with schools are a series of school-linked/service integration initiatives that also seek to make many community institutions responsive to the learning and development of children and families. Two closely allied efforts, school-linked services and services integration, are discussed below.

School-Linked Services

Among the most popular efforts are those that have been dubbed school-linked or school-based services. These seek to improve the "educational performance and well-being of at-risk, school-age children by addressing their multiple needs in a coordinated manner" (U.S. General Accounting Office, 1994, p. 1). Although many such efforts are envisioned primarily for at-risk, school-age children, there are also school-linked efforts that attend to the needs of non-risk populations, linking, for example, with community-based organizations for after-school care. There are also efforts that link younger-than-school-age populations with child care and other services.

The popularity of such programs is increasingly widespread. In 1993, the General Accounting Office estimated that they had taken root in more than 200 districts and at least eight states. Inherent in the concept of school-linked services is the need to streamline services so that access and efficiency will be maximized (Center for the Future of Children, 1992). To meet this need, services may be located on school grounds or in school facilities and administered either by the school itself or by other agencies or organizations. In most cases, these services are linked to the schools via contractual agreements and established systems of referral. Dryfoos (1994) has chronicled the evolution of many such efforts, noting that health clinics are finding homes in schools along with child care centers, family support groups, parenting education, and literacy training. She notes, however, that only a small percentage of such efforts are actually school administered (Dryfoos, 1994). Nonetheless, the efforts draw together community institutions in ways that create new opportunities for service and for learning.

Service Integration

Allied with efforts to lodge services in or near schools are additional efforts that are reshaping the fundamental design of all community services to increase effectiveness and efficiency (Kagan & Neville, 1993). These efforts, loosely termed *service integration,* begin with the premise that a broad realignment of community service delivery is necessary. Although it can be helpful to work with one institution to colocate or to expedite service access, such piecemeal efforts are insufficient to alter the long-term structure and conditions of human service. Service integrators are less concerned with a particular program or institution than they are with discerning ways to re-create the infrastructure and incentive systems to make durable, systemic (rather than programmatic) reform. As such, those concerned with issues of service integration are examining new ways to alter funding streams and governance and evaluation practices (Agranoff, 1991; Altman, 1991; Kagan, 1994; Kahn & Kamerman, 1992). These efforts complement school-linked reforms, seeking ways to alter the very structure of human services so that real community linkages—those that durably bind schools with other service organizations—can be fostered.

Although appealing in concept, the intellectual and functional overhaul that is necessary to accommodate service integration efforts is not easy. Further, such efforts tend to contradict the categorical modes of service delivery, in which each institution retains primary responsibility for its own efforts. Service integration demands collective accountability, and yet mechanisms that would effectively foster collective accountability are still quite embryonic. Generally speaking, service integration demands new governance and planning structures that are only just beginning to emerge.

Despite their difficulties, the increasing efforts toward school-linked and integrated service provision signal that schools and communities are recognizing that the responsibility for learning transcends schools. Cremin's (1976) triad of responsibility for learning—the school, the household, and the church—is being augmented to include a host of institutions and organizations performing an educative function in concerted rather than discrete fashion.

Family Support Efforts

Although little known and understood just two decades ago, family support efforts have grown remarkably to capture a prominent position on the American social agenda. Emanating from fields as diverse as health, education, welfare, prison reform, community development, parent education, social work, and organizational theory, family support efforts are often informal providers of services working simultaneously to reform the ways in which human services are conceptualized and delivered. Family support is rooted in commitments to building family strengths, prevention, diversity, peer support, and family integrity. Begun originally by program providers who were eager to learn and to share family support strategies, these efforts have always accorded prominence to egalitarian relationships among and between families and program staff (Kagan & Weissbourd, 1994). Ideally, family support programs are also embedded in, and contribute to, communities.

Through the years, as family support has adhered to these tenets, it has been particularly effective as a catalyst for change in diverse institutions. Institutions may adopt the principles of family support, thus infusing their normal operations with a family support perspective. In addition, large agencies may create special family support programs, operated under their aegis or in their facilities. It is not unusual for a health center, for example, to adopt a family support orientation that affects its basic institutional policies (such as visiting provisions) and also to establish a family support program either independently or in conjunction with a hospital. Similarly, schools have been particularly influenced by family support, with many using the movement's principles to reshape basic policies (e.g., report card conferencing). Many schools have created family support centers or family resource rooms in their facilities (Kagan, 1987).

Beyond the establishment of family support centers in schools, many state education departments and school districts have fostered the establishment of additional school-based family support programs, along with family support programs that reach into children's homes (e.g., "New Parents as Teachers" in Missouri and "Early Childhood and Family Education" in Minnesota). The commitment of schools to family support centers has been so strong that some states have, through legislation, established centers as cornerstones of educational reform (e.g., Kentucky Education Reform Act, Connecticut's Family Resource Centers, and Full-Service Schools in Florida). Other states have adopted a mixed delivery system for family support, including schools and other community-based organizations in the provision of services through family centers (e.g., Colorado's Family Development Centers). Fueled by federal dollars and local support, the family support movement is burgeoning, promising cutting edge reform of the ways that institutions and families interact and the ways in which families are supported in their multiple roles as parents and providers.

Lessons from the Reforms

Lessons in General

What have we learned from the plethora of efforts to reform services for children throughout the nation, particularly in inner cities, that can propel support systems toward better results? Several observations are noteworthy. First, there is growing recognition of the importance of evaluating such efforts; as a result, many evaluations exist. Second, there is growing concern about the evaluation enterprise. Evaluations often are methodologically flawed, with high attrition rates, control groups that are not comparable with intervention groups, program variation, and unspecified or unmeasurable outcomes. Moreover, the accountability systems being used to determine and assess outcomes is flawed, and some have called for its complete realignment (Kirst & Kelley, 1992). Others contend that we need new evaluation paradigms to examine systems efforts more appropriately (Knapp, 1995). In short, we have an abundance of information, some of it technically flawed, that can be used to provide clues to—rather than definitive answers regarding—the effects of systems efforts.

We have learned, for example, that the process for establishing support systems is often laborious, somewhat imprecisely conceived, and subject to contextual variables often beyond the control of program developers or implementers. Such efforts take time and may not be appropriate for every community (Annie E. Casey Foundation, 1995). Implementation is more likely to occur when there are outside patrons and supports for such services, and when there is a strong linkage among and between efforts. This has particularly been noted with regard to state and local initiatives (Kagan, Goffin, Golub, & Pritchard, 1995).

With regard to outcomes, there is less definitive material. Gomby and Larson (1992) noted that when efforts encourage parental support, results have been achieved in physical and behavioral domains, including improved cardiovascular fitness, weight loss, smoking reduction, and teen pregnancy prevention. Similarly, Wang, Haertel, and Walberg (1993) have found that integrated services do produce outcomes in frequently measured areas such as increased attendance, achievement, and self-esteem, along with reduced behavioral problems and drop-out rates. The authors caution, however, that the magnitude of such results is often not reported and that accomplishments vary by programmatic area and by specific project.

However promising, these accounts suggest that systems efforts are tough to evaluate not only because of their internal properties (e.g., design inconsistencies, participant variation, treatment variation) but also because of critical external factors including changes in the nature and level of support programs receive. All too often, system reform efforts are launched with considerable financial and political support, which then wanes over time. It appears, then, that our lessons about structure and organizational change outpace the lessons we need to learn about sustaining commitment to these efforts, that is, *attitudinal* change.

Structural Changes: The Good News

The above analyses suggest that much is happening structurally to realign learning and support services for children and families. Opportunities are being developed in and outside of schools, with new community institutions linking with schools to provide services. Family support programs are being created and developed throughout the nation to intervene before problems arise and to support contemporary families as they navigate life's responsibilities. Mainstream bureaucratic organizations are reforming themselves to be more accommodating and supportive, as well as more efficient.

Perhaps most impressive among the reforms are the changes taking place in schools and institutions formally charged with education. In addition to giving more attention to pedagogy and instructional practices, schools are refocusing their efforts on collaborative decision making that accords more power to staff and, in some cases, to parents. More than at any time in our history, schools are also becoming partners in the social agenda, working with other agencies and services. Whether linked as a result of an impetus from the business community or because of pressure from parents and consumers, schools are taking note.

This groundswell of structural reform is being precipitated as part of a national zeitgeist that seeks to reexamine our ways of doing business. Senge's (1990) powerful work on learning organizations, along with that of Osborne and Gaebler (1992) regarding the reinvention of government, is calling into question conventions of operations that we have long taken for granted. Today, change—not constancy—is an institutional prerequisite. The norm is to be driven by, and understood in terms of, mission and results, not categorical funding streams or input accountability.

In short, the changes in human service and educational institutions noted above, those that will help convert many settings to learning environments, are gaining currency. Schools stand the best chance of being joined in the educative role as at any time in our history. Indeed, schools as we know them today—isolated campuses used part-time, part-year by nonuniversal, age-segregated populations—may become relics replaced by learning communities coresponsible for the continuing educative function of the population.

Attitudinal Changes: The Bad News

That so much has been accomplished and that a zeitgeist for constructive reform exists is actually quite remarkable, given the state of our national conscience. We live in an era of deep and enduring tensions, with a widening ideological divide between haves and have-nots, urban and suburban, rich and poor, and Blacks, Whites, and others. Commitments to equality and social justice, once pervasive, are now waning. America has, it seems, put its equity blindfold on.

At the same time, but perhaps somewhat less consciously, America is closing its eyes to its children. Paradoxically, even as this nation *stands* as an economic and military superpower, it *stands by* as growing numbers of children and families develop without the hope of participating in the intellectual, spiritual, and economic wealth that many Americans take for granted. Daily, in our schools and in our mainstream institutions—good intentions and structural accomplishments aside—the covenant with the next generation is being broken. Today's children, growing numbers of them poor, are at risk of not becoming contributing members of society, reflective adults, or individuals capable of sustaining personal and employment relationships.

Education for democracy, upon which this nation's commitment to universal education was built, is eroding. It is not that we are making formal structural or policy changes such as doing away with compulsory school attendance. Rather, by informal moral and economic disinvestment, and by ignoring the need for sweeping attitudinal change, we discourage engagement and the kind of support for children that nurtures their creativity and human spirit. Despite some pedagogical reforms, much of today's education continues to quash inspiration in students. We perpetuate tedious, coercive activities that prepare American youths for assembly line jobs that were long ago exported to foreign nations. Often teachers know students as numbers, and they know each other as occupants of the next cubicle. We have depersonalized education as well as other human services. We wonder and worry about crime, building huge police forces and prisons as antidotes, but we abrogate responsibility for building a caring citizenry. We think back and wonder why Conant's (1961, 1964) prophecy is being fulfilled—we are building a nation of increasingly exploited, disconnected, dysfunctional people who will disrupt the social order. We read Kozol's (1992) *Savage Inequalities* and wonder, "Can this be us, contemporary America?"

Although not easy, structural, organizational, and pedagogical work is being called for and undertaken by those concerned about education and the human services (Grubb, 1995; Pallas, Natriello, & McDill, 1995). More difficult, however, is reforming the attitudinal and spiritual conditions that characterize and dissuade the American public from expending its commitments to nurture and protect all youngsters and to honestly prepare them for life in a 21st-century world. However difficult, disorganized, under-strategized, and underfunded, attitudinal and spiritual reform must play a part in the change agenda. Without attention in this domain, promising structural, organizational, and pedagogical reforms will be doomed to remain "demonstration" efforts, sequestered from the vast majority of youngsters. It is toward attitudinal change, then, that our efforts must be directed.

Creating Support Systems for Children and Families: Toward Attitudinal Change

Keep Up the Structural, Organizational, and Pedagogical Reforms

A focus on attitudinal reform is necessary but cannot alone achieve the kind of sweeping change of thinking needed. The most ardent skeptics are often those who need the most concrete evidence that greater commitment to, and greater public investment in, children's services will pay off. Without clear evidence that reform can be achieved and that investments matter, support for reform will not be forthcoming. Thus structural, organizational, and pedagogical reform must be sustained both to produce improved services and outcomes for children in the short term and to provide evidence for skeptics in the long term. As such, structural, organizational, and pedagogical reforms are the requisite tools—the ammunition—for attitudinal reform.

Reconceptualize Structural and Organizational Reform

Currently, most reforms are designed, developed, and implemented from the perspective of a single institution, whether the school or the social service agency. More rarely, reforms are conceptualized from the intersection of several agencies, so that a reform might emanate from community collaboration or from two organizations banding together for change. Only infrequently are reforms conceptualized from the perspectives of the consumers—the students, their parents, and the public. Indeed, if we envision a need for meaningful, successful, and durable reforms, then these consumers need to be engaged.

In crafting such engagement, it is important to distinguish between the *direct* consumers, children and parents of children who are enrolled in schools (or who receive services, and the *indirect* consumers, the broader public. Given the decreasing percentages of the population enrolled in schools, the mobilization of support for schools must, for several reasons, transcend those directly served and directly involved. First, from a functional perspective, the public must understand the nature of schooling and the challenges it poses; engagement in considering processes of reform is one effective strategy to accomplish this. Second, practically speaking, the public often has different perspectives, different kinds of knowledge, and different ways of knowing that can make their involvement a valuable addition. Third, if revised schools—schools that function in a democratic way in a democratic society—are to meet the public need, the public has a right and responsibility to become engaged.

Create Systems of Collective Accountability Around What Really Matters

If public attitudes are to change, schools and other public institutions must meet public expectations. The global performance of schools has been seriously questioned by the populace at a time when educational practitioners note some advances (National Center for Education Statistics, 1994). This schism of perception is fueled by different expectations, knowledge bases, and experiences. To engage public support and to change public attitudes toward education, there must be clarity and agreement on standards for, and outcomes of, education. Achieving such a consensus is, however, problematic and reflects the deep attitudinal divides that exist around education. Nonetheless, some states are achieving clarity around outcomes that include, but are not limited to, education, Engaging the public in coming to consensus regarding the ultimate goals of American education is a crucial task if public education is to commandeer public support.

Develops Mechanisms and Rituals for Community Collaboration

Attitudinal change is a process that is typically predicated on changes in knowledge or experience. Engaging professionals across systems and engaging the public are processes that will demand opportunities for both. Mechanisms for coming together should be created, as should be opportunities for different perspective taking and for knowledge building. In other words, attitudes will not change without some strategic thinking and planning and without mechanisms to frame such change. Ongoing activities, diverse projects, community gatherings, and celebrations all contribute to creating understanding within and across communities.

Engage the Media As a Partner and a Player

Public opinion is shaped dramatically by what is read and heard via the media. Prone to chronicling only the disasters, the media convey images of ineffective educational and social institutions. In so doing, they negate even neutral public attitudes. Alternative strategies to engage the media are clearly needed. In some communities, media executives sit on boards and committees, and are thus engaged in the hard process of educational restructuring. Media fellowships are being awarded to reporters who cover education beats. School systems and other human service organizations are working more closely with the media. In short, education and human service agencies are recognizing the necessity of using the instruments of society to their advantage. More of this needs to be done.

Train for the Three Cs—Change, Collaboration, Conviction

There is little in the professional training of educators and human service professionals to prepare them for the changed roles discussed herein. To accomplish this, new training approaches and new training objectives need to be developed and propagated. Training approaches need to be transdisciplinary so that workers with discrete skills will have knowledge and be less demanding of other fields and disciplines. Objectives for training must be reconstituted so that change, rather than being dreaded, will be regarded as the norm; adaptation and flexibility will be the new goals. Rather than assuming that collaboration with colleagues and the public is natural, new learnings must be infused into training so that collaborative problem solving, group consensus building, and amicable conflict resolution are part of the knowledge repertoire of human service professionals. Finally, individuals coming into human services must have passion and conviction that their work matters. Young people must be given opportunities to develop such passion and be exposed to role models who have conviction and dedication. Although training for passion and conviction is delicate, it is not so intricate and obtuse as to be impossible. The most inspirational professors should form the corps of preprofessional educators. They should be given opportunities for reflection and growth, and they should be compensated and rewarded justly. In short, we need to pay much more heed to the learnings of those coming in and those already in the professions if we expect them to deal with the challenges posed by 21st-century children and families, along with a recalcitrant public.

Conclusion

DuBois was correct: The most fundamental civil right is the right to learn. This article has suggested that in order for inner-city children to receive the educational and social services that will optimize their growth and development, new learnings are necessary. Constructive, important lessons for professionals about the structure, organization, and pedagogy of education and social services are evolving. What is sadly missing are the attitudes and spirit of the American public necessary to convert these learnings to a more positive reality for all youngsters.

References

Agranoff, R. A. (1991). Human services integration: Past and present challenges in public administration. *Public Administration Review, 51*(6), 533–542.

Altman, D. (1991). The challenges of service integration for children and families. In L. B. Schorr, D. Both, & C. Copple (Eds.), *Effective services for young children: Report of a workshop* (pp. 74–79). Washington, DC: National Academy Press.

Annie E. Casey Foundation. (1995). *The path of most resistance: Reflections on lessons learned from New Futures.* Baltimore, MD: Author.

Bruner, C. (1991). *Thinking collaboratively.* Washington, DC: Education and Human Services Consortium.

Caldwell, C. H., Greene, A. D., & Billingsley, A. (1994). Family support programs in Black churches: A new look at old functions. In S. L. Kagan & B. Weissbourd (Eds.), *Putting families first: America's family support movement and the challenge of change* (pp. 137–160). San Francisco: Jossey-Bass.

Center for the Future of Children. (1992). *The future of children: School-linked services.* Los Altos, CA: The David and Lucille Packard Foundation.

Chaskin, R. J., & Richman, H. A. (1992). Concerns about school-linked services: Institution-based versus community-based models. In *The future of children: School linked services.* Los Altos, CA: The David and Lucille Packard Foundation.

Children's Defense Fund. (1995). *The state of America's children yearbook, 1995.* Washington, DC: Author.

Conant, J. B. (1961). *Slums and suburbs.* New York: McGraw-Hill.

Conant, J. B. (1964). *Shaping educational policy.* New York: McGraw-Hill.

Crowson, R., & Boyd, W. (1993). Coordinated services for children: Designing arks for storms and seas unknown. *American Journal of Education,* 101, 141–179.

Cremin, L. (1976). *Public education.* New York: Basic Books.

Cremin, L. (1977). *Traditions of American education.* New York: Basic Books.

Dryfoos, J. (1994). *Full-service schools: A revolution in health and social services for children, youth and families.* San Francisco: Jossey-Bass.

DuBois, W.E.B. (1970). The freedom to learn. In P. S. Foner (Eds.), *W.E.B. DuBois speaks!* New York: Pathfinder.

Ellwood, D. (1988). *Poor support.* New York: Basic Books

Galston, W. A. (1993, Winter). Causes of declining well-being among U.S. children. *Administrative Quarterly.*

Gomby, D. S., & Larson, C. S. (1992). Evaluation of school-linked services. In *The future of children: School-linked services* (pp. 68–84). Los Altos, CA: The David and Lucille Packard Foundation.

Gordon, E. W. (1995). Commentary: Renewing familial and democratic commitments. In C. Rigsby, M. O. Reynolds, & M. Wang (Eds.), *School-community connections: exploring issues for research and practice* (pp. 45–57). San Francisco: Jossey-Bass.

Graham, P. A. (1993, February). What America has expected of its schools over the past century. *American Journal of Education, 101*(2), 83–98.

Grubb, N. (1995). The old problem of "new students": Purpose, content and pedagogy. In E. Flaxman & A. H. Passow (Eds.), *Changing populations: Changing schools* (pp. 4–29). Chicago: National Society for the Study of Education.

Heath, S. B., & McLaughlin, M. (1994). The best of both worlds: Connecting schools and community youth organizations for all-day, all-year learning. *Educational Administration Quarterly, 30*(3), 278–300.

Johnson, J., & Immerwahr, J. (1994). *First things first: What Americans expect from the public schools: A report from Public Agenda.* New York: Public Agenda.

Kagan, S. L. (1987). Home-school linkages: History's legacy and the family support movement. In S. L. Kagan, D. Powell, B. Weissbourd, & E. Zigler (Eds.), *America's family support programs* (pp. 161–181). New Haven, CT: Yale University Press.

Kagan, S. L. (1994). *Integrating services for children and families: Understanding the past to shape the future.* New Haven, CT: Yale University Press.

Kagan, S. L., Goffin, S., Golub, S., & Pritchard, E. (1995). *Toward systemic reform: Service integration for young children and their families.* Falls Church, VA: National Center for Service Integration.

Kagan, S. L., & Neville, P. (1993). *Family support services and school-linked services: Variations on a theme. An FRC report.* Chicago: Family Resource Coalition.

Kagan, S. L., & Weissbourd, B. (Eds.). (1994). *Putting families first: America's family support movement and the challenge of change.* San Francisco: Jossey-Bass.

Kahn, A., & Kamerman, S. (1992). *Integrating services integration: An overview of initiatives, issues, and possibilities.* New York: Columbia University School of Social Work and the National Center for Children in Poverty.

Kirst, M., & Kelley, C. (1992). *Collaboration to improve education and children's services: Politics and policymaking.* Paper presented at the Invitational Conference on School-Community Connections: Exploring Issues for Research and Practice, Philadelphia.

Knapp, M. S. (1995). How shall we study comprehensive, collaborative services for children and families? *Educational Researcher, 24*(4), 5–16.

Kozol, J. (1992). *Savage inequalities: Children in America's schools.* New York: Harper Perennial.

Lincoln, C. E., & Mamiya, L. (1990). *The Black church in the African-American experience.* Durham, NC: Duke University Press.

Lindner, E., Mattis, M., & Rogers, J. (1983). *When churches mind the children.* Ypsilanti, MI: The High/Scope Press.

Mintz, S. (1991). New rules: Postwar families (1955–present). In J. Hawes & E. Nybakken (Eds.), *American families: A research guide and historical handbook* (pp. 183–220). New York: Greenwood.

Mintz, S., & Kellogg, S. (1988). *Domestic revolutions: A social history of American family life.* New York: Free Press.

Morrill, W. (1992). Overview of service delivery to children. In *The future of children: School-linked services* (pp. 32–43). Los Altos, CA: The David and Lucille Packard Foundation.

National Center for Education Statistics. (1994). *The condition of education.* Washington, DC: U.S. Department of Education.

National Commission on Excellence in Education. (1983). *A nation at risk: The imperative for educational reform.* Washington, DC: Government Printing Office.

National Society for the Study of Education. (1953). *The 52nd yearbook of the National Society for the Study of Education, Part II: Community education.* Chicago: University of Chicago Press.

Osborne, D., & Gaebler, T. (1992). *Reinventing government.* Reading, MA: Addison-Wesley.

Pallas, A., Natriello, G., & McDill, E. (1995). Changing students/changing needs. In E. Flaxman & A. H. Passow (Eds.), *Changing populations: Changing schools* (pp. 30–58). Chicago: National Society for the Study of Education.

Richman, H. (1995). *Schools, social services, and communities.* Paper prepared for the Aspen Group.

Salamon, L. (1992). *America's nonprofit sector.* Baltimore: John Hopkins University, the Foundation Center.

Senge, P. M. (1990). *The fifth discipline: The art and practice of the learning organization.* New York: Doubleday.

Tyack, D. (1992). Health and social services in public schools: Historical perspectives. In *The future of children: School-linked services.* Los Altos, CA: The David and Lucille Packard Foundation.

U.S. General Accounting Office. (1994). *School-linked human services: A comprehensive strategy for aiding students at risk of school failure.* Washington, DC: Author.

Wang, M. C., Haertel, G. D., & Walberg, H. J. (1993). *School-linked services: A research synthesis.* Philadelphia: National Center on Education in the Inner Cities.

Wilson, W. J. (1987). *The truly disadvantaged: The inner city, the underclass, and public policy.* Chicago: University of Chicago Press.

Form at end of book

Integrating Early-Childhood and Family-Support Services with a School Improvement Process:
The Comer-Zigler Initiative

Matia Finn-Stevenson and Barbara M. Stern

Yale University

Abstract

In 1987, Edward Zigler conceptualized the School of the 21st Century, a child care and family-support model with 7 components linked to or based in public schools. In 1969, James Comer conceived of the School Development Program, which mobilizes adults in a school community to work together in planning a school program that promotes optimal student development. Independently, the School of the 21st Century and the School Development Program have been implemented in hundreds of U.S. schools. In 1992, a plan was developed at the Yale University Bush Center in Child Development and Social Policy to integrate the 2 models in a collaborative initiative termed CoZi. In this article, we present the background and description of the 2 models, the story of the first implementation of CoZi in an urban southeastern school, findings regarding implementation of the integrated model, an overview of the expansion to 3 pilot schools in different types of communities, and plans for evaluation and wider dissemination.

Societal Changes Leading to the School of the Twenty-First Century

In the past 30 years, the U.S. family has undergone numerous changes. By far the most dramatic has been the increasing number of mothers of young children who work outside the home. Currently, 57% of mothers with children under age 6 and 51% of mothers with infants under 1 years of age are employed outside the home (United States Department of Labor, 1988, 1993). The number of mothers with older children who are working is even higher (United States Department of Labor, 1993). Divorce, the increase in the number of single-parent families, and increased mobility of families, meaning that few parents can count on relatives and friends for assistance with child rearing and care, are examples of

Questions

What types of day- and child-care facilities exist in your local community?

Are they public or private?

What sites are used?

To what extent are parents and the larger community involved in these programs?

Who are the students served?

How are the programs funded?

How do the local programs compare with the twenty-first century, School Development Program (SDP), or Comer-Zigler programs?

Are there data to indicate the impact of the local programs on those enrolled?

Share your findings about various programs with classmates.

Matia Finn-Stevenson and Barbara M. Stern, *The Elementary School Journal*, Volume 98, Number 1. © 1997 by The University of Chicago. All rights reserved.

other factors affecting family life. Additionally, there has been an increase in the number of families with young children living in poverty and a decline in the median income of families, which pose stress and hardships, rendering parents and children vulnerable to mental health disorders (Tuma, 1989).

This increase in mothers working outside the home has brought about an unprecedented demand for child care, which far exceeds the supply (Committee on Economic Development, 1993; Willer, 1992). The lack of sufficient child care in the United States has been recognized for the last 2 decades by everyone, including working parents, corporate chief executive officers, educators, and legislators, and has been well reported in the media (Hofferth & Phillips, 1987). The 1970 White House Conference on Children voted the need for child care services as the most serious problem facing U.S. families. However, despite a few legislative attempts to improve the situation, such as the Child Care and Development Block Grant in 1990, each family still struggles to make its own arrangements as best it can, often in isolation and without the support of the traditional extended family. The child care system consists of a patchwork of fragmented services from a variety of sources (i.e., nonprofits, for-profits, family day-care offered in private homes) that are accountable to widely varying standards and not always easily accessible to the families that need them (Zigler & Lang, 1991).

The lack of a coherent child care system has three dimensions: availability, quality, and affordability. Availability of child care varies by region and socioeconomic class. Reisman, Moore, and Fitzgerald (1988) found that in affluent areas programs are available for one in five preschoolers as opposed to one in seven in the poorest communities. A more recent study (Fuller & Liang, 1995) showed that in Massachusetts, the state that spends more per capita on preschool programs than any other state, poor children have 40% fewer preschools available to them than wealthy children. In addition, if welfare mothers (65% of whom have children under the age of 5) are forced to go to work, the demand for preschools in the inner city will quickly overwhelm an already inadequate system (Fuller & Liang, 1995). For infants and toddlers, the situation is even worse (Fuller & Liang, 1995; Zigler & Lang, 1991). Essentially, parents fend for themselves in this environment, often leaving children in the care of neighbors or relatives, patching together a number of child care arrangements, or leaving school-age children alone in "self-care."

Quality of services also varies greatly and ranges from care that is developmentally appropriate for the age of the child and enhances growth in all developmental domains to that which is merely custodial and may in fact inhibit growth. During 1994 and 1995, two national studies documented this variation in quality, noting also that the majority of child care facilities, whether centers or home based, are of poor quality. A national study of family day-care and care by relatives indicated that only 9% of the homes sampled were of high quality whereas 56% were rated as custodial and 35% as poor (Galinsky, Howes, Kontos, & Shinn, 1994). In terms of center-based care, a recent national study of child care centers in four states indicated that most provided child care that is poor to mediocre (Helburn et al., 1995). This study showed that only one in seven centers provided a level of quality that is sufficient to promote healthy development and learning. A previous study on center-based child care yielded similar findings on the lack of quality, emphasizing that child care for preschoolers from working- and middle-class families is especially problematic (Whitebook, Phillips, & Howes, 1989).

Quality and affordability of child care are closely linked. High-quality care is usually defined as having stability, that is, a low staff turnover rate, high staff-to-child ratios, and staff trained in early-childhood and child development (Hayes, Palmer, & Zaslow, 1990). These indicators, however, translate into expensive child care. As a result, a tiered system of child care exists: the choices for low- and middle-income families are limited to low-cost and, most likely, low-quality child care, whereas more affluent families are able to purchase quality care (Zigler & Finn-Stevenson, 1994).

The effects of this tiered system are important because the experiences children have in these early settings influence their growth and development and, ultimately, their readiness for an academic program at age 5. It is well documented that good-quality preschool programs can provide children with the foundation for later academic success and can change their life trajectory (Berreuta-Clement, Schweinhart, Barnett, Epstein, & Weikart, 1984; Schweinhart, Barnes, & Weikart, 1993). Therefore, it is sensible to maximize the possibility that all children, regardless of socioeconomic level, have access to high-quality care during these critical years.

The important exceptions to Helburn et al.'s (1995) four-state study regarding the quality of child care centers were those centers operated by public agencies such as schools, colleges, and municipal agencies. These centers tended to be of higher quality and were less dependent on parent fees because of the in-kind support of the public agencies with which they were affiliated. This finding supports the idea that Edward Zigler has been promoting since 1987—that the child care system should be part of the public education system in order to make the best use of existing physical resources and to ensure quality, affordability, and equal access for all children. This feature serves as the foundation of the School of the Twenty-First Century.

The School of the Twenty-First Century

In response to the child care issues raised here, Zigler conceptualized the School of the Twenty-First Century (21C) in 1987. The goal of the program is to ensure the optimal development of children through the provision of good-quality child care and family-support services. The program calls for implementing a child care system within the already existing educational system and, where possible, using school buildings and administrative support services of local education agencies.

The 21C model includes two core child care components and several outreach services: all-day, year-round child care for children ages 3, 4, and 5; before-school, after-school, and vacation care for school-age children up to age 12; education and support for parents of children from birth to age 3, which is based on the Parents as Teachers or other home-visitation programs; information and referral; health and nutrition; and outreach to family day-care providers. This latter component is included to ensure that family day-care providers become part of the child care community and, as such, have access to training, social support, and other services they may need.

These components ensure a comprehensive array of services for children and families and make possible the continuity of care and support for children that provides the foundation on which subsequent learning occurs. The strength and potential of the program stem from its integration with the education system. By eliminating the distinction between child care and education, the model incorporates the view that learning begins at birth and occurs in all settings, not just within the traditional classroom. The school is no longer seen as a building delivering formal schooling during limited hours. Instead, the school becomes a place where formal schooling, child care, and the coordination of other services occur together from early morning until evening during 12 months of the year. Currently, 21C is being implemented in more than 400 schools in 13 states.

There is flexibility regarding the choice of components to implement. Based on a needs assessment, individual communities determine which components they will include in their program and often add others, such as adult education or social services. Though each program is unique, all 21C schools adopt a uniform set of principles that guide implementation from planning through stabilization and evaluation.

The first guiding principle calls for universal access to child care services and is achieved by instituting a sliding-scale fee system and subsidizing middle- and lower-income families. Second, the program must be noncompulsory, making available child care services to families who want

or need the services on a voluntary basis. Third, the program must focus on all developmental domains, including physical, cognitive, social, and emotional. This focus on the whole child is included because early-intervention and other services in the past emphasized cognitive development at the expense of other domains, although it is well known that children's social skills, their emotional status, and physical health as well as their cognitive development all play a role in predicting how well they will do in school. The fourth guiding principle is that all aspects of the program must be predicated on a partnership between parents and schools. Successful programs, such as Head Start, have demonstrated that much of their success can be attributed to the active participation of parents in the services provided to their children (Zigler & Muenchow, 1992; Zigler & Valentine, 1979). The fifth guiding principle requires increased recognition and support of child care providers through training, the provision of benefits, and pay upgrades. This is to underscore the critical role providers play in the quality of care children receive and their influence on children's development.

The School of the Twenty-First Century model was first implemented in Independence, Missouri, a midsize school district that implemented the program systemwide. The Yale Bush Center has nearly completed a 3-year outcome evaluation of the program (Finn-Stevenson, Chung, & Zigler, 1995). Preliminary results indicate that the program enjoys significant support from both parents and school personnel. Parents report an increase in the time they spend with their preschoolers and a decrease in the number of child care arrangements they use. Also, elementary schoolchildren who have participated in 21C child care programs in Independence achieved higher scores on standardized achievement tests than children in a matched comparison group.

During the same period that Zigler was studying the problems of young children and their families that were due to the lack of quality care during their early years, James Comer was formulating a process to help communities improve their schools. We now turn to the School Development Program and what led to its conceptualization.

Background of the School Development Program

The stressors cited earlier, especially those related to poverty, have had profound effects on inner-city schools. As early as 1969, Comer observed that children in New Haven's public schools were not achieving to their fullest potential. He also found that the organizational culture of the schools was not conducive to the students' optimal development or to the staff's sense of efficacy and comfort.

Parents felt unwelcome in the schools and had largely abandoned them (Comer, 1988, 1993).

Comer reflected on his own childhood in the 1940s when poor children seemed to fare better in school. He recalled that, in spite of poverty, communities were stronger and less mobile and adults could earn a living wage without higher education. He remembered what he termed a "conspiracy of adults," which included parents, school personnel, and community members, who had a common set of values, spoke with one voice, and were committed to supporting and protecting the children in their charge (Comer, 1988, 1993). Although it is unlikely there will ever be a return to the type of economy and community Comer remembers, he believes that schools, as the one public institution with which the majority of society still interacts, can provide a locus for change. With collaboration and a team effort, the school can become a place that bonds the community in order to create a growth-enhancing environment for its children. Based on this premise, Comer conceptualized the School Development Program.

The School Development Program

The School Development Program (SDP) is a process-oriented model that aims to build community and to support child development through a collaborative governance system that involves all the adult stakeholders in the school, including administrators, teachers, support staff, and parents. One belief on which the model rests is that learning occurs in the context of positive, nurturing relationships. Facilitators and principals are trained in how to establish and maintain those relationships. Another strong belief is that children develop along six pathways: physical, cognitive, psychological, language, social, and ethical (Comer, 1993). All school planning in SDP schools focuses on objectives that optimize growth along those pathways.

Unlike other school improvement efforts, SDP does not focus on one area of need; rather, the program is designed to facilitate a number of changes in the school so that school staff can work with one another and with parents in ways that benefit children. To achieve this goal, SDP has three teams, three operations, and three guidelines that make up its procedural core. The three teams include

1. the School Planning and Management Team (SPMT), which includes representatives of all adults in the school, makes policy decisions for the school, and annually develops and monitors a comprehensive school plan;

2. the Student and Staff Support Team, which addresses school climate and concerns of individual staff and students;

3. the Parent Team, which involves parents in all areas of school life. Parents are involved as members of the SPMT (along with representatives of teachers, administrators, and support staff), as members of a parent group that sponsors school projects, and as participants in school activities.

The SPMT conducts three operations:

1. it develops a comprehensive school plan that identifies goals in order to effect changes in academic areas and in the social climate of the school;

2. it conducts staff development activities that support the goals of the comprehensive school plan;

3. it conducts periodic assessments and modifications that allow the program to be adjusted as necessary.

The three process guidelines that facilitate implementation of the program are

1. a no-fault problem-solving policy that focuses on problems to be solved rather than placing blame for problems;

2. a consensus decision-making process in order to maximize commitment to decisions made;

3. a commitment to collaboration and an agreement to work together and not paralyze the process.

The implementation of these nine elements of SDP enables students, staff, and parents in the school to work together to improve the functioning of their school in a number of domains—academic and social development, school climate, and public relations. Like 21C, the program adapts to meet the needs of individual schools on the basis of data collected by the staff and parents. Schools implementing the program may differ in the goals and objectives they set and in the projects they undertake, but they have in common an adherence to the nine procedural elements of the program.

A number of studies have been conducted comparing the outcomes of SDP students with non-SDP students. Significant gains in math and reading achievement have been reported in several SDP school districts (Cauce, Comer, & Schwartz, 1987; Comer, 1993; Haynes, Comer, & Hamilton-Lee, 1988). Improvement has also been found in school attendance and school adjustment, as measured by number of suspensions, teachers' ratings of classroom behavior, attitudes toward authority, and group participation (Haynes et al., 1988), and in self-concept, as measured by the Piers-Harris Self-Concept Scale (Cauce et al., 1987).

Comer and Zigler developed SDP and 21C, respectively, as responses to two different problems they perceived. Their programs have the common goal of supporting the optimal development of children. Both recognized the importance of parents as active partners in the school, long a Head Start tradition. It seemed likely to the directors of both programs that, in combination, SDP and 21C would complement and extend the benefits associated with each. The SDP goals of creating a strong community and actively involving parents in the school are more easily achieved by starting earlier with young children and parents, such as those involved in CoZi. The SDP process provides a structure that would ensure that the components of 21C became an integral part of the school. If the concerns of the child care and family-support staff are discussed at the meetings of the three teams in the school, their "voice" becomes part of the tapestry of the school. Therefore, Edward Joyner, director of SDP, and Matia Finn-Stevenson, director of 21C, thought that the integration of both initiatives could result in a unique program that would enable schools to improve as well as provide families with a range of support services. With this expectation in mind, they agreed early in 1991 to explore the feasibility of implementing the combined model at one school.

CoZi: Addressing Child Care and School Improvement

School-Selection Criteria

Following the decision to explore the feasibility of the combined model, the program directors discussed whether to begin with a 21C school, an SDP school, or a school that had neither. They agreed to begin by integrating 21C into an existing SDP school in order to ensure a high probability of success. They reasoned that if the school had an established Comer program, the teams would be in place to communicate with staff, parents, and community members and garner support for the program. If the implementation was successful, the next step would be to experiment with CoZi in other contexts.

Before choosing the first school, a team at Yale University, representing both programs, developed a number of school-selection criteria. These included (1) a demonstrated need for child care and family-support services, (2) a strong principal and dedicated staff with a history of being innovative and comfortable with extending the traditional functions of the school, (3) a school that was firmly established in SDP, and (4) a superintendent and board who would support CoZi and who were committed to early-childhood programming.

After reviewing the list of schools in the SDP network, the Yale team selected the Bowling Park School in Norfolk, Virginia, and approached the district about participating. The superintendent and principal were very in-terested in the idea and several months later agreed that this school would be the first CoZi school. A grant proposal to support the initiative was developed and presented to the Carnegie Corporation of New York in December 1991. The grant was awarded in March 1992. What follows is a description of the school and a review of the planning and implementation steps taken to bring the program to fruition in Norfolk.

The First CoZi School

Bowling Park School is located in a low-income public housing community whose residents face the daily tolls associated with poverty—unemployment, substance abuse, crime, teen pregnancy, and hunger. Its 500 students are nearly all African American, and 92% are considered at risk, as measured by their eligibility for free or reduced-price lunch, qualifying the school as a Chapter 1 school-wide project. The principal reported that many of the students' parents were single, teenage mothers.

Many students entered kindergarten at this school without any preschool experience. Readiness, as measured by the Brigance Preschool Screening Test and by teachers' ratings, was traditionally low. The school also had some of the highest gain scores in the district, however, as evidenced on standardized tests given in the fifth grade. The Yale team's hypothesis was that if the readiness platform were raised due to the intervention of the CoZi early-childhood programs, the gains through elementary grades could be even greater.

The school had been using the Comer process for 4 years. Its planning and management team, student and staff support team, and parents' team were well established and running effectively. The SDP staff at the Yale Child Study Center suggested the Bowling Park School to test CoZi because they knew that the school needed the services provided by the program. They also knew that the principal and staff had a history of innovation, were held in high esteem by the community, and enjoyed strong support from parents. The principal was known to go beyond his traditional duties to improve the chances of students' success. He and his staff, for example, instituted an "adopt-a-child" program, whereby each staff member takes under his or her wing children identified as particularly at risk and needing additional one-on-one support. The school regularly held activities for parents and the community, such as the Black Plight Conference held at the school each spring. In addition, the district demonstrated a strong commitment to early-childhood programming and had recently opened an early-childhood center that provided full-day preschool for 84 3- and 4-year-olds as well as adult education for parents.

The Planning Process

Collaboration. The first stage of planning involved introductory meetings to inform all of the constituents about the plans for the program—the central office, school staff, parents, and community volunteers. At these meetings, important groundwork was laid for establishing a collaborative approach to defining the program goals and for developing a relationship between the Yale Bush Center and the school.

The first introductory meeting in Norfolk was attended by the Yale project managers, the principal, several teachers, a member of the central office staff, the newly hired Norfolk CoZi coordinator, two parents, and two community volunteers. All agreed that the principles of the Comer process would guide the effort: no-fault problem solving, collaboration, and consensual decisions. All attendees had an opportunity to express their hopes and dreams for this project, as well as their concerns, and agreed that the next step would be for the Norfolk representatives to hold a similar meeting for each of their constituencies and record their reactions. Over the next month, meetings were held with the school faculty as a whole, the parents group, the planning and management team, the student and staff support team, the community volunteers, and the superintendent's cabinet. At the same time, the principal and the CoZi coordinator developed a needs assessment, which the school's paraprofessionals administered, and conducted an organizational audit.

Needs assessment and organizational audit. The purpose of the needs assessment was to collect information about the child care and family-support needs in the community, what forms of child care families were currently using, the degree to which they would consider using such services at the school, and the kinds of adult programming they would like to have for themselves, such as adult education, job training, and parenting workshops.

The school's paraprofessionals went door to door in the public housing community where the school is located and surveyed parents for several days. Almost immediately parents started calling the school to ask when they could sign up their 3- and 4-year-olds for preschool. Excitement began to build in the neighborhood.

One of the interesting findings of the Norfolk needs assessment—besides the large number of parents (98% of the respondents) who indicated they would use child care services at the school if they were provided—was that 81% of respondents stated that if their children were in full-time care at the school, they would use this opportunity to finish their own education, attend job training, or find a job. Unlike the largely middle-class communities where 21C had been implemented previously to respond to the lack of child care, this community, largely unemployed, could use the program to improve parents' education and employment status.

Before beginning formal planning for the implementation of CoZi, an organizational audit was undertaken to ensure that the planning would be informed by a realistic understanding of the resources available and the gaps that needed to be filled. A number of people took responsibility for doing various aspects of the audit in preparation for a planning meeting that was to take place several months later. The principal took an inventory of physical space in the building. The CoZi coordinator researched existing child care services in the community and the number of children from Bowling Park who were using the services. The principal and several central office staff, including the senior coordinator of Chapter 1, reviewed such factors as funding opportunities and limitations, personnel, and in-kind services available from the school district.

Planning retreat. Once the introductory meetings, needs assessment, and organizational audit were completed, the information was brought to a planning retreat. Representatives of all stakeholder groups in the school and community participated in order to make sure all information needed was available and because one objective of this phase was to build support for the program and commitment to the final plans. In attendance were the Yale project managers, members of the 21C and SDP staffs, Norfolk administrators, teachers, parents, central office staff, and community members.

At the planning retreat, the team from Norfolk presented the results of the needs assessment, audit, and the reactions from their various constituencies. At the end of the day-long meeting, the following picture and time line emerged: an agreement to begin the following September with four full-day classrooms for 3- and 4-year-olds that would use the High Scope early-childhood curriculum; a before- and after-school child care program for school-age children to begin in mid-autumn; a home visitation program to serve parents of prenatal through 3-year-olds by January (based on Missouri's Parents as Teachers program); and a school-based health clinic to open the following year.

The financing of the program would come from a variety of sources. Chapter 1 funds would be used to finance three of the four classrooms (the local educational agency would cover the fourth), and the district would provide two modular units to the school to replace displaced classrooms. The Carnegie Corporation grant would support the district CoZi coordinator and secretary for the first 18 months. A grant for early-childhood programming from the Virginia State Department of Education would finance the Parents as Teachers component, staff development, technology, and new curriculum materials for the school. The next step was to plan the implementation of CoZi and prepare the physical space.

Implementation of CoZi

A work group was assembled in Norfolk to guide the implementation effort. This group was a subcommittee of the School Planning and Management Team and represented the interests of the school, both inside and outside. It was chaired by the CoZi coordinator and included classroom teachers, a guidance counselor, a special education teacher, the principal, a central office representative, a parent, and a community member. The work group participated in the development of program policies, a parent handbook, and enrollment forms for the preschool and school-age child care programs. The enrollment forms also provided baseline data for the later evaluation of the program.

The principal decided to put the preschool classrooms and CoZi office at one end of the primary wing and move upper-grade classrooms to the modular units outside. Over the summer, four classrooms clustered at one end of the primary wing were renovated and equipped for 3- and 4-year-olds. Certified early-childhood teachers and teaching assistants were hired and attended High Scope training in the summer. Enrollment began in August for the planned late-September opening of the preschool.

As parents started to enroll their children for preschool, it became clear that the classrooms could easily become over-crowded, and the preschool teachers were uneasy at this prospect. The principal assured teachers that the conditions of enrollment were that each parent had to attend a parent meeting to learn about the program, receive the handbook, and provide current immunization and health records. He predicted that this would reduce the number of children. However, every parent met these conditions, and the program opened in mid-September with 65 preschoolers enrolled and enthusiastic, cooperative parents. Approximately 30 children were on the waiting list. The average group size was 16 children with one certified teacher and one teaching assistant.

Over the next 3 years, the following components were added: before- and after-school child care, which provided child care from 7:30 A.M. until the opening of school and from the closing of school until 6:00 P.M.; a Parents as Teachers home-visitation program, which eventually enrolled 59 families; a 6-week summer vacation care program; an adult education class leading to a high school equivalency diploma; a family literacy program; and a school health clinic. These components were phased in one at a time as resources became available.

Training

Training for the CoZi model in Norfolk has taken several forms. The preschool teachers were trained in the High Scope early-childhood curriculum during the summer. Throughout the first year the work group received training from the state department of education on the change process and on meeting the needs of children through developmentally appropriate instruction. The state grant also supported a full-time staff developer for the first year. She and the work group developed a staff development schedule that used teachers at the school to present workshops to each other on such topics as cooperative learning and curriculum organization through thematic units. Over the next year, the principal and CoZi coordinator attended three training events at Yale that were related to SDP and 21C. Additionally, the Yale CoZi project managers conducted three training programs in Norfolk related to mission development and team building—the organization development work that would help CoZi become an integrated part of the school's conception of itself.

Training is an ongoing need, especially regarding an orientation to the philosophy of CoZi. There has been staff turnover at the school, and the CoZi coordinator has had to introduce new staff to the model as well as continually revisit the model with the entire faculty. Some preschool teachers have moved to higher grades with their students, and the new teachers have needed High Scope training. The School Planning and Management Team annually updates its training plans based on the goals and objectives of the comprehensive school plan.

We turn now to the evaluation of CoZi and preliminary learning regarding implementation.

Evaluation of CoZi

The first 3 years in Norfolk have focused on implementing the components of CoZi and stabilizing the program. An outcome evaluation, scheduled to begin in the fall of 1996, will involve measuring effects on a number of dimensions: students' academic and social achievement, readiness of entering kindergartners, reduction in stress for participating families because of the child care and family-support services, and an improved school climate for teaching and learning. Although the formal outcome evaluation has not been done, the four kindergarten teachers have reported some interesting anecdotal evidence. They claim that the "CoZi kids" stand out in their classrooms as being more verbal, better able to make choices and work independently, and as exhibiting more social skills. Approximately 70% of the kindergarten children in these classrooms attended the CoZi preschool.

In the meantime, the Yale Bush Center and Norfolk Public Schools have administered process evaluations independently to examine the implementation process and the degree to which the two models have become integrated in the school. Information has been collected through staff and parent surveys, quarterly reports from the CoZi coordinator, and the implementation journal of the Yale project manager. From these varied sources, a number of lessons have been learned that will inform future implementations of CoZi in other settings. A description of several of these lessons follows.

Importance of Team Building

Organizational change is often difficult. For this reason, it is important to pay as much attention to building relationships and developing a strong team as to developing good programs and raising the necessary resources. An ongoing staff development task during implementation in Norfolk was to focus on team building.

The work group took on a leadership role in the implementation and building of support for the program within and outside the school. The teachers in the work group represented the range of grade levels, which turned out to be a critical factor later. The decision to move the fifth grades into modular classrooms so that the preschool classes could be inside the building in the primary wing could have resulted in a drop in support from the upper-grade teachers. However, one of them was a member of the work group. She was committed to the success of the venture because she participated in the decision and saw its merits. A decision that could have lowered internal support for the program did not because of the inclusion of and support by the upper-grade teachers.

Before the first day of school, a day was devoted to community building with the entire staff, including the food personnel and office and custodial staff. A ribbon was cut, speeches were made, and the work group performed a skit celebrating change. The session concluded with the entire group boarding a bus and going to eat at a local restaurant.

At the end of the year, 2 staff development days were set aside for reviewing the year, strengthening the team, and assessing and modifying the school's internal communication system. This decision was based on feedback from the staff reporting that breakdowns had occurred during the year. Clearly, an emphasis on team building and communication is vital. In spite of everyone's best efforts, improvements needed to be made in these areas and continue to be a focus.

Developing Partnerships

CoZi requires an initial investment of capital either to renovate existing space, create new space, or subcontract with other service providers. It also needs new staff members whose salaries are not likely to be paid by district funds. Although many operating expenses can be covered by parent fees and child care subsidies for low-income children, ongoing fund-raising is still necessary. Bowling Park has been entrepreneurial and creative in attracting outside funders to offset the costs of the program. They also have put considerable effort into developing good relationships with the community and its various organizations, which has attracted resources to the school, gained access to enriching experiences for the students, and nurtured a base of support during budget development time in the district. Today many schools look beyond their district funds for innovative programming, but this program *requires* grant writing and fund-raising savvy. The stronger the relationship is with the community, the more likely the school is to be aware of external funding opportunities.

Integration of the School of the Twenty-First Century and the School Development Program

Clearly, new services are being offered in this school, and the halls are regularly traveled by parents of infants, toddlers, and preschoolers. But are they add-on services or truly part of the school? We next discuss this question.

During the summer after the first year of operation, the Yale Bush Center surveyed the entire staff and relevant central office personnel regarding their perceptions of the success of the CoZi implementation and the benefits of the program. When asked about the degree to which the school had integrated the Comer and Zigler models, 73% agreed that the model was fully integrated, and 27% thought it was partly integrated. There was general agreement that the school community had adopted the philosophy that these service components belonged in the school and that the staff development focusing on team building was helpful to this change in philosophy. Additionally, 81% of the staff said that they felt more positive about their jobs since CoZi began because of the changed atmosphere in the school, an increase in parent involvement, and the prevailing sense that the school was reaching out to families to promote the healthy development of children (Briggs, 1994). Some of the problems survey respondents noted were the need for more space, the continual need to find funding to maintain the program, resistance to change, and occasional communication breakdowns in the school.

Independently of this effort, Norfolk Public Schools also completed their own process evaluation of CoZi. They found that the school had achieved 18 of its 19 process objectives and declared the program "a considerable success during its first year" in terms of implementation of planned components. Parent surveys showed that between 80% and 100% agreed or strongly agreed with statements that indicated that they felt welcome in the school, were encouraged to volunteer in classrooms, found teachers available to them, and were assisted in their parenting skills (Moore, 1993).

Although these findings are preliminary and will be amplified further in the planned outcome evaluation, an abundance of anecdotal evidence from the observations and journals of the Norfolk CoZi coordinator and the Yale CoZi project manager indicates that CoZi is integrated into the fabric of Bowling Park School. The name of the school has been changed to the Bowling Park CoZi Community School, for example. Parents of preschoolers, infants, and toddlers, along with parents of school-age students, are constantly present in classrooms, at school-sponsored activities, in the family literacy breakfast program, in the adult education program, and, informally, as visitors in the CoZi parent room. The principal and CoZi coordinator note a marked increase in parent involvement in the school. The CoZi coordinator is a member of all of the SDP teams in the school, continues to provide staff development regarding CoZi, and consults regularly with the principal. The school-age children and the preschoolers interact during the day in reading, social, and recreational activities. Also, unlike many 21C schools, the preschool staff are certified teachers on the same salary scale and with the same training as the rest of the faculty. We believe that this equivalence in status makes it easier for the preschool teachers to become full partners on the faculty.

Another critical element of integration is that the staff of the CoZi program are represented on the School Planning and Management Team. Their voice is a regular part of the adult discussion in the school, and the needs of the children they represent are taken into account when the team makes policy decisions and develops the comprehensive school plan.

Service integration has become somewhat of a movement in this country, and a number of initiatives nationally link family-support, social, and health services to the school. The initiatives are described variously as "integrated services," "seamless services," "full-service schools," or even "one-stop shopping." New Beginnings in San Diego, the Beacon Schools in New York, and Walbridge Caring Communities in St. Louis are three such examples. The evaluation of these initiatives is still preliminary, and there are discussions in the literature regarding the appropriateness of schools taking on these functions, whether they should be school based or school linked, who should be served, and effective and ineffective ways of collaboration among service providers, among other topics (Chaskin & Richman, 1992; Levy & Shepardson, 1992). Levy and Shepardson noted in their analysis that a formal

connection with the decision-making body of the school is necessary if the effort is to be integrated well with the regular operations of the school. We believe that this element is a distinguishing feature of CoZi. The governing teams of the SDP model can ensure that the model becomes instilled in the school culture. The full extent to which this has happened will be examined further in the outcome evaluation.

The Norfolk implementation has provided an understanding of how to proceed with an SDP school in an urban environment. The Yale Bush Center next determined that it needed to experiment with implementation of the model in varying circumstances in order to gain the knowledge needed to disseminate CoZi further.

Wider Dissemination

To learn more about implementation of CoZi under varying conditions, the Carnegie Corporation of New York awarded a continuation grant in March 1994 to expand CoZi to three new demonstration schools, each having unique characteristics. All three had approached the Yale Bush Center about participating in the initiative, so a self-selection bias exists. However, the purpose of the expansion was to learn more about implementation, and we believed that the commitment and enthusiasm of the district were important. Our intent was not to convince a school that it needed CoZi but to work collaboratively with interested schools to develop plans that met their needs and afforded the Yale Bush Center further information about the model. Brief descriptions of the three schools follow.

Hagemann Elementary School

Hagemann Elementary School is a public school located in Mehlville, Missouri. This suburban school has an enrollment of 430 students, the majority of whom are Caucasian children from middle-class families. Ten percent of the students are African American children from St. Louis who attend as a school-choice option. In the fall of 1994, this new school opened with two 21C components already in place—the before- and after-school child care program, operated in the building by the Young Men's Christian Association, and Parents as Teachers, a statewide program in Missouri available to all members of the community through the school district.

During its first year and a half, the focus at Hagemann has been first to develop the Comer process, in order to build a strong community of staff and parents, and second to add the preschool component. The school presented an opportunity to learn about implementing CoZi in a suburban setting that, unlike Norfolk, already had some of the 21C elements in place but did not have collaborative governing teams. This school also afforded the Comer organization the opportunity to demonstrate the wide applicability of the SDP model, which is often associated solely with inner-city schools.

The Six to Six Interdistrict Magnet School

The Bridgeport, Connecticut, school is an interdistrict desegregation magnet school with a 50-50 mix of urban/suburban and minority/Caucasian students. The school draws its students from four suburban school districts and the city of Bridgeport. Its managing agency is Cooperative Educational Services (CES), an intermediary agency of the state department of education. The school's director reports to the director of CES, who also presides over a board of trustees made up of representatives of each participating district. Its initial operational plan, developed by two educational consultants, was to provide a full-day, year-round program governed by a school-based management structure for a racially balanced group of children ages 3–12. As the consultants did their research and planning, they realized that what they were describing mirrored the CoZi model. Therefore, they decided to call the program CoZi and formally requested assistance from the Yale Bush Center in July 1993.

The Six to Six School (named for its 6:00 A.M. to 6:00 P.M. hours of operation) opened its doors with 40 preschoolers in September 1993. By the fall of 1995, the school had extended to third grade with a total enrollment of 180 students. During the next 3 years, the school will extend the program to grade 6.

In the third year of operation, the Bush Center assisted the school in developing the elements of the School Development Program, team building among the entire staff, developing a nutrition component, and promoting parent involvement. From the process evaluation at this school, we hope to extend the understanding of how the Comer and Zigler models can be implemented simultaneously. There is also an opportunity in Bridgeport to study how a community develops from a diverse group of students and families who do not live in the same community but who share the wish for their children to be educated in an integrated setting.

Wexler Family Resource Center

In 1988 the Connecticut legislature developed and passed legislation to support the creation of three 21C schools, one in an urban, one in a rural, and one in a suburban setting. The state named its program the Family Resource Center (FRC) and since that time has expanded its support to 18 centers. New Haven's Wexler School was awarded a grant to create an FRC in April 1994.

Wexler's demographics are similar to Bowling Park's; it is situated in a public housing community with the majority of its students considered at risk, as measured by their eligibility for free and reduced-price lunch. Like Bowling Park, Wexler was already an SDP school. However, the preschool component at Wexler will likely be a collaboration with Head Start or a community agency. In addition, the program will be included in a larger initiative in New Haven called the Family Campus, a collaboration between Yale, the city of New Haven, and the board of education. The "campus," as it is being designed, will have CoZi at its core and will also include a partnership with the housing authority, a community agency, adult education, a health clinic, a tenants' association, and a police substation. From this ambitious project, the Yale Bush Center hopes to learn about integrating Head Start and these numerous other providers into the school community and to glean lessons about organizational change from bringing this diverse group of people from separate areas toward a common mission.

All of these schools are at different stages of implementation and need different forms of technical assistance. The Yale Bush Center's approach to assistance is not to be prescriptive but to help the community mold the program according to its own situation. Each school determines which components to implement on the basis of its needs and resources. What are nonnegotiable are the integration of the program into the whole school and a commitment to providing high-quality services. The CoZi model's governance structure and guiding principles make these goals more easily achievable. The model provides process guidelines and a built-in forum for the community to reflect about its operations—its academic program as well as its child care and family-support services.

Next Steps

The experience with CoZi to date has demonstrated the feasibility of combining two complex and distinct initiatives. By early 1996, having completed the demonstration phase at Norfolk and having seen the initial phases of implementation at the additional schools, the Yale Bush Center staff believe that CoZi is ready for wider dissemination and can benefit many more children and their families. Norfolk is already expanding to a second school and has plans to phase in several others as resources become available. New Haven is in the planning stage for several more CoZi schools.

In the next 3–5 years, the Yale Bush Center intends to focus on two areas: outcome evaluation at the initial pilot schools mentioned earlier and increasing the capacity in order to assist school districts interested in the implementation of CoZi. Regarding further dissemination, the plan is to increase the Yale Bush Center's capacity to offer schools information, technical assistance, and training, all of which enable the growth of the program. This will be accomplished through the identification of training requirements under varying school district conditions (e.g., schools that have the Comer but not the Zigler model, the Zigler but not the Comer model, or neither), the development of the corresponding training protocol and materials, the hiring and training of regional implementation associates to assist schools in their implementation of the program, and the development of informational and promotional materials.

Conclusion

Blending the services of the School of the Twenty-First Century with the process of the School Development Program results in a school reform model that addresses the concerns of Comer and Zigler and makes each of their goals more achievable. The Yale Bush Center sees this initiative as "school reform" because, when faithfully replicated, it substantially changes the definition of the elementary school and the way it operates. The school serves as the hub of a community where formal schooling, child care, and family-support services are provided during all hours of the day, 12 months a year, for children from birth through age 12 and their families. The distinction between child care and education, in terms of their importance for the development of children, is eliminated. Decisions about the scope of services and the social and academic programs are made by a representative group committed to working collaboratively. This represents a significant departure from the traditional elementary school.

Educational reform in the United States has been marked by a series of initiatives sparked by events such as the Sputnik landing in the 1950s and the release of the landmark report *A Nation at Risk* in 1983 (National Commission on Excellence in Education, 1983). Typically, the approaches to reform focus on a single aspect of education, such as curriculum, assessment, climate, teacher preparation, or governance or on a single group in the school, such as students, teachers, or parents. Examples abound and include philosophical and organizational approaches such as Theodore R. Sizer's Coalition of Essential Schools, Henry M. Levin's Accelerated Schools, and Ron Edmond's Effective Schools as well as curricular approaches such as Robert E. Slavin's Success for All, thematic instruction, constructivism, cooperative learning, and authentic assessment, to name a few of the most noted. The CoZi model can contribute to the effects of other reform initiatives, and we are exploring its compatibility with a number of them.

On its own, CoZi stands out as being more comprehensive in scope and depth than most reform initiatives. The services CoZi offers span birth through age 12 and include not only children but also their families. Additionally, the Comer process targets the entire school and involves all adult stakeholders in a continuous change process that responds to the academic and social needs identified by the people who are closest to the school program and the students. Many school reform efforts have failed because of their piecemeal nature or the lack of attention paid to continual renewal once a change has been instituted (Fullan, 1991). Through the collaborative development of the annual comprehensive school plan and its regular assessment and modification when new information is collected, the CoZi school has a built-in mechanism that can protect it from the fade out so often seen in well-intentioned but superficial school reform efforts.

We anticipate that the outcome evaluations at the pilot schools will provide evidence that this approach to schooling enhances the academic success of children and the lives of the families served. The initial signs from the first pilot school in Virginia point in that direction. As the program is replicated elsewhere, the Yale Bush Center will work to further its understanding of how implementation proceeds under various conditions and how best to provide the corresponding assistance needed.

References

Berrueta-Clement, J., Schweinhart, L. J., Barnett, W. S., Epstein, A. S., & Weikart, D. P. (1984). *Changed lives: Effects of the Perry preschool program on youths through age 19.* Ypsilanti, MI: High/Scope Press.

Briggs, M. (1994). *The CoZi community school demonstration project of Norfolk, Virginia: Process evaluation part 1.* New Haven, CT: Yale University, Bush Center in Child Development and Social Policy.

Cauce, A. M., Comer, J. P., & Schwartz, B. A. (1987). Long term effects of a system-oriented school intervention program. *American Journal of Orthopsychiatry, 57*(1), 127–131.

Chaskin, R. J., & Richman, H. A. (1992). Concerns about school-linked services: Institution-based versus community-based models. *Future of Children, 2*(1), 107–117.

Comer, J. P. (1988). *Maggie's American dream.* New York: New American Library.

Comer, J. P. (1993). *School power* (Rev. ed.) New York: Free Press.

Committee on Economic Development. (1993). *Why child care matters.* New York: Author.

Finn-Stevenson, M., Desimone, L., & Chung, A. E. (1997). *Linking child care with the school: Pilot evaluation of the School of the 21st Century.* Unpublished manuscript, Yale University, Bush Center in Child Development and Social Policy, New Haven, CT.

Fullan, M. G. (1991). *The new meaning of educational change.* New York: Teachers College Press.

Fuller, B., & Liang, X. (1995). *Can poor families find child care? Persisting inequality nationwide and in Massachusetts* (Report from the Harvard Child Care and Family Policy Project). Cambridge, MA: Harvard University, Graduate School of Education.

Galinsky, E., Howes, C., Kontos, S., & Shinn, M. B. (1994). *The study of children in family child care and relative care.* New York: Families and Work Institute.

Hayes, C. D., Palmer, J. L., & Zaslow, M. (Eds.). (1990). *Who cares for America's children?* Washington, DC: National Academy Press.

Haynes, N. M., Comer, J. P., & Hamilton-Lee, M. (1988). The School Development Program: A model for school improvement. *Journal of Negro Education,* 57(1), 11–21.

Helburn, S., Culkin, M., Howes, C., Bryant, D., Clifford, R., Cryer, D., Peisner-Feinberg, E., & Kagan, S. (1995). *Cost, quality, and child outcomes in child care centers* (Final report). Denver: University of Colorado.

Hofferth, S. L., & Phillips, D. A. (1987). Child care in the United States, 1970–1995. *Journal of Marriage and the Family,* 49(3), 559–579.

Levy, J. E., & Shepardson, W. (1992). A look at current school-linked service efforts. *Future of Children,* 2(1), 44–55.

Moore, D. S. (1993). *Bowling Park Community School program (Comer/Zigler program)* Norfolk, VA: Norfolk Public Schools Program Evaluation.

National Commission on Excellence in Education. (1983). *A nation at risk: The imperative for educational reform.* Washington, DC: United States Department of Education.

Reisman, B., Moore, A., & Fitzgerald, K. (Eds.). (1988). *Child care: The bottom line.* New York: Child Care Action Campaign.

Schweinhart, L., Barnes, H., & Weikart, D. (1993). *Significant benefits: The High/Scope Perry Preschool study through age 27.* Ypsilanti, MI: High/Scope Press.

Tuma, J. M. (1989). Mental health services for children. *American Psychologist,* 44, 188–189.

United States Department of Labor, Bureau of Labor Statistics. (1988). Labor force participation among mothers with young children. *News,* 88–431.

United States Department of Labor. (1993). *Employment and earnings,* 40(1).

Whitebook, M., Phillips, D., & Howes, C. (1989). *Who cares? Child care teachers and the quality of care in America* (National Child Care Staffing Study). Oakland, CA: Child Care Employee Project.

Willer, B. (1992, January). Overview of demand and supply of child care in the 1990's. *Young Children,* 47(1), 19–22.

Zigler, E., & Finn-Stevenson, M. (1994). Schools' role in the provision of support services for children and families: A critical aspect of program equity. *Educational Policy,* 8(4), 591–606.

Zigler, E., & Lang, M. (1991). *Child care choices: Balancing the needs of children, families, and society.* New York: Free Press.

Zigler, E., & Muenchow, S. (1992). *Head Start: The inside story of America's most successful educational experiment.* New York: Basic.

Zigler, E., & Valentine, J. (Eds.). (1979). *Head Start: The legacy of the war on poverty.* New York: Free Press.

FRAME the DEBATE

Form at end of book

School-Linked Services

Many board members, our survey shows, tread gingerly in giving school-linked services their full support.

Priscilla M. Hardiman, Joan L. Curcio, and Jim C. Fortune

Priscilla M. Hardiman is an assistant principal at Lake Braddock Secondary School in Fairfax County, Va. Joan L. Curcio and Jim C. Fortune are professors of Education at Virginia Tech, Blacksburg, Va.

School board members aren't sure just how entangled they want to get in the web of social problems children bring to school. It might be true that schools can't "do it alone" any longer, given the complex social and economic factors that put many children at risk of educational failure. In fact, many school districts already are acting as brokers for an array of social and health services being provided to children and families through collaborative partnerships between schools and other public agencies.

Even so, in a recent research study we conducted (see page 58), board members sent mixed messages about their comfort level with the role they play in promoting school-linked services within their districts. The survey, which included two separate mailings, defined school-linked services as "the coordinated linking of school and community resources to support the needs of school-aged children and their families. The services may be delivered at the school building, at a site near the school, or at another agency, but the delivery must be coordinated in some way with the local school."

This article reports the results of our survey, describing the perceptions and opinions of a sample of board members across the country on school-linked services, the availability of services, the range of services provided, and the impact of these services on local school districts.

The Need Is There

We asked board members whether their communities supported the development of school-linked services and whether they believed such services were necessary to meet the needs of children and families in their districts. A substantial majority of the districts represented by board members from both survey mailings (75.3 and 84.5 percent respectively) support the development of school-linked services, and a majority of respondents from both groups (73.9 and 80.4 percent) say such services are necessary to meet the needs of children and families in their school districts. (Note that throughout this article, we are reporting the results of the two survey mailings separately; in many cases, the results are similar.)

When we gave respondents an opportunity to make individual com-

Available school-linked services (percent of districts).

Survey Group One		Survey Group Two
62.0	Substance abuse services	63.8
60.1	Psychological services	53.6
59.5	Education services	57.7
51.3	Health services	52.6
51.0	Social services	51.5
47.6	Job training	51.5
40.8	Teen pregnancy	53.6
42.2	Child welfare	47.4
38.0	Juvenile probation	49.5
30.9	Family welfare	35.1
22.2	Housing services	32.0

ments, though, some said that such services were not supported or needed: "My district is not involved in school-related services," one wrote. "This has no bearing on anything my district does." Another board member made a similar observation: "It is a full-time effort to educate our students. We cannot be all things to all people."

Respondents to both mailings acknowledged the presence of existing school-linked programs and services in their school districts. The range of services provided and the variety of approaches to school-linked services are broad, reflecting the diversity of needs and resources in each community. The following services are found in the majority of responding school districts in both groups: substance abuse services (62.0 and 63.8 percent respectively); psychological services (60.1 and 53.6 percent); education services (59.5 and 57.7 percent); health services (51.3 and 52.6 percent); and social services (51.0 and 51.5 percent).

Job training (47.6 and 51.5 percent) and teen pregnancy services (40.8 and 53.6 percent) are offered in slightly less than the majority of the first group surveyed and in the majority of the districts responding in the second group. Child welfare (42.2 and 47.4 percent), juvenile probation (38.0 and 49.5 percent), family welfare (30.9 and 35.1 percent), and housing services (22.2 and 32.0 percent) are found in even fewer responding school districts. Board members report that their school districts collaborate with many different agencies and organizations to provide these services. Most are supported by partnerships with agencies at the state and local level, but some involve partnerships with federal programs.

Governance and Policy

Creating and implementing school-linked services are complex endeavors for a school district to undertake. Division of labor, lines of responsibility, and policies surrounding multi-agency collaboration tend to be hazy, overlapping, and hard to formulate, analyze, or summarize. Perhaps it should not be surprising, then, that many school board members in both survey groups (60.3 and 49.5 percent) say their districts have no policies governing all school-linked services.

What's more, a majority of respondents say their boards do not have to waive or change regulations to enable service providers to serve children and families. Just under 50 percent of the school districts surveyed in both groups do not permit agencies to collect data on students and their families in order to assess their needs. Following this same pattern, school districts do not collect data to assess the effectiveness of the school-linked services provided to school children. Interestingly, advocates of school-linked services say that for those services to be effective, it is necessary both to involve and support families as a whole and to collect data about what was attempted and achieved.

When asked if their school districts sponsor or support legislation at the federal, state, or local level favoring school linkages with other services, almost three-fourths of the respondents in both groups say their districts do not. Existing national, state, and local initiatives and legislation supporting school-linked services vary widely in

Funding support for school-linked services (percent of districts).

Survey Group One		Survey Group Two
53.5	Federal funds	52.6
64.9	State funds	65.0
59.6	Local government funds	56.7
25.5	Local nongov't funds	27.8
22.9	Private donations	27.8
15.6	Fundraisers	15.5
3.7	Others — grants	2.1

intensity and expansiveness and combine both formal and informal arrangements. Asked which arrangements support school-linked services in their districts, board members list the following: legislative mandates, state-level task forces and commissions, formal agreements with other state agencies, formal and informal agreements with local government agencies, in-kind (nonmonetary) support of local government and nongovernment agencies, formal and information agreements with local nongovernment agencies, formal and informal referral network, and the school administrator's prerogative.

Funding and Evaluation

Pulling together the funding sources necessary to support a strong program of school-linked services might present a challenge to school board members. As one board member said, "School boards face difficult decisions allocating dollars for school-linked services when there are so many demands for programs and activities for the general school population." Another made a similar point: "We have limited school-linked services because we have no $$$ for anything not directly related to academic achievement."

These comments apparently represent atypical opinions, however, because more than half of the respondents in the first group surveyed and 47 percent from the second group say no changes in school district funding have been necessary to support school-linked services.

So where does the money come from? In response to a question about the multiple sources of funding districts use to support school-linked services, school board members list the following: federal funds, state funds, local government agency funds, local nongovernment agency funds, private donations, fund-raisers, and grants.

However, these services are funded, efforts to evaluate them appear to be sporadic, with few in-depth evaluations to date. The majority of respondents from both

groups (55.8 and 59.7 percent) say their school districts do have some means of reviewing the effectiveness of existing school-linked services. But in almost half the school districts represented, the results of those reviews are not used to modify services.

When asked to rate the effectiveness of the services provided, the majority (58.4 and 58.7 percent) perceive that the school-linked services provided within the district are good and are meeting the client's needs. The respondents generally based their ratings on feedback received from clients, the community in general, and the service providers.

Obstacles and Issues

The final questions on the survey were designed to discover obstacles and critical issues related to school-linked services. Respondents from both survey groups clearly identified inadequate funds as the major obstacle to implementing services. This perception is supported by a 1995 report from the U.S. Department of Education, which found that school-linked collaborative services are built on fragile financial foundations that are both insufficient and inconsistent. But this complaint does not synchronize well with the respondents' claim that no changes in school district funding have been necessary to support school-linked services. A possible explanation is that the respondents are distinguishing between services provided to date, which have not required funding changes, and additional services that could be provided only with additional funding.

Other obstacles were also cited, among them the limited availability of services as well as a reluctance among children and families to seek services. Another obstacle (or, more accurately, an issue) is the perception that schools should not get involved in providing social services. One board member called such services a "subversion of the purpose of schooling." And another wrote

Major obstacles to implementation (percent of districts).

	Survey Group One		Survey Group Two	
Inadequate funds	59.2			44.3
Belief that schools should not be involved	37.1		30.9	
Reluctance to seek services	32.0		32.0	
Limited availability of services	35.1		32.0	
Insufficient awareness by client population	26.1		32.0	
Inadequate coordination and communication	25.5		25.8	
Lack of qualified personnel	18.1		10.3	
State or federal regulations	13.6		13.4	
Inadequate/unclear agency policies	11.9		10.3	
Services not needed	11.9		11.4	
Cumbersome accounting procedures	8.2		13.4	

emphatically, "Health clinics should not be in schools. Parents should feed the child, not the school. Before long, we will be building dormitories for students so they can report to school on Monday and go home on the weekend."

Board members in both survey groups overwhelmingly agreed that schools and communities should collaborate to assist students and families on controversial issues. But many respondents reacted negatively to the idea of using schools as the sites for drug treatment programs (55.3 and 47.4 percent), social service programs for families (48.8 and 43.2 percent), health clinic services for families (55.8 and 48.5 percent), or offices for probation officers (69.1 and 61.9 percent). As one board member commented, "I believe we are in the business to educate students and not to deal with social issues and provide health care. These are family issues, and we do not need to get involved."

At the end of the survey, we asked board members to list the three areas where school-linked services are most critically needed in their school district. Both groups ranked substance abuse services (32.9 and 35.1 percent), health services (25.5 and 21.6 percent), and parenting classes (20.7 and 17.5 percent) as the top three most press-

ing needs. Those selections were not unexpected, given that drug and alcohol use has increased among teens; that many children live in poverty and are not immunized against diseases; and that teenage pregnancy, while declining, remains common. What is less clear is the reluctance many respondents express to providing services on school grounds.

School board members recognize that many of today's children do not come to school prepared to learn, but some possible solutions for this problem appear to create as many dilemmas as they solve. As these survey results suggest, many board members support the development of school-linked services. On the basis of our results, however, we cannot say this trend enjoys the full support of boards. While we have consensus that many of our children are not succeeding in school for deep-seated sociological, economic, and perhaps even political reasons, we do not have consensus about what part the school should play in addressing those issues that go beyond schoolhouse gates into the family and the community.

Both state and local grass-roots efforts have advanced the idea of linking human services and public agencies with schools in more effective and collaborative ways to boost a child's chances of being ready to learn. The

Most critical areas of need (percent of districts).

	Survey Group One		Survey Group Two
Substance abuse services	32.9		35.1
Health services	25.5		21.6
Parenting classes	20.7		17.5
Social services	12.8		11.4
Teen pregnancy	12.8		9.3
Job training	11.9		8.2
Psychological services	11.6		11.4
Child welfare	9.9		9.3
Family welfare	9.1		5.2
Education	8.8		6.2
Juvenile probation	7.4		10.3
Day care	6.5		3.1
At-risk programs	4.2		7.2

findings of this research, however, would suggest that although school districts are selectively embracing school-linked services as one way to help students achieve, questions about funding, policy, governance, and the purpose of schooling cause some school board members to tread gingerly in giving school-linked services their full support.

About the Study

In this nationwide research study, *The American School Board Journal* and Virginia Polytechnic Institute and State University collaborated to seek the opinions of board members across the country. A questionnaire was sent to a stratified random sample of 6,000 school board members who subscribe to *The American School Board Journal*.

A total of 353 board members (or 5.9 percent of the target population) responded to the survey. In an effort to obtain a higher final return rate, a second mailing using coded return envelopes was sent to 492 randomly selected school board members based on a proportional representation of the subscriber list. This mailing resulted in a 19.7 percent response rate, giving the survey results what statisticians call a 98 percent confidence rate and a maximum possible error of plus or minus 2 percentage points.

Form at end of book

Character Education

Questions

Reading 7. Doyle argues that schools "cannot be value-free; they must . . . model, exemplify and reinforce . . . honesty, forbearance, toleration, respect for others, courage, integrity." He also argues for including religion in schools. If you were a school board member, would you want the schools in your district to have this explicit curriculum?

Reading 8. For the most part Kohn is not a strong supporter of character education. Based on the reading, why do you think he has come to these conclusions? To what extent should or should not character education be an overarching umbrella for the school day? Why or why not?

Reading 9. As you consider definitions, descriptions, and applications of character education in school settings, first take the time to reflect on such questions as: What is a good person? What is the good citizen? What is virtue? What is a just society? As you reflect on these questions, write your thoughts in your journal for review at a later time.

After reading all of the articles on this issue, comment on William Bennett's quotation (this page). Also, working with classmates, decide what role the school should have in teaching values. Ask yourself and teachers in a school where you may be volunteering the following two questions: Can you avoid the teaching of values? Are there implicit values behind every instructional choice a teacher makes?

What should be the role of the school and other social institutions in developing character education in young learners?

The history of education in the United States is replete with examples of the explicit teaching of moral values. For example, the McGuffey Readers featured stories that not only taught children to read but also taught a moral lesson. Almost all countries have coupled the didactic teaching of moral values with the educational curriculum, and many countries still do. In these countries, however, virtually all of the citizens embrace the values of one strong religious faith.

In the United States, problems have risen regarding whether public schools should transmit values that might be seen as religious in nature. Problems have also arisen due to the pluralistic nature of American life. Because of the number of religions in the United States, suspicions are aroused whenever a community's moral values seem to favor one religion over others. Legal battles over what role public schools should play in transmitting either religious or moral values have often ended up being argued in the U.S. Supreme Court. The rulings in almost all of these cases have been that the U.S. Constitution calls for the separation of church and state.

Should schools teach moral values? Should the shaping of character be as important as the passing on of knowledge? Schools are seen as the transmitters of a knowledge of democracy and civic education; why shouldn't they transmit moral values as well? In his best-selling tome, *The Book of Virtues*, William Bennett says: "If we want our children to possess the traits of character we most admire, we need to teach them what those traits are and why they deserve both admiration and allegiance."

Dennis Doyle presents a conservative view of education and notes that life is about making moral choices about important issues and practices of good behavior. Alfie Kohn, on the other hand, recommends that students need quality literature, followed by in-depth classroom conversations to encourage reflection. Kohn disagrees with the notion of character education as being indoctrination.

The final reading in this section was written by a leader in the field of character education, Thomas Lickona. Lickona suggests several examples of classrooms and schools that have developed character education programs, which are said to have helped young people develop positive habits of mind to enable them to help others in need of support, encouragement, and compassion.

The readings on this issue have been chosen to place the debate within you: As you read the articles and answer the questions, share your thoughts with your classmates.

Education and Character:
A Conservative View

Good character education is made up of three elements, Mr. Doyle avers—example, study, and practice. In the final analysis life is about moral choices, not about technique or spontaneous unfolding.

Denis P. Doyle

Denis P. Doyle is the founder of Doyle Associates, an education consulting firm in Chevy Chase, Md. His most recent book (with Louis V. Gerstner et al.) is Reinventing Education *(Dutton, 1994). This article draws on a work in progress,* Reclaiming the Legacy: In Defense of Liberal Education, *to be published by the Council for Basic Education in 1997.*

From the time of the ancient Greeks to sometime in the late 19th century, a singular idea obtained: education's larger purpose was to shape character, to make men (and later, women) better people. Education and training were not confused. Education was "liberal" from *liberalis,* the Latin for "free," as distinct from slave. Training was (as it remains today) narrow and functional. Education imparted fundamental knowledge—or content, as we would think of it today. It was both essential and instrumental. Mastery of content was the device by which one achieved mastery of self and, in turn, mastery over nature. Born naked and ignorant, humans had neither the tools—teeth that rip, claws that tear, wings that soar, or fins that swim— nor the instincts to survive on their own.

No animal is so dependent for so long as the human animal. Yet humans need more than nurturing parents; we need a supportive social order in which to live and thrive. As Aristotle knew, we are political animals: it is our fate—which is to say, our opportunity and our obligation—to live in the *polis.* Without it we cannot survive. We also need time. Time and the city: we cannot live without culture. Which is to say we cannot live without language. Finally, we cannot live without values. While these three threads are analytically distinct, they are inexorably woven together.

Obvious? Perhaps, but in the present climate of education it bears repeating. Culture. Language. Values. In the beginning was the word. A religious conception, to be sure, but an anthropological one as well. One need not believe John to appreciate his insight. Culture is the set of social arrangements we have chosen to organize our lives. Language is culture's quintessential tool, for it permits us to communicate with one another and across time and space. It permits culture to come into existence and to remain over time. And values are the engine that defines and drives culture. We choose Athens or Sparta, tolerance or belligerence, the way of Cato the Elder or that of Cincinnatus.

Values are the embodiment of choices; we can choose to forbear or to indulge. Or, as the ancient Greeks

Questions

Doyle argues that schools "cannot be value-free; they must . . . model, exemplify and reinforce . . . honesty, forbearance, toleration, respect for others, courage, integrity." He also argues for including religion in schools. If you were a school board member, would you want the schools in your district to have this explicit curriculum?

Denis P. Doyle is the founder of Doyle Associates, a firm that specializes in education "change management." Copyright 1997. Reprinted with permission from the author and *Phi Delta Kappan.*

and later Romans knew so well, we can choose *when* to forbear and *when* to indulge. Dionysus, the Greek god of wine (from whose name the modern name Denis is derived), stands in counterpoise to Apollo, god of reason. They exist in sharp tension: one, the god of abandon; the other, the god of restraint. Such is the enduring power of myths that they embody living truths today no less than yesterday. Today, of course, the political scientist more readily thinks of Rousseau and Hobbes—the modern exemplars of self-indulgence and self-restraint—than of Dionysus and Apollo. Indeed, as E. D. Hirsch so ably and persuasively demonstrates in his new book, *The Schools We Need,* it is the legacy of Rousseau, filtered through romanticism, that explains today's educational wilderness. This heritage does much to explain our cultural wilderness as well.

Self-expression rather than self-restraint, a belief that the child knows more than the adult, a conviction that children are innately good and need only to be nourished for a spontaneous unfolding to occur—these are the ideas of Rousseau and the romantic (whether Schiller or Whitman). To any parent they even have the ring of partial truth; to be sure, there is in every child a divine spark. There is in every child the capacity for truth and beauty. Indeed, so far as we can tell, every child is hard-wired for language. But this is an incomplete list of the child's potential. It is at best fatuous, at worst dangerous, to ignore the other side of the ledger.

Children—and the adults they become—have the potential for dreadful behavior as well as good. While children have a spontaneous capacity to listen and speak, they have no such untutored capacity to read, write, and count. So too, they have the capacity to distinguish between pleasure and pain but no untutored capacity to make moral judgments. Just as children must learn to read, they must learn to be good. Like faith, morality must be acquired. The social and psychological restraints imposed by culture are what dissuade children from "bad" behavior and incline them toward good.

As Thomas Huxley so aptly said:

Perhaps the most valuable result of all education is the ability to make yourself do the thing you have to do, when it ought to be done, whether you like it or not; it is the first lesson that ought to be learned; and however early a man's training begins, it is probably the last lesson that he learns thoroughly.

It is no accident that, after the Fall, the first moral question to emerge in the Judeo-Christian (and Islamic) tradition is played out between the world's first two children. After the first child kills the second, he asks, "Am I my brother's keeper?" That is the fundamental moral issue before us all. Are we our brothers' keepers? The lesson must be learned. The problem with romantics is not their poetry but their philosophy.

At issue here is not sociobiology, or scientific theories about altruism, or modern behavioral psychology, but our history as a species. Nowhere is this history drawn more vividly or fearfully than in the 20th century. The "banality of evil," Hannah Arendt called it. To abandon education's historic mission to shape character—to fail to try to turn boys into men and girls into women—flies in the face of history and reason. It is the ultimate romantic fallacy. To build a pedagogy on romanticism, as Hirsch shows, not only invites failure; it courts disaster. It is equally dangerous to build a theory of character formation on such grounds. Even if, in some narrow, strict, scientific sense the question is still open—who is right, Rousseau or Hobbes?—we cannot frame social policy on the slender possibility that the answer may be Rousseau.

And that, put most simply, is the issue. That is the cultural divide that conservatives talk about (and, one hopes, liberals worry about). It is the case of *Rousseau* v. *Hobbes,* and the court is public opinion. Whom do you believe, Primo Levi (*Survival in Auschwitz* or, in the Italian, *If This Be a Man*) and William Golding (*Lord of the Flies*) or Ralph Waldo Emerson, Walt Whitman, and William Heard Kilpatrick?

Indeed, the issue of moral education, or character education, or values education—by whichever name it may be called is really no more and no less than the issue that pervades modern theories of pedagogy. It is process rather than content, form rather than substance. It is "critical-thinking skills" as opposed to thinking critically about content; it is "learning to learn" rather than learning something substantive. Just as "rote" learning of subject matter is derided, so too is "rote" learning of values.

Derision, however, misses the point. Poorly conceived or weakly executed character education does not condemn the enterprise entire. To be sure, teaching and learning about character—just as about content—ought not to be exclusively a matter of didactic instruction or catechistic learning (though it includes both); rather, fundamental values must be internalized to the point of habituation. The child's instinctual desire to grab what he likes or hit what she dislikes is profoundly antisocial. It is not a matter of indifference; these "natural" impulses will not spontaneously resolve themselves in a socially beneficial way. To the contrary, to trust to innate goodness is to invite evil, just as to ignore Thracymacus' assertion (in *The Republic*) that "justice is the right of the stronger" is to invite its realization.

A conservative view of education and character formation, then, has two elements that are simply framed. First, there is no such thing as a "value-free" school. (An academy for nihilists would be as close as one could come to a value-free school, and even nihilists think that "nothing" is something to value.) The issue is not whether or not a school will have values, but what those values will be. Like it or not, schools shape character.

Second, there are "good" values and "bad" values, or "right" values and "wrong" values. Or, as Aristotle knew, good knowledge and bad knowledge. These are inextricably embedded in our institutions. Like it or not, schools shape character for good or ill.

Think, for example, of the values of science and the learned professions: honesty in collecting evidence, in conducting research and analysis, and in reporting results; fidelity to the scientific method and the canons of professional ethics; accuracy and reliability in execution; openness to new ideas; avoidance of dogmatism; willingness to change conclusions upon the presentation of new evidence or analysis; and respect for the subject, for colleagues, and for self. The scientist, the doctor, the attorney, or the teacher who lies is profoundly immoral. In short, these are the values of the academic enterprise. They can be taught; they must be taught. It is a moral imperative.

How are values taught, and how do schools shape character? To be sure, there is more than content at stake. There is the question of general application as well. We cannot anticipate every contingency. Just as it is both desirable and useful to know how to think critically, it is desirable and useful to act virtuously. But as Aristotle knew that people become virtuous by behaving virtuously, so too he knew that we acquire the capacity to think critically by thinking critically. Not surprisingly, when it comes to character education, the two often blur. The most egregious example of the genre of character education is, of course, the teaching of "self-esteem" a popular concept imbued with near-mythic power in the modern era. Who could deny the importance of self-esteem? What is at issue is how one acquires it. Not through fiat or edict. There is no magic wand that can impart it. True self-esteem is acquired the old-fashioned way, by hard work. Mastery. Genuine accomplishment. Accolades and praise are both appropriate and desirable, but they must be earned. Indeed, to act otherwise is to work a cruel hoax on youngsters, leading them to believe, at least in passing, something that is patently untrue.

But if I have described what good character education is not, then of what is it constituted? Of three elements: example, study, and practice. First is the role of virtuous men and women, who, by example, model virtuous behavior. Parents first, then teachers and friends. It is no accident that the Hebrew honorific *rabbi* and the Japanese honorific *sensei* mean teacher. It is the highest compliment that can be paid by a people who honor the book and revere learning. In *Fiddler on the Roof,* what would Tevye do "if he were a rich man"? He would study. He would not buy a summer cottage on the Crimean Sea.

He would not buy a new horse and buggy. He cares not for material things. That is example.

Remember your best teachers; odds are they were not the easiest or the least demanding. To the contrary, it is almost certain that the teachers who left an enduring impression on you, the ones who changed your life, were men and women of high moral purpose. They were teachers because they believed in their calling and the importance of the subject they were teaching, whether it was physics, soccer, or shop. Indeed, it is the high expectations the best teachers have for us that induce us to give our best. Education, in the original Latin, means to draw out. What do good teachers "draw out" of us? Not Latin or algebra or history—they fill us with those subjects. Not virtue and morality. We are not spontaneously good. Without guidance we are at best an ethical tabula rasa. No, good teachers draw out energy, enthusiasm, verve, and spirit—even courage as they impart knowledge and model virtue.

Second, study. The basics, to be sure, but only as a vehicle to bring the exalted within reach. We learn to read not to acquire a disembodied skill called "reading" but to engage with worthwhile texts. People do not read phone books for pleasure. In school and after, they should read the ancients (*The Iliad, The Odyssey, The Aeneid,* Ovid's *Metamorphoses,* the Old and New Testaments); the great documents of citizenship (the Magna Carta, the Bill of Rights, Lincoln's Second Inaugural, Martin Luther King's "Letter from Birmingham Jail"); the great classics of prose and poetry (Sophocles, Shakespeare, Donne, Marlowe, Spenser); and more recent storytellers (Hemingway and Steinbeck, Melville and Twain, Cather and Brontë).

It is at this point that the connection between content and character formation is most starkly evident. These books and these writers endure precisely because they wrestle with the moral dilemmas that we all confront. They force the careful reader to engage in a dialogue about right and wrong, to make decisions and choices. But they do so in a context: they are embedded in content, just as our own moral dilemmas are. They are not disembodied.

By way of contrast, imagine the "moral development" both implicit and explicit in the "open boat" exercise urged on the young by Kohlberg's moral relativists. Students are asked to role-play, to imagine what they could ethically do if they were lost at sea in an open lifeboat with little or no food and water and only a remote hope of early rescue. Removed from the context of morality, historical experience, and maritime law, this can be no more than a shadow exercise. May starving survivors eat one of their own to stay alive? May they eat only someone who has already died, or may they extract a higher sacrifice? May they kill and eat the cabin boy because he is presumably the tastiest (and the weakest)?

As it happens, these are not idle questions, just as there are no right answers. But there are carefully thought-through answers. The Roman Catholic Church does not sanction killing someone to survive, but it does sanction consuming the body of one already dead if there is no other recourse. The British, as a preeminent maritime power, reached a different conclusion. British Admiralty Law holds that a survivor may be dispatched so that others might live, as long as he is selected in an evenhanded way. Lots must be drawn. In that open boat, the short straw has real significance. This is context with meaning. British fair play is not an empty boast.

Consider as well our Fifth Amendment, which protects us from self-incrimination. No one in America may be compelled to testify against himself. Why? Absent historical context, the right has little meaning. Why should a well-known mobster or child molester not be expected to testify about his activities and behavior? It is the long tradition of the rack and thumbscrew, of forced confession, of gross abuse of police power by the state that makes the Fifth Amendment a pearl beyond price. History offers few more compelling moral lessons. To advance the idea that children should not be instructed in these and similar areas is to profoundly misconceive the purposes of education. They will not invent this knowledge on their own, any more than they will invent algebra or English grammar. There is a body of shared moral and ethical information, fact, story, myth, and history that we must all possess.

We gain access to this information through proper study. We do not reinvent the world anew; we learn from our teachers, living and dead. This is not to say that acts of the imagination are bad. Indeed, much of what we know is acquired by acts of imagination; we read *The Red Badge of Courage* and share with Stephen Crane the horrors of battle, or we read his great stories *Maggie: A Girl of the Streets* or "The Open Boat" and appreciate the horrors of sexual exploitation and the terror of being lost at sea. Crane is a particularly apt example: one of the first realists, he nonetheless wrote his most enduring work about the Civil War, which was over before his fifth birthday. His magnum opus was an act of the imagination for him as it is for us.

Finally, there is practice. It makes perfect. Whether it is the repetition of scales or the shooting of baskets, practice is the key to success. Lab work, fieldwork, open heart surgery, oral argument, lecturing—all are improved by practice. At this level practice reveals that perseverance and hard work are singular virtues that are rewarded. And practice produces habit, one of the greatest gifts nature confers. Imagine having to remember how to tie your shoes every morning, having to relearn scales each day, or having to learn to read the newspaper anew each day. But practice has more elevated dimensions—it also means real experience, as in medical or legal practice.

The more advanced student writes expository prose and conducts organized research, performs lab work, undertakes fieldwork, interviews sources, learns the "language" of various disciplines. But the most important form of practice is the exercise of being a good person. It includes such simple things as being accurate, honorable, and punctual; respecting teachers, classmates, and self. Such behavior builds on the inner logic of scholarship and academic mastery—hard work, honesty, integrity.

The most telling point is that, as George Santayana said, "something not chosen must choose." In the final analysis, life is about moral choices—it is not about technique or spontaneous unfolding. Science and technology are servants, not masters. They are given scope and justification by their humane purposes. Not the reverse. The first lesson of culture is that children are not wildflowers; they are domestic flowers, and they require careful tending in both the academic and moral spheres. They cannot be left to their own devices; adults do know more than children—that is what school is all about.

As the great critic of romanticism Arthur Lovejoy (aptly named) pointed out, the romantic failure—its Achilles heel—is its inability to inform and inspire itself. Romanticism is received; it does not project. Put most simply, a romantic in a good mood (or a bad mood, for that matter) remains in one only till external circumstances change. Romanticism is a posture, not a policy; it is a view of the world, not a philosophy with which to shape the world. And as it does not work as a philosophy for adults, it works even less well with children.

One fundamental point remains. Recognizing that there is no small risk in raising the question of religion in a diverse and secular society, I feel that it is an issue that cannot be ignored in the context of education and values. The central question is deceptively simple: can man be good without God? No doubt some people can, though I expect their numbers are few. The larger issue is that the great wisdom traditions (as theologian Huston Smith calls them) are the source of moral and ethical life for most citizens of the globe, past and present. Recognizing this truism does not make life easier for schools, but ignoring it makes schooling nearly impossible. Think, for example, of explaining the civil rights movement without referring to its religious foundations: Martin Luther King was a pastor, his ministry was social justice, and the enemy was the government. The last bears repeating. The enemy was the government. The policeman was not his friend.

Schools that serve a heterogeneous population are properly nonsectarian. But they cannot ignore religion.

Schools that serve a heterogeneous population are properly nonsectarian. But they cannot ignore religion, nor can they ignore the fact that all the great religions seek to better the human lot: they are value-laden. Because schools cannot be value-free, they must at minimum model, exemplify, and reinforce the homespun virtues of democratic capitalism: honesty, forbearance, toleration, respect for self and others, courage, integrity.

In *The Aims of Education,* written in 1911, Alfred North Whitehead—mathematician, philosopher, teacher—wrote what is arguably the most compelling essay about education in the history of the genre. He concludes with these words:

The essence of education is that it be religious. Pray, what is religious education? A religious education is an education that inculcates duty and reverence. Duty arises from our potential control over the course of events. Where attainable knowledge could have changed the issue, ignorance has the guilt of vice. And the foundation of reverence is this perception, that the present holds within itself the complete sum of existence, backwards and forwards, that whole amplitude of time, which is eternity.

Although one of the first lessons we learn in philosophy is not to judge the message by the messenger, in the case of Rousseau it would be irresponsible to ignore his behavior. He practiced what he preached. His life is metaphor. As he cruelly exploited his weak-minded housekeeper, using her for his sexual pleasure, he blithely consigned their children to foundling homes, asserting that they were better off for being spared the evils of a bourgeois upbringing. In his case, at least, that may have been true. But our children are not better off for being consigned to the education foundling homes that are his legacy.

Finally, as a true conservative, I must conclude in the best liberal tradition. As I do not want to have Rousseau's views imposed on me, I do not propose to force my Hobbesian views on hapless romantics. Let us agree to that. That is what liberty—or liberalism—is supposed to be about. The logic of liberalism is to leave people free to pursue the aims that suit their values. Let the followers of Rousseau and Hobbes compete in the marketplace of both ideas and practice. The schools of Rousseau for those that want them, the schools of Hobbes for the rest.

Form at end of book

How Not to Teach Values:
A Critical Look at Character Education

What goes by the name of character education nowadays is, for the most part, a collection of exhortations and extrinsic inducements designed to make children work harder and do what they're told, Mr. Kohn maintains. He subjects this approach to careful scrutiny, arguing that there are better ways to promote social and moral development.

Alfie Kohn

Alfie Kohn writes and lectures widely on education and human behavior. His five books include Punished by Rewards *(Houghton Mifflin, 1993) and, most recently,* Beyond Discipline: From Compliance to Community *(Association for Supervision and Curriculum Development, 1996). He lives in Belmont, Mass.*

Teachers and schools tend to mistake good behavior for good character. What they prize is docility, suggestibility; the child who will do what he is told; or even better, the child who will do what is wanted without even having to be told. They value most in children what children least value in themselves. Small wonder that their effort to build character is such a failure; they don't know it when they see it.

—John Holt
How Children Fail

Were you to stand somewhere in the continental United States and announce, "I'm going to Hawaii," it would be understood that you were heading for those islands in the Pacific that collectively constitute the 50th state. Were you to stand in Honolulu and make the same state-

ment, however, you would probably be talking about one specific island in the chain—namely, the big one to your southeast. The word *Hawaii* would seem to have two meanings, a broad one and a narrow one; we depend on context to tell them apart.

The phrase *character education* also has two meanings. In the broad sense, it refers to almost anything that schools might try to provide outside of academics, especially when the purpose is to help children grow into good people. In the narrow sense, it denotes a particular style of moral training, one that reflects particular values as well as particular assumptions about the nature of children and how they learn.

Unfortunately, the two meanings of the term have become blurred, with the narrow version of character education dominating the field to the point that it is frequently mistaken for the broader concept. Thus educators who are keen to support children's social and moral development may turn, by default, to a program with a certain set of methods and a specific agenda that, on reflection, they might very well find objectionable.

My purpose in this article is to subject these programs to careful scrutiny and, in so doing, to highlight the possibility that there are other ways to achieve our broader objectives. I address myself not so much to those readers who are avid proponents of character education (in the narrow sense) but to those who simply want

Questions

For the most part, Kohn is not a strong supporter of character education. Based on the reading, why do you think he has come to these conclusions?

To what extent should or should not character education be an overarching umbrella for the school day?

Why or why not?

to help children become decent human beings and may not have thought carefully about what they are being offered.

Let me get straight to the point. What goes by the name of character education nowadays is, for the most part, a collection of exhortations and extrinsic inducements designed to make children work harder and do what they're told. Even when other values are also promoted—caring or fairness, say—the preferred method of instruction is tantamount to indoctrination. The point is to drill students in specific behaviors rather than to engage them in deep, critical reflection about certain ways of being. This is the impression one gets from reading articles and books by contemporary proponents of character education as well as the curriculum materials sold by the leading national programs. The impression is only strengthened by visiting schools that have been singled out for their commitment to character education. To wit:

A huge, multiethnic elementary school in Southern California uses a framework created by the Jefferson Center for Character Education. Classes that the principal declares "well behaved" are awarded Bonus Bucks, which can eventually be redeemed for an ice cream party. On an enormous wall near the cafeteria, professionally painted Peanuts characters instruct children: "Never talk in line." A visitor is led to a fifth-grade classroom to observe an exemplary lesson on the current character education topic. The teacher is telling students to write down the name of the person they regard as the "toughest worker" in school. The teacher then asks them, "How many of you are going to be tough workers?" (Hands go up.) "Can you be a tough worker at home, too?" (Yes.)

* * *

A small, almost entirely African American school in Chicago uses a framework created by the Character Education Institute. Periodic motivational assemblies are used to "give children a good pep talk," as the principal puts it, and to reinforce the values that determine who will be picked as Student of the Month. Rule number one posted on the wall of a kindergarten room is "We will obey the teachers." Today, students in this class are listening to the story of "Lazy Lion," who orders each of the other animals to build him a house, only to find each effort unacceptable. At the end, the teacher drives home the lesson: "Did you ever hear Lion say thank you?" (No.) "Did you ever hear Lion say please?" (No.) "It's good to always say . . . what?" (Please.) The reason for using these words, she points out, is that by doing so we are more likely to get what we want.

* * *

A charter school near Boston has been established specifically to offer an intensive, homegrown character education curriculum to its overwhelmingly white, middle-class student body. At weekly public ceremonies, certain children receive a leaf that will then be hung in the Forest of Virtue. The virtues themselves are "not open to debate," the headmaster insists, since moral precepts in his view enjoy the same status as mathematical truths. In a first-grade classroom a teacher is observing that "it's very hard to be obedient when you want something. I want you to ask yourself 'Can I have it—and why not?'" She proceeds to ask the students, "What kinds of things show obedience?" and, after collecting a few suggestions, announces that she's "not going to call on anyone else now. We could go on forever but we have to have a moment of silence and then a spelling test."

Some of the most popular schoolwide strategies for improving students' character seem dubious on their face. When President Clinton mentioned the importance of character education in his 1996 State of the Union address, the only specific practice he recommended was requiring students to wear uniforms. The premises here are first, that children's character can be improved by forcing them to dress alike, and second, that if adults object to students' clothing, the best solution is not to invite them to reflect together about how this problem might be solved, but instead to compel them all to wear the same thing.

A second strategy, also consistent with the dominant philosophy of character education, is an exercise that might be called "If It's Tuesday, This Must Be Honesty." Here, one value after another is targeted, with each assigned its own day, week, or month. This seriatim approach is unlikely to result in a lasting commitment to any of these values, much less a feeling for how they may be related. Nevertheless, such programs are taken very seriously by some of the same people who are quick to dismiss other educational programs, such as those intended to promote self-esteem, as silly and ineffective.

Then there is the strategy of offering students rewards when they are "caught" being good, an approach favored by rightwing religious groups[1] and orthodox behaviorists but also by leaders of—and curriculum suppliers for—the character education movement.[2] Because of its popularity and because a sizable body of psychological evidence germane to the topic is available, it is worth lingering on this particular practice for a moment.

In general terms, what the evidence suggests is this: the more we reward people for doing something, the more likely they are to lose interest in whatever they had to do to get the reward. Extrinsic motivation, in other words, is not only quite different from intrinsic motivation but actually tends to erode it.[3] This effect has been demonstrated under many different circumstances and with respect to many different attitudes and behaviors. Most relevant to character education is a series of studies showing that individuals who have been rewarded for doing something nice become less likely to think of themselves as caring or helpful people and more likely to attribute their behavior to the reward.

"Extrinsic incentives can, by undermining self-perceived altruism, decrease intrinsic motivation to help others," one group of researchers concluded on the basis of several studies. "A person's kindness, it seems, cannot be bought."[4] The same applies to a person's sense of responsibility, fairness, perseverance, and so on. The lesson a child learns from Skinnerian tactics is that the point of being good is to get rewards. No wonder researchers have found that children who are frequently rewarded—or, in another study, children who receive positive reinforcement for caring, sharing, and helping—are less likely than other children to keep doing those things.[5]

In short, it makes no sense to dangle goodies in front of children for being virtuous. But even worse than rewards are *a*wards—certificates, plaques, trophies, and other tokens of recognition whose numbers have been artificially limited so only a few can get them. When some children are singled out as "winners," the central message that every child learns is this: "Other people are potential obstacles to my success."[6] Thus the likely result of making students beat out their peers for the distinction of being the most virtuous is not only less intrinsic commitment to virtue but also a disruption of relationships and, ironically, of the experience of community that is so vital to the development of children's character.

Unhappily, the problems with character education (in the narrow sense, which is how I'll be using the term unless otherwise indicated) are not restricted to such strategies as enforcing sartorial uniformity, scheduling a value of the week, or offering students a "doggie biscuit" for being good. More deeply troubling are the fundamental assumptions, both explicit and implicit, that inform character education programs. Let us consider five basic questions that might be asked of any such program: At what level are problems addressed? What is the underlying theory of human nature? What is the ultimate goal? Which values are promoted? And finally, How is learning thought to take place?

1. At What Level Are Problems Addressed?

One of the major purveyors of materials in this field, the Jefferson Center for Character Education in Pasadena, California, has produced a video that begins with some arresting images—quite literally. Young people are shown being led away in handcuffs, the point being that crime can be explained on the basis of an "erosion of American core values," as the narrator intones ominously. The idea that social problems can be explained by the fact that traditional virtues are no longer taken seriously is offered by many proponents of character education as though it were just plain common sense.

But if people steal or rape or kill solely because they possess bad values—that is, because of their personal characteristics—the implication is that political and economic realities are irrelevant and need not be addressed. Never mind staggering levels of unemployment in the inner cities or a system in which more and more of the nation's wealth is concentrated in fewer and fewer hands; just place the blame on individuals whose characters are deficient. A key tenet of the "Character Counts!" Coalition, which bills itself as a nonpartisan umbrella group devoid of any political agenda, is the highly debatable proposition that "negative social influences can [be] and usually are overcome by the exercise of free will and character."[7] What is presented as common sense is, in fact, conservative ideology.

Let's put politics aside, though. If a program proceeds by trying to "fix the kids"—as do almost all brands of character education—it ignores the accumulated evidence from the field of social psychology demonstrating that much of how we act and who we are reflects the situations in which we find ourselves. Virtually all the landmark studies in this discipline have been variations on this theme. Set up children in an extended team competition at summer camp and you will elicit unprecedented levels of aggression. Assign adults to the roles of prisoners or guards in a mock jail, and they will start to become their roles. Move people to a small town, and they will be more likely to rescue a stranger in need. In fact, so common is the tendency to attribute to an individual's personality or character what is actually a function of the social environment that social psychologists have dubbed this the "fundamental attribution error."

A similar lesson comes to us from the movement concerned with Total Quality Management associated with the ideas of the late W. Edwards Deming. At the heart of Deming's teaching is the notion that the "system" of an organization largely determines the results. The problems experienced in a corporation, therefore, are almost always due to systemic flaws rather than to a lack of effort or ability on the part of individuals in that organization. Thus, if we are troubled by the way students are acting, Deming, along with most social psychologists, would presumably have us transform the structure of the classroom rather than try to remake the students themselves—precisely the opposite of the character education approach.

2. What Is the View of Human Nature?

Character education's "fix the kids" orientation follows logically from the belief that kids need fixing. Indeed, the movement seems to be driven by a stunningly dark view of children—and, for that matter, of people in general. A "comprehensive approach [to character education] is based on a somewhat dim view of human nature," acknowledges William Kilpatrick, whose book *Why Johnny Can't Tell Right from Wrong* contains such assertions as: "Most behavior problems are the result of sheer 'willfulness' on the part of children."[8]

The character education movement seems to be driven by a stunningly dark view of children—and of people in general.

Despite—or more likely because of—statements like that, Kilpatrick has frequently been invited to speak at character education conferences.[9] But that shouldn't be surprising in light of how many prominent proponents of character education share his views. Edward Wynne says his own work is grounded in a tradition of thought that takes a "somewhat pessimistic view of human nature."[10] The idea of character development "sees children as self-centered," in the opinion of Kevin Ryan, who directs the Center for the Advancement of Ethics and Character at Boston University as well as heading up the character education network of the Association for Supervision and Curriculum Development.[11] Yet another writer approvingly traces the whole field back to the bleak world view of Thomas Hobbes: it is "an obvious assumption of character education" writes Louis Goldman, that people lack the instinct to work together. Without laws to compel us to get along, "our natural egoism would lead us into 'a condition of warre one against another.' "[12] This sentiment is echoed by F. Washington Jarvis, headmaster of the Roxbury Latin School in Boston, one of Ryan's favorite examples of what character education should look like in practice. Jarvis sees human nature as "mean, nasty, brutish, selfish, and capable of great cruelty and meanness. We have to hold a mirror up to the students and say, 'This is who you are. Stop it.' "[13]

Even when proponents of character education don't express such sentiments explicitly, they give themselves away by framing their mission as a campaign for self-control. Amitai Etzioni, for example, does not merely include this attribute on a list of good character traits; he *defines* character principally in terms of the capacity "to control impulses and defer gratification."[14] This is noteworthy because the virtue of self-restraint—or at least the decision to give special emphasis to it—has historically been preached by those, from St. Augustine to the present, who see people as basically sinful.

In fact, at least three assumptions seem to be at work when the need for self-control is stressed: first, that we are all at war not only with others but with ourselves, torn between our desires and our reason (or social norms); second, that these desires are fundamentally selfish,

aggressive, or otherwise unpleasant; and third, that these desires are very strong, constantly threatening to overpower us if we don't rein them in. Collectively, these statements describe religious dogma, not scientific fact. Indeed, the evidence from several disciplines converges to cast doubt on this sour view of human beings and, instead, supports the idea that it is as "natural" for children to help as to hurt. I will not rehearse that evidence here, partly because I have done so elsewhere at some length.[15] Suffice it to say that even the most hard-headed empiricist might well conclude that the promotion of prosocial values consists to some extent of supporting (rather than restraining or controlling) many facets of the self. Any educator who adopts this more balanced position might think twice before joining an educational movement that is finally inseparable from the doctrine of original sin.

---

3. What Is the Ultimate Goal?

It may seem odd even to inquire about someone's reasons for trying to improve children's character. But it is worth mentioning that the whole enterprise—not merely the particular values that are favored—is often animated by a profoundly conservative, if not reactionary, agenda. Character education based on "acculturating students to conventional norms of 'good' behavior . . . resonates with neoconservative concerns for social stability," observed David Purpel.[16] The movement has been described by another critic as a "yearning for some halcyon days of moral niceties and social tranquillity."[17] But it is not merely a *social* order that some are anxious to preserve (or recover): character education is vital, according to one vocal proponent, because "the development of character is the backbone of the economic system" now in place.[18]

Character education, or any kind of education, would look very different if we began with other objectives—if, for example, we were principally concerned with helping children become active participants in a democratic society (or agents for transforming a society *into* one that is authentically democratic). It would look different if our top priority were to help students develop into principled and caring members of a community or advocates for social justice. To be sure, these objectives are not inconsistent with the desire to preserve certain traditions, but the point would then be to help children decide which traditions are worth preserving and why, based on these other considerations. That is not at all the same as endorsing anything that is traditional or making the preservation of tradition our primary concern. In short, we want to ask character education proponents what goals they emphasize—and ponder whether their broad vision is compatible with our own.

4. Which Values?

Should we allow values to be taught in school? The question is about as sensible as asking whether our bodies should be allowed to contain bacteria. Just as humans are teeming with microorganisms, so schools are teeming with values. We can't see the former because they're too small; we don't notice the latter because they're too similar to the values of the culture at large. Whether or not we deliberately adopt a character or moral education program, we are always teaching values. Even people who insist that they are opposed to values in school usually mean that they are opposed to values other than their own.[19]

And that raises the inevitable question: Which values, or whose, should we teach? It has already become a cliché to reply that this question should not trouble us because, while there may be disagreement on certain issues, such as abortion, all of us can agree on a list of basic values that children ought to have. Therefore, schools can vigorously and unapologetically set about teaching all of those values.

But not so fast. Look at the way character education programs have been designed and you will discover, alongside such unobjectionable items as "fairness" or "honesty," an emphasis on values that are, again, distinctly conservative—and, to that extent, potentially controversial. To begin with, the famous Protestant work ethic is prominent: children should learn to "work hard and complete their tasks well and promptly, even when they do not want to," says Ryan.[20] Here the Latin question *Cui bono?* comes to mind. Who benefits when people are trained not to question the value of what they have been told to do but simply to toil away at it—and to regard this as virtuous?[21] Similarly, when Wynne defines the moral individual as someone who is not only honest but also "diligent, obedient, and patriotic,"[22] readers may find themselves wondering whether these traits really qualify as *moral*—as well as reflecting on the virtues that are missing from this list.

The character education programs—and theorists who promote them—seem to regard teaching as a matter of telling and compelling.

Character education curricula also stress the importance of things like "respect," "responsibility," and "citizenship." But these are slippery terms, frequently used as euphemisms for uncritical deference to authority. Under the headline "The Return of the 'Fourth R' "—referring to "respect, responsibility, or rules"—a news magazine recently described the growing popularity of such practices as requiring uniforms, paddling disobedient students, re-

warding those who are compliant, and "throwing disruptive kids out of the classroom."[23] Indeed, William Glasser observed some time ago that many educators "teach thoughtless conformity to school rules and call the conforming child 'responsible.' "[24] I once taught at a high school where the principal frequently exhorted students to "take responsibility." By this he meant specifically that they should turn in their friends who used drugs.

Exhorting students to be "respectful" or rewarding them if they are caught being "good" may likewise mean nothing more than getting them to do whatever the adults demand. Following a lengthy article about character education in the *New York Times Magazine,* a reader mused, "Do you suppose that if Germany had had character education at the time, it would have encouraged children to fight Nazism or to support it?"[25] The more time I spend in schools that are enthusiastically implementing character education programs, the more I am haunted by that question.

In place of the traditional attributes associated with character education, Deborah Meier and Paul Schwarz of the Central Park East Secondary School in New York nominated two core values that a school might try to promote: "empathy and skepticism: the ability to see a situation from the eyes of another and the tendency to wonder about the validity of what we encountered."[26] Anyone who brushes away the question "Which values should be taught?" might speculate on the concrete differences between a school dedicated to turning out students who are empathic and skeptical and a school dedicated to turning out students who are loyal, patriotic, obedient, and so on.

Meanwhile, in place of such personal qualities as punctuality or perseverance, we might emphasize the cultivation of autonomy so that children come to experience themselves as "origins" rather than "pawns," as one researcher put it.[27] We might, in other words, stress self-determination at least as much as self-control. With such an agenda, it would be crucial to give students the chance to participate in making decisions about their learning and about how they want their classroom to be.[28] This stands in sharp contrast to a philosophy of character education like Wynne's, which decrees that "it is specious to talk about student choices" and offers students no real power except for when we give "some students authority over other students (for example, hall guard, class monitor)."[29]

Even with values that are widely shared, a superficial consensus may dissolve when we take a closer look. Educators across the spectrum are concerned about excessive attention to self-interest and are committed to helping students transcend a preoccupation with their own needs. But how does this concern play out in practice? For some of us, it takes the form of an emphasis on *compassion;* for the dominant character education approach, the alternative value to be stressed is *loyalty,* which is, of course, altogether different.[30] Moreover, as John Dewey remarked at the turn of the century, anyone seriously troubled about rampant individualism among children would promptly target for extinction the "drill-and-skill" approach to instruction: "The mere absorbing of facts and truths is so exclusively individual an affair that it tends very naturally to pass into selfishness."[31] Yet conservative champions of character education are often among the most outspoken supporters of a model of teaching that emphasizes rote memorization and the sequential acquisition of decontextualized skills.

Or take another example: all of us may say we endorse the idea of "cooperation," but what do we make of the practice of setting groups against one another in a quest for triumph, such that cooperation becomes the means and victory is the end? On the one hand, we might find this even more objectionable than individual competition. (Indeed, we might regard a "We're Number One!" ethic as a reason for schools to undertake something like character education in the first place.) On the other hand, "school-to-school, class-to-class, or row-to-row academic competitions" actually have been endorsed as part of a character education program,[32] along with contests that lead to awards for things like good citizenship.

The point, once again, is that it is entirely appropriate to ask which values a character education program is attempting to foster, notwithstanding the ostensible lack of controversy about a list of core values. It is equally appropriate to put such a discussion in context—specifically, in the context of which values are *currently* promoted in schools. The fact is that schools are already powerful socializers of traditional values—although, as noted above, we may fail to appreciate the extent to which this is true because we have come to take these values for granted. In most schools, for example, students are taught—indeed, compelled—to follow the rules regardless of whether the rules are reasonable and to respect authority regardless of whether that respect has been earned. (This process isn't always successful, of course, but that is a different matter.) Students are led to accept competition as natural and desirable, and to see themselves more as discrete individuals than as members of a community. Children in American schools are even expected to begin each day by reciting a loyalty oath to the Fatherland, although we call it by a different name. In short, the question is not whether to adopt the conservative values offered by most character education programs, but whether we want to consolidate the conservative values that are already in place.

5. What Is the Theory of Learning?

We come now to what may be the most significant, and yet the least remarked on, feature of character education: the way values are taught and the way learning is thought to take place.

The character education coordinator for the small Chicago elementary school also teaches second grade. In her classroom, where one boy has been forced to sit by himself for the last two weeks ("He's kind of pesty"), she is asking the children to define tolerance. When the teacher gets the specific answers she is fishing for, she exclaims, "Say that again," and writes down only those responses. Later comes the moral: "If somebody doesn't think the way you think, should you turn them off?" (No.)

Down the hall, the first-grade teacher is fishing for answers on a different subject. "When we play games, we try to understand the—what?" (Rules.) A moment later, the children scramble to get into place so she will pick them to tell a visitor their carefully rehearsed stories about conflict resolution. Almost every child's account, narrated with considerable prompting by the teacher, concerns name-calling or some other unpleasant incident that was "correctly" resolved by finding an adult. The teacher never asks the children how they felt about what happened or invites them to reflect on what else might have been done. She wraps up the activity by telling the children, "What we need to do all the time is clarify—make it clear—to the adult what you did."

The schools with character education programs that I have visited are engaged largely in exhortation and directed recitation. At first one might assume this is due to poor implementation of the programs on the part of individual educators. But the programs themselves—and the theorists who promote them—really do seem to regard teaching as a matter of telling and compelling. For example, the broad-based "Character Counts!" Coalition offers a framework of six core character traits and then asserts that "young people should be specifically and repeatedly told what is expected of them." The leading providers of curriculum materials walk teachers through highly structured lessons in which character-related concepts are described and then students are drilled until they can produce the right answers.

Teachers are encouraged to praise children who respond correctly, and some programs actually include multiple-choice tests to ensure that students have learned their values. For example, here are two sample test questions prepared for teachers by the Character Education Institute, based in San Antonio, Texas: "Having to obey rules and regulations (a) gives everyone the same right to be an individual, (b) forces everyone to do the same thing at all times, (c) prevents persons from expressing their individually [sic]"; and "One reason why parents might not allow their children freedom of choice is (a) children are always happier when they are told what to do and when to do it, (b) parents aren't given a freedom of choice; therefore, children should not be given a choice either, (c) children do not always demonstrate that they are responsible enough to be given a choice." The correct answers, according to the answer key, are (a) and (c) respectively.

The Character Education Institute recommends "engaging the students in discussions," but only discussions of a particular sort: "Since the lessons have been designed to logically guide the students to the right answers, the teacher should allow the students to draw their own conclusions. However, if the students draw the wrong conclusion, the teacher is instructed to tell them why their conclusion is *wrong*."[33]

Students are told what to think and do, not only by their teachers but by highly didactic stories, such as those in the Character Education Institute's "Happy Life" series, which end with characters saying things like "I am glad that I did not cheat," or "Next time I will be helpful," or "I will never be selfish again." Most character education programs also deliver homilies by way of posters and banners and murals displayed throughout the school. Children who do as they are told are presented with all manner of rewards, typically in front of their peers.

Does all of this amount to indoctrination? Absolutely, says Wynne, who declares that "school is and should and must be inherently indoctrinative."[34] Even when character education proponents tiptoe around that word, their model of instruction is clear: good character and values are *instilled in* or *transmitted to* students. We are "planting the ideas of virtue, of good traits in the young," says William Bennett.[35] The virtues or values in question are fully formed, and, in the minds of many character education proponents, divinely ordained. The children are—pick your favorite metaphor—so many passive receptacles to be filled, lumps of clay to be molded, pets to be trained, or computers to be programmed.

Thus, when we see Citizen-of-the-Month certificates and "Be a good sport!" posters, when we find teachers assigning preachy stories and principals telling students what to wear, it is important that we understand what is going on. These techniques may appear merely innocuous or gimmicky; they may strike us as evidence of a scatter-shot, let's-try-anything approach. But the truth is that these are elements of a systematic pedagogical philosophy. They are manifestations of a model that sees children as objects to be manipulated rather than as learners to be engaged.

Ironically, some people who accept character education without a second thought are quite articulate about the bankruptcy of this model when it comes to teaching academic subjects. Plenty of teachers have abandoned the use of worksheets, textbooks, and lectures that fill children full of disconnected facts and skills. Plenty of administrators are working to create schools where students can actively construct meaning around scientific and historical and literary concepts. Plenty of educators, in short, realize that memorizing right answers and algorithms doesn't help anyone to arrive at a deep understanding of ideas.

And so we are left scratching our heads. Why would all these people, who know that the "transmission" model fails to facilitate intellectual development, uncritically accept the very same model to promote ethical development? How could they understand that mathematical truths cannot be shoved down students' throats but then participate in a program that essentially tries to shove moral truths down the same throats? In the case of individual educators, the simple answer may be that they missed the connection. Perhaps they just failed to recognize that "a classroom cannot foster the development of autonomy in the intellectual realm while suppressing it in the social and moral realms," as Constance Kamii and her colleagues put it not long ago.[36]

In the case of the proponents of character education, I believe the answer to this riddle is quite different. The reason they are promoting techniques that seem strikingly ineffective at fostering autonomy or ethical development is that, as a rule, they are not *trying* to foster autonomy or ethical development. The goal is not to support or facilitate children's social and moral growth, but simply to "demand good behavior from students," in Ryan's words.[37] The idea is to get compliance, to *make* children act the way we want them to.

Indeed, if these are the goals, then the methods make perfect sense—the lectures and pseudo-discussions, the slogans and the stories that conk students on the head with their morals. David Brooks, who heads the Jefferson Center for Character Education, frankly states, "We're in the advertising business." The way you get people to do something, whether it's buying Rice Krispies or becoming trustworthy, is to "encourage conformity through repeated messages."[38] The idea of selling virtues like cereal nearly reaches the point of self-parody in the Jefferson Center's curriculum, which includes the following activity: "There's a new product on the market! It's Considerate Cereal. Eating it can make a person more considerate. Design a label for the box. Tell why someone should buy and eat this cereal. Then list the ingredients."[39]

If "repeated messages" don't work, then you simply force students to conform: "Sometimes compulsion is what is needed to get a habit started," says William Kilpatrick.[40] We may recoil from the word "compulsion," but it is the premise of that sentence that really ought to give us pause. When education is construed as the process of inculcating *habits*—which is to say, unreflective actions—then it scarcely deserves to be called education at all. It is really, as Alan Lockwood saw, an attempt to get "mindless conformity to externally imposed standards of conduct."[41]

When education is construed as the process of inculcating habits, then it scarcely deserves to be called education at all.

Notice how naturally this goal follows from a dark view of human nature. If you begin with the premise that "good conduct is not our natural first choice," then the best you can hope for is "the development of good habits"[42]—that is, a system that gets people to act unthinkingly in the manner that someone else has deemed appropriate. This connection recently became clear to Ann Medlock, whose Giraffe Project was designed to evoke "students' own courage and compassion" in thinking about altruism, but which, in some schools, was being turned into a traditional, authoritarian program in which students were simply told how to act and what to believe. Medlock recalls suddenly realizing what was going on with these educators:

"Oh, *I* see where you're coming from. You believe kids are no damn good!"[43]

The character education movement's emphasis on habit, then, is consistent with its view of children. Likewise, its process matches its product. The transmission model, along with the use of rewards and punishments to secure compliance, seems entirely appropriate if the values you are trying to transmit are things like obedience and loyalty and respect for authority. But this approach overlooks an important distinction between product and process. When we argue about which traits to emphasize—compassion or loyalty, cooperation or competition, skepticism or obedience—we are trafficking in value judgments. When we talk about how best to teach these things, however, we are being descriptive rather than just prescriptive. Even if you like the sort of virtues that appear in character education programs, and even if you regard the need to implement those virtues as urgent, the attempt to transmit or instill them dooms the project because that is just not consistent with the best theory and research on how people learn. (Of course, if you have reservations about many of the values that the character educators wish to instill, you

may be *relieved* that their favored method is unlikely to be successful.)

I don't wish to be misunderstood. The techniques of character education may succeed in temporarily buying a particular behavior. But they are unlikely to leave children with a *commitment* to that behavior, a reason to continue acting that way in the future. You can turn out automatons who utter the desired words or maybe even "emit" (to use the curious verb favored by behaviorists) the desired actions. But the words and actions are unlikely to continue—much less transfer to new situations—because the child has not been invited to integrate them into his or her value structure. As Dewey observed, "The required beliefs cannot be hammered in; the needed attitudes cannot be plastered on."[44] Yet watch a character education lesson in any part of the country and you will almost surely be observing a strenuous exercise in hammering and plastering.

For traditional moralists, the constructivist approach is a waste of time. If values and traditions and the stories that embody them already exist, then surely "we don't have to reinvent the wheel," remarks Bennett.[45] Likewise an exasperated Wynne: "Must each generation try to completely reinvent society?"[46] The answer is no—and yes. It is not as though everything that now exists must be discarded and entirely new values fashioned from scratch. But the process of learning does indeed require that meaning, ethical or otherwise, be actively invented and reinvented, from the inside out. It requires that children be given the opportunity to make sense of such concepts as fairness or courage, regardless of how long the concepts themselves have been around. Children must be invited to reflect on complex issues, to recast them in light of their own experiences and questions, to figure out for themselves—and with one another what kind of person one ought to be, which traditions are worth keeping, and how to proceed when two basic values seem to be in conflict.[47]

In this sense, reinvention is necessary if we want to help children become moral people, as opposed to people who merely do what they are told—or reflexively rebel against what they are told. In fact, as Rheta DeVries and Betty Zan add (in a recent book that offers a useful antidote to traditional character education), "if we want children to resist [peer pressure] and not be victims of others' ideas, we have to educate children to think for themselves about all ideas, including those of adults."[48]

Traditionalists are even more likely to offer another objection to the constructivist approach, one that boils down to a single epithet: *relativism!* If we do anything other than insert moral absolutes in students, if we let them construct their own meanings, then we are saying that anything goes, that morality collapses into personal preferences. Without character education, our schools will just offer programs such as Values Clarification, in which adults are allegedly prohibited from taking a stand.

In response, I would offer several observations. First, the Values Clarification model of moral education, popular in some circles a generation ago, survives today mostly in the polemics of conservatives anxious to justify an indoctrinative approach. Naturally, no statistics are ever cited as to the number of school districts still telling students that any value is as good as any other—assuming the program actually said that in the first place.[49] Second, conservative critics tendentiously try to connect constructivism to relativism, lumping together the work of the late Lawrence Kohlberg with programs like Values Clarification.[50] The truth is that Kohlberg, while opposed to what he called the "bag of virtues" approach to moral education, was not much enamored of Values Clarification either, and he spent a fair amount of time arguing against relativism in general.[51]

If Kohlberg can fairly be criticized, it is for emphasizing moral reasoning, a cognitive process, to the extent that he may have slighted the affective components of morality, such as caring. But the traditionalists are not much for the latter either: caring is seen as an easy or soft virtue (Ryan) that isn't sufficiently "binding or absolute" (Kilpatrick). The objection to constructivism is not that empathy is eclipsed by justice, but that children—or even adults—should not have an active role to play in making decisions and reflecting on how to live. They should be led instead to an uncritical acceptance of ready-made truths. The character educator's job, remember, is to elicit the right answer from students and tell those who see things differently "why their conclusion is *wrong*." Any deviation from this approach is regarded as indistinguishable from full-blown relativism; we must "plant" traditional values in each child or else morality is nothing more than a matter of individual taste. Such either/or thinking, long since discarded by serious moral philosophers,[52] continues to fuel character education and to perpetuate the confusion of education with indoctrination.

To say that students must construct meaning around moral concepts is not to deny that adults have a crucial role to play. The romantic view that children can basically educate themselves so long as grown-ups don't interfere is not taken seriously by any constructivists I know of—certainly not by Dewey, Piaget, Kohlberg, or their followers. Rather, like Values Clarification, this view seems to exist principally as a straw man in the arguments of conservatives. Let there be no question, then: educators, parents, and other adults are desperately needed to offer guidance, to act as models (we hope), to pose challenges that promote moral growth, and to help children understand the effects of their actions on other people, thereby tapping and nurturing a concern for others that is present in children from a very young age."[53]

Character education rests on three ideological legs: behaviorism, conservatism, and religion. Of these, the third raises the most delicate issues for a critic; it is here that the charge of *ad hominem* argument is most likely to be raised. So let us be clear: it is of no relevance that almost all of the leading proponents of character education are devout Catholics. But it is entirely relevant that, in the shadows of their writings, there lurks the assumption that only religion can serve as the foundation for good character. (William Bennett, for example, has flatly asserted that the difference between right and wrong cannot be taught "without reference to religion."[54]) It is appropriate to consider the personal beliefs of these individuals if those beliefs are ensconced in the movement they have defined and directed. What they do on Sundays is their own business, but if they are trying to turn our public schools into Sunday schools, that becomes everybody's business.

Character education rests on three ideological legs: behaviorism, conservatism, and religion. The third raises the most delicate issues.

Even putting aside the theological underpinnings of the character education movement, the five questions presented in this article can help us describe the natural constituency of that movement. Logically, its supporters should be those who firmly believe that we should focus our efforts on repairing the characters of children rather than on transforming the environments in which they learn, those who assume the worst about human nature, those who are more committed to preserving than to changing our society, those who favor such values as obedience to authority, and those who define learning as the process of swallowing whole a set of preexisting truths. It stands to reason that readers who recognize themselves in this description would enthusiastically endorse character education in its present form.

The rest of us have a decision to make. Either we define our efforts to promote children's social and moral development as an *alternative* to "character education," thereby ceding that label to the people who have already appropriated it, or we try to *reclaim* the wider meaning of the term by billing what we are doing as a different kind of character education.

The first choice—opting out—seems logical: it strains the language to use a single phrase to describe practices as different as engaging students in reflecting about fairness, on the one hand, and making students dress alike, on the other. It seems foolish to pretend that these are just different versions of the same thing, and thus it may be unreasonable to expect someone with a constructivist or progressive vision to endorse what is now called character education. The problem with abandoning this label, however, is that it holds considerable appeal for politicians and members of the public at large. It will be challenging to explain that "character education" is not synonymous with helping children to grow into good people and, indeed, that the movement associated with the term is a good deal more controversial than it first appears.

The second choice, meanwhile, presents its own set of practical difficulties. Given that the individuals and organizations mentioned in this article have succeeded in putting their own stamp on character education, it will not be easy to redefine the phrase so that it can also signify a very different approach. It will not be easy, that is, to organize conferences, publish books and articles, and develop curricular materials that rescue the broad meaning of "character education."

Whether we relinquish or retain the nomenclature, though, it is vital that we work to decouple most of what takes place under the banner of "character education" from the enterprise of helping students become ethically sophisticated decision makers and caring human beings. Wanting young people to turn out that way doesn't require us to adopt traditional character education programs any more than wanting them to be physically fit requires us to turn schools into Marine boot camps.

What does the alternative look like? Return once more to those five questions: in each case, an answer different from that given by traditional character education will help us to sketch the broad contours of a divergent approach. More specifically, we should probably target certain practices for elimination, add some new ones, and reconfigure still others that already exist. I have already offered a catalogue of examples of what to eliminate, from Skinnerian reinforcers to lesson plans that resemble sermons. As examples of what to add, we might suggest holding regular class meetings in which students can share, plan, decide, and reflect together."[55] We might also provide children with explicit opportunities to practice "perspective taking"—that is, imagining how the world looks from someone else's point of view. Activities that promote an understanding of how others think and feel, that support the impulse to imaginatively reach beyond the self, can provide the same benefits realized by holding democratic class meetings—namely, helping students become more ethical and compassionate while simultaneously fostering intellectual growth.[56]

A good example of an existing practice that might be reconfigured is the use of literature to teach values. In principle, the idea is splendid: it makes perfect sense to select stories that not only help students develop reading skills (and an appreciation for good writing) but also raise moral issues. The trouble is that many programs use simplistic little morality tales in place of rich, complex literature. Naturally, the texts should be developmentally appropriate, but some character educators fail to give children credit for being able to grapple with ambiguity. (Imagine the sort of stories likely to be assigned by someone who maintains that "it is ridiculous to believe children are capable of objectively assessing most of the beliefs and values they must absorb to be effective adults."[57])

Perhaps the concern is not that students will be unable to make sense of challenging literature, but that they will not derive the "correct" moral. This would account for the fact that even when character education curricula include impressive pieces of writing, the works tend to be used for the purpose of drumming in simple lessons. As Kilpatrick sees it, a story "points to these [characters] and says in effect, 'Act like this; don't act like that.' "[58] This kind of lesson often takes the form of hero worship, with larger-than-life characters—or real historical figures presented with their foibles airbrushed away held up to students to encourage imitation of their actions.

Rather than employ literature to indoctrinate or induce mere conformity, we can use it to spur reflection. Whether the students are 6-year-olds or 16-year-olds, the discussion of stories should be open-ended rather than relentlessly didactic. Teachers who refrain from tightly controlling such conversations are impressed again and again by the levels of meaning students prove capable of exploring and the moral growth they exhibit in such an environment. Instead of announcing, "This man is a hero; do what he did," such teachers may involve the students in *deciding* who (if anyone) is heroic in a given story—or in contemporary culture[59]—and why. They may even invite students to reflect on the larger issue of whether it is desirable to have heroes. (Consider the quality of discussion that might be generated by asking older students to respond to the declaration of playwright Bertolt Brecht: "Unhappy is the land that needs a hero.")

More than specific practices that might be added, subtracted, or changed, a program to help children grow into good people begins with a commitment to change the way classrooms and schools are structured—and this brings us back to the idea of transcending a fix-the-kid approach. Consider the format of classroom discussions. A proponent of character education, invoking such traditional virtues as patience or self-control, might remind students that they must wait to be recognized by the teacher, But what if we invited students to think about the best way to conduct a discussion? Must we raise our hands? Is there another way to avoid having everyone talk at once? How can we be fair to those who aren't as assertive or as fast on their feet? Should the power to decide who can speak always rest with the teacher? Perhaps the problem is not with students who need to be more self-disciplined, but with the whole instructional design that has students waiting to be recognized to answer someone else's questions. And perhaps the real learning comes only when students have the chance to grapple with such issues.

One more example. A proponent of character education says we must make students understand that it is wrong to lie; we need to teach them about the importance of being honest. But why do people lie? Usually because they don't feel safe enough to tell the truth. The real challenge for us as educators is to examine that precept in terms of what is going on in our classrooms, to ask how we and the students together can make sure that even unpleasant truths can be told and heard. Does pursuing this line of inquiry mean that it's acceptable to fib? No. It means the problem has to be dissected and solved from the inside out. It means behaviors occur in a context that teachers have helped to establish; therefore, teachers have to examine (and consider modifying) that context even at the risk of some discomfort to themselves. In short, if we want to help children grow into compassionate and responsible people, we have to change the way the classroom works and feels, not just the way each separate member of that class acts. Our emphasis should not be on forming individual characters so much as on transforming educational structures.

Happily, programs do exist whose promotion of children's social and moral development is grounded in a commitment to change the culture of schools. The best example of which I am aware is the Child Development Project, an elementary school program designed, implemented, and researched by the Developmental Studies Center in Oakland, California. The CDP's premise is that, by meeting children's needs, we increase the likelihood that they will care about others. Meeting their needs entails, among other things, turning schools into caring communities. The CDP offers the additional advantages of a constructivist vision of learning, a positive view of human nature, a balance of cognitive and affective concerns, and a program that is integrated into all aspects of school life (including the curriculum).[60]

Is the CDP an example of what character education ought to be—or of what ought to replace character education? The answer to that question will depend on tactical, and even semantic, considerations. Far more compelling is the need to evaluate the practices and premises of contemporary character education. To realize a humane and progressive vision for children's development, we may need to look elsewhere.

Notes

1. See, for example, Linda Page, "A Conservative Christian View on Values," *School Administrator,* September 1995, p. 22.

2. See, for example, Kevin Ryan, "The Ten Commandments of Character Education," *School Administrator,* September 1995, p. 19, and program materials from the Character Education Institute and the Jefferson Center for Character Education.

3. See Alfie Kohn, *Punished by Rewards: The Trouble with Gold Stars, Incentive Plans, A's, Praise, and Other Bribes* (Boston: Houghton Mifflin, 1993); and Edward L. Deci and Richard M. Ryan, *Intrinsic Motivation and Self-Determination in Human Behavior* (New York: Plenum, 1985).

4. See C. Daniel Batson et al., "Buying Kindness: Effect of an Extrinsic Incentive for Helping on Perceived Altruism," *Personality and Social Psychology Bulletin,* vol. 4, 1978, p. 90; Cathleen L. Smith et al., "Children's Causal Attributions Regarding Help Giving," *Child Development,* vol. 50, 1979, pp. 203–10; and William Edward Upton III, "Altruism, Attribution, and Intrinsic Motivation in the Recruitment of Blood Donors," *Dissertation Abstracts International* 34B, vol. 12, 1974, p. 6260.

5. Richard A. Fabes et al., "Effects of Rewards on Children's Prosocial Motivation: A Socialization Study," *Developmental Psychology,* vol. 25, 1989, pp. 509–15; and Joan Grusec, "Socializing Concern for Others in the Home," *Developmental Psychology,* vol. 27, 1991, pp. 338–42.

6. See Alfie Kohn, *No Contest: The Case Against Competition,* rev. ed. (Boston: Houghton Mifflin, 1992).

7. This statement is taken from an eight-page brochure produced by the "Character Counts!" Coalition, a project of the Josephson Institute of Ethics. Members of the coalition include the American Federation of Teachers, the National Association of Secondary School Principals, the American Red Cross, the YMCA, and many other organizations.

8. William Kilpatrick, *Why Johnny Can't Tell Right from Wrong* (New York: Simon & Schuster, 1992), pp. 96, 249.

9. For example, Kilpatrick was selected in 1995 to keynote the first in a series of summer institutes on character education sponsored by Thomas Lickona.

10. Edward Wynne, "Transmitting Traditional Values in Contemporary Schools," in Larry P. Nucci, ed., *Moral Development and Character Education: A Dialogue* (Berkeley, Calif.: McCutchan, 1989), p. 25.

11. Kevin Ryan, "In Defense of Character Education," in Nucci, p. 16.

12. Louis Goldman, "Mind, Character, and the Deferral of Gratification," *Educational Forum,* vol. 60, 1996, p. 136. As part of "educational reconstruction," he goes on to say, we must "connect the lower social classes to the middle classes who may provide role models for self-discipline" (p. 139).

13. Jarvis is quoted in Wray Herbert, "The Moral Child," *U.S. News & World Report,* 3 June 1996, p. 58.

14. Amitai Etzioni, *The Spirit of Community: The Reinvention of American Society* (New York: Simon & Schuster, 1993), p. 91.

15. See Alfie Kohn, *The Brighter Side of Human Nature: Altruism and Empathy in Everyday Life* (New York: Basic Books, 1990); and "Caring Kids: The Role of the Schools," *Phi Delta Kappan,* March 1991, pp. 496–506.

16. David E. Purpel, "Moral Education: An Idea Whose Time Has Gone," *The Clearing House,* vol. 64, 1991, p. 311.

17. This description of the character education movement is offered by Alan L. Lockwood in "Character Education: The Ten Percent Solution," *Social Education,* April/May 1991, p. 246. It is a particularly apt characterization of a book like *Why Johnny Can't Tell Right from Wrong,* which invokes an age of "chivalry"

and sexual abstinence, a time when moral truths were uncomplicated and unchallenged. The author's tone, however, is not so much wistful about the past as angry about the present: he denounces everything from rock music (which occupies an entire chapter in a book about morality) and feminism to the "multiculturalists" who dare to remove "homosexuality from the universe of moral judgment" (p. 126).

18. Kevin Walsh of the University of Alabama is quoted in Eric N. Berg, "Argument Grows That Teaching of Values Should Rank with Lessons," *New York Times*, 1 January 1992, p. 32.

19. I am reminded of a woman in a Houston audience who heatedly informed me that she doesn't send her child to school "to learn to be nice." That, she declared, would be "social engineering." But a moment later this woman added that her child ought to be "taught to respect authority." Since this would seem to be at least as apposite an example of social engineering, one is led to conclude that the woman's real objection was to the teaching of *particular* topics or values.

20. Kevin Ryan, "Mining the Values in the Curriculum," *Educational Leadership*, November 1993, p. 16.

21. Telling students to "try hard" and "do their best" begs the important questions. *How*, exactly, do they do their best? Surely it is not just a matter of blind effort. And *why* should they do so, particularly if the task is not engaging or meaningful to them, or if it has simply been imposed on them? Research has found that the attitudes students take toward learning are heavily influenced by whether they have been led to attribute their success (or failure) to ability, to effort, or to other factors—and that traditional classroom practices such as grading and competition lead them to explain the results in terms of ability (or its absence) and to minimize effort whenever possible. What looks like "laziness" or insufficient perseverance, in other words, often turns out to be a rational decision to avoid challenge; it is rational because this route proves most expedient for performing well or maintaining an image of oneself as smart. These systemic factors, of course, are complex and often threatening for educators to address; it is much easier just to impress on children the importance of doing their best and then blame them for lacking perseverance if they seem not to do so.

22. Edward A. Wynne, "The Great Tradition in Education: Transmitting Moral Values," *Educational Leadership*, December 1985/January 1986, p. 6.

23. Mary Lord, "The Return of the 'Fourth R,'" *U.S. News & World Report*, 11 September 1995, p. 58.

24. William Glasser, *Schools Without Failure* (New York: Harper & Row, 1969), p. 22.

25. Marc Desmond's letter appeared in the *New York Times Magazine*, 21 May 1995, p. 14. The same point was made by Robert Primack, "No Substitute for Critical Thinking: A Response to Wynne," *Educational Leadership*, December 1985/January 1986, p. 12.

26. Deborah Meier and Paul Schwarz, "Central Park East Secondary School," in Michael W. Apple and James A. Beane, eds., *Democratic Schools* (Alexandria, Va.: Association for Supervision and Curriculum Development, 1995), pp. 29–30.

27. See Richard de Charms, *Personal Causation: The Internal Affective Determinants of Behavior* (Hillsdale, N.J.: Erlbaum, 1983). See also the many publications of Edward Deci and Richard Ryan.

28. See, for example, Alfie Kohn, "Choices for Children: Why and How to Let Students Decide," *Phi Delta Kappan*, September 1993, pp. 8–20; and Child Development Project, *Ways We Want Our Class to Be: Class Meetings That Build Commitment to Kindness and Learning* (Oakland, Calif.: Developmental Studies Center, 1996).

29. The quotations are from Wynne, "The Great Tradition," p. 9; and Edward A. Wynne and Herbert J. Walberg, "The Complementary Goals of Character Development and Academic Excellence," *Educational Leadership*, December 1985/January 1986, p. 17. William Kilpatrick is equally averse to including students in decision making, he speaks longingly of the days when "schools were unapologetically authoritarian," declaring that "schools can learn a lot from the Army," which is a "hierarchial [sic], authoritarian, and undemocratic institution" (see *Why Johnny Can't*, p. 228).

30. The sort of compassion I have in mind is akin to what the psychologist Ervin Staub described as a "prosocial orientation" (see his *Positive Social Behavior and Morality*, vols. 1 and 2 [New York: Academic Press, 1978 and 1979])—a generalized inclination to care, share, and help across different situations and with different people, including those we don't know, don't like, and don't look like. Loyally lending a hand to a close friend is one thing; going out of one's way for a stranger is something else.

31. John Dewey, *The School and Society* (Chicago: University of Chicago Press, 1900; reprint, 1990), p. 15.

32. Wynne and Walberg, p. 17. For another endorsement of competition among students, see Kevin Ryan, "In Defense," p. 15.

33. This passage is taken from page 21 of an undated 28-page "Character Education Curriculum" produced by the Character Education Institute. Emphasis in original.

34. Wynne, "Great Tradition," p. 9. Wynne and other figures in the character education movement acknowledge their debt to the French social scientist Emile Durkheim, who believed that "all education is a continuous effort to impose on the child ways of seeing, feeling, and acting which he could not have arrived at spontaneously. . . . We exert pressure upon him in order that he may learn proper consideration for others, respect for customs and conventions, the need for work, etc." (See Durkheim, *The Rules of Sociological Method* [New York: Free Press, 1938], p. 6.)

35. This is from Bennett's introduction to *The Book of Virtues* (New York: Simon & Schuster, 1993,), pp. 12–13.

36. Constance Kamii, Faye B. Clark, and Ann Dominick, "The Six National Goals: A Road to Disappointment," *Phi Delta Kappan*, May 1994, p. 677.

37. Kevin Ryan, "Character and Coffee Mugs," *Education Week*, 17 May 1995, p. 48.

38. The second quotation is a reporter's paraphrase of Brooks. Both it and the direct quotation preceding it appear in Philip Cohen, "The Content of Their Character: Educators Find New Ways to Tackle Values and Morality," *ASCD Curriculum Update*, Spring 1995, p. 4.

39. See B. David Brooks, *Young People's Lessons in Character: Student Activity Workbook* (San Diego: Young People's Press, 1996), p. 12.

40. Kilpatrick, p. 231.

41. To advocate this sort of enterprise, he adds, is to "caricature the moral life." See Alan L. Lockwood, "Keeping Them in the Courtyard: A Response to Wynne," *Educational Leadership*, December 1985/January 1986, p. 10.

42. Kilpatrick, p. 97.

43. Personal communication with Ann Medlock, May 1996.

44. John Dewey, *Democracy and Education* (New York: Free Press, 1916; reprint, 1966), p. 11.

45. Bennett, p. 11.

46. Wynne, "Character and Academics," p. 142.

47. For a discussion of how traditional character education fails to offer guidance when values come into conflict, see Lockwood, "Character Education."

48. Rheta DeVries and Betty Zan, *Moral Classrooms, Moral Children: Creating a Constructivist Atmosphere in Early Education* (New York: Teachers College Press, 1994), p. 253.

49. For an argument that critics tend to misrepresent what Values Clarification was about, see James A. Beane, *Affect in the Curriculum* (New York: Teachers College Press, 1990), pp. 104–6.

50. Wynne, for example, refers to the developers of Values Clarification as "popularizers" of Kohlberg's research (see "Character and Academics," p. 141), while Amitai Etzioni, in the course of criticizing Piaget's and Kohlberg's work, asserts that "a typical course on moral reasoning starts with something called 'values clarification' " (see *The Spirit of Community*, p. 98).

51. Kohlberg's model, which holds that people across cultures progress predictably through six stages of successively more sophisticated styles of moral reasoning, is based on the decidedly nonrelativistic premise that the last stages are superior to the first ones. See his *Essays on Moral Development, Vol. 1: The Philosophy of Moral Development* (San Francisco: Harper & Row, 1981), especially the essays titled "Indoctrination Versus Relativity in Value Education" and "From *Is to Ought.*"

52. See, for example, James S. Fishkin, *Beyond Subjective Morality* (New Haven, Conn.: Yale University Press, 1984); and David B. Wong, *Moral Relativity* (Berkeley: University of California Press, 1984).

53. Researchers at the National Institute of Mental Health have summarized the available research as follows: "Even children as young as 2 years old have (a) the cognitive capacity to interpret the physical and psychological states of others, (b) the emotional capacity to effectively experience the other's state, and (c) the behavioral repertoire that permits the possibility of trying to alleviate discomfort in others. These are the capabilities that, we believe, underlie children's caring behavior in the presence of another person's distress. . . . Young children seem to show patterns of moral internalization that are not simply fear based or solely responsive to parental commands. Rather, there are signs that children feel responsible for (as well as connected to and dependent on) others at a very young age." (See Carolyn Zahn-Waxler et al., "Development of Concern for Others," *Developmental Psychology,* vol. 28, 1992, pp. 127, 135. For more on the adult's role in light of these facts, see Kohn, *The Brighter Side.*)

54. "Education Secretary Backs Teaching of Religious Values," *New York Times,* 2 November 1985, p. B-4.

55. For more on class meetings, see Glasser, chaps. 10–12; Thomas Gordon, *T.E.T.: Teacher Effectiveness Training* (New York: David McKay Co., 1974), chaps. 8–9; Jane Nelsen, Lynn Lott, and H. Stephen Glenn, *Positive Discipline in the Classroom* (Rocklin, Calif.: Prima, 1993); and Child Development Project, op. cit.

56. For more on the theory and research of perspective taking, see Kohn, *The Brighter Side,* chaps. 4–5; for practical classroom activities for promoting perspective-taking skills, see Norma Deitch Feshbach et al., *Learning to Care: Classroom Activities for Social and Affective Development* (Glenview, Ill.: Scott, Foresman, 1983). While specialists in the field distinguish between perspective taking (imagining what others see, think, or feel) and empathy (*feeling* what others feel), most educators who talk about the importance of helping children become empathic really seem to be talking about perspective taking.

57. Wynne, "Great Tradition," p. 9.

58. Kilpatrick, p. 141.

59. It is informative to discover whom the proponents of a hero-based approach to character education themselves regard as heroic. For example, William Bennett's nominee for "possibly our greatest living American" is Rush Limbaugh. (See Terry Eastland, "Rush Limbaugh: Talking Back," *American Spectator,* September 1992, p. 23.)

60. See Victor Battistich et al., "The Child Development Project: A Comprehensive Program for the Development of Prosocial Character," in William M. Kurtines and Jacob L. Gewirtz, eds., *Moral Behavior and Development: Advances in Theory, Research, and Applications* (Hillsdale, N.J.: Erlbaum, 1989); and Daniel Solomon et al., "Creating a Caring Community: Educational Practices That Promote Children's Prosocial Development," in Fritz K. Oser, Andreas Dick, and Jean-Luc Patry, eds., *Effective and Responsible Teaching* (San Francisco: Jossey-Bass, 1992). For more information about the CDP program or about the research substantiating its effects, write the Developmental Studies Center at 2000 Embarcadero, Suite 305, Oakland, CA 94606.

Form at end of book

Becoming a School of Character:
What It Takes

Thomas Lickona

Thomas Lickona is a developmental psychologist and professor of education at the State University of New York at Cortland, where he directs the Center for the 4th and 5th Rs (Respect and Responsibility). He serves on the Board of Directors of the national Character Education Partnership and is author of several books on moral development and character education, including Educating for Character: How Our Schools Can Teach Respect and Responsibility *(Bantam Books).*

In her article "Raising Children for an Uncivil Society," social historian Kay Hymowitz begins: "Recently I rebuked my nine-year-old daughter for some especially obnoxious back talk. 'It's a free country,' she retorted with that know-it-all sneer second nature to her generation. Her words, familiar ammunition in living room wars for decades now, point to one of the cultural contradictions of American childhood. In order to become individuals capable of freedom, we need years of surveillance, orders, and control. It's a free country, maybe, but it takes a heavily regulated living room."[1]

It also takes, character educators would add, a heavily regulated classroom and school. "Regulated" in the sense there are social norms—such as courtesy, honesty, responsibility, fairness, and obedience to legitimate rules and authority—to which adults hold children accountable. This is what sociologist Norbert Elias calls

"the civilizing process," and it is one we have, as a nation, been neglecting. "I just don't have the energy to keep hassling the kids," one father says. "We have more pressing issues to attend to," says a high school principal when asked by a colleague how his school deals with students' inappropriate displays of affection. A headmaster of a private high school says "it would be daunting" to do something about the well-known, widespread violations of his school's honor code. ("I will not lie, cheat, or steal or tolerate such acts performed in my presence").

Even worse than these acts of omission are those cases where adults are drawn into aiding and abetting the young's immorality. I recently spoke with the mother of a high school girl who recounted a conversation she had with the mother of a girl from another high school. The second mother had said, "We're so relieved about the prom. The dance is at the hotel, the parties afterward are at the hotel, and the kids all have rooms at the hotel for the night." The first mother had swallowed hard and said, "But don't you realize the signal that sends to kids—what it gives them permission to do?" The other mother had sighed and said, "Well, at least they're not drinking and driving." The first mother, in sharing this exchange with me, observed: "We draw a line, and then we cross that.

Questions

As you consider definitions, descriptions, and applications of character education in school settings, first take the time to reflect on such questions as:

What is a good person?

What is the good citizen?

What is virtue?

What is a just society?

As you reflect on these questions, write your thoughts in your journal for review at a later time.

We draw another line, and then we cross that. Pretty soon we've compromised our standards to the point of disappearing."

Today, Hymowitz asserts, the civilizing process needs to be more, not less, demanding. The heart of this civilizing process is inculcating "dependable controls." As the political theorist Clifford Orwin observes, "Every scheme of ethics demands that we practice self-restraint."

Where's the Restraint?

Consider two areas where adolescents' absence of self-restraint is all too evident: language and sex. Language is an index of a civilization. Teachers everywhere comment on the foul language that is increasingly part of high school culture. In a workshop I recently conducted, a high school English teacher in a suburban system told of having to step outside her class because "the F-word was flying" from a group of boys and girls in the hallway. Foul language has become so habituated, she says, that some students even use it in their English journal entries.

With sex, the lack of inner controls is equally pronounced. Fifty percent of seniors say they are currently sexually active; half of those say they have had four or more partners; the United States has the highest teen pregnancy rate and teen abortion rate in the industrialized world, according to the federal government's 1995 National Survey of Family Growth; teenage girls are now having their first sex with males who are at least three years older than they are (in one survey, 70 percent of the girls said their first sex was involuntary); by the Centers for Disease Control estimates, there are at least 12 million new cases of sexually transmitted diseases each year, most of them in young persons under 25; and according to a study published in the February 1991 issue of *Pediatrics,* teen sex is increasingly part of a syndrome of troubled behaviors that include drug and alcohol abuse, riding with a drug-using driver, getting suspended from school, running away from home, and committing suicide.

These behaviors should give us pause. Kids hold up a mirror to society; in it, we see ourselves. Disturbed by that image, many people have decided they need to take action to reverse our downward moral spiral. In a rapidly growing movement that transcends politics and religion, schools and their communities are coming together to return schooling to what has historically been its most important mission—the formation of good character.

What Is Character Education?

Character education is a deliberate effort to cultivate virtue. It is not allowing kids to decide for themselves what is right and wrong; rather, the school stands for virtues and promotes them explicitly. It is not an "add-on" or even an elective class, it is a whole-school effort to create a community of virtue, where moral behaviors such as respect, honesty, kindness, hard work and self-control are modeled, taught, expected, celebrated, and continuously practiced in everyday interactions. Although thinking and discussing issues are important, character education is not just talk. Its guiding principle is the Aristotelian idea that virtues are not mere thoughts but habits developed by performing virtuous acts.

The Content of Character

Good character is the constellation of virtues, or objectively good human qualities, a person possesses. Virtues are good for the individual because they help a person lead a fulfilling life. They are good for the whole human community because they enable us to live together harmoniously and productively. Virtues are different from "values." Values are whatever you or I subjectively consider to be important. You may value being a good person; I may value getting ahead at any price. Everyone has values, but not everyone has virtues. As the columnist George Will quipped, Hitler had values, but he did not have virtues. Moreover, virtues, unlike, "values," do not change. Justice, honesty, and patience always have been and always will be virtues. Virtues transcend time and culture.

Every virtue, like character as a whole, has three parts: moral knowing, moral feeling, and moral behavior. To possess the virtue of justice, for example, I must first understand what justice is and what justice requires of me in human relations (moral knowing). I must also care about justice—be emotionally committed to it, have the capacity for appropriate guilt when I behave unjustly, and be capable of moral indignation when I see others suffer unjustly (moral feeling). Finally, I must practice justice—have the habit of acting fairly in my personal relations and carrying out my obligations as a citizen to help build a just society (moral behavior). Thus, teachers, in order to develop virtuous character in their students, must help them know what the virtues are, appreciate their importance and want to possess them, and practice them in their day-to-day conduct.

A National Movement

Within the past five years character education has mushroomed into a national movement. The 1990s have seen a spate of books on the subject; the emergence of three national organizations—the Character Education Partnership (of which NASSP is a member), the Character Counts Coalition, and the Communitarian Network—dedicated to putting character development at the top of the nation's educational agenda; U.S. Department of Education funding of statewide character education projects; four White House Conferences on Character Building for a Democratic and Civil Society; state mandates requiring schools to spend time on character education; the creation of university-based centers and summer institutes in character education; and grassroots initiatives by schools that have developed home-grown, low-cost character education programs that are having a positive impact on school climate and student behavior.

The premise of the character education movement is straightforward. Irresponsible and destructive youth behaviors such as violence, dishonesty, drug abuse, sexual promiscuity, and a poor work ethic have a common core: the absence of good character. Character education, unlike piecemeal reforms, offers the hope of improvement in all these areas.

Character Education in the Classroom

How can schools educate for character? Most character education advocates recommend a comprehensive approach. This approach uses all phases of the school's moral life to promote character development, including the teacher as moral model and mentor, creating a caring classroom community, using discipline as a tool for moral growth, teaching virtues through the curriculum, cooperative learning, high standards of academic responsibility, ethical reflection, conflict resolution, service learning, creating a positive moral culture in the school, and recruiting parents and the wider community as partners in promoting good character.

Consider how one high school teacher implements many of these strategies. Hal Urban is an award-winning instructor of American history, government, and psychology at Woodside High School, a multi-ethnic public school in the San Francisco Bay Area. Every day, before every class period, he stands at the classroom door and greets and shakes hands with each of his students as they come into class. "It's time I could be using for other things," he says, "but I want to make a personal connection, and I want them to learn how to return a handshake."

For the first 5–6 weeks of school, Urban has his students pair up at the beginning of class and do a two-minute interview. "I give them the question—Who do you live with? What's an achievement you're proud of? A goal you have? A hobby or special interest? A hero?—and a sheet on which to record their partners' answers." These partner interviews lay groundwork for how teacher Urban begins class during the rest of the year. He explains: "First, I ask, 'What's something good that has happened in your life recently?' Next I ask, 'Is there someone in the class right now you could say something positive about?' Then,

'What is something you are thankful for?' Finally, I ask students to take a new seat and spend a minute talking with their new neighbor. All this takes about five minutes and creates a sense of community and a climate for learning." On the final exam, when he asks students what they think they'll remember about the course 10 years from now, many write they will remember the way he started each class.

In order for it to contribute to character development, classroom and school discipline must foster mutual respect, personal responsibility, and self-discipline. A key element of Urban's discipline policy is his "Memorandum of Agreement," which each student, or their parents or guardians, and he signs. (See next page.)

A major challenge is to convince students that character matters—that it's in their own best interest to do the right thing, that being a person of good character is essential if you want to lead a happy and fulfilling life. How, for example, do you get teenagers to believe honesty is the best policy when so many people seem to get ahead by lying, cheating, and stealing? To help his students understand how being honest will help them in their lives, Urban begins by asking students to write their thoughts in response to 15 questions about honesty, 6 of which follow.

1. A prospective employer or college writes to one of your teachers for a recommendation. They ask, "We know this student has good grades but what about his/her character?" What is character?

2. How do you gain the trust of another person? How do you destroy trust in a relationship?

3. Is "everybody's doing it" a valid reason to do something dishonest?

4. What are some of the rewards of being honest?

5. What are some of the consequences of being dishonest?

6. Do you see any threats to our present society from dishonesty?

Students then discuss their answers in small groups and as a whole class. Next, Urban gives them an essay he has written entitled "Honesty Is Still the Best Policy." It discusses seven costs of dishonesty (dishonesty is a vicious circle, turns us into phonies, can't be hidden, eventually catches up with us, ruins relationships, attacks our nervous systems, and prevents our fulfillment) and six reasons for being honest (peace of mind, character and reputation, strong relationships, wholeness, mental and physical health, and authenticity).

After reading this essay, students once again write their thoughts in response to the questions about honesty they answered earlier. Last, students compare their two sets of responses and discuss the reasons for any changes.

This activity, Urban finds, gets students to really think about the character trait of honesty and how it will help them achieve self-respect and satisfying relationships.

Developing student character, however, must go beyond improving moral understanding to fostering moral commitment and moral habits. One way to do this is to help students become aware of their own behavior in a way that inspires them to want to improve it.

Most high school teachers have seen a marked decline in student courtesy. Troubled by this trend in his own classes, Urban decided to address the issue in a provocative and explicit way (two of the hallmarks of character education). At the beginning of the fall semester, he gave his students a handout entitled "Whatever Happened to Good Manners?" He prefaced this by saying, "In my experience, I've found that people are capable of courteous behavior when they know clearly what is expected of them. Second, the classroom is a more enjoyable place for all when everyone treats everyone else with respect and consideration."

Listed on this handout, under the heading "How Things Were Different Not Too Many Years Ago," was a series of Urban's observations of changes in student behavior, such as:

"Students rarely came late to class. When they did, they apologized. Today many come late. Only rarely does one apologize." Another: Students used to listen when the teacher was talking. Today many students feel they have a right to ignore the teacher and have a private conversation with their friends."

Under this list of behavioral observations were several questions like: "Why is this happening?" "Is a society better when people treat each other with respect?" "Is a classroom better when both students and teacher show mutual respect?" Each student was asked to think about these questions and write a paragraph in response. Urban then collected the students' written responses and used them as a springboard for a class discussion of manners.

Urban comments: "This simple exercise made a noticeable difference in the behavior of my students. Later in the semester, several students told me they wished all of their teachers would discuss manners in the classroom, because it improved the atmosphere for learning." At the end of the course one student wrote, "That manners page you handed out really made me think. Sometimes we do rude things and aren't even aware we're being rude."

Schoolwide Character Education

Not every teacher, obviously, will be as committed and creative a character educator as Hal Urban. But all teachers, regardless of subject matter or grade level, have the

---

As the Classroom Teacher, I Agree to Do the Following:

- Treat all my students with courtesy and respect
- Be organized and well-prepared for every class session
- Make myself available for extra help (personal or academic) when needed
- Return all parent phone calls within 24 hours

Signature of teacher

As a Student in Mr. Urban's Class, I Agree to:

- Attend class regularly and on time (unless valid excuse)
- Be courteous and respectful toward my classmates and teacher
- Stay "on task" while in class; do the work which is expected of me
- Let Mr. Urban know if I am having personal problems that are affecting my performance in school

Signature of the student

As a Parent/Guardian of a Student in Mr. Urban's Class, I Agree to:

- Do what I can to ensure that my student attends class regularly and on time
- Encourage my student to develop good study habits
- Stay informed as to what my student is learning and the progress he or she is making
- Call Mr. Urban when I have questions or concerns

Signature of parent/guardian

---

potential to make a significant contribution to the character development of their students. What can a high school administrator do to help all school staff members realize their potential as character educators?

The first step is to make time. At a faculty meeting (better still, a retreat) small groups can be given butcher paper, magic markers, and this task: "Make a list of six character traits that are so basic thoughtful people everywhere would agree schools should develop these traits in students." Groups then post their lists. Invariably, there will be a striking similarity in what different groups come up with. The traits named will invariably include qualities such as good judgment, honesty, caring, respect, responsibility, courage, self-control, perseverance, and the capacity for hard work. Staff can then reach a decision on which

6–10 traits to make the focus of the school's character effort by having all persons vote for their top choices.

The next question is: "What are we already doing to foster these traits in our students?" In workshops I've done, I give faculty members a list of "100 Ways to Promote Character Education," available from Kevin Ryan's Center for the Advancement of Ethics and Character at Boston University.[2] The instructions: "Take seven minutes to read through the list; circle those things you already do; star those things you do not already do but would be willing to try (e.g., hang pictures of local heroes in the halls and classrooms; promote service clubs with a real mission for the school or community; study and promote a different virtue each month; have students bring in and discuss newspaper and magazine clippings illustrating character qualities and their opposites). With a partner, take five minutes to discuss one of your circled items and one of your starred items." Through this simple exercise, faculty members quickly see there are many kinds of character education they already do—important to acknowledge lest character education seem like another "add-on"—and many other things they might do to enhance their efforts in this area.

Forming a leadership group is another important step. Wasatch High School in Heber, Utah, is an example of a school that has an effective character education committee, chaired by John Moss, an 11th-grade English teacher. Moss says, "We started slowly, with just those faculty who wanted to participate. We didn't mandate it. Little by little, other faculty started to come to us. Our message to faculty is that character education will make your life better. We believe that all good teachers teach character. We're just helping people do it in a more focused way." Moss's committee has just completed a 45-minute video detailing Wasatch's eight-point, building-wide character education initiative that embraces cocurricular as well as curricular activities.[3]

Another step is helping teachers develop the character dimension of lessons they already teach. "For high school faculty," Moss says, "the key is showing them how they can do this through their subject matter, without a lot of extra time."[4] Small, interdisciplinary sharing groups—for example, four faculty members who teach different subjects—is one way to brainstorm possibilities and share ideas.

Becoming a School of Character

Besides reaching consensus on its target character traits, a school needs to define these traits in terms of observable behaviors in the moral life of the school. Montclair

Kimberly Academy, a pre-K through grade 12 independent school in Montclair, N.J., has the following seven character expectations for all of its students: (1) **RESPECTFUL** (civil in their relations to other persons); (2) **FRIENDLY** (showing goodwill and compassion in their relations with others); (3) **RESPONSIBLE** (doing assigned tasks diligently and volunteering to do things that are worthwhile); (4) **CONFIDENT** (not afraid to decline invitations to join in hurtful behavior); (5) **TEMPERATE** (intelligent managers of their time and talents and able to deal prudently with both temptations and challenges); (6) **FAIR** (cultivating speech and behavior that can be consistently maintained in both public and private without prejudice or embarrassment); and (7) **INFORMED** (knowledgeable about the workings of the world around them and reflective about their own experiences.[5] When a school posts such expectations, shares them with parents, and continually uses them as a reference point in staff discussions and faculty-student dialogue (e.g., in discipline or counseling situations) they will come over time to define its moral culture.

Becoming a school of character also requires that the school staff be a moral community in which all share responsibility for the character education effort and attempt to adhere to the same character expectations that guide the education of students. Three things need attention here. First, all staff members—teachers, administrators, counselors, coaches, secretaries, custodians, cafeteria workers, and bus drivers—must be involved in learning about, discussing, and taking ownership of the character education effort. All of these adults must try to model the character traits in their own behavior and take advantage of the other everyday opportunities they have to influence the character of students.

Second, the same character expectations established for students must govern the collective life of the adult members of the school community. If students are to be treated as constructive learners, so must staff members. They must have opportunities for meaningful staff development. If students are given opportunities to work collaboratively and participate in decision making, so must staff members. If a school's staff members do not experience mutual respect, fairness, and cooperation in their adult relationships, they are less likely to commit to teaching these virtues to students.

Third, the school must protect time for staff members' ongoing reflection on moral matters. In faculty meetings, for example, staff members should be regularly asking: What positive, character-building experiences is the school already *providing* for its students? What negative moral experiences (e.g., academic dishonesty, peer cruelty, adult disrespect of adults, littering of the grounds) is the school currently *permitting,* or at least not addressing effectively? And what important moral experiences (e.g., cooperative learning, service learning, opportunities to learn about and interact with people from different racial, ethnic, and socioeconomic backgrounds) is the school now *omitting?* Finally, what current school practices are at odds with its professed character goals? Reflection of this nature is an indispensable condition for developing an effective character education initiative.[6]

Involving Students As Character Leaders

How can high schools mobilize the peer culture in support of a character effort? To do this, students must be brought into a leadership role. How to do that is illustrated by Brentwood High School in St. Louis County, Mo. In 1993–94, Brentwood formed a committee of students and parents that came up with the following goals for its character education program: (a) **PERSONAL GOALS:** accountability, honesty, perseverance, and respect for self, (b) **SOCIAL GOALS:** abstinence from drugs, alcohol, and sex; caring about others; commitment to family; positive work ethic; respect for others; and service; and (c) **CIVIC GOALS:** equality, freedom, justice, respect for authority, and respect for property.

Each quarter of the school year, a different class is responsible for a project promoting respect and responsibility throughout the school and shares this with the entire student body. A student task force has organized a Corridor of Respect showcasing students, staff members, and community members who have displayed respect and responsibility in exemplary ways. The same student task force has also hosted a Respect and Responsibility Conference and invited students from other area high schools to discuss how they might promote character education in their schools as well. At Brentwood, faculty and students alike report more respectful attitudes and responsible behavior on the part of students.[7]

Finally, it's good news for the character education movement that Phi Delta Kappa (PDK) with the help of a Templeton Foundation grant, has launched a League of Value-Driven Schools.[8] The League consists initially of some 50 high schools and eventually, PDK hopes, of hundreds (recruitment is still underway). Member schools will focus on promoting seven core values: *learning, honesty, cooperation, service to others, freedom, responsibility, and civility.* The goal is to incorporate these values deeply into the culture of a school—into its mission statement, stu-

dent handbook, student orientation, back-to-school night for parents, posters for classrooms and hallways, student assignments, bulletin boards, thoughts for the day, assembly programs, student projects, school-business partnerships, and academic curriculum. This far-ranging effort will include, according to PDK's Jack Frymeier, a "major student project"—involving "as many students, faculty, parents, and community members as possible"—that will seek to improve the school environment in a significant way. At the end of each two-year period, PDK plans to host a national conference at which these student projects will be reported by students and faculty, every school will receive recognition, and some schools will receive special distinction.

Dealing with Diversity

One of the challenges facing all secondary schools is how to deal with "diversity issues." Character education's basic philosophy rejects moral relativism, asserts that right and wrong do exist, and holds that good character means understanding what is right, caring about what is right, and doing what is right. Compare that philosophy to the relativism implicit in one state education department's policy that "each student will develop the ability to understand, respect, and accept people of different races, sex, cultural heritage, national origin, religion, and political, economic, and social background, and their values, beliefs, and attitudes."[9] As the late Albert Shanker, then president of the American Federation of Teachers, commented, "This goal sounds very broad-minded, very reasonable. Of course we don't want students to be prejudiced. But do we really want them to 'respect and accept' the 'values, beliefs, and attitudes of other people,' no matter what they are?"[10]

In *Why Johnny Can't Tell Right From Wrong,* William Kilpatrick writes, "From the extreme multiculturalist point of view, all cultures are created equal and no system of values is less valid than another. [However] few cultures are free of racial or ethnic antagonisms. In many parts of the world, women are almost totally subject to men. Clitoridectomies are still performed among some African tribes. Wife beating is considered a minor matter in India and some Latin societies. Child prostitution is not uncommon in some parts of the world. Slavery still exists in Mauritania and the Sudan. Infanticide is practiced in parts of China. In dozens of societies, civil rights and free speech are only words. What is a child supposed to make of these multicultural items? What *can* he make of them if he is taught there are no right or wrong ways, just different ways?"[11]

The tension between nonjudgmental multiculturalism and character education is compounded when multiculturalism or "diversity" is expanded, as it increasingly is, to include "sexual orientation." People who argue for this expansion often do so out of a concern about the unjust persecution of non-heterosexual persons. Tolerance, this argument goes, must be defined to include "acceptance of diverse sexual life styles." From an ethical standpoint, however, tolerance doesn't mean *acceptance of a person's beliefs or behavior,* sexual or otherwise. Tolerance means *respect for a person's dignity and basic human rights,* including freedom of conscience. We are all obliged to respect each other as persons even if we profoundly disagree about the behavioral choices we make.

How high schools negotiate the sexual diversity minefield will affect their ability to marshall faculty and community support for character education or any other effort that touches on the moral domain. In dealing with the controversial issue of non-heterosexual life styles, schools will be within the bounds of truth, respect for pluralism, and sound character education if they teach the following: A promiscuous life style is not healthy—regardless of who your partner is. For teens who are outside a committed, long-term, monogamous relationship, genital sexual activity is dangerous, whether it is heterosexual, homosexual, or bisexual.

Regardless of sexual orientation, the best way for young people to avoid AIDS and other STDs is to follow the recommendation made by the U.S. Department of Education's guidebook, *AIDS and the Education of Our Children:* "To refrain from sexual activity until as adults they are ready to establish a mutually faithful monogamous relationship."[12]

The factors influencing homosexuality and bisexuality are not fully understood and continue to be debated. In seeking to identify factors contributing to homosexuality, for example, researchers have cited genetic disposition, family upbringing, personal sexual experiences, or a combination of these factors.

A homosexual *orientation* is not the same thing as homosexual *activity.* Some persons who have a homosexual orientation decide—for health, moral, or religious reasons—to refrain from all genital sexual activity. Homosexual sex and bisexual sex are highly controversial in our society, with some people regarding them as acceptable and other people regarding them as contrary to what is right and normal. Many persons of religious conscience, for example, believe that sexual intimacy is reserved by God for a husband and wife united in marriage. By this standard, any sex outside of heterosexual marriage—regardless of whether the sex is premarital, extramarital, homosexual, or bisexual—is wrong. If this is the conviction of a person's conscience, it is not fair to accuse that person of being "prejudiced" for so believing. A prejudice is a judgment that someone is inferior *as a person* because he or she is a member of a certain race, gender, or other group; by contrast, judgments about homosexual sex, bisexual sex, or premarital heterosexual sex are judgments about the healthfulness or rightness of certain sexual *behaviors,* not judgments about the worth of persons.

All persons, whatever their conscience tells them about homosexual or bisexual activity, are obliged to respect the basic human rights and dignity of all other individuals, regardless of their sexual orientation. For that reason, name-calling, degrading graffiti, harassment, violence, and any other malicious conduct directed against homosexual or bisexual persons are always morally wrong. All persons of good will agree that everyone's basic *human* rights must be guaranteed regardless of sexual orientation, but people of good conscience can and do disagree about what *civil* rights should be extended to non-heterosexual persons. Inalienable human rights, such as the right to life and liberty, are recognized by the Declaration of Independence; the government does not confer these rights and cannot take them away. By contrast, civil rights, such as the right to marry or adopt children, are granted to citizens at the discretion of society.[13]

Character-Based Sex Education

Handling sexual diversity issues is, of course, only part of a much broader challenge: the sexual moral education of the young. Sex, as we have noted, is the area of young people's lives where they often display the poorest character—the lowest levels of respect, responsibility, and self-control. As adults, we are gradually emerging from the sexual revolution to recover the wisdom that chastity, which enables us to govern our sexual desires, is part of the constellation of virtues that serve human dignity and the individual and common good. When it comes to sex education, however, many schools still practice a kind of educational schizophrenia. In most areas of school life, they are appropriately directive, guiding students to morally correct conclusions (it's wrong to lie, cheat, steal, be racist, etc.), as character education recommends. But in the sex education curriculum they send a mixed moral message ("Don't have sex, but here's a way to do it fairly safely"), use relativistic values clarification methodology (where students simply clarify their personal values), and end up being non-directive ("You have to decide what's right for you").

Happily, two groups, the Character Education Partnership and the Medical Institute for Sexual Health (MISH), have each recently issued documents designed to help schools apply character education principles to the sexual domain. The MISH publication *National Guidelines for Sexuality and Character Education* states, "Premature sexual activity is destructive toward self and others . . . The destructive effects of premature sexual activity include pregnancy and its consequences, sexually transmitted diseases, emotional hurt, potential difficulty in future relationships, and the development of disrespectful and irresponsible behavior patterns that are antithetical to good character."[14] *Character-Based Sex Education in Public Schools,* the position paper of the Character Education Partnership, states: "Sex education should reach students to see sexuality as an area of their lives that calls for the presence of virtues. They should be taught that their sexuality must be supported by self-control, a strong sense of responsibility, prudence, and often courage to withstand strong sexual desires . . . Students should also realize that learning to bring self-discipline to their sexuality is a means of developing character and preparing themselves for a deep, loving relationship as an adult."[15]

"Character is destiny," wrote the Greek philosopher Heraclitus. The American Founders affirmed that belief "Nothing is more important for the public weal," Ben Franklin said, "than to train up our youth in wisdom and virtue." In recent decades, we have neglected that task. If we wish to flourish as a society in the next century, the character development of our children must once again become a priority for all schools and communities. In that civilizing process, high schools have an indispensable role to play.

References

1. Kay S. Hymowitz, "Raising Children for an Uncivil Society," *City Journal,* Summer 1997, 57–66.
2. For a copy of "100 Ways to Promote Character Education," write to the Center for the Advancement of Ethics and Character, School of Education, Boston University, 605 Commonwealth Avenue, Boston, MA 02215.
3. A copy of the Wasatch character education video can be ordered from John Moss, Wasatch High School, 64 E. 600 South, Heber City, UT 84032 (801-654-4615).
4. Resources that will help high school teachers make the connections between character and academic content include: *Core Values in the Classroom* (teacher-designed lesson plans for many different subject areas), available from the Tempe Union High School District, 500 W. Guadalupe Rd., Tempe, AZ 85283 (602-839-0292); and *Creating a Values-Based Literature Program,* available from the Center for Learning, P.O. Box 910 Villa Maria, PA 16155-0910 (800-767-9090).
5. For Montclair's newsletter, contact Linda Clark, Montclair Kimberly Academy, 201 Valley Rd., Montclair, NJ 07042 (201-746-9800).
6. Taken from *Eleven Principles of Effective Character Education.* For a free copy of this four-page document, contact the Character Education Partnership (800-988-8081). For a 40-minute video on the 11 principles, contact National Professional Resources, P.O. Box 1479, 25 South Regent St., Port Chester, NY 10573 (914-937-8879).
7. The story of Brentwood High School is featured in the publication, *Character Education in U.S. Schools. A New Consensus* (Alexandria, Va.: The Character Education Partnership, 1996).
8. For more information on the League of Values Driven Schools, contact Phi Delta Kappa, Eighth and Union, P.O. Box 789, Bloomington, IN 47402-0789 (800-766-1156).
9. Quoted in Ben Wildavsky, "Can You *Not* Teach Morality in Public Schools?", *The Responsive Community,* Winter 1991–92, pp. 46–54.
10. Ibid.
11. William Kilpatrick, *Why Johnny Can't Tell Right from Wrong* (New York: Simon & Schuster, 1992), pp. 127–128.
12. *"AIDS and the Education of Our Children* (Washington, D.C.: U.S. Department of Education, 1987).
13. *National Guidelines for Sexuality and Character Education* (Austin, Tex.: Medical Institute for Sexual Health, 1996).
14. Ibid.
15. The Character Education Partnership, *Character-Based Education in Public Schools. A Position Statement* (Alexandria, Va.: Character Education Partnership, 1996).

Form at end of book

WiseGuide Wrap-Up

Issues related to the current reform efforts in education extend across a broad continuum of perspectives. Many of these perspectives are worthy of thoughtful consideration as schools are being reshaped. Education should challenge people to answer such questions as, "What is the good to society?" What obligations do I have to society?" "What values do we as a society want to preserve?" These and similar questions are not easy to answer and demand careful consideration of education reform efforts.

R.E.A.L. Sites

This list provides a print preview of typical **Coursewise** R.E.A.L. sites. (There are over 100 such sites at the **Courselinks**™ site.) The danger in printing URLs is that web sites can change overnight. As we went to press, these sites were functional using the URLs provided. If you come across one that isn't, please let us know via email to: webmaster@coursewise. com. Use your Passport to access the most current list of R.E.A.L. sites at the **Courselinks** site.

Site name: Sudbury Valley School

URL: http://www.sudval.org/

Why is it R.E.A.L.? According to information at the Sudbury Valley School site: "The fundamental premises of the school are simple: that all people are curious by nature; that the most efficient, long-lasting, and profound learning takes place when started and pursued by the learner; that all people are creative if they are allowed to develop their unique talents; that age-mixing among students promotes growth in all members of the group; and that freedom is essential to the development of personal responsibility."

Key topic: democratic society

Try this: Read the "About Sudbury Valley" information that explains the approach of the school. How do educational theories that you are aware of (cognitivist, constructivist, behaviorist) support or contradict this approach?

Site name: The Comer School Development Program

URL: http://infor.med.yale.edu/comer/

Why is it R.E.A.L.? This site provides an overview of how the Comer School Development Program works in schools for the betterment of student achievement through family involvement. Sites and dates for regional training in implementing the Comer School Development Program in schools are also provided. Links are available to schools, districts, and states that use the Comer School Development Program, as well as to research on school climate.

Key topics: parental involvement, parents as partners

Try this: Browse the information on the site to find the discussion about research strategies and evaluation. What three methods have been used?

Site name: The Character Education Partnership

URL: http://www.character.org/

Why is it R.E.A.L.? Character education in public schools has been a controversial topic for some time and continues to be as we approach the twenty-first century. This web site provides a brief explanation of what character education is, as well as links to resources and references.

Key topic: character education

Try this: Search the CEP Resource Center Database. What organizations are located in your home state?

section 2 Teaching As a Profession

Learning Objectives

By studying the issues related to teaching as a profession, students will:

- Realize that teachers have numerous roles and responsibilities as they meet job requirements and expectations.

- Seek to become lifelong learners and use new information based on research in their classrooms for effective teaching.

- Respond to criticisms of education and offer their perspectives of teaching as a profession.

WiseGuide Intro

People often assert that teaching is not a true profession and that teachers are not considered professionals. We dispute this assertion and believe that teaching is a profession and should be regarded as such. The roles and responsibilities of teachers have changed over the years, as have society's perceptions of teachers.

In earlier times, teachers in the United States and elsewhere were respected members of the community and generally held in high regard. Today, those advocating school reform are often critical of teachers and hold them as partially responsible for low student performance on international and national standardized tests. Critics of teachers and teacher education demand reforms that include higher standards for teacher education programs and for teachers personally. These critics believe that teachers, like their students, should be more accountable. Most agree that society wants well-prepared, high-quality teachers, and various proposals have been suggested to accomplish this goal.

The issues in this section address a range of perspectives about teachers and teacher education. For a person just entering the profession, you should keep your professional eye on such issues as revised certification and relicensing proposals, assessment of student learning, social promotion of students who fail to pass standardized tests, the inclusion of diverse learners in classroom learning activities, and so forth. The profession of teaching is not easy and challenges teachers on a daily basis.

Teacher Education

Questions

Reading 10. Irwin-DeVitis and DeVitis analyze the writings of William Ayers's *To Become a Teacher* and David Hansen's *The Call to Teach* and suggest two perspectives of teaching. As you analyze this reading, identify the major arguments that Ayers and Hansen offer about teaching. Based on your experiences to date, which aspects of each perspective would you be willing to adhere to today and with which perspective might you disagree? Share your current thinking and reflections with classmates and experienced teachers.

Reading 11. What types of mentor supports are likely to be of value to new teachers? What help would you likely want during your first year of teaching? Ask teachers in a neighborhood school what help they would have welcomed during their first year of teaching.

Reading 12. Why are government officials and community leaders challenging teacher education programs? What are some strengths and weaknesses of the teacher education program at the college/university you attend? What suggestions do you have for strengthening your program? Discuss this issue in your class(es) and offer constructive comments to teacher education leaders on campus.

Why are teacher education programs being criticized? What are some ways that teacher education programs are responding to these criticisms?

Teacher education programs are in a state of change, and this will most likely continue in the immediate future. People outside of education often fail to recognize the many added responsibilities that classroom teachers have today. In addition, experienced teachers frequently indicate that newer teachers are much better prepared for teaching than they themselves were during the initial years of their careers.

In Reading 10, Linda Irwin-DeVitis and Joseph L. DeVitis provide an overall review of education over the years. In Reading 11, Joan Montgomery Halford suggests that mentoring programs help new teachers to be socialized into the profession. Kit Lively reports in Reading 12 on initiatives by states to increase requirements and/or standards for teachers in light of criticisms of teacher education programs. In Reading 13, Alison Black and Linda Davern describe one of the newer roles for teachers—that of working with other adults in classroom settings. Landon Beyer reminds us in Reading 14 that teachers have moral responsibilities as professionals.

Reading 13. School districts across the country are increasingly looking to hire teachers who have developed the knowledge, skills, attitudes, and values necessary to work collaboratively and effectively with peers, parents, and community members. Black and Davern describe ways in which pre-service teachers such as yourselves can gain the experience to meet this qualification. Is your teacher preparation program allowing you similar opportunities to develop the knowledge and skills necessary for effective collaboration? Assess your abilities in this area now and throughout the rest of your teacher preparation program.

Contact schools in the area where you are; find out what collaborative efforts are underway and what degree of success has been achieved.

Reading 14. Beyer poses six groups of fundamental questions (p. 113) that invite thoughtful reflection and discussion. Within a small group setting, grapple intellectually with these questions as you prepare for your professional responsibilities as an educator. As you complete your teacher education requirements, including student teaching, look back over your notes and/or reflections on these questions. Have you changed your thinking about your earlier responses? Why or why not?

What Is This Work Called Teaching?

Linda Irwin-DeVitis and Joseph L. DeVitis

Linda Irwin-DeVitis is Associate Professor of Education at Binghamton University. Her preferred mailing address is 107 Balford Dr., Oneonta, NY 13820. Her primary areas of scholarship are the gendered nature of the literacy curriculum and reading interests, and visual strategies that promote thinking and learning.

Joseph L. DeVitis is Professor of Education and Human Development at Binghamton University. His preferred mailing address is 107 Balford Dr., Oneonta, NY 13820. His primary areas of scholarship are moral development, educational policy, and service-learning.

Teacher education has rarely challenged young people and instilled a sense of mission. Rather, it is most often a theory-laden, inconsistent rubric—helpful but insufficient without the modeling of the call and the passion that make teaching worthwhile. In William Ayers's *To Become a Teacher* and David Hansen's *The Call to Teach*, the teacher and teacher educator can find provocative challenges to the essentialist concept of teaching.[1] Both Ayers and Hansen explore the challenge and uncertainty, the personal creativity and commitment, and the uniquely individual aspect of each teacher's practice. Hansen provides the ethnographer's nuanced judgment as he sketches the practice of four teachers. Ayers assembles the voices of a varied group of educators and thinkers who share a deep commitment to the practice of teaching.

How can we understand the work of teachers and the motives, aspirations, struggles and daily realities of the teaching life? Both books have value to those who are engaged in or considering a career in teaching. In their recognition of teaching as practice, both Ayers and Hansen explore the spaces where theoretical constructs collide with the complexities of working in schools. Joseph Featherstone, et al., capture this tension in their contribution to Ayers's volume:

Knowing what we believe in theory doesn't mean we are equipped to carry it out. More likely, we'll fall back on what we "know." Two years of intense learning has to contend with a life of living and doing school. New teachers are pressured to give up ideals either to fit into a school or because they don't know how to reconcile idealism, theory, and learning with the real world. The scary part is that it happens without us knowing (*TBT*, p. 202).

Ayers and Hansen recognize the need for teacher education programs that recognize and operate in the complexities, political and social, of actual life in classrooms. Hansen's book is the culmination of a three-year study of the teaching life through four case studies. His well-grounded discussion illuminates the realities of teaching and, perhaps more important, recognizes the genuine commitment and caring of teachers whose work may appear unexceptional to the casual observer. Ayers's collection of writings by a number of well-respected educators also illuminates the motives and values of those called to teach. While many entries are outstanding, the collection is uneven. In discussing these two books, we have chosen to ask three questions:

What are the philosophical roots of their analyses?

How do Ayers and Hansen define and characterize teaching and its place in public and private spheres?

What are the metaphors that shape and define their visions of teachers and teaching?

Aristotelian and Deweyan Philosophical Roots

According to Hansen, "a person cannot 'will' a sense of service into existence, nor wake up one day and 'decide' to be of service. Those dispositions grow and take shape over time, through interaction with people and through the attempt to perform the work well" (*CTT*, p. 4). Hansen's theory of conduct is thus compatible with Aristotle's notion of the development of a "master craft." Aristotle describes that craft as a "function of . . . a certain form of life" combined with "excellence or virtue."[2] But he is careful to underline that "this activity must occupy a complete lifetime; for one swallow does not make spring, nor does one fine day."[3]

Ayers's contribution is also crafted from cognitive, affective, and moral bases reminiscent of Aristotelian foundations. As he explains his own vocation as a onetime kindergarten teacher, "It's the most intellectually demanding thing I've ever done. And it's also *ethical* work. I make decisions constantly, all day long, that impact the well-being of children and the direction their lives will take" (*TBT*, p. 2). The wondrous mix of human dispositions and classroom interaction becomes richly textured in Ayers's introduction—one that takes on obvious Aristotelian dimensions: "Every day in every classroom, a teacher's personality, preferences, capacities, judgment, and values are on display" (*TBT*, p. 3). As with Aristotle's craft, which assumes uncertain paths of investigation, Ayers's definition of teaching is "an act of inquiry . . . and research into the lives of children" (*TBT*, p. 6).

Amidst such uncertainties and perplexities, Ayers's and Hansen's teachers grow pragmatically toward virtue through habit, practice, and reflection. As Hansen puts it "Vocation cannot exist as a state of mind alone, disembodied or removed from practice" (*CTT*, p. 5). In such passages he appears starkly Aristotelian in his empiricism: "The call to teach comes from what [teachers] have seen

and experienced in the world, not solely from what they may have 'heard' in their inner heart and mind" (*CTT*, p. 6).

Like Aristotle, Hansen refers to the teacher's influence as particular to the practical ways in which she conducts her practice. Those ways "have to do with the ethos of the person, his or her characteristic conduct when in the presence of students" (*CTT*, p. 11). Likewise, Hansen's (and Aristotle's) teachers are "attentive to detail and nuance" (*CTT*, p. 13); they are realists within possibility rather than pure romanticists. Indeed, Hansen is plainly Aristotelian when he summarizes, "A teacher's intellectual and moral influence on others can derive as much from a kind of everyday continuity in his or her practice as from heroic efforts" (*CTT*, p. 14).

In terms of concrete classroom examples, Hansen's Ms. Payton pays close attention to "the often mundane chores," works to "patiently organize and arrange . . . materials" (*CTT*, p. 28), and realizes that meticulous planning can be crucial to successful pedagogy (*CTT*, p. 41). Meanwhile, Hansen's Mr. James is appropriately pragmatic in defining "success" in teaching in view of "one's circumstances" and the "expectations one can reasonably fulfill" (*CTT*, p. 76). Echoing Aristotle, Mr. James exudes "a persistent reasonableness, as if he would provide his own model of how to conduct oneself" (*CTT*, p. 87). His character and identity, so integral to his teaching, have been mined from lifelong experiences in practice and reflection (*CTT*, p. 90).

John Dewey also focuses on the shaping of human dispositions, over time, through the cultivation of habit, conduct, and reflective thought and action. For him, education is fundamentally moral and social—much in the manner that Hansen characterizes teaching as "to be potentially meaningful, as the way to instantiate one's desire to contribute to and engage with the world" (*CTT*, p. 10). Dewey's vision of human calling is strikingly similar: "What [one] gets and gives as a human being . . . is not external possessions, but a widening and deepening of conscious life—a more intense, disciplined, and expanding realization of meanings."[4]

Hansen's notion of teaching, like Dewey's, implies an openness to experience and change, a vulnerability to doubt and uncertainty, a pragmatic yearning to adjust conditions to solve problems and make decisions. At the same time, they both view the school as a laboratory for social inquiry—in a mode similar to that of Hansen's Ms. Payton. The latter continually seeks to "distinguish school from other environments and to render the former into its own special and valued place" (*CTT*, p. 22).

Ayers's and Hansen's teachers typically want to observe, to experiment, to communicate with students, that is, to practice in many ways that Dewey would appreciate.

And they are largely able to adjust their practice within an atmosphere of flux and contingency, thus reminding us of Dewey's sobering admonition: "The poignancy of situations that evoke reflection lies in the fact that we really do not know the meaning of the tendencies that are pressing for action."[5]

Ayers's and Hansen's teachers also discover themselves in the act of teaching: They press on in fluid spaces; they create different meanings in challenging circumstances; sometimes they fall and lift themselves up again; and they learn to use critical reflection to make innumerable decisions in their everyday classroom lives.

Through their habitual actions in the classroom, refined simultaneously by reflective thinking, these teachers engage in a subtle presaging of the ends themselves. In the words of political philosopher David Steiner:

[In Dewey's theory of democratic education] . . . there is no epistemic separation between self, others, and world. The "mindful" choice of a path of action must be based on an understanding of how one's own character ("the interpenetration of habits") is at once a product of the world that forged that character and the source of a set of possible futures through which we can transform that interconnected world.[6]

Ayers's "reinvented schools" also speak to the Deweyan need to "treat youngsters and adults as if we live in a democracy" (p. 126). Reviving Dewey's quest for educative experience wherever we can find and nurture it, Ayers writes eloquently of such treasure:

Teachers will work to create classrooms that are places where people can think, question, speak, write, read critically, critique freely, work cooperatively, consider the common good, and link consciousness to conduct. In other words, classrooms will be places where democracy is practiced, not ritualized (TBT, p. 126).

In Ayers's collection of essays, Featherstone, in his "Letter to a Young Teacher," perhaps best embodies the Deweyan ideal of education as cultural development. Featherstone stresses "the ongoing creation of professional forms of community," of forging "links between the kind of culture [students] are enacting in school and the cultures of their communities" (TBT, p. 19). In an age in which liberal and radical public intellectuals seem scarce, indeed, Featherstone prods beginning teachers to "start the lifetime work of becoming a practical intellectual who can help the people progress culturally" (TBT, p. 20).

Maxine Greene, another of Ayers's contributors, evokes images of Dewey's "eclipse of the public" from his *The Public and Its Problems* as she writes of those "consuming audiences" who "let their own voices be silenced under the drumbeat and patter of certainties and packaged truths" (TBT, p. 69).[7] Greene recommends a decentralized form of democracy and education in which local changes would become increasingly important.

Dewey's communitarian impulse is further highlighted in Ayers's volume by Mara Sapon-Shevin's paper, "Building a Safe Community for Learning." She argues that "communities are built over time, through shared experience, and by providing multiple opportunities for students to be themselves, know one another, and interact in positive and supportive ways" (TBT, p. 111). In Sapon-Shevin's eyes, community-building becomes "a central organizing value" for collaborative teacher/student decisionmaking (TBT, p. 112). Similarly, Bruce Kanze's "Democratic Classrooms, Democratic Schools" elaborates on the theme of concrete democracy and pedagogy by offering specific practical suggestions for sharing meaning and expertise among students, faculty, and parents (TBT, pp. 169–170).

Profession or Vocation: What Is the Work Called Teaching?

Hansen examines teaching from the Aristotelian perspective of a vocation, that is, "a form of public service to others that at the same time provides the individual a sense of identity and personal fulfillment" (CTT, p. 2,). This analysis is in opposition to the notion of professionalism that has held center stage throughout the last decade in much of the literature on teaching. Hansen espouses a secular definition of vocation, although he does rely upon the notion of a *calling*, or a growing awareness of what it means to be *of service*. Vocation is essentially a personal, psychological notion. Thus, the author is not concerned with issues of credentialing, licensure, public recognition, and defined standards in the collective sense. Rather, Hansen stresses the individual commitment, vision, and sense of identity that are inherent in the practice of teaching itself. Hansen's vision of teaching stresses the individual, the unique and personal instantiation of the role: "The role or occupation itself does not teach students. It is the person *within* the role and who *shapes* it who teaches students, and who has impact on them, for better or worse" (CTT, p. 17). Doubts, failures, and uncertainty are to be expected. Thus the vision of teaching as vocation is not singular, the path is not predefined, and the results are not preordained. Many of Ayers's contributors also stress the teacher as singular, the artist who creates and shapes, inspired by a unique and solitary vision. For instance, Jonathon Kozol, while urging teachers to join with children, does not speak of joining with other teachers. Ayers himself, harkening to his grandmother's wisdom, advises teachers to "fight the atomization, isolation, and alienation endemic in teaching" (*TBT*, p. 63), to "join up with other teachers" (*TBT*, p. 21). Yet, on the same page, he cautions teachers to remember W. E. B. DuBois's dictum to "keep your soul and know your roots" (*TBT*, p. 21).

Ayers speaks of teaching as "highly personal" (*TBT*, p. 3) and he acknowledges that there are no guarantees. He describes teaching as "the least certain of professions" (*TBT*, p. 3) and stresses that it is demanding—intellectually, emotionally, and physically. While Ayers does refer to teaching as a calling, he does not explore the implications of that term. One of Ayers's contributors, Lillian Weber, bemoans the shallowness of the professionalism that has dominated university teacher education programs in recent years. She asks questions that relate to Hansen's notion of vocation, questions of commitment and possibility, complexity and caring. She and many other contributors focus on the teacher as a committed, caring, reflective practitioner whose practice is both art and science, highly individual and constantly evolving.

Both books acknowledge that teacher education has rarely challenged young people and has often failed or abrogated its responsibility to instill and nurture a sense of mission and moral commitment. It is the sense of calling and passion that makes teaching appealing. But what is the focus of that individual commitment and passion? On what stage will this teaching occur?

Private or Public Sphere: What Is the Focus of Teaching?

Hansen clearly situates his concept of vocation within a larger social context, but his focus is on the person of the teacher within the classroom. He defines teaching as a social practice within, yet independent of, the institutions where it occurs. Like Paulo Freire, Hansen situates the motivation to teach in the world outside the school.[8] However, the world that Hansen discusses is far less political than Freire's; thus his vision is far less radical. Freire and those who share his vision of education look outward. Their morality speaks of oppression, dominance, collective relations, and the recognition and deconstruction of social relations. If Freire's praxis is inextricably centered in teaching and learning for a transformed society, Hansen's teachers situate their work in the private sphere. The concept of vocation that is central to Hansen's analysis is built upon a number of tenets: taking teaching seriously; expanding ambitions; an ability to accept disappointment without losing faith; a sense of mission; a sense of efficacy; and an ability to savor the rewards teaching brings (*CTT*, p. 84). Hansen and the teachers he profiles situate their moral vision and their vocation within classrooms: their morality speaks of the relation of teacher and students, in-

dividual and collective. Yet, relations within the classroom are not immune to external realities. In her recent research on middle school girls, Margaret Finders concludes:

the girls' perceptions of the social consequences of their actions directly affected their classroom behaviors. Social roles beyond the classroom directly influence those within, Yet, the discourse of student-centered pedagogy creates filters that hide the contamination of the classroom by other contexts and social roles.[9]

There is a strong assumption by the four teachers profiled in *The Call to Teach* that their work centers on preparing students for the world, rather than explicitly involving them in efforts to change it. Mr. Peters, Mr. James, Ms. Payton, and Ms. Smith are sensitive to the troubles and needs of students. They are also acutely aware of the need for students to be independent thinkers capable of critical judgment. Yet, these teachers do not challenge their institutions or the larger society. Indeed, Hansen acknowledges teachers' obligations and accountability to the institutions in which they practice.

Like Hansen, Ayers's own contributions to the edited collection focus on the classroom and the relations within that room. He stresses the individual—teacher and student. While he recognizes the reality of "children at risk" and the myriad cultures and capacities of children, Ayers locates the teacher and her work in the classroom. However, Ayers and Nancy Balaban, Patricia Redd Johnson, and Hubert Dyasi acknowledge the need for teachers to be aware of larger societal issues and to look beyond the stereotypes and revel in the uniqueness and promise of each of their children. Mary Anne Raywid urges teachers to be aware of their power, but she locates that power strictly within the classroom and in relation to students. While Raywid encourages teachers to use and share their power in constructive ways within their classrooms, she describes teachers as powerless in the larger system and even within their own schools and districts. Raywid portrays teachers as individuals who recognize the injustice of society, and the impact of that injustice upon their students, but that impact is bounded by the classroom walls.

Lisa Delpit's chapter in Ayers's book, "I Just Want to Be Myself: Discovering What Students Bring to School 'in Their Blood,'" cautions teachers about replicating the disempowering assumptions and stereotypes of the larger society within the classroom. Delpit urges teachers to shape classrooms that recognize and value individual differences. Although Delpit challenges teachers to avoid recreating an unjust society within their classrooms, she also situates the teacher's role within the classroom environment. Rita Tenorio, like Delpit, acknowledges the societal realities that govern the lives of children and suggests that for many children school is a place, perhaps the only place, where there is safety and structure. Both Delpit and Tenorio stress the private sphere and suggest that the teacher must protect and nurture in spite of the larger society. The image is one of the classroom as safe haven, as womb. Ms. Payton, one of the teachers profiled by Hansen, explains, "School should be a place where you can leave your problems behind, where you can find good, regular activity, a structured place. . . . I should give them a place where they can *work*" (*CTT,* p. 22). The teacher's role is to create safe places in which to prepare students to survive and succeed in a world that may be unfair and unjust.

The creation of safe spaces, risk-free environments, and learning communities are common themes in current educational theory and research. Is it possible for teachers to create safe havens that are immune to external realities? Is it desirable? Such aspirations ignore the realities of power relations within and beyond the classroom. As Margaret Finders states,

Those students who appeared to feel most comfortable, whose voices were loudest and quickest, were those who were generally regarded by their peers as holding popular power. Such power was attained through physical appearance, socioeconomic status, and athletic prowess—attributes all gained beyond the classroom walls.[10]

Teachers must deconstruct assumptions about comfort and risk in light of such findings. Safe havens and risk-free environments cannot exist within societies where injustice, bias, and inequity are ubiquitous.

Maxine Greene pushes teachers to look and teach beyond the classroom. Greene sees teachers as players in the public sphere. She, like Freire and other radical educators, sees the teacher as a political actor on a larger stage. Teaching becomes activism. Recalling the transitional years of the 1930s and the 1960s, Greene locates her own desire to become a teacher in a belief, a hope, that the world could be better (*TBT,* pp. 67–68). She clearly defines an outward focus, a dream of possibilities, and potential that goes beyond individual students: "Learning itself may have as much to do with bringing about changes in a locality as it does with preparing for the upward climb to whatever constitutes success" (*TBT,* p. 69). Greene goes on to define her personal calling, "to become . . . a teacher who can awaken people, who can make a difference . . . to create myself and construct a reality that demands a mode of thought and action that reaches beyond the private sphere" (*TBT,* p. 70). Greene's eloquent memories and her certainty that teaching impacts the larger sphere raises concerns about the dangers of failing to look beyond the safe haven of the classroom. These concerns are shared by several of the teachers in Hansen's book. Mr. Peters states, "We don't know what education is doing. . . . We could

be just bringing about 'American machines.' We could be cogs in the system that's just keeping people in order. Maybe that's all I'm doing, just kind of keeping control of the masses" (*CTT,* pp. 118–119). Ms. Smith is also concerned. She fears that she is not teaching students to think for themselves. While Hansen reports these concerns, he does not explicitly deal with a focus on the public sphere as a defining characteristic of the vocation of teaching.

In failing to make those links to the external world, its diverse realities, and multiple perspectives more explicit, Hansen risks universalizing schools and classrooms like the one in which Delpit was a student teacher:

The school was located just on the border of those two communities [Society Hill, mostly upper-middle class and white and the South Side, poor and African American]. The front door opened onto Society Hill, and the back door opened onto the South Side. The problem is, the back door never opened. It was permanently locked. All the African American kids had to literally and figuratively leave their community in order to come to school (*CTT,* p. 35).

Delpit's story is a cautionary allegory and teachers must recognize, as did Mr. Peters, that a sense of vocation requires a commitment to know and understand the cultures of students. Hansen asserts that research has not clarified the role of the cultural or social milieu in shaping individuals' beliefs, values, and perceptions (*CTT,* p. 129). He suggests that we think of teachers and students as individuals who are "much more than the sum of the social, cultural, and economic forces at work in [their] environment" (*CTT,* p. 129). Yet, this extreme focus on the individual may undermine the critical perspective advocated by Greene, Ayers, and Tenorio. Hansen documents Mr. Peters and Ms. Smith's fears that they are agents in social reproduction. Those fears and reflections are evidence of critical perspectives, but Hansen attributes them to individual ethical and moral judgment and commitment. Hansen suggests that teachers' perceptions shape the world in which they live, the meaning and the possibilities, but he does not problematize the nature of that perception. His faith in teacher reflection and the call to serve students, in personal agency and vision, are central to his argument. Issues of power, realities of dominance and institutional bias, are subsumed or ignored. There is danger in such a myth attributing all success and all failure to personal efforts. As Deborah Britzman warns,

Individualizing the social basis of teaching dissolves the social context and dismisses the social meanings that constitute experience as lived. These forces are displaced by the supposed autonomy and very real isolation of the teacher in the current school structure. . . . The value of individualism, inhering in each myth, requires the overreliance on the self. . . . Consequently, a significant social outcome of the individualization of learning to teach is the reproduction of school structure through pedagogy and the suppression of any differences that can move one toward a dialogic understanding of pedagogy and the self.[11]

Reflection and agency focused solely on the classroom are not always sufficient. While viewing challenges and obstacles as "sources of interest" rather than frustrations may invite imagination and creativity in the classroom, some of those obstacles and challenges need to be catalysts for activism and change within and beyond the classroom (*CTT*, p. 144).

Future teachers and teacher educators will find that while both of these books raise issues about the teacher's role and power in society, they do not resolve those issues. Perhaps both Ayers and Hansen would argue that there is no answer. Each teacher's individual and unique practice and the specific classroom and societal context of that practice suggest the appropriate response. In shaping appropriate responses, a balance between teacher's identity and teacher's role must be negotiated. Teachers must recognize and value teaching as tradition, but also reflect critically upon "taken for granted ways of knowing."[12] Thus, individual teachers move between the public and private spheres as their own calling and circumstances evolve and change.

In his introduction to *To Become a Teacher,* Kozol writes,

I think that teachers *ought* to be political, at least in the sense of being ardent and ingenious advocates for kids in all respects. But I also urge these students to look hard for something in—and not beyond—the act of teaching as a reason in itself, apart from politics, apart from *higher* purposes of any other kind. I urge them to be teachers so that they can join with children as the co-collaborators in a plot to build a little place of ecstasy and poetry and gentle joy (*CTT*, p. xi).

Warrior and Architect: What Are the Metaphors of Teaching?

Metaphor, "the embodiment of an idea in concrete particulars . . . is nearer to *showing* than to *telling*," according to James Britton.[13] He characterizes the metaphorical aspect of human language as an ability to organize experience into images we cannot relate, but can only show. Metaphor is a type of psycholinguistic shorthand that allows us to share complex and illuminating similarities in poetic and parsimonious constructions. Yet, metaphors may operate beyond what is conscious and thus furnish insight into the implicit assumptions and beliefs of the creator: "All teachers have their own images and symbols to capture their feelings of loss, hurt, anguish and frustra-

tion, as well as those of joy and success" (*CTT*, p. 59). What are the images and metaphors that shape the discourse of the teachers and scholars in these two books and what insights can be obtained when we deconstruct and compare those metaphors?

The teachers in Hansen's study are described by themselves and the author through a series of vivid metaphorical images. From Ms. Payton's role as architect to Mr. James self-description as "plague-fighter," the educators in To Become a Teacher tell the story of their reflection through metaphorical images. These metaphors capture the reflective and critical thought each teacher devotes to self-examination and self-definition.

A recurrent metaphor in Ayers is the notion of teacher as warrior and school as battleground. Monroe Cohen uses the term "free-er" for the liberatory nature of teaching (*TBT*, p. 98). Similarly, Mr. James, one of the teachers Hansen studied, feels that schools are a "battleground of values," and he must advocate, defend, and "heal" the special education students who are marginalized even by the power structure within his inner-city school. The exclusion of Mr. James and his students is marked. They exist in a room without windows tucked away on the third floor. In many ways, the room also lacks the doors to the mainstream world, the opportunities and the rewards of this institution and the society it serves. Yet, Mr. James feels, in a perverse way, "free, maybe, by my marginality" (*CTT*, p. 84). Hansen describes him as a "baseball catcher behind the plate. He takes in whatever the students throw his way behaviorally. He has to scoop some of their actions 'out of the dirt,' while many others are 'high and wild'" (*CTT*, p. 76). Often, Hansen notes, the students, like the pitcher, dictate the game. Thus, Mr. James continues to fight the battle, but the battle plan is in the hands of his students. His commitment to the rights and worth of his students suggests his right to the title of warrior and champion, but his abdication of his role to educate, at least in the sense of traditional academic instruction, suggests a general who is so busy fighting on one front that he is not able to help his troops advance and achieve their ultimate goal—education that will prepare them to succeed. In truth, this metaphor is the more apt. Mr. James is not a player in a game. The stakes are too high, and the battle too important. His students need a warrior and an advocate, but they must also learn the skills and strategies they will need to fight and win in the wider arena where they will not write the rules of engagement, nor be allowed to control the action.

Featherstone extends the battleground metaphor beyond the school and community to encompass society: "Education is a battleground on which different visions of the future are struggling" (*TBT*, p. 17). In his conclusion,

Ayers tells of John Taylor Gatto's disturbing words to the audience at his teaching award presentation. Gatto described his work as a losing battle, a guerrilla war against genocide in the classroom (*TBT*, p. 215). In each of these metaphors, the image of the teacher leading, taking center stage, bearing solitary, heavy, and crucial responsibility resonates.

Less frequent is the metaphor that evokes images of collaborator, especially in Hansen's study. The description of teacher as activist and community-builder is espoused by Ayers and Sapon-Shevin. Yet Ayers returns the responsibility to the individual teacher when he speaks of building bridges between "the broader culture and the local neighborhood culture" (*TBT*, p. 228).

Hansen's teachers also use metaphorical images that highlight the individual nature of teaching and the sobering responsibility and moral obligation teaching entails. He describes Ms. Payton as the "architect of a structured setting" (*CTT*, p. 21). Teaching is the creation of a sense of space—unique, functional, distinctive, and insulated. Ms. Payton attempts to build "a place you can leave your problems behind" (*CTT*, p. 22). In her attempt to build a space for learning, Ms. Payton describes a shelter, separate from the chaos of her students' lives. Yet, in constructing this safe haven, Ms. Payton has raised walls between the school and the outside world.

As Hansen and Ms. Payton herself recognize, she has orchestrated the details, shaped the space to support learning, but severed connections beyond the walls. Has she doomed her efforts because students see school and community culture as separate? Is she forcing students to choose between their heritage and the school because there are no doors in her walls? Has she constructed a classroom that transforms its surroundings or one that ignores them? Ms. Payton "appears to resent having to play the role of nurturer and caregiver" (*CTT*, p. 32). She wants all baggage left outside her walls. As she herself admits, this is much more difficult for her high school students than for her seventh graders. In her determination to ignore the constraints imposed by the outside world and her belief that students can transcend those constraints, Ms. Payton has not found a workable blueprint for her high school classes. Yet, like the architect who continually seeks perfection in the marriage of function and space, construction and site, Ms. Payton continues to reflect and struggle with the complexities of her practice.

Mr. Peters does not use metaphors in describing himself, but Hansen does emphasize one of Mr. Peters's own analogies to illuminate his practice, the notion of boundaries. Mr. Peters has some clear borders, a strong faith, an unshakable desire to teach, and a faith that he can

learn to teach well. Other lines are problematic: how to examine issues of faith without preaching; how to balance freedom and structure; how to interact and understand students whose cultural background is different from his own; how to share one's own beliefs and ideals and yet allow students to negotiate their own understandings. In his first year, Mr. Peters was unable to assemble the *givens,* the boundaries of his own philosophy and beliefs, into a coherent shape. Hansen writes of Mr. Peters "[He] had much to learn about teaching" and "goals sometimes eluded him, although never entirely" (*CTT*, p. 44). Yet, he continued to believe that a shape would emerge. That belief and dedication allowed him to look beyond traditional images and commonly drawn borders. The classroom boundaries he sought to draw reflected a less common, but more exciting classroom. With continued faith, reflection and willingness to take risks, Mr. Peters's boundaries assumed a more easily discernible shape. These newly defined boundaries encompassed a world of thinking and growing far more exciting than the neat borders that demarcate life in traditional classrooms. There is no meaningful attempt to examine or alter the structure of the school and society. Mr. Peters draws and redraws evermore exciting boundaries, but he does not look beyond them.

Hansen documents an image of a place (Mr. Peters's classroom) constructed with some fundamental lines based on beliefs and values. Mr. Peters adjusts the angles, balance, and position of each line as he negotiates appropriate borders. Once again, however, Hansen emphasizes Mr. Peters's agency. Hansen acknowledges the pressures that impinge upon the classroom shape and design Mr. Peters constructs and the teacher he is becoming, but he attributes (as does Peters) his ultimate success or failure to his own efforts.

This notion of teaching as "becoming" is a central metaphor throughout both books. Continuing images "of the possible" are central to the descriptions of the best teaching practice. Mr. James talks of his students not as they are, but as "the people they might become" (*CTT*, p. 81). Ms. Smith talks of a growing realization of "how much there is to learn" and she feels that teachers "can make a huge difference" (*CTT*, p. 113). Featherstone suggests, "Teaching is, after all, more like taking part in a religion or political movement than anything else—the whole thing rests on what the old theologians called the virtue of hope" (*TBT*, p. 16). Delpit captures the image of possibilities in her anecdote about an older African American teacher: "You see that little boy over there? He's either going to grow up to be my doctor or hit me in the head and steal my purse. My job is to make sure he's my doctor" (*TBT*, p. 47).

These vivid images of possibility are closely linked with Greene's notion of teaching as project, "reaching beyond what is to what might or ought to be" (*TBT*, p. 65). Imagination and creativity are essential to teaching as project. Both Kozol and Greene cite Wallace Steven's metaphor of "blue guitars" to capture the romantic imagination, the music of social and political potential, the belief that magic and loveliness are within reach and capable of transcending the desperation of urban despair and rural isolation. These themes of hope and romance are essential ones for teaching, according to Susan Edgerton (*TBT*, p. 182). Indeed, the language and metaphor we use to describe the vocation of teaching is reflexive and teachers are shaped by the words and images they use to describe themselves and their work.

Implicitly building on the philosophical traditions of Aristotle and Dewey, highlighting images of teachers as creative, reflective intellectuals called to a service of practice, Hansen shares portraits of ordinary teachers and their extraordinary vocation. For aspiring teachers, the sense of vocation and the quiet dedication of these teachers is inspiration without intimidation. The perspectives and advice in Ayers's book will extend and challenge thinking about the work of teaching, the larger contexts in which teaching occurs, and the roles of teachers in educational change. Both books explore teaching as a moral act and offer advice and challenge to those who are studying to teach and those who strive to teach more thoughtfully.

Notes

1. William Ayers, ed., *To Become a Teacher: Making a Difference in Children's Lives* (New York: Teachers College Press, 1995) and David T. Hansen, *The Call to Teach* (New York: Teachers College Press, 1995). These books will be cited as *CTT* and *TBT* in the text for all subsequent references.
2. Aristotle, *Nicomachean Ethics,* trans. John Rockham (1916; reprint, Cambridge: Harvard University Press, 1980), 369.
3. Ibid.
4. John Dewey, *Democracy and Education* (1922; reprint, Cambridge: Harvard University Press, 1957), 201.
5. Dewey, *Human Nature and Conduct* (1922; reprint, New York: Modern Library, 1957), 201.
6. David M. Steiner, *Rethinking Democratic Education: The Politics of Reform* (Baltimore: Johns Hopkins University Press, 1994), 143. See also Dewey, *Human Nature and Conduct,* 29.
7. Dewey, *The Public and Its Problems* (1927; reprint, Athens, Ohio: Swallow Press, 1954), 184.
8. Paulo Freire, *Pedagogy of the Oppressed* (New York: Seabury Press, 1970).
9. Margaret J. Finders, *Just Girls: Hidden Literacies and Life in Junior High* (New York: Teachers College Press, 1996), 118.
10. Ibid., 119.
11. Deborah P. Britzman, *Practice Makes Practice: A Critical Study of Learning to Teach* (Albany: State University of New York Press, 1991), 218.
12. Ibid., 21.
13. James Britton, *Language and Learning,* 2d. ed. (Portsmouth, N.H.: Boynton Cook Publishers, 1993), 217.

Form at end of book

Easing the Way for New Teachers

How can schools support novice educators so they not only survive, but thrive?

Joan Montgomery Halford

Joan Montgomery Halford is Senior Associate Editor of Educational Leadership.

Julia Archer was elated when she accepted her first job teaching social studies at Whitman Middle School. She had just completed a graduate-level teacher preparation program at a prestigious university, and she was eager to make a difference with students as a permanent staff member.

Julia's first week, however, quickly dampened her enthusiasm. Although the principal held a brief orientation for new teachers, the meeting was a perfunctory overview of school procedures, not a chance to build a support network or discuss the school's vision. Julia then learned that she would have four different course preparations for her five classes—and that the classes had become "dumping grounds" for students with chronic behavior, attendance, and learning difficulties. Her new colleagues in the social studies department were friendly, but few had time to help Julia address the serious challenges in her classroom. As a new teacher, Julia also soon realized that she lacked an adequate repertoire of teaching materials.

Nothing in her teacher preparation program, including her one-year internship at another school, had prepared Julia for the isolation she would experience during her first months at Whitman. As a new teacher in a probationary period, Julia was concerned that seeking assistance for her classroom problems would be viewed as a sign of incompetence. She also began to question whether her colleagues shared her philosophy of teaching and learning, and this compounded her concerns. As the school year wore on, Julia wore out. Teaching left her with feelings of disillusionment and failure, shattering her idealism. By June, Julia decided to leave teaching and pursue another career.

The Profession That Eats Its Young

Julia's story encapsulates the thousands behind the staggering teacher attrition rate in the United States today. Nearly 30 percent of teachers leave in the first five years, and the exodus is even greater in some school districts. Further, research indicates that the most talented new educators are often the most likely to leave (Gonzales and Sosa 1993). Given comparisons to fields such as medicine and law, which recognize the needs of new professionals more fully, some observers have dubbed education "the profession that eats its young."

Teacher turnover threatens school reform, which requires years of sustained staff effort. And even for teachers who remain in the classroom, difficulties in the formative professional years can have a continuing negative effect. "When we don't ease the way into schools, it's a signal about

J. M. Halford (1998). "Easing the Way for New Teachers," *Educational Leadership,* v55, n5, 33–36. Reprinted with permission of the Association for Supervision and Curriculum Development. Copyright © 1998 by ASCD. All rights reserved.

how people—including teachers, parents, and the kids—are valued," notes Mary E. Diez, director of the Master of Arts in Education program at Alverno College In Milwaukee, Wisconsin. Ultimately, students suffer the consequences of inadequate support for beginning teachers.

Nearly two million new teachers are projected to enter U.S. schools in the next decade, and the challenge of supporting them effectively has become a critical issue. "The demand for new teachers is a real concern—and an opportunity," says James Rowley, associate professor at the University of Dayton. "It's a chance to bring in fresh young minds." But recruiting talented, competent educators is only a first step; schools must also help novice teachers develop staying power. Linda Darling-Hammond, executive director of the National Commission on Teaching and America's Future, asserts, "To retain new teachers, we must do two things: design good schools in which to teach and employ mentoring."

Schools That View New Teachers As Learners

The need to design schools that are good places for educators, novice and experienced, is a perennial concern. In many cases, creating a positive induction experience for new teachers is an essential component of this reform. At the core of such support efforts is the recognition that all teachers, particularly new teachers, are learners. In addition to learning how to effectively work with a variety of students, new teachers are in the throes of developing a professional identity and navigating a new school culture. As Fuller's classic (1969) research suggests, new educators often progress through predictable, developmental stages of concern, gradually shifting from a primary focus on student learning.

Education leaders who understand the typical realities of new teachers can anticipate and address the needs of these novices. Class assignments are a starting point. North Carolina Governor James B. Hunt Jr., chair of the National Commission on Teaching and America's Future, notes, "Teachers with the least training are assigned to teach the most disadvantaged students." Schools can often avoid setting beginning teachers up for failure by more carefully considering their teaching schedules.

Schools and universities are also seeking ways to build a better bridge from preservice preparation to the early years of teaching. Diez points out that beginning teachers often experience problems when the beliefs they developed during their university-based teacher preparation stand in contrast to the school culture they encounter in their first teaching assignments. "We need to work with new teachers to help them articulate their beliefs—not so they can be argumentative, but so they can advocate," she states. "New people need an orientation during which they

can begin to discuss the vision and the mission of the school, not just 'here are the keys, here are the procedures.'" Recruiting practices that enable beginning teachers to consider the curricular approaches of individual schools are another way to ensure more appropriate teaching assignments for novices.

New teachers also benefit when universities work more closely with school districts. Although university faculty sometimes assist beginning teachers after preservice preparation, some school districts and universities are establishing more formalized partnerships. Among these partnerships are collaborations that develop cadres of trained mentors to bolster beginning teachers.

Mentoring: Relationships to Grow On

From classrooms to commission chambers, education leaders are recognizing the power of mentoring. In California, a state study found that among the many approaches to supporting new teachers, the most effective focused on the relationship between the new teacher and a support provider (California Commission on Teacher Credentialing 1992). "Simply put, new teachers need somebody to talk to," says Terry Janicki, consultant at the California Commission on Teacher Credentialing. As part of the California Beginning Teacher Support and Assessment Program, the state recently earmarked $17 million toward mentors (technically called "support providers") for beginning teachers.

Support programs that focus on mentoring relationships have caught on at the state and district level nationwide. The chance to connect to a veteran peer is a powerful resource," Rowley says. As instructional leaders and master teachers, mentors can be a professional lifeline for their new colleagues.

The success of mentoring new teachers hinges on systemic support of the mentoring program.

For Mindy Cline, a kindergarten teacher in Centerville, Ohio, mentor Barb Roberts smoothed the initial transition into teaching. From the mundane to the philosophical, Roberts lent a hand—and an ear—in Cline's new classroom. She helped Cline arrange her room, reviewed her early lesson plans, and introduced her to other school staff. Even though Cline had participated in a five-year preparation program with a full-year internship, she still benefited from Roberts's gentle guidance.

As a requirement of the Centerville mentoring program, Roberts and Cline observed each other teaching. They also had four days of release time, which they used to visit other schools and gather instructional ideas. During the course of her induction year, Cline frequently sought Roberts's input on her classroom practice. "Barb made me feel real successful, but she also let me fall a few times,"

Cline admits. "She supported me, yet she gave me the space to try new things and see how they worked."

At one point, Cline experienced classroom management difficulties and sought Roberts's assistance. Together, they devised a new classroom management program, and within three weeks, Cline's class exhibited significant improvement. "Barb also helped me to avoid burning out," Cline says. "When she saw that I was constantly working quite late, she advised me to go home. She told me that I might have flawless bulletin boards, but if I was physically exhausted, I wouldn't be very good for my students."

Making Mentoring Meaningful

Roberts, who serves on the Centerville School District mentoring committee, believes that the success of mentoring new teachers hinges on systemic support of the mentoring program. In Centerville, the union local negotiated release time and $1,000 stipends for mentor teachers. "The stipends and credit hours are a real incentive for our mentors," Roberts says. "They also formalize the program, give it credibility, and communicate that the program is valued." For Cline, Roberts's protégé, the stipend also made a difference. "Knowing she was being paid kept me from feeling I was imposing on her," she says.

As instructional leaders and master teachers, mentors can be a professional lifeline for their new colleagues.

Although schools have developed many models of mentoring, successful programs share key components. "Having leaders, particularly principals, who are committed to the notion of helping beginning teachers find success, makes a critical difference," says Rowley, who serves as a university connection with mentor teachers in Centerville.

In addition to tangible incentives and district support, mentors also require specialized professional development. "Educators need to be trained to know how to effectively help new teachers," Roberts says. In Centerville, experienced teachers apply to become mentors and participate in coursework. And each year, the district mentoring committee gives careful consideration to the matches between mentors and new teachers. Mindy Cline believes she benefited from the careful selection process. "As a reading resource teacher, Barb really understood my content concerns," she says. "But because she wasn't a member of my teaching team, I felt comfortable seeking her advice on my team's dynamics."

Feedback and Time

Many mentoring training programs focus on teaching how to provide appropriate feedback to new teachers. "The support providers give descriptions, not value judg-ments, about what they observe in the new teacher's classroom," Janicki explains. Although mentors may help new teachers learn and understand state standards for teacher practice, the role of the mentors is to be confidential support providers—not formal evaluators. In California, this supportive role is exemplified through the individual induction plans that mentors develop with the teachers based on the state's standards for teaching.

For Janicki, time is the fundamental resource for effective teacher support programs. "Doing this well requires a time commitment on the part of schools," he says. "Policymakers need to recognize that support providers need time to work with beginning teachers. Not allowing adequate time can doom a program. You can't do this on the fly."

Professional Payoffs

Although mentoring a new teacher in California costs nearly $5,000 (including administrative expenses), studies show that the approach is financially effective. By reducing the teacher dropout rate, the California New Teacher Project, the precursor to today's state effort, saved money on recruitment and rehiring (California Commission on Teacher Credentialing 1992).

The budget books tell only part of the story, however. The greatest benefits of supporting new teachers can be found in the classroom. "I wouldn't be the same teacher today if it weren't for my mentor," says Cline. "Reflection is a large part of my teaching today, because Barb modeled the importance of reflecting on my practice." Mentors, too, benefit from their relationships with beginners. "Mindy brought a lot to me in the area of new curriculum," Roberts notes. "We all become better teachers through these relationships." Following Roberts' lead, Cline, now in her seventh year of teaching, recently pursued the training to become a mentor herself—and continue the cycle of support.

Author's note: Julia Archer and Whitman Middle School are pseudonyms.

References

California Commission on Teacher Credentialing. (1992). *Success for Beginning Teachers: The California New Teacher Project.* Sacramento: California Department of Education.

Fuller, F. F. (1969). "Concerns of Teachers: A Developmental Conceptualization." *American Educational Research Journal* 6, 2: 207–226.

Gonzales, F., and A. S. Sosa. (March 1993). "How Do We Keep Teachers in Our Classrooms? The TNT Response." *IDRA Newsletter* 1, 6–9.

States Move to Toughen Standards for Teacher-Education Programs

Many politicians see emphasis on test scores as overdue; some critics say it is simplistic.

Kit Lively

Policy makers in states across the country are taking a hard look at prospective teachers and the colleges that train them. In some instances, they're threatening to crack down on programs that don't make the grade.

New York's Board of Regents, for example, voted this month to consider closing teacher-training programs next year if 80 per cent of their graduates can't pass state certification exams.

Texas will start placing teacher-education programs on a kind of probational accreditation in September if at least 70 per cent of their students don't pass certification exams in one year, or 80 per cent don't pass over two years. Colleges that fail to meet those standards within three years risk losing their accreditation.

And in Massachusetts, where 59 per cent of prospective teachers learned this month that they had failed a new certification exam, college officials have been instructed to come up with concrete steps for improving teacher education. This tough love is getting high-profile support from Acting Gov. A. Paul Cellucci, a Republican, who is seeking re-election in November.

Other states, while not experiencing such fallout, are adopting policies and programs to insure that teachers are well trained. New Hampshire is requiring new teachers to pass a test to be licensed, and Pennsylvania is raising standards for teacher preparation and certification.

The University System of Georgia has adopted a set of guarantees that its teachers will meet school systems' expectations for quality—and has promised free retraining, at their alma maters, to any new teachers who fall short. California State University has voted to improve and expand its programs so that they will graduate 25 per cent, or 3,000, more teachers by 2000.

College officials in those states are eager to show that they are making such efforts. "I would rather take the responsibility than have it mandated from the Legislature," said Charles B. Reed, chancellor of the California State system. "In most one-on-one meetings I had with legislators, almost everyone raised the issue of teacher education."

Questions

Why are government officials and community leaders challenging teacher education programs?

What are some strengths and weaknesses of the teacher education program at the college/university you attend?

What suggestions do you have for strengthening your program?

Discuss this issue in your class(es) and offer constructive comments to teacher education leaders on campus.

Proposed Reporting Requirement

The pressure on teacher-training programs is likely to increase if Congress passes legislation requiring states to report to federal officials the rates at which teachers pass licensure exams. The provisions are part of bills to extend the Higher Education Act that are now before Congress.

People who watch trends in teacher education say the scrutiny is a natural outgrowth of the public-school reforms that have been growing in popularity for more than a decade. Strong teacher-education programs, they say, are necessary if school reforms are to succeed.

Researchers who praise efforts to improve teacher training don't necessarily applaud all of the approaches that states are using. Some critics say scores on teacher-certification tests do not, by themselves, provide enough information to warrant denying teaching licenses or closing training programs. Others charge that state politics can play too big a role, as some say it did in Massachusetts.

Still, even experts who dislike some of the steps states have taken say the efforts have forced the public to confront important issues. The furor over test scores in Massachusetts, for example, raises questions about whether standards for teachers are, in fact, rigorous enough, said Linda Darling-Hammond, executive director of the National Commission on Teaching & America's Future, and an education professor at Columbia University's Teachers College.

"We are busily setting standards for students and raising the bar for the content of courses and creating tests students will have to pass in all states without paying attention to whether teachers know how to teach to the new standards," she said.

Kati Haycock, director of the Education Trust, a Washington-based group that works to improve elementary and secondary education, said: "It's good that people are being forcibly shaken. Higher education particularly is being shaken out of its somnolence."

The tremors are being felt in New York, where the crackdown, which takes effect next year, threatens four of the eight training programs at the City University of New York, one at the State University of New York, and several at private colleges.

Graduates must now pass three tests, measuring their proficiency in the liberal arts and sciences, their knowledge in their content areas, and their pedagogical skills. Programs with low passing rates can remain certified only if they show "significant" improvement, the state regents said.

CUNY's City, Lehman, Medgar Evers, and York Colleges didn't meet the 80-percent threshold in 1996–97.

Brooklyn, Hunter, and Queens Colleges, and the College of Staten Island did meet the standards.

Louise Mirrer, CUNY's vice-chancellor for academic affairs, said most CUNY students who failed the tests had faltered on language skills, because English is not their first language. The colleges are helping those students improve their skills, she said. The deficient programs already have begun to tighten admissions standards for students beginning this fall, and to require certain academic standards for students to remain in the programs, she added.

Those moves will shrink the programs at a time when New York City faces a teacher shortage, Ms. Mirrer acknowledged. But, she said, the university also is introducing scholarships to attract bright students to teaching. "We are going to get very aggressive to attract the best students. We think it is a good thing for everyone."

The one SUNY campus that fell short was the College at Old Westbury, which had a 79-per-cent pass rate on one of the tests.

Declines in Massachusetts

In Massachusetts, the institutions where graduates scored best on the state teaching exam included several elite private colleges. But even among that group, pass rates fell off sharply beyond Wellesley College and the Harvard University Graduate School of Education, which had 100-per-cent pass rates. Boston University had the eighth-highest pass rate out of 56 institutions reporting scores, with 65.7 of its test-takers passing both parts of the eight-hour exam. The test measures reading comprehension, writing skills, spelling, punctuation and grammar, and knowledge of the subjects the students planned to teach.

People who watch trends in teacher education say the scrutiny is a natural outgrowth of the public-school reforms that have swept the country for more than a decade.

John Silber, Boston University's chancellor and chairman of the state Board of Education, which adopted the cutoff score for the test, called his institution's results "not satisfactory to us at all."

"The dean of the school who has these results for his school has already called his faculty together and informed them that the school will have two years in which to reach the result that more than 90 per cent of our graduates who take the test will pass it," said Mr. Silber, who defends the tough standard. "If we don't reach that objective within two years, that more than 90 per cent pass, he will recommend to the trustees of Boston University that the school be closed. And I can tell you he will have my support for this recommendation."

Other Massachusetts institutions have been put on notice, too. In a searing letter last month, James F. Carlin, chairman of the state Board of Higher Education, told college presidents to produce ideas for improving teacher education by the middle of this month. "Rightly/wrongly," he wrote, "fairly/unfairly," let's, for this task, build on a premise/assumption that far too many education school graduates are not prepared to teach in our K–12 classrooms."

"Unless we put extraordinarily capable, competent and well-prepared teachers in the classrooms, everyone is getting shortchanged," he wrote. "We all talk about our young people being 'America's future.' Well, if we believe it, let's roll up our sleeves and deal with this problem."

The Board of Education settled on the cutoff scores only after internal wrangling and charges of political interference. In late June, the board adopted a cutoff slightly lower than the one recommended by a panel of teachers, school administrators and college professors. Members said the lower standard, under which 44 per cent of the test-takers would have failed, was fair, since the exam was new this year.

But at the urging of Governor Cellucci, the board reconvened on July 1 and adopted the higher standard, recommended by the advisory panel, which 59 per cent of test-takers did not meet. Also at that meeting, the board accepted the resignation of the state's interim Commissioner of Education, Frank W. Haydu III, who had supported the lower standard.

Mr. Silber bristled at charges of meddling by the Governor, saying that board members could vote as they wished.

Disputes about approaches aside, many educators and researchers say providing the best-prepared and brightest teachers possible should be a top national priority. Ms. Haycock, of the Education Trust, said some recent research shows that the quality of teachers has more influence on student achievement than does any other reform, including reduced class sizes.

Willis Hawley, executive director of the National Partnership for Excellence and Accountability in Teaching, says teacher-training programs shouldn't bear the full blame for scores on certification tests.

"They don't learn all that stuff in education schools," said Mr. Hawley, who also is a former dean of education at the University of Maryland at College Park. "They should learn grammar and spelling in the English department. Somehow, they passed college-level courses in English. It is a problem of the university."

Form at end of book

When a Preservice Teacher Meets the Classroom Team

Preservice teachers accept the challenges of educating children, but how do they learn to work collaboratively with other adults?

Alison Black and Linda Davern

Alison Black is Instructor in the Education Department at SUNY-Oneonta.

Linda Davern is Assistant Professor in the Education Division at the Sage Colleges. The authors can be reached care of Alison Black, SUNY-Oneonta, Education Department, 215 Alumni Hall, Oneonta, NY 13280 (e-mail: blackka@oneonta.edu).

Patrice had been excited to begin her first field placement—a 4th grade classroom at a large urban school. But now a particular teaching strategy employed in the classroom was beginning to disturb her. Both Jamake, her host teacher, and Deena, the paraprofessional, declined to answer students' questions. Instead, they turned questions back to the class or the individual. Patrice expressed doubts about Jamake's ability as a teacher and a mentor.

"He doesn't give the students any information, and Deena just follows along," she told her college supervisor. "They're not teaching anything. I thought teaching was conveying knowledge!"

"Is their teaching style successful?" asked the supervisor.

"If you mean are the students learning? I don't know. It's hard to tell."

When Patrice later requested that her placement be changed, her supervisor advised her to give it more time.

Beyond First Impressions

What was going on? A preservice teacher became so distracted by a specific teaching style that she was unable to see innovative aspects of the classroom, for example, the intriguing learning centers or the fact that her host teacher was highly skilled at teaching reading. Had Patrice asked her host teacher about his rationale for his approach to students' questions, she would have discovered that Jamake saw himself as carefully facilitating his students' use of their own critical thinking skills. Seeing Deena's role as simply a mimic, Patrice failed to appreciate the strategies needed to reinforce the classroom teacher and to create a classroom community.

Her supervisor, advising Patrice to give it more time, was of little use in helping the student reflect upon her experiences and her own perspectives. Taking a more proactive role—listening, then questioning—the supervisor could have enabled Patrice to move beyond her initial resistance to a teaching strategy she did not fully understand.

In today's public schools, a variety of teaming structures—such as grade-level teams, classroom teams,

Questions

School districts across the country are increasingly looking to hire teachers who have developed the knowledge, skills, attitudes, and values necessary to work collaboratively and effectively with peers, parents, and community members. Black and Davern describe ways in which preservice teachers such as yourselves can gain the experience to meet this qualification. Is your teacher preparation program allowing you similar opportunities to develop the knowledge and skills necessary for effective collaboration?

Assess your abilities in this area now and throughout the rest of your teacher preparation program.

Contact schools in the area where you are; find out what collaborative efforts are underway and what degree of success has been achieved.

and vertical teams (for example, grades K–3)—are renewing an emphasis on collaboration, a teaming strategy with which many preservice teachers often are unfamiliar. Teacher educators can do a great deal to parlay frustration into highly valued collaborative skills. They can help preservice teachers realize that some level of disagreement in philosophy and practice between themselves and their host team members is inevitable. At the same time, they can help preservice teachers appreciate a variety of attributes and skills displayed by team teachers and eventually choose which to incorporate into their own instructional repertoires. The challenge for preservice teachers is to tactfully work with team members and manage conflicts, so that the whole team can build on shared perspectives.

The preservice teacher's challenge is to tactfully work with team members and manage conflicts, so that team members can build on shared perspectives.

Conflict Enhances Reflection

Christopher's first experience in an urban setting was rewarding. His host teacher, Marissa, and a paraprofessional, Rivka, invited him to arrive early and greeted him warmly. As the children entered the classroom, so did Arnold, a speech therapist, who joined the team three mornings a week for the first hour. From that first day, Christopher was impressed with the manner in which the three adults interacted. The paraprofessional, who volunteered at the local historical museum, led a class discussion on New York State and its role in the Revolutionary War, while the teacher monitored several students who had difficulties with self-control during large group activities. Arnold, the speech therapist, added several comments during the whole-class component of the activity, and then joined a small group for the cooperative learning component. There, two children in this temporary group of five received the speech therapy described in their individualized education plans.

After this activity, the students stayed in cooperative groups to review for a math test. Marissa presented a series of problems and challenged each group to be the first with the correct answer. The winning group would be able to plan free time for Friday. To win, any member picked randomly had to be able to explain how the group reached its solution.

A groan was heard from Group Four "Oh, great, and we've got Michael!" (a student with a disability). Christopher was taken aback. After observing a very effective cooperative activity the preceding hour, he watched as the climate of helpfulness and mutual learning degenerated into name-calling. The following week, a similar sce-

nario unfolded, and Christopher called his college supervisor to discuss his concerns.

She listened closely to his observations and then asked Christopher several questions to help him reflect upon the various teaching strategies he had observed. "What have you seen thus far that you admire?" she asked. Hearing the question framed in this manner, Christopher easily came up with an extensive list: the use of cooperative groups, the sophisticated teaming skills, the use of a related service provider in the general class, a general climate of respect and concern for students. The supervisor asked whether Christopher thought the team would expect him to design competitive activities.

"No," he replied, "the team has given me freedom to initiate any design I please. We plan regularly on Wednesdays and Fridays, and I run my ideas by them. They've been very open and encouraging." The supervisor urged him to ask the team about the use of competitive structures to better understand the rationale for them. Even if Christopher disagreed with the perspective (and it was likely that he would), he would at least have better insight into how the team was thinking about instruction.

Critiquing Can Start with the Good

By leading Christopher through an analysis of the overall character of the class, the supervisor helped him refocus on what he admired about the team and its approach to teaching. Once he realized that his ability to critique teaching practices was an invaluable skill, he reentered the classroom able to make distinctions between those practices he would ultimately incorporate into his own repertoire and those he would not.

Without appearing judgmental, he was able to question each team member about why he or she chose a specific teaching strategy. Becoming aware of his team members' perspectives freed Christopher to learn from many other aspects of their teaching.

Strategies for Success

Successfully negotiating conflicts with team members and building on similarities are aspects of the practicum experience over which teacher educators can exert a great deal of influence. The following strategies can help.

- *Listen carefully to concerns* of the preservice teacher. Through active listening, both the college supervisor and the college classroom instructor show that they value the preservice teacher's experiences and concerns. The preservice teacher needs to receive the message that he or she may discuss issues freely, regularly, and constructively, whether in the college classroom or in the field.

- *Model respect and appreciation* for the challenges that school staff experience. The teacher educator's attitudes and behaviors can powerfully model a fundamental respect for the challenges of teaching and teaming. The preservice teacher may need to be reminded of the resources teachers need, such as staff development opportunities to explore varied approaches to heterogeneous groupings.

- *Explore the strengths of the current placement.* By balancing discussions of problems and concerns with reflective talk about team members' skills and strengths, the teacher educator may divert students from teacher-bashing or from constantly venting complaints. Open-ended, guided questioning can uncover elements of a common vision with the team. This vision, in turn, may provide a starting point for discussion and a sharing of concerns in a professional manner.

- *Encourage preservice teachers to articulate* their own teaching and teaming philosophies and practices. Developing the critical ability and reflection that characterizes a good teacher will help preservice teachers identify and explore their own teaching philosophy. By nurturing this spirit of independent thought, teacher educators can create an environment where preservice teachers are able to raise differences they may have with the host team.

- *Practice skillful ways of raising difficult subjects.* Differences will be inevitable in any setting. The question becomes: Is it productive to raise a specific concern and perhaps create unnecessary tension? or Can my concern be negotiated in other ways? The teacher educator can provide opportunities to practice addressing such concerns without alienating the team.

Becoming aware of his team members' different perspectives freed Christopher to learn from many other aspects of their teaching.

Asking the preservice teacher to reverse roles is effective: "Imagine that you have been teaching for 10 years, and that a new practicum student questions you about a particular practice. What kinds of questions would you find offensive, and what kinds would lead to a discussion that is respectful of the teachers and their extensive experience with children? What is the difference between questions such as, How can you use competitive games when some students will always lose? and questions that are likely to lead to a sharing of perspectives rather than a debate: Do you use games very often? How do you feel about the way they work?"

A renewed emphasis on collaboration and the growing number of inclusive classrooms make it important that teacher preparation programs develop new teachers' teaming skills. Such skills will help the preservice teacher reflect on her or his own philosophy and actions and enable teacher educators and host teams to communicate more fully about their partnerships. Most important, adults who are able to model collaboration for their students will find that, in so doing, they can meet the needs of all individuals within that classroom.

FRAME the DEBATE

Form at end of book

The Moral Contours of Teacher Education

Landon E. Beyer

Landon E. Beyer is associate dean for Teacher Education at Indiana University, Bloomington. His specializations include alternative teacher education program design, curriculum studies, and social foundations.

In this article, I describe the nature of and necessity for moral reasoning in everyday life and in programs in teacher education, consider ways teacher educators can consider moral issues with their students, and provide examples of how some educators have incorporated such issues in actual and proposed programs.

Exchanges over school issues with moral connotations often focus on controversies such as censorship of books, appropriateness of sex education, or the legitimacy of creationism versus evolutionism. The Christian Coalition, other fundamentalist organizations, and groups with different perspectives have provoked controversies like these. Some recent efforts of the New Right have sought to regain what they perceive as lost intellectual ground, with cultural and ethical repercussions (Bennett, 1989; Cheney, 1988; Wynne, 1987; Wynne & Ryan, 1993). This ground was lost, so the argument goes, because of changes in the canon in higher education; progressive alternatives to more mainstream educational programs in public schools, especially during the 1960s; movements that promoted greater diversity and inclusiveness within the curriculum as well as

among students; and a focus on issues of race, class, gender, and sexual orientation in public school and college classrooms. Those with alternative intellectual and political commitments (Asante, 1991–1992; Delpit, 1995; Gates, 1992; hooks; 1994; Kozol, 1991) have, in turn, challenged the perspective and agenda of the New Right.

Such debates demonstrate that education is an ethically and politically contested domain, that the articulation of different points of view on basic moral questions is a central element of the educative process (Beyer & Liston, 1996). At the same time, these debates may be misleading, for they tend to be characterized by particularly heated, even inflammatory exchanges, accompanied by shrill, sometimes personalized accusations and counter-accusations that divide people into sides that talk past, rather than to or with, each other. Debates that grab headlines in the local and national media like those between proponents of creationism and evolutionism may hide the fact that value-laden perspectives underlie a good deal of the commonplace in education, and indeed help shape daily school practice.

Moral Issues and Moral Reasoning

Moral discourse operates on questions or dilemmas resolved neither by

Questions

Beyer poses six groups of fundamental questions (p.113) that invite thoughtful reflection and discussion. Within a small group setting, grapple intellectually with these questions as you prepare for your professional responsibilities as an educator. As you complete your teacher education requirements, including student teaching, look back over your notes and/or reflections on these questions. Have you changed your thinking about your earlier responses?

Why or why not?

reference to empirical realities nor by logical or linguistic analyses, though the latter may clarify the relevant issues involved in moral disagreements. Moral questions arise whenever we ponder what is the right thing to do, or when we are puzzled about competing claims to action and the values on which those claims rest. Moral deliberation is central to daily lives as well as to decisions about social justice; for instance, in issues ranging from how I treat others on a day-to-day basis, to what my obligations are to members of my community, to what public policies will most help the least advantaged members of society.

We may disagree about what makes for a good, responsible, or fulfilling life, as well as about the actions most likely contributing to the realization of that life. Discussion of alternative conceptions of the good life may not be commonplace outside some university classrooms and religious institutions, but issues concerning the politics of affirmative action and the legitimacy of capital punishment frequently contain implicit conceptions of what a good or worthwhile life is. Similarly, concrete classroom questions like those concerning which curriculum content should be selected, what student socialization patterns should be reinforced, what pedagogical practices should be emphasized, and when, how, and by whom evaluative activities should be incorporated, must be understood in relation to ideas about what constitutes a good or rewarding life (Beyer & Apple, in press; Macdonald, 1975).

Because everyday social and educational experiences contain moral dimensions, philosophers, as well as others, have always considered how moral questions may be resolved. People have sought ways to ground or justify moral judgments from the search for a metaphysical grounding for action fundamentally connected to *the Good,* which exists in itself, in a nonphysical realm, and yet provides a more permanent or transcendent basis for the direction of human life (see Plato's *Republic* in Hamilton & Cairns, 1961); to more modern, less metaphysical approaches to moral questions and action that have attempted to articulate a moral framework from nonmoral, empirically verifiable, natural features of the physical and psychological worlds (Boyd, 1956); to efforts to develop the implications of Kant's *categorical imperative,* which says we are to *act only according to that maxim by which you can at the same time will that it should become a universal law* (Beck, 1959, p. 39; also see Singer, 1971).

Such efforts underline an important point about the nature of moral reasoning. When we entertain a range of possible actions within a particular setting, consider arguments in favor of this or that option, gather relevant evidence, and then ask, *What is the right thing to do?* we are considering the situation from a moral point of view. Furthermore, individuals who wish to be thoughtful, con-

scious, *wide-awake* (Greene, 1978) agents of their own action must adopt such a view. Adopting a moral point of view—interrogating what others have thought, reflecting on and reconsidering the bases for value disputes and decisions, taking a stand on certain principles, and so forth—is one of the capacities that makes us human. A. J. Ayer (1990) writes, *An attitude of moral indifference is . . . not easily maintained. For since we are constantly faced with the practical necessity of action, it is natural for most of us to act in accordance with certain principles; and the choice of principles implies the adoption of a positive set of values. . . . In the last resort, therefore, each individual has the responsibility of choice; and it is a responsibility that is not to be escaped* (p. 13).

When we take a moral stand, we believe that some actions, some decisions, are more justifiable than others and that we can use arguments, appropriate evidence, and particular reasons to support that belief. We adopt a *moral point of view* (Baier, 1965) when we believe that we can give reasons for the choices we make concerning our actions. In reflecting on a situation, thinking about the implications of our actions, and considering the reasons that support or detract from them, we are making moral judgments about our obligations as moral beings. *To one who is trying to decide whether something ought or ought not to be done, it is no help to be told that moral judgments are all subjective, or merely expressive of attitudes* (Singer, 1971, p. 7), because we must still choose. We must choose wisely; to do so, we must carefully consider facts and cogently construct arguments and articulate defensible conceptions of what it means to live in the world.

These few remarks about moral reasoning make clear that moral questions are part of day-to-day human life, based on the need to make choices about matters requiring action; that reasoning about moral questions—considering relevant evidence, arguments, and alternatives, focusing on what one ought to do—is important because it can help us make choices that are defensible if not capable of incontestable proof; and that our obligations as moral beings require us to consider the moral character of our situations, perhaps necessitating the articulation of certain principles that provide direction for actions.

If moral reasoning is an inevitable part of human life, we might wonder why it has not always been central to the professional preparation of teachers. Several plausible reasons exist for this. First, a widespread understanding of professionalism in teaching has focused on the possession of specialized and typically isolated skills, techniques, and forms of knowledge to be acquired through teacher education programs and school experience. A decontextualized, technical approach to learning, classroom management, student achievement, teacher competency, standards-driven instruction, and the like implies that reflections on the moral significance of teachers' actions are unimportant aspects of school practice. Second, at least since the time of Horace Mann (Cremin, 1957), schools have been seen as places that blunt sharp differences in outlook or ideology and avoid contentious issues surrounding value conflicts. The idea that students need to share a common perspective, one in keeping with whatever is thought to be the mainstream, too often dominates. Third, the guiding and interlocking logics of certainty, predictability, and control, often thought central to school life, militate against teachers and students taking moral issues seriously (Beyer, 1989). To entertain moral issues and engage in moral reasoning is to engage in more open-ended forms of inquiry that some may perceive as too undirected or ungoverned, or simply too removed from the facts that ought to guide the curriculum (Beyer, 1996). Fourth, the culture and structure of the school itself frequently work against the incorporation of moral deliberation into classrooms. Facing the demands on their time and the need to keep up with a daunting pace of decision making, teachers may legitimately believe understanding the technical-managerial dimensions of block scheduling, for example, is more urgent than understanding the moral complexities of classroom decisions. Fifth, moral issues and reasoning are central to political ideas and possibilities. A good deal of moral theory deals with the requirements for social justice and its meaning for social and educational activities (Barber, 1992; Jackson, Boostrom, & Hansen, 1993; Liston & Zeichner, 1991; Noddings, 1992; Rawls, 1971). A quite widespread belief, however, is that schools, and teachers in their professional roles, ought to be politically and, hence, morally neutral.

Yet when teachers do not consider the moral dimensions of education, or the moral qualities of educative experience, other people and agencies including textbook publishers, individuals and organizations representing business and industry, politicians, and special interest groups have a relatively unobstructed hand in determining the moral perspectives communicated to students (Molnar, 1996). Lack of teacher, student, and community involvement in the discussion, articulation, and implementation of moral directions for schools is especially problematic in a democracy. When teacher educators refrain from helping prospective teachers think through the moral dimensions of classroom practice, they countenance the moral perspectives of others and deny teachers' moral responsibility and agency.

Moral Issues in Teacher Education

The following example illustrates how moral questions are integral to everyday school activities. (Pseudonyms are

used for all people and places in this incident.) A school district in the midwestern United States some time ago adopted a K–12 program called, *Polite Is Right.* The program is designed to socialize students into those habits, manners, and modes of interaction that, in the view of the school administration, are required to ensure decorum in the classroom and civility in the larger community. Ann, a student teacher working in a first grade classroom at James Madison Elementary School, taught a lesson within this program at the request of her cooperating teacher; Kathy, the college supervisor, observed the lesson. Ann instructed the class on the proper etiquette of table place settings—where to place the knife, fork, and spoon, how to fold and place the napkin—as well as how to pour juice and serve and eat bread appropriately. In the conference following the observation, Kathy asked Ann what she thought of the activity and raised questions about the sort of knowledge being conveyed, the values tacitly communicated and how they might affect students from different social class and racial/ethnic backgrounds, and the value of this activity compared with other possibilities. The cooperating teacher, absent on the day Ann conducted this lesson, was later told about the conference and became agitated about the questions Kathy posed. While Kathy's general aim was to help Ann reflect on her activities, the cooperating teacher conveyed the view that *there is no need to question everything* and that student teachers *need direction.* During a subsequent meeting at the school district office, the assistant superintendent relayed his view that supervisory comments should be guided by *a non-'global' perspective* and that raising the kinds of questions Kathy raised is inappropriate during student teacher supervision. It was suggested instead that Kathy should base the evaluation of Ann's student teaching activities on technical concerns such as her poise and voice quality as well as the structure, but not the *content,* of lessons.

The perspectives of the participants involved in this story reflect long-standing and often deep-seated differences that will not be smoothed over through the adoption of new techniques of supervision or alternative school procedures. They relate to central moral and political issues concerning the purposes and meaning of schooling, the nature and politics of school knowledge, the types of character development necessary and appropriate, and the purposes of teacher education. These issues, like other moral questions, are ultimately connected to the kind of world we want to construct with students.

On a larger scale, some countries are threatening to take teacher education out of the university precisely because of its political and value-laden perspectives. This has taken many forms, some aided by overt political agendas and others seemingly generated more spontaneously. In the former category are attempts to deregulate education consistent with the political and cultural conservatism apparent in Australia, the United Kingdom, the United States, Canada, and other industrialized nations. In such contexts, support for a free market economy teamed with a more conservative political and pedagogical orientation has led to movements that would suspend both teacher education and patterns of schooling as once known.

The view that teaching is a profession requiring technical competence rather than moral reasoning and practical wisdom is one reason some are attempting to de-institutionalize teacher education (Beyer, Feinberg, Pagano, & Whitson, 1989). Another rationale is that the theoretical, and especially political/moral, investigations the university is concerned with have become infused with a perspective that integrates schooling and wider social contexts while challenging the educational and social status quo (Stones, 1992).

The rejection of any substantive theoretical background for prospective teachers, and the substitution of an apprenticeship-oriented program, relates to the morally sensitive nature of teaching and teacher education. One important dimension of certain forms of educational inquiry is raising questions about the justifiability of current practices. In fostering such inquiry, teacher educators and their students may, in the process, generate critical analyses of current situations and provide alternative ideas and practices for classrooms and larger social arenas. This may well call into question dominant educational activities and the values on which they rely. Situating schooling in larger cultural and social contexts, encouraging thoughtful consideration of the ends it serves, and examining alternative moral, social, and political possibilities school practices might embrace may result in students challenging prevailing ideas and values.

Teacher Education As Moral Action

I have come to regard teaching as a *field of reflective moral action*. This phrase provided the unifying theme for a teacher preparation program with which I was involved. (For discussions of this program, see Beyer, 1992; Liston & Zeichner, 1991.)

When teacher educators regard the ends of education and schooling as unproblematic or irrelevant, they limit students to an instrumentalism that eliminates opportunities for moral engagement. To avoid such instrumentalism, teacher educators must provide opportunities for reflection on current school practice and the ends it serves, as well as support for articulating alternative visions and practices that respect students' integrity as moral beings and their abilities as social agents. When teachers and teacher educators regard schools and teacher preparation as comprising closed systems within which the major issues have been resolved and the most crucial questions answered, they promote a perspective for which there is little evidence, and one that denies moral responsibility to students and themselves.

Appreciating the moral dimensions of teaching requires that teacher educators and their students see educational studies and teaching relationally. This entails making clear how the dilemmas and questions that have social consequences and moral parameters constitute the ebb and flow of classroom life. The language and orientation of teacher education as a moral enterprise include an integrative, synoptic vision within which schools are elements of actual or possible social, economic, political, and cultural worlds (Ross, Cornett, & McCutcheon, 1992). This orientation must encourage prospective teachers to develop a social vision, a vision of what is required for a socially just society that can help construct a platform for teaching.

A crucial ingredient missing from many teacher education efforts is a theory of social power to help teachers understand the dynamics of student interaction, curriculum theory and development, pedagogy, evaluation, professionalism, and so on, as these arise in classrooms. Such a theory is vital to understand the school/society nexus and undertake moral actions leading to significant change to democratic and egalitarian classrooms and social contexts. The issues this perspective brings to the fore need not be abstract, theoretical, and disconnected from the practices occurring in schools. For the reality and meaning of moral decisions to be salient for them, public school teachers and pupils must perceive them in the context of their own activities.

Efforts of some of my former students make clear the possibilities of this sort of integration. The work of Ushma Shah illustrates these possibilities. Throughout her undergraduate coursework, as well as her student teaching and other experiences, Ushma not only found, but actively constructed, opportunities for morally informed, reflective action. Concerning her student teaching placement, Ushma writes:

Throughout the term I had a feeling of being trapped between packaged objectives and the search for ways to implement a worthwhile curriculum, one that would value controversy and instigate thought in the classroom. I also struggled to assert my understanding that a teacher is a curriculum designer and not a mere conveyer of someone else's information. Since I myself was struggling with the narrow nature of the curriculum texts, I decided to use [them] as a launching point for students to begin to critique their own texts.

Students were asked to read an article entitled, 'Blacks only one group ignored in history class,' written by Jennifer Thompson (1992), from *New Expressions,* a newspaper published by Chicago public school students. We then worked in cooperative learning groups to discuss: 'Was the writer of this article . . . off-base? Is it possible that our history books are inaccurate? Why would this be? Is everything in our history books true or fair?' In an active discussion about these questions, students approached critical issues regarding differences in perspective, the meaning of the truth when people have different understandings of an event, and the reasons some groups may be left out of or unfairly portrayed in, in this case, our history books (Shah, 1996, pp. 51–52).

Ushma could imagine and work toward alternative values, nonmainstream activities in schools, and altered social worlds without becoming naively utopian; she could develop a comprehensive understanding of current school practices and current society without becoming pessimistic. Ushma rejected the conventional either/or dualisms of theory and practice, mainstream and conventional, facts and values, and so on. She kept a foot in both the ideal world to which she was committed and in the real world in which she worked.

A second example shows how teachers and students can explicitly consider how moral issues form an integral part of everyday school life. Mary Cunat, an experienced teacher, graduated several years earlier from the same program as Ushma. Mary outlines the dynamics of power in her classroom and the moral issues they raise for herself and her students:

[We have a rule in our school] about silence in the hallways. The students understand the reason for this: not to disturb other rooms. However, because they are a group of lively ten-year-olds, we are frequently bumping into power struggles. . . . There are three flights of stairs to quietly climb up and down. I have found there is only one truly honest and democratic way I can handle this: by engaging my students in reflective dialogue about the rules. We discuss the value of following rules for the sake of appearances. I present my own difficulty with the situation. We think about our responsibility to the community. . . . We reflect on the personal responsibility of each individual in relation to me, their teacher, a relationship that most of them come to value. We reflect on the problems they will face should they decide not to respect this particular rule. Even though I cannot change the rule or my own personal discomfort, the students have a vital experience of reflection and evaluation. We are faced with such political and moral issues every time we trudge up and down those stairs (Cunat, 1996, p. 131).

For teachers to incorporate moral deliberation into their professional lives, teacher educators must prevent moral discourse from being sequestered in foundations courses and peripheral or irrelevant to courses in educational psychology, curriculum, teaching, and human development and to field experiences in schools and the community. The moral aspects of teacher education must be prevalent in all areas of the education of teachers, including courses in the arts and sciences.

Many educators struggle to put into practice this perspective on teaching and teacher education. Students and teachers attempt to articulate positions and create projects, sometimes against powerful forces, to remake their classrooms so that moral discourse and values are present (Apple & Beane, 1995; Beyer, 1996). Such efforts provide evidence that schools may help revitalize notions of a morally informed, democratic practice for the revitalization of not only education, but civic life and the public good (Elshtain, 1995).

Principled Actions to Reconceptualize Teacher Education: One Program

For 3 years, the reconceptualization of teacher education and the redesign of programs have been central activities within the School of Education at Indiana University, Bloomington. Faculty continue to discuss and act on a number of efforts as the School of Education creates new programs and revises continuing ones.

Efforts to reconsider teacher education began in earnest in January 1995, when a schoolwide retreat focused on identifying redundancies, overlaps, and gaps in existing programs and began to consider a new conceptual framework for teacher education. Coincident with that retreat, a Teacher Education Steering Committee (TESC) was assembled and began conversations necessary to articulate a new orientation to teacher education.

Seven commitments guided these conversations:

- to include people representing all the constituencies involved in teacher education;

- to ensure that the process of creating a new direction for teacher education was as open, inclusive, and democratic as we could make it;

- to look to the creation of a vision for the future of teacher education at Indiana University, and not to look at current courses, aims, and experiences to see if they are working;

- to help rejuvenate a sense of community, without which any program of teacher education, regardless of how novel or invigorating it may be, cannot fully succeed;

- to outline a cohesive vision and set of principles for all teacher education programs;

- to not shrink from disagreement, but to debate issues openly, collegially, and seriously, and to see if a consensus would emerge; and

- to assume that every component and phase of teacher education—from courses to field experiences to standards for admission and retention to relations with people and groups outside the School of Education—may be changed, that nothing is sacred, and that the School can collectively forge a new beginning in teacher education. Conversations focused on considering diverse ideas, a wide array of possibilities, aims, and issues that could ground teacher education, and ultimately on reinventing teacher education from the ground up.

From the discussions and activities in spring 1995, through a series of open forums, intensive and numerous small group discussions, and inquiry by members of the TESC, a framework for teacher education emerged that included the following six principles:

- **Community:** Our teacher education programs will foster a sense of community among students, among faculty members, between faculty members and students, and between the university and the schools.

- **Critical Reflection:** Our teacher education programs will encourage students to develop their own social and educational visions that are connected to critically reflective practice.

- **Intellectual, Personal, and Professional Growth:** Our teacher education programs will foster intellectual curiosity and encourage an appreciation of learning through, among other avenues, intuition, imagination, and aesthetic experience.

- **Meaningful Experience:** Our teacher education programs will include early and continuous engagement—through direct immersion or simulation—with the multiple realities of children, teaching, and schools.

- **Knowledge and Multiple Forms of Understanding:** Our teacher education programs will help students acquire a *practical wisdom* that integrates forms of understanding, skilled action within and outside classrooms, and a particular sensitivity to the diversity of students.

- **Personalized Learning:** Our teacher education programs will give students a significant measure of control over how, when, and where their learning takes place, thus enabling their interests and values to shape major portions of their work.

A second retreat, in February 1996, was a major step by all members of the teacher education community to take collective ownership of their professional identity and chart a course of action consistent with our six principles that would best serve current and future students. Those attending the retreat met in license area and subject matter groups to consider the meaning and implications of the

six principles for the curriculum, pedagogy, and field experiences of teacher education programs. The final segment of the retreat produced an outline of subsequent steps to continue the process of creating new programs and a timetable for that process including interim reports submitted later that spring and submission of final reports by January 1997.

In sum, the process undertaken to generate a new orientation to teacher education at Indiana University was principled, thoughtful, unglamourous, democratic, and undertaken by many people with long-standing commitments to teacher education. It was oriented to the generation of morally informed, democratic, collegial ideals and to the articulation of their meaning for the practice of teacher education.

As a result of these efforts, several new programs are in the process of being created, while the others are being significantly revised in ways consistent with our conceptual framework and related ideas and values. One of the new programs, *Democracy, Diversity, and Social Justice,* will provide an option for elementary education students. This program has as central foci emphases on social justice, democratic practices, morally informed inquiry, and interdisciplinary activities. The program is based on four interconnected commitments:

- the centrality of inquiry to teaching and education at all levels;

- the necessity of creating communities within which democratic ideas and practices can be created;

- the need to critically reflect on experiences, ideas, and actions so that we can examine their moral consequences and consider alternatives; and

- the idea that educational and other institutions, as well as individuals and groups, must be grounded by a comprehensive understanding of social justice.

This program, like all educational endeavors, is not value-neutral. The central value commitments include, first, the rejection of dualisms that have confounded educational ideas and practices in the West for centuries (theory and practice, knowing and doing, reflection and action, and so on) and have negatively influenced conceptions of teaching. This program will highlight and interrogate these dualisms. The program is based on a commitment to praxis: the integration of theoretical understandings and action in and on the world, and enlivened with an understanding of the dynamics of power as these affect our ideas and actions.

The program will be oriented around a number of fundamentally moral questions that all teachers and prospective teachers must face. We will take these questions up with our future students and with the teachers with whom we will be involved in our partnership:

- What knowledge and forms of experience are most worthwhile? Important issues here include complex epistemological questions and assumptions regarding, for instance, the nature of knowledge, knowing, and justification. Moral questions that always surround judgments of worth will also be considered, necessitating a set of values within which alternative ways of constructing and valuing knowledge can be considered and evaluated.

- What is the relationship between the knowledge encoded in the curriculum and those who are involved in enacting it? What are the implications, for example, of the view that knowledge, rather than being discovered, is always created? What are the implications of thinking about a transmission versus a constructivist orientation to knowledge and pedagogy?

- What types of educational and social relationships are required or desirable to facilitate classroom experiences? The enactment of any curriculum will affect the human and social relationships in the university and in the public school classroom, raising a series of moral questions. For example, to what extent should interactions among students be based on individual activities or on shared experience? In the case of the latter, should they be focused on competitive or cooperative activities?

- How do larger social and cultural identities affect the experiences students have with the curriculum? How do and should the complex and interacting realities of race, social class, ethnicity, gender, sexual orientation, cultural identity, and the like affect the understandings and the curricular experiences that public school and university students have? How are these understandings in turn related to the opportunities for social justice to be acted upon?

- Within educational practices, what are the implicit (and explicit) conceptions of democracy, and how are these related to the aims of education generally and to school practices in particular? Within modern democratic societies, education and a system of public schooling have come to be viewed as central means for ensuring the vitality and cohesiveness of a democratic way of life. Universities are also increasingly seen as providing this cohesiveness. Yet there are a number of conceptions of democracy itself that are incompatible with each other. Moreover, these conceptions are related in one way or another to conceptions of social justice. How are these things to be understood and addressed in educational environments?

- Within the practices of educational institutions, what are the implicit (and explicit) visions of students' social, political, and economic futures, and how does the school and university prepare students for these futures?

As individuals in a morally sensitive enterprise, teacher educators must examine traditional and alternative forms of knowledge, values, dispositions, and habits of heart and mind; they must also be critically aware of the social future they help create with their students. At the same time, teacher educators must remain sensitive to who students are, in terms of their individual experiences, histories, ways of seeing the world, and so on, as well as how they learn, the ways they construct meaning in their lives, and their hopes and dreams regarding their futures.

This program will emphasize both critical and contextual reflection and consider options to the dominant values and culture of the school, the university, and other institutions. In so doing, faculty members, teachers, and students in this elementary education program will inevitably engage a series of moral questions requiring choices and actions. When teacher educators do this, they regard students, teachers, and themselves as people with moral and political agency, people capable of thinking in new terms and acting in unconventional ways. Emphasizing the centrality of the dynamics of moral reasoning and social justice, we bring to the fore the moral questions educators must, in one way or another, deal with. We move, in short, to a conception of teaching as a form of inquiry-driven reflective moral action aimed at educational and, perhaps, social change.

Conclusions

Although moral questions inevitably accompany normative activities like teaching, they have not always been central to the preparation of future teachers or the continued development of professionals. When moral questions arise, they often signal heated, prolonged disputes over headline-grabbing issues or perennial controversies. Such disputes may cloud how daily classroom life is filled with decisions with moral connotations. If future teachers are to acknowledge and respond reflectively and sensitively to the moral questions that are equally a part of daily classroom and social/civic life, teacher educators must focus on helping students understand the contours and implications of those issues.

Teacher educators must help prospective and continuing teachers develop a vision for teaching and schooling that recognizes their moral meanings and implications. When teacher education programs aim narrowly at replicating the status quo, focus exclusively on technical measures of success, look to decontextualized standards for guidance, or confuse process for substance, they unwittingly contribute to the continuation of moral perspectives in classrooms that are both unarticulated and harmful. As people capable of thoughtfully and carefully considering moral questions and principles, and acting on conviction, teachers as moral agents engage in practices contributing to the creation of a better educational and social world. Such teachers are, indeed, genuine professionals.

Public schools and programs for the preparation of teachers can be fully understood or acted on only by seeing the ways, sometimes contradictory, in which they are related. For example, powerful segments of the economy are currently trying to reshape the curricula of both the public schools and colleges to align them with their interests. Examples include Choice proposals, School to Work programs in high schools such as General Motors' *Youth Educational Systems* (1996), and other efforts to privatize schools and the broader aims of education. At the university level, Total Quality Management ideas, programs for retraining workers in the private sector, and courses leading to the further deskilling of teachers as they are regarded as mere technicians must be critically assessed by teacher educators and their students.

Teachers and others can resist, transform, or ignore dominant influences such as these. They can create spaces for liberating, empowering, democratic ideas, moral actions, and educational experiences. Schools and teachers are not helplessly caught in a web of influences over which they have little or no control but can sometimes resist and transform those very influences.

References

Apple, M. W., & Beane, J. A. (1995). *Democratic schools.* Washington, DC: Association for Supervision and Curriculum Development.

Asante, M. (1991–1992). Afrocentric curriculum. *Educational Leadership, 49*(4), 28–31.

Ayer, A. J. (1990). *The meaning of life.* New York: Charles Scribner's Sons.

Baier, K. (1965). *The moral point of view.* New York: Random House.

Barber, B. R. (1992). *An aristocracy of everyone: The politics of education and the future of America.* New York: Ballantine.

Beck, L. W. (Trans.). (1959). *Foundations of the metaphysics of morals.* New York: Liberal Arts Press.

Bennett, W. (1989). *Our children and our country: Improving America's schools and affirming the common culture.* New York: Touchstone.

Beyer, L. E. (1989). *Critical reflection and the culture of schooling: Empowering teachers.* Victoria: Deakin University Press.

Beyer, L. E. (1992). Educational studies, critical teacher preparation, and the liberal arts. *Journal of Education for Teaching 18*(2), 131–148.

Beyer, L. E. (1996). *Creating democratic classrooms: The struggle to integrate theory and practice.* New York: Teachers College Press.

Beyer, L. E., & Apple, M. W. (in press). *The curriculum: Problems, politics, and possibilities*(2nd ed.). Albany: State University of New York Press.

Beyer, L. E., Feinberg, W., Pagano, J. A., & Whitson, J. A. (1989). *Preparing teachers as professionals: The role of educational studies and other liberal disciplines.* New York: Teachers College Press.

Beyer, L. E., & Liston, D. P. (1996). *Curriculum in conflict: Social visions, educational agendas, and progressive school reform.* New York: Teachers College Press.

Boyd, W. (1956). *The Emile of Jean Jacques Rousseau.* New York: Teachers College Press.

Cheney, L. V. (1988). *American memory: A report on the humanities in the nation's public schools.* Washington, DC: U.S. General Accounting Office.

Cremin, L. A. (1957). *The republic and the school: Horace Mann on the education of free men.* New York: Teachers College Press.

Cunat, M. (1966). Vision, vitality and values: Advocating the democratic classroom. In L. E. Beyer (Ed.), *Creating democratic classrooms: The struggle to integrate theory and practice* (pp. 127–149). New York: Teachers College Press.

Delpit, L. (1995). *Other's people's children: Cultural conflict in the classroom.* New York: The New Press.

Elshtain, J. B. (1995). *Democracy on trial.* New York: Basic Books.

Gates, H. L. (1992). *Loose canons: Notes on the culture wars.* New York: Oxford University Press.

General Motors Corporation (1996). *Youth educational systems.* Detroit: General Motors Corporation.

Greene, M. (1978). *Landscapes of learning.* New York: Teachers College Press.

Hamilton, E., & Cairns, H. (1961). *The collected dialogues of Plato.* Princeton, NJ: Princeton University Press.

hooks, b. (1994). *Outlaw culture.* New York: Routledge.

Jackson, P. W., Boostrom, R. E., & Hansen, D. T. (1993). *The moral life of schools.* San Francisco: Jossey-Bass.

Kozol, J. (1991). *Savage inequalities: Children in America's schools.* New York: Crown.

Liston, D. P., & Zeichner, K. M. (1991). *Teacher education and the social conditions of schooling.* New York: Routledge.

Macdonald, J. D. (1975). Curriculum and human interests. In W. Pinar (Ed.), *Curriculum theorizing: The reconceptualists* (pp. 283–294). Berkeley, CA: McCutchan.

Molnar, A. (1966). *Giving kids the business: The commercialization of America's schools.* Boulder, CO: Westview Press.

Noddings, N. (1992). *The challenge to care in schools.* New York: Teachers College Press.

Rawls, J. (1971). *A theory of justice.* Cambridge, MA: Harvard University Press.

Ross, E. W., Cornett, J. W., & McCutcheon, G. (1992). *Teacher personal theorizing: Connecting curriculum practice, theory, and research.* Albany: State University of New York Press.

Shah, U. (1996). Creating space: Moving from the mandatory to the worthwhile. In L. E. Beyer (Ed.), *Creating democratic classrooms: The struggle to integrate theory and practice* (pp. 41–61). New York: Teachers College Press.

Singer, M. G. (1971). *Generalization in ethics: An essay in the logic of ethics, with the rudiments of a system of moral philosophy.* New York: Atheneum.

Stones, E. (1992). Mindless imperatives and the moral profession. *Journal of Education for Teaching, 18*(2), 111–113.

Thompson, J. (1992). Blacks only one group ignored in history class. *New Expressions, 16*(2), 5.

Wynne, E. (1987). Students and schools. In K. Ryan & G. McLean (Eds.), *Character development in schools and beyond.* New York: Praeger.

Wynne, E., & Ryan, K. (1993). *Reclaiming our schools.* New York: Macmillan.

Form at end of book

Professional Issues and Standards for Teachers

Questions

Reading 15. To what extent is the process of securing NBPTS (National Board for Professional Teaching Standards) advanced certification likely to improve teaching and learning? Critique the five general propositions about teaching identified in the reading. What propositions should be retained, modified, or deleted? What other propositions for improving teaching, if any, should be added?

Reading 16. Check with your local school district leaders and state education officials to find out about the status of the National Board for Professional Teaching Standards in your state. How many teachers are NBPTS certified? What incentives do they receive? If an NBPTS-certified teacher is in or near your area, arrange an interview with her or him to discuss the board certification process. Share the results of your interview with classmates. At this point in your life, do you think you will want to earn national certification in your field? Why or why not?

Traditionally, there were only four recognized professions: the ministry, law, medicine, and the military. To what extent will national standards and board certification lead to a recognition of teaching as a profession?

Many view accreditation and higher professional standards as a means of motivating teachers to be more effective in promoting higher student learning outcomes. Readings 15 and 16 on national standards and licensing (certification) are an indication of continuing discussions concerning teacher preparation programs and expectations for experienced teachers.

Our schools need well-prepared, competent, and highly qualified teachers in our classrooms. Our role as a nation in the coming millennium depends on today's students, who will lead our nation. We prepare for the future by effectively teaching our students of today.

The NBPTS Sets Standards for Accomplished Teaching

Issued for the first time in January 1995, National Board Certification distills the experience and the ideals of excellent teaching practice.

Barbara C. Shapiro

Barbara C. Shapiro is a Teacher-in-Residence, National Board for Professional Teaching Standards, 1900 M St., N.W., Suite 210, Washington, DC 20036.

Everyone knows the old myths about teaching—for instance, that a few pedagogical tricks plus the ability to stay a chapter ahead of the class will suffice. As an essential step to shedding outworn notions about the nature of teaching, the profession requires a set of standards that can measure and recognize exemplary practice. Systems of advanced certification are well established in other professions, such as medicine or accounting, but only recently have educators begun to define standards for judging advanced teaching.

In its 1986 report, *A Nation Prepared: Teachers for the 21st Century*,[1] the Carnegie Task Force on Teaching as a Profession called for the creation of a National Board for Professional Teaching Standards (NBPTS), which was formed the following year. NBPTS is governed by a 63-member board of directors—a majority of them K–12 teachers. It also includes school administrators and curriculum specialists, state and local officials, union and business leaders and scholars from colleges and universities. The certification system based on National Board guidelines represents "the first formal new structure to be introduced into public education since the early part of the 20th century," former *New York Times* education editor Ted Fiske recently noted.

Certification promises to have a profound impact on both educational institutions and the teaching profession itself. Schools will be able to devise teaching assignments that capitalize on the wisdom, ability, and commitment of the most accomplished teachers—so that a school can marshal its precious resources (for example, time, people, and money) more effectively. Advanced professional standards and certification also create a new and more attractive vocational path for all teachers. The profession can thus attract and retain talented young people and minorities who are often drawn to other careers offering greater promise of advancement, better compensation, more congenial working environments, and higher prestige.

Certification complements, but does not replace, mandatory state licensing.

National Board Certification complements, but does not replace, state systems of mandatory licensure. While mandatory state licensing is

Barbara C. Shapiro (1995). "The NBPTS Sets Standards for Accomplished Teaching," *Educational Leadership*, v52, n6, 55–57. Reprinted with permission of the Association for Supervision and Curriculum Development. Copyright © 1995 by ASCD. All rights reserved.

Questions

To what extent is the process of securing NBPTS (National Board for Professional Teaching Standards) advanced certification likely to improve teaching and learning?

Critique the five general propositions about teaching identified in the reading. What propositions should be retained, modified, or deleted?

What other propositions for improving teaching, if any, should be added?

designed to assure that beginning teachers meet certain basic requirements, National Board Certification is voluntary. And unlike licensing standards, which vary from state to state, National Board Certification is uniform across the country. It also attests to a level of accomplishment far surpassing basic state licensing requirements.

The Basics of Excellence

The National Board certificates will cover more than 30 fields, categorized by both subject matter and developmental level of students. A teacher may choose to become National Board Certified either as a generalist (responsible for advancing student learning across the curriculum) or a specialist in a subject area (for example, English language arts, vocational education, or music). The National Board also is designing certificates for specialists who work with children having exceptional needs, or with students for whom English is a new language. The National Board recognizes four developmental levels: early childhood (age 3–8); middle childhood (age 7–12); early adolescence (age 11–15); and adolescence and young adulthood (age 14–18+).

Each set of standards is grounded in the National Board's policy statement, "What Teachers Should Know and Be Able To Do," with its five general propositions about accomplished practice:

1. *Teachers are committed to students and their learning.* They understand how students grow and mature within a certain developmental level. They are skilled at coming to know students' interests, views, and communities. They are committed to equitable practice and act accordingly.

2. *Teachers know the subjects they teach and how to teach those subjects to students.* They grasp the major ideas and key facts within their disciplines. They keep up with the emerging theories and debates in their field. They possess a repertoire of analogies, experiments, tasks, metaphors, and the like—and so can help students recognize key dilemmas and grasp important concepts, events, or phenomena.

3. *Teachers are responsible for managing and monitoring student learning.* They create an environment that encourages risk-taking, inquiry, persistence, and collaboration, and that fosters democratic values. They can assess student progress—and they teach students how to evaluate their own progress. They are adept at grouping students and at regulating the pace of instruction. They recognize the teachable moment and know how to seize it.

4. *Teachers think systematically about their practice and learn from experience.* They reflect on their practice to strengthen and improve it. They seek the advice of students, colleagues, administrators, parents, teacher educators, and others to reexamine and rethink their own approach.

5. *Teachers are members of learning communities.* They work well not only with students but also with adults—both parents and professional colleagues. They contribute to the intellectual life of the school. And they advance the profession in a variety of ways: for example, mentoring, presenting, publishing, serving on task forces and committees at the local, state, or national level.

Defining and Refining Standards

These five general principles provide a broad overview of accomplished practice. Based on that vision, standards committees are working out the specific requirements for judging high performance within each certification field. Teachers make up the majority of each committee. Other members include scholars and experts in child development, curriculum development, teacher education, and the relevant subject disciplines. To date, 17 standards committees have been formed to develop standards for 21 certification fields.

Over the course of a year, committee members draft a set of standards. They then circulate these standards throughout the professional and public policy communities for discussion and critique. Members solicit opinions of teachers from all parts of the country. Following the comment period, the committee reconvenes to consider how best to address the results of this review process and makes a final recommendation to the National Board.

A set of standards is not a cookie cutter. The committees are sensitive to the range of circumstances in which teachers work: the variety of resources and professional support available to them, for example. The standards committees recognize that school populations are diverse in ethnicity, home language, and gender—and that classes are made up of students with a wide array of knowledge, interest, and motivation. Given these circumstances, an accomplished teacher can call upon a repertoire of good practices, acting on the conviction that there are multiple ways to reach the same end.

Each standard is described through an explanation of what teachers must know and do to satisfy that requirement at a high level. This often includes the provision of a range of examples and case histories illustrating exemplary practice. The standards avoid being either so general that they have no "bite," or so specific that they prescribe a single method of practice.

Assessing the Exemplary

With these standards as a foundation, the National Board is developing a new generation of teacher assessments. Its performance-based, two-part assessment system requires one school year to complete. Unlike multiple-choice tests—which trivialize the evaluation of teaching—this approach is sensitive to the complexities of exemplary practice.

Over the course of the academic year, candidates assemble a body of work. Portfolios include samples of their students' work and videotapes of their interaction with students, as well as written reflections on student progress and on their own instructional choices. The following summer, candidates spend two days at an assessment center where teachers may defend their portfolios and engage in other activities, such as interviews, and written essay examinations. Fellow teachers from within the same field make all judgments about the quality of a candidate's practice.

The National Board's Field Test Network provides access to a nationally representative sample covering 7 percent of the country's teachers. In 1993–94, approximately 540 teachers field-tested the first two assessments. As of January 1995, 81 candidates successfully completed the Early Adolescence/Generalist certificate to become the first-ever National Board Certified teachers. Candidates for the Early Adolescence/English Language Arts certificate will be notified this summer. These two certificates were available for the first time in 1995. In addition, four new assessments are being tested this school year: Adolescence and Young Adulthood/Mathematics; Early Adolescence/Social Studies-History; Early Childhood/Generalist; and Middle Childhood/Generalist.

The Rigorously Flexible Professional

We are taking much care to keep certification standards flexible but not diffuse, rigorous without becoming rigid. All standards are based on a body of scholarly work that will shift in the years ahead as new research brings forth new information about learning, teaching, and knowledge in the disciplines. They draw on the wisdom of practice and—most important—on the steadily developing professional consensus about exemplary practice. After all, both standards and the process of their review and revaluation are central to any profession. Over the years, cardiologists' sense of best practice has changed. Likewise teachers' views have developed over time, and so will the National Board's standards.

The National Board's certification system stresses collegiality, self-reflection, and intellectual challenge. School supervisors and curriculum specialists can look to the National Board standards as a starting point for serious professional conversations about efforts to advance teaching and learning in their own schools.

Clearly, if we want to provide high-quality learning for all our students, our understanding of what it means to be an accomplished teacher must change. The National Board's standards introduce a new and challenging conversation about practice. Certification promises to bring to the nation's schools a new level of professionalism that will advance teaching and improve learning.

Note

1. Carnegie Task Force on Teaching as a Profession, (1986), *A Nation Prepared: Teachers for the 21st Century,* (New York: Carnegie Forum on Education and the Economy).

Form at end of book

National Board Certification:
Increasing Participation and Assessing Impacts

The authors present the findings of one of the first studies of teachers who have participated in the certification process of the National Board for Professional Teaching Standards, and they offer recommendations for assessing the impact of such certification and for making it a more effective and widely used part of the education system.

Iris C. Rotberg, Mary Hatwood Futrell, and Joyce M. Lieberman

Iris C. Rotberg is a research professor of education policy in the Department of Education Leadership, Graduate School of Education and Human Development, George Washington University, Washington, D.C., and co-principal investigator of the project described in this article. Mary Hatwood Futrell is dean of the Graduate School of Education and Human Development, George Washington University, and co-principal investigator of the project. Joyce M. Lieberman, a doctoral student and former research associate with the project, is a senior project associate with the Council of Chief State School Officers, Washington, D.C. The authors gratefully acknowledge the important contributions of the Pew Charitable Trusts, which funded the project, and of Elaine P. Witty, Barbara C. Browne, Kathleen Anderson Steeves, and Colette Bukowski. The views expressed in this article are those of the authors.

Conventional wisdom holds that student achievement will improve if we develop curriculum standards, give students more tests, and make teachers accountable for test scores. Among the fallacies underlying that wisdom is the assumption that accountability will enable teachers to apply new curriculum standards and teaching methods even if they are inconsistent with the teachers' previous training, with contemporary school practice, and with the accountability measures themselves. We have always tended to underestimate the gap between developing curriculum standards and implementing them in the classroom.

In the past decade, several education organizations have tried to address this problem by developing programs that would make teacher education and certification more consistent with the new standards. One of these, the National Board for Professional Teaching Standards, sets standards for teachers and certifies those who meet the standards. The National Board was highlighted in President Clinton's 1997 State of the Union address, which described its role this way:

[T]o have the best schools, we must have the best teachers. . . . For years, many of our educators, led by North Carolina's Governor Jim Hunt and the National Board for Professional Teaching

Questions

Check with your local school district leaders and state education officials to find out about the status of the National Board for Professional Teaching Standards in your state. How many teachers are NBPTS certified?

What incentives do they receive?

If an NBPTS-certified teacher is in or near your area, arrange an interview with her or him to discuss the board certification process. Share the results of your interview with classmates. At this point in your life, do you think you will want to earn national certification in your field?

Why or why not?

Reprinted from *Phi Delta Kappan*, v79, n6, pp. 462–466.

Standards, have worked very hard to establish nationally accepted credentials for excellence in teaching. . . . We should reward and recognize our best teachers.[1]

In this article we present the findings of one of the first studies of teachers who have participated in the certification process, and we offer recommendations for assessing the impact of National Board certification and for making it a more effective and more widely used part of the education system.

Background

The National Board for Professional Standards was established in 1987 on the recommendation of the Carnegie Task Force on Teaching as a Profession.[2] The mission of the National Board is "to establish high and rigorous standards for what accomplished teachers should know and be able to do, to develop and operate a national voluntary system to assess and certify teachers who meet these standards, and to advance related education reforms for the purpose of improving student learning in American schools."[3] It is governed by a board of 64 directors, the majority of whom are classroom teachers. A related goal of the National Board is to collaborate with other reform efforts to improve schools by increasing the supply of highly qualified teachers (with special emphasis on teachers from racial and ethnic minority groups) and by improving teacher training and professional development.

To achieve these goals, the certification process requires a substantial commitment on the part of applicants.[4] In the first part of the assessment, teachers seeking certification submit portfolios based on student work, videotapes, and other examples of their teaching. The second part, conducted at an assessment center, requires teachers to perform a set of exercises, including evaluation of texts and teaching materials, analysis of teaching situations, and assessment of student learning based on knowledge of subject matter, teaching methods, and student needs.[5]

Under a grant funded by the Pew Charitable Trusts, George Washington University and Norfolk State University worked with teachers who were seeking certification from the National Board. The findings reported below are based on telephone interviews conducted in 1997 with 28 of 38 teachers who had been supported by the Pew grant project team over the previous three years. The teachers were interviewed to determine their views about the incentives to go through the certification process, the contribution of the process to their teaching skills, and the consistency between National Board standards and current teaching practices.

Policy and Research Issues: Benefits and Challenges

The case study findings show both the potential benefits of National Board certification and the challenges posed by attempting to expand participation nationally. Most of the teachers interviewed found that preparing for National Board certification provided a strong professional development experience. They described the process this way:

- "The most meaningful self-evaluation."

- "The most dramatic and transforming experience."

- "The most concentrated professional development."

- "One of the best professional development experiences—it gave me lots of self-confidence."

- "The certification process was a real eye-opener. I realized I've done an awful lot—the process helps document your accomplishments."

- "It was like the final stages of a major graduate course or a cumulative comprehensive exam or thesis."

- "The certification process far exceeds everything I've ever done, including my M.A."

- "The certification process was more focused than a master's program and more valuable because it was what I was really doing in the classroom."

Although most teachers responded favorably to the certification process as a professional development activity, a minority found it less useful in certain respects:

- "The process was an add-on—there were extra things I had to do that detracted from my classroom teaching."

- "Going through the process was more strenuous and lots of extra work."

- "I'm used to a one-day workshop where you get information. I didn't get much out of it. We weren't taught information."

Teachers were also asked about what changes, if any, they perceived in their teaching since completing the certification process. Most teachers reported positive changes:

- "I reflect more on what I am teaching and how it affects the kids."

- "I am much more aware of standards."

- "I've increased collaboration with other teachers."

- "I think more about why I'm doing something. I think more of the objectives—what I want to cover and why."

- "I have changed—definitely. It has made me a more insightful and aware teacher. I evaluate my teaching technique."

A few of the teachers interviewed did not perceive changes in their teaching as a result of having gone through the process. One teacher stated that the process did not teach her how to teach differently because no one gave her information on ways to improve instruction. Another perceived negative changes in her teaching and stopped because she felt the process was taking her in the wrong direction. A third teacher noted that, "even though the theory behind the process is good, you don't need to go through the National Board certification process to gain reflective skills."

The case study findings are supported by anecdotal evidence from teachers nationally. A large proportion of those who go through the certification process find it a powerful learning experience.[6]

Despite the generally positive reviews, participation and success rates nationally are low. Between 1993 and 1997, 911 teachers nationwide achieved National Board certification. The average success rate in the first three years of the assessment was about 35%; in the last year the rate increased to 45%. Without major gains in teacher participation, National Board certification is unlikely to have a significant impact on the quality of education, although it may be valuable for the relatively few teachers who participate.

In short, the process of National Board certification has recognized a small number of expert teachers rather than leading to the sort of broad participation that could contribute to general improvements in teaching. Several factors limit the program's potential to expand to the point of having a significant impact on the quality of education across the nation.

The case study findings show the potential benefits of National Board certification and the challenges it poses.

Many educators are either unfamiliar with the certification process or give it low priority. Successful completion of the process requires expertise in applying the standards, strong analytic skills, and a significant time commitment. The case study shows that most teachers had little prior information about either the skill or the time requirements of National Board certification. An additional impediment was the lack of support from colleagues. While some teachers reported that principals and peers were supportive by providing help with videotaping, granting leave time, or setting a positive tone, others felt that they received little or no support. Some teachers believed that their principals were simply unaware of the process; others noted that principals, while aware of the process, did not consider National Board Certification a priority. As one principal put it, "I have too many other priorities. National Board certification goes to the bottom of the pile." A teacher commented, "My peers thought I was crazy." Thus National Board Certification is rarely one of the primary options considered when teachers and administrators seek opportunities for professional development.

Only limited incentives exist to encourage teachers to take part. Relatively few teachers nationally receive salary incentives that would induce them to participate in National Board certification, although recently eight states and 25 school districts have provided some support. The following states offer salary increases to teachers who achieve Board certification. Georgia offers a one-time 5% increase in salary, and South Carolina offers a one-time bonus. The other six states offer a salary supplement each year for the life of the certificate: Delaware, $1,500 for a maximum of 30 teachers; Kentucky, an average of about $2,000; Mississippi, $3,000; North Carolina, 12% of the state-paid salary; Ohio, $2,500; and Oklahoma, $5,000. In addition, some states and school districts provide other types of incentives—fee supports, licensure renewal, continuing education credits, and license portability.[7]

There were no financial incentives for candidates in the case study except for payment of the fee for taking the assessment. Teachers who chose to participate cited other factors—opportunities for professional development, the prospect of increasing the professionalization of teachers, and the importance of national standards—as their main incentives. It is questionable whether these incentives are sufficient to attract a much larger set of teachers nationally.

There also are disincentives to participation—the process is long and difficult, and many candidates do not achieve National Board certification. It is not surprising, therefore, that the number of participating teachers remains a small proportion of the total eligible teaching force.

Many teachers do not have access to support services. Review materials (such as those routinely provided to students studying for law, business, or medical boards) are not yet available to teachers seeking National Board certification. Indeed, there are few support services of any kind available to teachers nationwide, although universities and school systems in some regions have begun to sponsor workshops, and efforts are also under way to develop training manuals to assist teachers preparing for the certification process.

Teachers participating in the case study, who had received support services from the Pew grant project team, reported that services were essential in a number of different areas—for example, learning the standards; reviewing subject matter, teaching methods, and developmental theory; studying assessment strategies for different learning styles; practicing writing and videotaping skills; and understanding the complexities of the assessment format and the criteria by which the assessment is scored. Teachers also expressed interest in having access to examples of successful portfolios. The current lack of support services and training materials nationally further reduces teachers' incentives to participate and diminishes the likelihood of success.

Board standards are often inconsistent with teachers' educational experience and contemporary school practice. Wide discrepancies exist between the standards and current practice in many colleges of education, professional development programs, and school districts.[8] And, in some cases, discrepancies exist between the National Board standards and the standards and assessments currently being implemented by states and school districts in developing accountability measures. Thus many teachers have not had the prior training and experience needed to meet the requirements for National Board certification. Beginning teachers lack the preparation for the assessment, and they often do not gain that experience as part of their teaching responsibilities or in subsequent professional development programs.

While most teachers in the case study felt that the National Board standards were consistent with their own teaching practices, some reported inconsistencies between the standards and the practices within their schools. These discrepancies arose either because of differences in educational philosophy or simply because the realities of the school environment—for example, large class sizes—made the standards difficult to implement. Further, one teacher raised a concern about the potential lack of congruity between the National Board standards and the new standards for learning scheduled to be implemented in Virginia in 1997–98. If, indeed, there is to be consistency between the two, the overlap would need to be more specifically delineated if it is to be helpful to teachers and administrators.

It is not surprising that to date less than half of the teachers who have completed the process have actually obtained certification. That proportion may increase, however, as the National Board institutes its new "banking" policy, which permits teachers who do not achieve certification to retake only those sections of the assessment for which they did not meet the standards. The banking policy, however, does not address the basic problem: the discrepancy between National Board standards and teachers' other experiences.

Research information is not yet available about the impact of the certification process on the quality of teaching. While most of the teachers who participated in the case study were positive about the process as a professional development experience, no research evidence exists about its impact on the quality of teaching either for individual teachers or for schools that have a critical mass of teachers taking part in the process. If research showed a positive impact, teachers would have a stronger incentive to go through the process, and states and school districts would have the data to justify allocating resources to encourage the participation of large numbers of teachers.

Implications

While evidence from the case study suggests that the process of participating in National Board certification provides a potentially powerful learning experience, current constraints severely limit teacher participation and, in turn, our ability to assess the impact on school quality of a national certification program. We do not have the critical mass of teachers needed to document the effect of the program even on the standard of education in an individual school district, much less on the quality of education in school districts and states nationwide.

The point is that National Board certification can have little impact on the quality of education nationwide without substantial increases in participation and success rates. These rates, in turn, can increase significantly only with major increases in incentives, greater consistency between National Board standards and contemporary school practice, and a wider availability of support services. Thus it would be useful to provide the research evidence that school systems and universities need in order to assess the merits of allocating substantial resources for this purpose.

The following interrelated activities are designed to increase participation of teachers in National Board certification. Such an increase would, in turn, make it possible to acquire the research data needed to demonstrate the impact of the National Board standards on school improvement.

1. *Develop and disseminate materials that will assist schools of education in incorporating the standards for National Board certification into their course offerings.* While some schools of education have begun to incorporate the National Board standards into their course offerings, it would be useful to assist a larger number of schools in accomplishing this goal and to assess the impact on the quality of teacher education. Any effort along these lines could be designed to address one of the basic impediments to large-scale participation in National Board certification: the lack of prior training needed to meet certification requirements. The work would be consistent with current policies of the National Council for Accreditation of Teacher Education, which has aligned its standards with those of the National Board.

2. *Develop and disseminate information that will assist school systems in aligning their professional development programs with National Board standards.* The lack of congruence between teacher education programs and National Board standards is often observed when teachers enter the work force and take part in professional development programs. Many of these programs do not focus on the skills that are assessed by the National Board certification process. While review materials designed specifically to support teachers preparing for national certification can be helpful, they are not a substitute for professional development programs that reach a wide range of teachers throughout their careers. Some school systems have begun to incorporate the standards for National Board certification into their professional development activities. We might draw on this experience to help school systems align their professional development activities with the standards.

3. *Design professional development materials that support teachers preparing for National Board certification.* This work could build on the two activities described above to develop courses for teachers preparing for National Board certification.

4. *Conduct research to assess the contribution of the certification process to teachers' professional development and to the quality of educational programs in schools with large proportions of Board-certified teachers.* The purpose would be to assess the contribution of the certification process both to the expertise of individual teachers and to overall school quality.

With so few teachers currently participating in National Board certification, schools do not have the critical mass of nationally certified teachers needed to make a difference in the overall education program. The program now functions as if it were based on a "master" or "lead" teacher concept rather than on the type of broad-based certification that exists, for example, in the legal, medical, or financial communities.

The few Board-certified teachers can have little catalytic effect on the school environment. Previous experience shows that an individual teacher (no matter how expert) is unlikely to have a significant impact on overall school quality unless specific steps are taken to incorporate the teacher's skills into the general educational environment. In a recent study of innovative educational models, for example, teachers and administrators recommended that "training should be widespread— available to all staff, not just a few. Teachers leveled strong criticisms at teams that provided training to only a narrow set of teachers . . . which use lead-teacher or train-the-trainer models."[9]

Teachers could receive strong incentives to go through the process in the form of course credits and bonuses.

Thus it is important to assess the impact of the certification process on schools with large proportions of teachers who have completed the process. It could be helpful to develop a pilot project and assess the contribution of Board-certified teachers to the quality of education in selected schools. Such a project would need to have a critical mass of Board-certified teachers in the project schools (and in selected certification areas within these schools). For example, all or most of the teachers in an elementary school might undergo the certification process and take the early childhood/generalist or the middle childhood/generalist assessment. Teacher participation would be voluntary, of course, but only schools with a large enough proportion of teachers interested in participating would be selected for study. Teachers could receive strong incentives to go through the process in the form of course credits and bonuses.

5. *Disseminate the findings to states and school districts.* The research findings could be used by school systems to weigh the costs and benefits of allocating resources to the National Board certification process. School systems currently have little research evidence on whether the professional development opportunities offered by national Board certification lead to significant improvements in the quality of education.

Funds now used for professional development offer a potential revenue source. The report of the National Commission on Teaching and America's Future describes the status of current professional development programs this way:

District staff development is still characterized by one-shot workshops that have very little effect on practice, rather than more effective approaches that are linked to concrete problems of practice and built into teachers ongoing work with colleagues. These workshops tend to offer ideas for classroom management or teaching that are not tied to specific subject areas or problems of practice, that do not offer follow-up help for implementation, and that are replaced at the next workshop with another idea— the new "flavor of the month"—offering little continuity in building practice. . . . As one New York teacher commented of his frustration with his district's top-down approach to managing staff development: "They're offering me stress reduction workshops when I need to learn how to help students meet these new standards. My stress comes from not having the tools to help my students succeed!"[10]

The objective of National Board certification is to help provide the tools that a teacher needs. It can become an integral part of the U.S. education system only if substantial numbers of teachers have both the incentives to participate and the expertise to succeed.

Notes

1. *State and Local Action Supporting National Certification* (Southfield, Mich.: National Board for Professional Teaching Standards, October 1997), p. 1.
2. Carnegie Task Force on Teaching as a Profession, *A Nation Prepared: Teachers for the 21st Century* (New York: Carnegie Forum on Education and the Economy, 1986).
3. *Leading the Way: 10 Years of Progress, 1987–1997* (Southfield, Mich.: National Board for Professional Teaching Standards, 1997).
4. National Board certification was offered in the following fields during the period of this study: 1993–94: early adolescence/generalist and early adolescence/English language arts: 1994–95; early adolescence/generalist, early adolescence/English language arts, early childhood/generalist, and middle childhood/generalist; 1995–96; early childhood/generalist, middle childhood/generalist, early adolescence and young adulthood/art, and adolescence and young adulthood/mathematics. In 1996–97, National Board Certification was offered in each of the six fields listed above, and a seventh, adolescence and young adulthood/science, was added. Additional areas for Board certification will be offered in subsequent years.
5. *What Matters Most: Teaching for America's Future* (New York: National Commission on Teaching and America's Future, 1996).
6. Ibid.
7. *State and Local Action.*
8. *What Matters Most.*
9. Susan Bodilly, with Susanna Purnell, Kimberly Ramsey, and Sarah J. Keith, *Lessons from New American Schools Development Corporation's Demonstration Phase* (Santa Monica, Calif.: RAND, 1996).
10. *What Matters Most,* pp. 40–41.

Form at end of book

WiseGuide Wrap-Up

Parents and communities regularly seek to reform education to promote higher student accomplishments. These school reform efforts have resulted in imposition of higher standards for both students and teachers and the strengthening of teacher education programs. Teachers are being encouraged to meet national teaching standards and to seek advanced certification. States are also in the process of revising initial and continuing teacher certification requirements.

R.E.A.L. Sites

This list provides a print preview of typical **Coursewise** R.E.A.L. sites. (There are over 100 such sites at the **Courselinks™** site.) The danger in printing URLs is that web sites can change overnight. As we went to press, these sites were functional using the URLs provided. If you come across one that isn't, please let us know via email to: webmaster@coursewise.com. Use your Passport to access the most current list of R.E.A.L. sites at the **Courselinks** site.

Site name: National Board for Professional Teaching Standards
URL: http://www.nbpts.org/
Why is it R.E.A.L.? Today, many states offer considerable financial incentives to teachers who gain NBPTS certification in addition to state licensure. This site explains the five propositions created by the NBPTS and provides links to sites that explain the performance assessments that comprise the certification process.
Key topic: professional standards for teachers
Try this: Summarize the process for becoming NBPTS certified.

Site name: Council of Chief State School Offices
URL: http://www.ccsso.org/
Why is it R.E.A.L.? This site gives information about the Interstate New Teacher Assessment and Support Consortium (INTASC), which is an initiative of the Council of Chief State School Offices to professionalize teaching. The ten INTASC standards for initial licensure are given, broken down by the knowledge, performances, and dispositions required to maintain certification in the teaching profession. Other information available at this site is on Goals 2000 and on content-area assessments in the states requiring them thus far.
Key topic: evaluation of initially licensed teachers
Try this: Look up the member(s) of the Council of Chief State School Offices in your home state. How were they selected?

Site name: Beginning Teacher Induction: Collaboration for Success
URL: http://teachnet.org/docs.cfm/Network/PolicyInstitute/Research/TPNTI/Regan/
Why is it R.E.A.L.? This site describes the teacher induction process in most schools and the plight of beginning teachers, gives the common criteria for state licensure, and describes how programs for beginning teachers are assessed.
Key topic: teacher induction
Try this: How are beginning teacher induction programs evaluated?

section | Academic Standards
3 | and Assessment

Learning Objectives

By studying the issues related to academic standards and assessment, students will:

- Recognize that high-quality standards are tools for enhancing student learning through decisions related to selecting important content and instructional choices.

- Analyze various assessment measures and determine which of these measures are appropriate for use in the classroom and why.

 **WiseGuide Intro**

Since the 1989 Governors' Education Summit in Charlottesville, Virginia, called by President George Bush, terms such as *standards* and *assessment* have become a part of many discussions related to educational reform, student learning, and the need to change. Most professional organizations have developed academic standards in their disciplines (for example, social studies, science, mathematics, and the arts). Almost concurrent with these developments has been a national call for assessment that identifies what individual students should know and be able to do. At this time, forty-nine states have standards in place or are in the process of developing or revising existing standards. Over half of those states have policies and mandates regarding assessment of student learning; many are high-stakes tests that deny student promotion to a higher grade level (for example, from fourth grade to fifth grade) or that deny a high school diploma to a student who has not met the required high school graduation competencies. Such testing may motivate students to learn more and teachers to teach more effectively. Many such policies and practices, however, are politically motivated.

There are several reasons for concerns about assessing student learning. For example, when President Bill Clinton in 1997 proposed that his administration would prepare national tests in reading for fourth-graders and in mathematics for eighth-graders, he most likely did not anticipate the opposition that the proposal would generate. Issues regarding the proposal included whether or not the reading test meant reading in English or in the child's first language, what the real purpose of such tests was, how test scores would be used (individual vs. group), what the format of the test would be (depth coverage vs. time constraints), whether or not the test would be fair and the results credible, and what the effects of assessment would be on curriculum development, implementation, and the selection of instructional activities and materials. Thus far, there are no specific right/wrong answers to these questions. At best, educators are working their way through such issues. As states move into the areas of standards, assessment, curriculum, and instruction, challenges to these decisions will likely result in court cases, perhaps leading to hearings and decisions by the U.S. Supreme Court. Teachers and other educational leaders will need to keep a close eye on what is happening (or not happening) at the local district/state level (education in the United States is a state responsibility). The approximately sixteen thousand school districts functioning across the nation will face these issues, and the decisions made will affect you as teachers and parents.

Academic Standards

Questions

Reading 17. If the United States as a whole, or if your state were to develop and adopt "world-class" or "state-class" standards for all students in your discipline content focus, what would these standards look like? What would they emphasize? How would student learning be assessed? Share the standards you develop with classmates for discussion. What commonalities, if any, are evident among the standards? If there are no commonalities, why not?

Reading 18. Explain the differences between "content" standards and "performance" standards. Examine state and national standards documents in your discipline focus area (for example, social studies, the arts, science, etc.), and write three to five "content" standards and three to five "performance" standards on a specific topic. How will these standards help to promote student learning? In small groups, discuss your standards in terms of assessability.

Reading 19. Virtually all content-area disciplines have developed and disseminated standards and standards-related documents. Secure a copy of a standards document published by your professional organization and state education agency and compare the standards in terms of specificity, regarding content, concepts, skills, and attitudes/values expressed. What are some overall conclusions you can make based on an examination of these standards materials? To what extent should school districts use the McREL generic database rather than developing their own standards to meet district objectives?

How will the development and use of academic standards promote student learning?

The development of academic standards is intended to help educators communicate more effectively with many audiences: peers, students, parents, and the larger community, including the media. In many states, critics of proposed discipline-oriented standards gathered in public forums and focus groups to voice their concerns and/or support for standards in general or for specific expectations (for example, the teaching of evolution, the titles of books to be read, whether or not social studies should have a global orientation, and so forth). For the most part, those who were writing standards listened to public comments and made revisions as appropriate. State boards of education or state legislatures adopted standards that were then signed into law. Teachers are expected to teach and assess student learning based on the approved standards. These are two major challenges that teachers face as society moves into the twenty-first century.

In Reading 17, Lauren Resnick and Kate Nolan describe world-class standards and note that a review of curriculum and standards documents does not reveal the entire story. For example, the New Standards Project headed by Resnick and colleagues at the University of Pittsburgh did not include social studies due, in part, to controversy over content with meaningful categories.

W. James Popham, one of the early leaders in the development and use of instructional standards, asks the reader in Reading 18 to consider how current content standards differ from instructional or behavioral objectives. He argues that many instructional objectives have a narrow focus, while content standards are broader and most likely will receive fairly broad support.

The development and implementation of standards pose problems for many educators because the standards are often detailed and controversial. Teachers who need to implement the standards for their students are often overwhelmed with both the quality and quantity of standards and ask, "How can I possibly teach all of these standards?" In Reading 19, Robert J. Marzano and John S. Kendall suggest the use of the McREL (Midcontinent Regional Educational Laboratory) database. Those using the McREL data should keep in mind that the McREL database is generic and that they will want to revise/adjust/modify those standards to meet the learning needs of their students in their specific setting.

Note: Many professional organizations and state education agencies have web sites and information about standards available for downloading.

Where in the World Are World-Class Standards?

Countries known for their outstanding students have several practices in common; clear, consistent, demanding public education standards head the list.

Lauren Resnick and Kate Nolan

Lauren B. Resnick is Director of the New Standards Project. Kate Nolan is Coordinator for International Benchmarking with the project. They can be reached at the Learning Research and Development Center, University of Pittsburgh, 3939 O'Hara St., Pittsburgh, PA 15260.

A current television ad portrays a neatly dressed young girl walking into a middle school classroom, a pile of books cradled in her arms. With a pleasant voice, the teacher calls roll. The scene is genial and familiar, until we notice that there is only one long row of chairs, and that the names being called are the names of countries: "Taiwan, Korea, Switzerland. . . ." As the girl takes her place in the very last seat, the teacher intones ominously, "the United States of America."

The ad expresses our national concern over how well U.S. students are doing in school. Readers of an article on international standards typically expect a similarly gloomy perspective, buttressed with handy charts comparing students from around the world. Because the international standing of U.S. children is well-known, we will spare you another such chart. Instead, we want to look at countries known for producing high-performing students to discover why these school systems look so good on the honor roll of nations.

Documents Don't Tell the Story

At a recent forum on 21st century education, a co-panelist asked us to send him a copy of the world-class standards in education. We had to chuckle; would that it were so easy! If world-class standards were defined and available in the local library's reference section, researchers and policymakers alike would make frequent use of it. Unfortunately, no such volume exists.

In 1993, when the New Standards Project at the University of Pittsburgh began its international benchmarking efforts, we hoped to collect and analyze the standards documents of other countries. We began by concentrating on mathematics, thinking it might suffer less from cultural differences than do other areas.

The countries that interested us fell into the following categories:

- those whose students perform well in international tests (for example, France),

- those whose educational systems enjoy international esteem (for example, Netherlands),

- those with a federal structure much like our own (for example, Germany), and

Lauren Resnick and Kate Nolan (1995), "Where in the World Are World-Class Standards?" *Educational Leadership*, v52, n6, 6–10. Reprinted with permission of the Association for Supervision and Curriculum Development. Copyright © 1995 by ASCD. All rights reserved.

- those representing major economic competitors of the United States (for example, Japan).

We quickly discovered that standards are not in neat volumes on the shelves of education ministries, but instead arise out of a complex interaction of curriculums, textbooks, exams, classroom practice, and student work.

When we aim for world-class standards, we are not aiming at a target that is standing still and waiting for us.

Moreover, when we sought to compile a library of materials, teachers, both at home and abroad, warned us that documents alone cannot tell the whole standards story. After all, teachers do not teach all and only what is in a textbook. They advised us to (1) find out what happens to kids who do *not* meet the standards, and (2) look at student work, which is where one really finds out what is expected of students.

We realized we had to answer six important questions to get a clear picture of world-class performance:

- What is the structure of the education systems in other countries?

- What are students expected to know and be able to do at key junctures in their schooling careers?

- What kinds of performances are used to demonstrate competence?

- What counts as "good enough" in these performances?

- What percentage of the students is meeting the standards?

- What reform efforts are under way or on the horizon?

The answers to these questions were often fascinating, and, at times, startling. For example, students in France, Japan, and the Netherlands have traditionally done very well on international mathematics tests (Educational Testing Service 1993, McKnight et al. 1987). In addition, international experts hold these systems in high esteem. At first glance, these systems differ dramatically from one another, but a closer look yields two important lessons:

- There is more than one way to help students achieve excellence.

- To successfully serve a large number and variety of students, schools must work as systems whose parts are focused on coherent, consistent, publicly articulated goals.

Let's look at mathematics education in Japan, France, and the Netherlands.

Tracking: Results Are Mixed

Historically, U.S. schools were among the first to provide secondary schooling for all students. Many argue that this is why the United States fares poorly in international comparisons: while we are committed to the education of all children, other countries practice strict ability tracking that creams off the best students. Hence, our average students are compared with their best students.

In fact, our research shows that things are no longer that simple. Other developed nations have caught up with and even surpassed us in terms of retaining students throughout the years of secondary schooling (Centre for Educational Research and Innovation 1993). Further, tracking practices do not correlate in any straightforward way with high performance internationally. In such comparisons, tracking and achievement appear to be independent of one another.

In practice, U.S. students are often tracked into classes for the gifted and talented, vocational education, and the like. On the other hand, those systems in which students outperform ours include both highly tracked and highly untracked systems.

Tracking is common in the Netherlands, where secondary school students elect one of four levels of study based on both their career goals and their past experience in school. French students are untracked through age 13; thereafter, about 85 percent of students are in a single track. In Japan, there is no tracking throughout the years of compulsory schooling.

In other words, tracking and education's availability to the whole populace cannot by themselves explain away the poor performance of U.S. students on international tests.

We have, however, learned some important lessons while examining tracking.

Japan

Japanese schools prefer heterogeneous grouping because it seems to produce higher performance all around: High performing students actually learn more, it is argued, by serving as tutors to their classmates. Further, a central focus of Japanese schools is to help form the moral and cultural character of students. High performance is valued because it contributes to the well-being of the group. In school, this means that students see their own excellence as compromised by another student's failure! One of the standards for all Japanese students, then, is to be a contributing member of an effective work group.[1]

The Netherlands

Tracking in the Netherlands is not determined by achievement tests, which are a predominant means of sorting students in the United States. In fact, achievement tests are not used in the Netherlands. Instead, secondary students, in consultation with parents, teachers, and—sometimes—school administrators, choose the track that is most appropriate for them.

The major factor in the student's choice of track is his or her career goals, because each of the four tracks in Dutch secondary schools leads to a broad set of careers and levels of specialization. Further, throughout the first two years of secondary school, and in some cases beyond that, students may switch tracks if their goals change. Early on, then, Dutch students have a clear sense that their studies are directly connected with life after school.

A defining characteristic of tracking in Dutch schools is that *all* students are expected to perform well. Mathematics exams at the conclusion of high school are a case in point: Although students who intend to go on to a university are asked to perform at a more sophisticated level than those who wish to enter the work force, the latter group faces very difficult exams. As Figure 1 shows, these exams involve complex applications of algebra and geometry. Students are also expected to show how they arrived at their answers; there is more than one right way. Dutch educators have been developing a mathematics program geared to helping all students perform well.

The Dutch approach contrasts sharply with that used in the United States today, where educators are hotly debating the relationship between tracking and achievement. Some argue that tracking results in a weak curriculum for students whose work has been weak in the past; others argue that a failure to track means holding back highly motivated students, forcing them into heterogeneous groups with a dumbed-down curriculum.

Curriculums: Common Goals Are Crucial

Many countries whose schools have achieved academic excellence have a national curriculum. Many educators maintain that a single curriculum naturally leads to high performance, but the fact that the United States values local control of schools precludes such a national curriculum. This argument would have us throw in the towel regarding raising achievement.

Our research has shown that national curriculums are a diverse group of documents. Some express the edu-

Figure 1 Exercise from a Dutch leaving exam In mathematics designed for 16-year-olds who will not go on to college (Dutch National Institute for Educational Measurement).

Exercise 4

A swimming pool of 16 x 50 meters has a shallow part A (depth 1 meter) and a deep part C (depth 4 meters). In between, the depth increases regularly from 1 meter to 4 meters. (See the drawing.) All measurements are given in meters. The swimming pool is filled up to the edge.

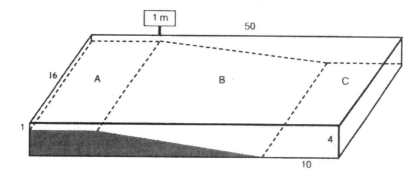

- Calculate how many m³ of water are in the swimming pool.

On the border between part A and Part B is a sign that indicates the depth (see the drawing). The lifeguard wants to put another sign on the edge saying "depth 1.80 meters."

- Calculate the distance between the two signs.

cational philosophy or traditions of the country, while others concentrate on prevailing cultural needs. Some describe teaching strategies or content considered important. Most are very sketchy. They do not detail lesson plans that mandate uniform classroom practice throughout the country.

In Japan, for example, the curriculum includes brief objectives for each grade and content level, and a few specific items that should be mastered. Teachers must and do go far beyond the guidelines. The same is true in France and in the Netherlands.

Still, a centrally articulated set of goals, even if vaguely stated, plays important roles: It organizes the development of exams and curriculums, informs textbook writing, and determines the direction of teacher training. As a result, high-stakes exams, texts, curriculums, and lesson plans do not work at cross-purposes. When all parties involved in these diverse activities have their eyes on the same set of goals, students get a consistent message about what they should know to be well educated.

France

France offers the clearest example of this convergence of goals. In texts and exams, the influence of the national curriculum is obvious, For example, a French math text

Figure 2 Portion of a Swedish mathematics exam for 16-year-olds (PRIM Group of the School Administration for the Stockholm Teacher Training Institute).

Part B. For exercises 12–15, complete solutions must be given.
NOTE! If you only give the answer you will get 0 points.

---

12. What is the price of a piece of ham weighing 6 hg if the price is 150 krona per kilogram?

---

13. How much is the telephone bill for a quarter of the year if it shows 300 units of use for that time? Each unit costs 23 Öre. In addition, there is a charge of 187 krona per quarter in subscription fees.

---

for 16-year-olds begins by spelling out the national curriculum for the year so that all 16-year-olds know what they are expected to study. The book's similar table of contents shows that the text developers referred to the curriculum. Moreover, the text makes frequent references to math exams the regional school districts have given in the past. Students practice on these exams to help them prepare for the exam they will face; they know where to concentrate to meet the standard.

One could draw a tempting but fallacious inference from these examples. Can simply having a coherent system of curriculums, texts, and exams produce excellent student performance? In fact, coherence is not enough; Sweden offers the counter-example.

Sweden

As in France, the Swedish national curriculum strongly influences texts and exams, giving students a clear message about what is expected. Still, the mathematics exam for Swedish 16-year-olds shows that a clear message, too, can set a low standard (see fig. 2). Unlike its Dutch counterpart, the Swedish exam does not ask for complex mathematical reasoning, but focuses instead on relatively low-skill computation. The lesson here: Unless coherent schooling elements set high academic standards, we can't expect student achievement to rise.

Exams: Upholding Standards

To understand how certain systems produce excellence, we also must find out how students demonstrate what they know and can do. Many countries give an exam at the end of compulsory schooling, at about age 16, and that exam often is the last measure we have of how *all* students are performing. After this point, not all students are expected to work to high standards.

France

In France, virtually all students attempt to qualify for the *Brevet* certificate at the end of middle school, and more than 75 percent succeed. This qualification is awarded on two bases: final exams in several subjects, and classroom teachers' continuous assessment during the last two years. The exams differ among the country's 27 regional school districts, but multiple choice is virtually unknown. Students must write essays, argue for positions, and solve problems while giving evidence of their reasoning. Texts and curriculums support these practices. This means that students can prepare for the *Brevet*, because it reflects the very same skills and knowledge they have been honing in school.

The Netherlands

In the Netherlands, all students take high school leaving exams. The final grade is the average of the exam's two parts: one generated nationally, the other compiled by the school. Dutch schools have four tracks and give four corresponding national exams in most subjects. As in France, multiple-choice and short-answer questions are rare.

U.S. teachers often marvel at these exams that require a lot of writing. "How are they graded?" they want to know. Obviously, with few exceptions, machine grading is impossible. By and large, teachers do it. If selected as graders, they are either freed from other duties for a time, paid a stipend, or both. To be sure grades are given fairly across regions, all scorers receive scoring guides, and auditors check a random sample of scores.

Germany

In Hessen, Germany, however, teachers both compile and grade the exam for their own students. When questioned about the possibility of teachers artificially inflating grades or helping their students cheat, one university professor seemed puzzled. "Why would they cheat," she asked us, "when they are professionals who care about their work?" This trust in and respect for teachers as professionals is common in countries whose students are noted for excellence.

What We've Learned

These shared practices and common threads among apparently very different approaches to education teach important lessons:

- Setting clear, consistent, demanding, public standards helps students perform well.

- Tracking and grouping practices must make sense in the culture of the school and for both the student's and community's future goals.

- Exams should test what students have been asked to learn, preferably in the same ways they must perform in class.

- Exams that call for complex, demanding tasks can be given to a wide range of students, perhaps to all students.

- As the front-line professionals in the education process, teachers should have much to say about what goes into exams and how they are graded.

None of these results is surprising. They represent what good teachers in good programs with hard-working students have always done. For the New Standards Project, the good news from international comparisons is that it is possible to set high standards and expect all students to work to achieve them.

One caveat is in order: The route to high performance is not necessarily to simply implement the good practices of other countries. When we aim for world-class standards, we are not aiming at a target that is standing still and waiting for us. Far from it.

Concerns about preparing students for the challenges of work and community in the 21st century are not unique to the United States. The Netherlands continues to stress the development of improved mathematics curriculums as a national priority. Around the world, schools are seeking to improve the technological abilities of all students.

Sweden and France are piloting creative means for teaching children of immigrants. All over the world, in fact, educators are working to improve school services to traditionally marginalized groups, including children from low-income families and girls of all economic classes. Issues of equity, or the performance of language, racial, and ethnic minorities are not unique to the United States.

The challenge for the United States is to create a national agenda of excellence that can raise the performance of all students without creating a national exam or curriculum. Each community must adapt the agenda in unique ways that nonetheless work in unison.

The image of a symphony comes to mind: each instrument has its own score, its own qualities, its own goals, but the scores must harmonize if a satisfying performance is to result. Just so with state and local reforms: they must and will vary in ways that make sense to local schools and communities. But they must also share a common vision of the high performance we must expect from all students.

Note

1. For more on Japanese attitudes toward ability, effort, and grouping, see H.W. Stevenson and J. W. Stigler, (1992), The Learning Gap, (New York: Summit Books); K. Okamoto, (1992), Education of the Rising Sun, (Tokyo: Monbusho); H. W. Stevenson, C. Chen, and S. Lee, (1993), "Motivation and Achievement of Gifted Children in East Asia and the United States," Journal for The Education of the Gifted 16, 3: 223–250.

References

Centre for Educational Research and Innovation. (1993). *Education at a Glance: OECD Indicators.* Paris: Organisation for Economic Co-operation and Development, p. 116.

Educational Testing Service. (1993). *NAEP 1992 Mathematics Report Card for the Nation and the States,* IAEP/NAEP Cross-linking Study. Washington, D.C.: U.S. Government Printing Office.

McKnight. C., F. Crosswhite, J. Dossey, E. Kifer, J. Swafford, K. Travers, and T. Cooney. (1987). *The Underachieving Curriculum: Assessing U.S. School Mathematics from an International Perspective.* Champaign, Ill.: Stipes Publishing Company.

Form at end of book

The Standards Movement and the Emperor's New Clothes

Then a small voice called out from the crowd, "But the emperor's not wearing new standards at all; he's wearing old objectives!" According to a classic but uncorroborated fairy tale, a ruler can be persuaded to parade around in the buff if he's made to believe he is wearing wonderful but invisible garments. The moral of the fable, of course, is that a ruler is not apt to redress his state of undress unless someone forcefully informs him he's naked as a jaybird.

W. James Popham

W. James Popham is director of IOX Assessment Associates and professor emeritus, UCLA School of Education, Los Angeles, Calif.

"Standards" is a warmth-inducing word. Although perhaps not in the same league with "motherhood," "democracy," and "children," I suspect that "standards" ranks right up there with "oatmeal," "honor," and "excellence." It's really tough not to groove on "standards," especially if they're high. Everyone wants students to reach high standards. And, because high standards are so intrinsically praiseworthy, if educators are pursuing such standards, then educators can sleep tranquilly at night. Educators are clearly questing after that which, like the Holy Grail, clearly warrants such questing.

Problems in the Apple Pie

But, therein lies the peril. Many people concerned with education, ranging from parents to educational policymakers, have become so entranced with educational standards that they sometimes fail to recognize the raft of problems still waiting for those who must deal with educational standards.

Marzano and Kendall (1996) have done an outstanding job in describing the serious conceptual problems educators face when they start swimming in the standards stream. They point out, for example, that educators must still wrestle with the problem of the optimum level of generality at which our standards should be stated. Then there's the confusion induced because different standards-determination groups have come up with decidedly different levels of subordination. Sometimes standards sit there all by themselves; sometimes a standard is sliced into a number of sub-levels. Finally, it's all too clear that there are different meanings of educational standards roaming the land.

But before I start adding to the conceptual confusion I often encounter regarding educational standards, let me indicate how I'm using the term "standard." I want to focus on content standards, and by those I mean descriptions of the knowledge and skills we want our students to learn. I'm not talking about performance standards, that is, the level of proficiency at which we wish the knowledge and/or skill to be displayed. So, in the remainder of this brief essay I'll relentlessly toss in the modifier "content" whenever I use the word "standard." I promise.

What I intend to do in the following paragraphs is deal with only one of the still unresolved problems facing educators who are trying to base their programs on content standards. I'll then close by addressing the all-too-frequent misuse of rubrics as ways of determining whether students have attained content standards.

Content Standards and Educational Aims

If by the expression content standards we refer to the knowledge and skills we want our students to achieve as a consequence of education, how is a content standard different than an instructional objective? The answer (All emperors and emperors-in-training take heed) is that there really is no difference between instructional objectives and content standards. Both phrases describe the educational intentions we have for our students.

. . . how is a content standard different than an instructional objective?

But there are two subtle yet important differences between instructional objectives and content standards. First, the instructional objectives movement of the '60s stumbled seriously because its architects equated specificity with utility. The more specifically an instructional objective was stated, especially in the form of a behavioral objective that delineated students' post-instruction behavior, the more useful it was thought such objectives would be to teachers. Because of behavioral objectives' hyperspecificity, however, classroom teachers were overwhelmed by hundreds of teensy objectives. It was a clear case of teachers' not seeing the educational forest because of the profusion of sapling-sized behavioral objectives they were being asked to address. As a consequence, any attempt to link serious educational reform to instructional objectives would be quite rightly dismissed with such phrases as "Been there, done that. And done it badly."

A second reason a content standard is much more appealing to almost everyone than an instructional objective is that content standards are warmth-inducing. Instructional objectives are not. What right-minded politician or educational policymaker would not leap with enthusiasm to be "in solid support of high content standards." It's far less exciting to be a supporter of instructional objectives, even high-level ones.

So, for both these reasons, I foresee continued widespread support for the identification and promotion of defensible content standards. As I listen to today's enthusiastic endorsements of content standards and their pivotal role in educational improvement, however, I find myself doing a bit of mental juggling so I know I'm really dealing with instructional objectives.

All the educational prizes we hope to win with first-rate content standards, and all the problems we will encounter as we employ them, have been with us since we began seriously to articulate our educational aims several decades ago. I'm not offended by the use of new, more appealing descriptors for educational intentions. Whatever works to improve the caliber of schooling is fine with me. What I'm fearful of is that the recent converts to the content standards catechism will believe their adoption of a new warmth-inducing descriptor for educational aims will automatically make the problems we first encountered with instructional objectives disappear.

A second reason a content standard is much more appealing to almost everyone than an instructional objective is that content standards are warmth-inducing. Instructional objectives are not.

Let me give you a few examples of perils that have not evaporated simply because we've now dolled up our educational aims as content standards:

- *Inadequate descriptive rigor.* In the past, many instructional objectives were stated so vaguely or so generally that they provided insufficient clarity for teachers. Many content standards still are.

- *Overwhelming numbers.* In the past, because those who created instructional objectives were so enamored of their field's content, instructional objectives were often set forth in such large numbers that teachers were overwhelmed. Many content standards still are.

- *Absence of assessments.* In the past, because it was not recognized that objectives without assessments are little more than empty rhetoric, objectives were often advocated without corollary assessment procedures. Many content standards still are.

Rubrics Running Rampant

Because the kinds of content standards that are more often touted as praise-worthy are those calling for students to respond to complex tasks, we frequently see the use of scoring rubrics closely linked to the educational standards movement. Even though content standards can describe either skills or knowledge, it's the skill-focused content standards that most often excite us.

But just as was true with instructional objectives, we still need to devise ways of scoring students' responses to demanding tasks such as being able to communicate orally or design, conduct, and report a scientific experiment. And the scoring scheme most frequently employed to judge the adequacy of students' responses, these days, is almost always a scoring rubric.

But, and here's the most important point of this essay: Many of the rubrics now being used to determine students' mastery of significant content standards are educationally dysfunctional.

A scoring rubric, at bottom, consists of:

1. Evaluative criteria by which to judge the caliber of a student's response

2. Quality descriptions for each evaluative criterion indicating how, for that criterion, qualitative differences between student responses are determined

3. Procedural guidelines such as whether the evaluative criterion should be considered in concert, that is, holistically; or on a criterion-by-criterion basis, that is, analytically.

Briefly, let me describe several serious shortcomings of rubrics I've seen being used in schools during the past few years.

1. Hyper-General Rubrics

These rubrics spell out different levels of quality in such broad terms that teachers receive little more guidance than "good responses are wonderful, weak responses are bad." Hyper-general rubrics do little more than define traditional grading systems, from A to F, in words. Hyper-general rubrics, because they are so amorphously general, provide no genuine guidance to teachers about the design of instruction for the promotion of the skill identified in the content standard.

2. Skill-Specific Rubrics

A skill-specific rubric gives teachers ample guidance to evaluate students' responses, but only to a particular task. For instance, if a student were asked to write a descriptive essay summarizing the major findings of three scientific data tables, the rubric's evaluative criteria would be directly linked to those three data tables, not to the skill set forth in the content standard. The rubric, in short, is task-linked, not skill-linked. A skill-specific rubric, as was true with a hyper-general rubric, offers teachers no instructional guidance because the rubric's elements are based on a particular task, not on the content standard's skill.

3. Lengthy, Off-Putting Rubrics

Finally, I've run across far too many excessively detailed rubrics that soon induce a cerebral numbing that, over the long haul, will not lead to widespread rubric use by teachers. The creators of many of today's scoring rubrics forget that teachers are busy folk who might put up with a one-page or two-page rubric, but will soon forget about an eight-page rubric with seven evaluative criteria and five different quality levels per criterion. If rubrics are going to provide the kind of clarity classroom teachers need to plan instruction that helps students master content standards, those rubrics must be used by teachers. Some of the rubrics I've encountered in schools are less suitable for planning than they are for penance.

If rubrics are going to supply support for students' acquisition of content standards, these rubrics must be organized around a skill (not a task), focus on a small number of evaluative criteria that are instructionally addressable, and be sufficiently brief that overtaxed teachers will want to use them. Such rubrics are currently the exception, not the rule. I have elaborated on these views elsewhere (Popham, 1997).

Friend or Foe?

I am a solid supporter of the educational standards movement. I like where it's headed and I think the curricular interest it has created will, over the years, prove beneficial to children. What I am opposed to, however, is the unthinking adulation of standards I find among too many educators—adulation that presumes we now have solved most of the traditionally vexing problems originally associated with the use of educational objectives and the determination of whether those objectives have been achieved.

We have, indeed, latched onto a generally appealing concept in content standards. But there are still problems to be solved. Ask any emperor.

References

Marzano, Robert J., and Kendall, John S. *A Comprehensive Guide to Designing Standards-Based Districts, Schools, and Classrooms.* Alexandria, Va.: Association for Supervision and Curriculum Development, 1996.

Popham, W. James. "Rubrics, What's Right, What's Wrong?" *Educational Leadership,* September 1997.

Form at end of book

National and State Standards:
The Problems and the Promise

How can schools, principals, and teachers address the daunting problem of implementing all the standards that have been promulgated in recent years? How can they ensure that their students are prepared to meet all the standards? Can it even be done?

Robert J. Marzano and John S. Kendall

Robert J. Marzano is vice president of the McREL Institute and John S. Kendall is senior program associate, McREL, Aurora, Colo.

Most teachers are aware of the documents that identify standards in their subject areas of expertise. For example, most social studies teachers are familiar with *Expectations of Excellence: Curriculum Standards for Social Studies* published by the National Council for the Social Studies in 1994. Similarly, most health education teachers are aware of the *National Health Education Standards: Achieving Health Literacy* developed by the Joint Committee on National Health Education Standards in 1995. Few educators are aware of standards documents outside their subject areas, however, nor are they aware of the character and purpose of the standards movement as a whole.

Efforts at the National Level

Many educators see the publication of *A Nation at Risk* (National Commission on Excellence in Education, 1983) as the initiating event of the modern standards movement. Ramsay Seldon, director of the State Assessment Center at the Council of Chief State School Officers, notes that after this highly damaging exposé on public education, educators set out to change what they could through new policies, such as those that increased the rigor of graduation requirements. Researcher Lorrie Shepard explains that with the publication of *A Nation at Risk*, the rhetoric of education reform changed drastically. Proponents of reform began to make a close link between the financial security and economic competitiveness of the nation and our educational system.

These growing concerns about the educational preparation of the nation's youth prompted President Bush and the nation's governors to call an Education Summit in Charlottesville, Va., in September 1989. Shepard (1993) explains that at this summit, President Bush and the governors, including then-governor Bill Clinton, agreed on six broad goals for education to be reached by the year 2000.

These goals and the rationale for them are published under the title *The National Education Goals Report: Building a Nation of Learners* (National Education Goals Panel [NEGP], 1991). Two of those goals (3 and 4) related specifically to academic achievement:

. . . President Bush and the governors, including then-governor Bill Clinton, agreed on six broad goals for education to be reached by the year 2000.

Goal 3: By the year 2000, American students will leave grades 4, 8, and 12 having demonstrated competency in challenging subject matter including English, mathematics, science, history, and geography; and every school in America will ensure that all students learn to use their minds well, so they may be prepared for responsible citizenship, further learning, and productive employment in our modern economy.

Goal 4: By the year 2000, U.S. students will be first in the world in science and mathematics achievement. (p. 4)

One tacit purpose of the Education Summit was to motivate educators to set challenging standards within all major subject areas. This purpose was quickly realized. In a relatively short period of time, standards documents were generated for all major academic areas. For example, the documents listed in Figure 1 are the result of efforts by groups that either were funded by the U.S. Department of Education or identify themselves as representing the national consensus in their subject areas. Thus, these documents could be said to articulate the "official" version of standards in the respective subject areas. (For a detailed discussion of the status of standards development in various subject areas, see Kendall and Marzano, 1996.)

Given this impressive list of what might be called national "standards" documents, one might assume that U.S. educators now have clear direction regarding what should be taught in the core subject areas. Unfortunately, this is not the case. Although the standards documents as a set represent a powerful resource for teachers, these documents are not readily useful in their present state. As a group, they represent at least four major problems to the user.

Figure 1

Science	National Research Council. *National Science Education Standards.* Washington, D.C.: National Academy Press, 1996.
Foreign Language	National Standards in Foreign Language Education Project. *Standards for Foreign Language Learning: Preparing for the 21st Century.* Lawrence, Kans.: Allen Press, 1996.
English/ Language Arts	National Council of Teachers of English and the International Reading Association. *Standards for the English Language Arts.* Urbana, Ill.: NCTE, 1996.
History	National Center for History in the Schools. *National Standards for History for Grades K–4: Expanding Children's World in Time and Space.* Los Angeles, Calif.: NCHS, 1994.
	———. *National Standards for United States History: Exploring the American Experience.* Los Angeles, Calif.: NCHS, 1994.
	———. *National Standards for World History: Exploring Paths to the Present.* Los Angeles, Calif.: NCHS, 1994.
	———. *National Standards for History: Basic Edition.* Los Angeles, Calif.: NCHS, 1996.
Arts	Consortium of National Arts Education Associations. *National Standards for Arts Education: What Every Young American Should Know and Be Able To Do in the Arts.* Reston, Va.: Music Educators National Conference, 1994.
Health	Joint Committee on National Health Education Standards. *National Health Education Standards: Achieving Health Literacy.* Reston, Va.: Association for the Advancement of Health Education, 1995.
Civics	Center for Civic Education. *National Standards for Civics and Government.* Calabasas, Calif.: CCE, 1994.
Economics	National Council on Economic Education. *Content Statements for State Standards in Economics, K–12* (Draft). New York: NCEE, August 1996.
Geography	Geography Education Standards Project. *Geography for Life: National Geography Standards.* Washington, D.C.: National Geographic Research and Exploration, 1994.
Physical Education	National Association for Sport and Physical Education. *Moving into the Future, National Standards for Physical Education: A Guide to Content and Assessment.* St. Louis: Mosby, 1995.
Mathematics	National Council of Teachers of Mathematics. *Curriculum and Evaluation Standards for School Mathematics.* Reston, Va.: NCTM, 1989.
Social Studies	National Council for the Social Studies. *Expectations of Excellence: Curriculum Standards for Social Studies.* Washington, D.C.: NCSS, 1994.

Problem 1: Multiple Documents

A number of subject areas have multiple documents that address the standards in that domain. For example, *Curriculum and Evaluation Standards for School Mathematics,* published by NCTM (1989), is certainly considered the "official" description of what students should know and be able to do in the field of mathematics. However, mathematics standards and benchmarks are also explicitly and implicitly articulated in each of the following documents:

- *Benchmarks for Science Literacy,* by Project 2061 of the American Association for the Advancement of Science (AAAS), 1993

- *Framework for the 1994 National Assessment of Educational Progress Mathematics Assessment,* by the National Assessment of Educational Progress, 1992

- New Standards. *Performance Standards: English Language Arts, Mathematics, Science, Applied Learning, Volume 1, Elementary School.* Washington, D.C.: National Center on Education and the Economy, 1997a.

- ———. *Performance Standards: English Language Arts, Mathematics, Science, Applied Learning, Volume 2, Middle School.* Washington, D.C.: National Center on Education and the Economy, 1997b.

- ———. *Performance Standards: English Language Arts, Mathematics, Science, Applied Learning, Volume 3, High School.* Washington, D.C.: National Center on Education and the Economy, 1997c.

- International Baccalaureate. *Group 5 Mathematics Guide* (Edition 1.2). Geneva, Switzerland: IB, 1993.

- ———. *Middle Years Programme: Mathematics* (Edition 1.1). Geneva, Switzerland: IB, 1995e.

Science provides another example of the problem of multiple documents. At least three documents have gained recognition as descriptions of what students should know and be able to do in science. The official effort to identify science standards was led by the National Committee on Science Education Standards and Assessment (NCSESA) and published in 1996 by the National Research Council (NRC) as *National Science Education Standards.* The document contains some 200 pages of standards written at three levels: K–4, 5–8, and 9–12. Twenty-five standards are articulated at the K–4 level, 28 standards at the 5–8 level, and 34 standards at the 9–12 level. A second science standards document comes from AAAS's Project 2061: *Benchmarks for Science Literacy* (1993). This publication articulates 60 "literacy goals" across four levels: K–2, 3–5, 6–8, and 9–12. In addition to these publications, the National Science Teachers Association (NSTA) has published *The Scope, Sequence, and Coordination of National Science Education Content Standards* (Aldridge and Strassenburg, 1995) as an addendum to *Scope, Sequence, and Coordination of Secondary School Science, Volume 1: The Content Core: A Guide for Curriculum Designers* (Pearsall, 1993).

In short, a district or school would need to consult a number of documents to review mathematics and science comprehensively. Based on our review of important text materials that address student content knowledge and skills, we have concluded that a school or district would have to consult 112 documents to make a comprehensive review of the arts, civics, economics, the English language arts, foreign languages, geography, health, history, mathematics, physical education, science, social studies and technology. For example, the district or school should review 10 documents in history, 8 documents in mathematics, and 24 documents in English language arts.

Problem 2: Too Much Information

Even if a school or district were to consult only the official documents listed in Figure 1, it would be faced with a difficult task. In the beginning of the effort, the hope for the standards documents was that they would represent a concise set of statements about what students should know and be able to do in core subject areas. However, as the standards drafts and final documents were produced, it became clear that the standards were far from concise. Education researcher Chester Finn, Jr., noted that "the professional associations, without exception, lacked discipline. They all demonstrated gluttonous and imperialistic tendencies" (in Diegmueller, 1995, p. 6).

At the time of Finn's statement in 1995, the standards documents, taken together, weighed about 14 pounds, stood six inches tall, and contained more than 2,000 pages. Since then, more documents, more pounds, and more inches have been added to the total mass of standards. By contrast, the Japanese national curriculum fits into "three slender volumes, one for elementary schools, one for lower secondary schools, and one for upper secondary schools" (Ravitch, 1995, p. 15). Ron Brandt (1995), executive editor of the Association for Supervision and Curriculum Development, acknowledged the problem of the sheer volume of the standards:

I would describe them as an ambitious conception of what professional educators, most of whom are advocates or specialists in the various school subjects, want students to learn in those subjects. It's the classic curriculum dilemma faced by every principal, central administrator, and generalist teacher: specialists naturally expect a lot; they love their subject and they know its possibilities. Taken as a whole, however, such statements of aspirations are overwhelming. (p. 5)

Problem 3: Controversial Content

At least two subject areas have produced documents that generated quite a bit of controversy regarding their content: history and the language arts.

In the fall of 1994, Lynne Cheney, a fellow of the American Enterprise Institute, unleashed a blistering attack on the History Standards Project, which, along with science, was the first standards project to receive funding from the U.S. Department of Education in 1991. Cheney alleged that the history standards portrayed the United States and its white, male-dominated power structure as an oppressive society that victimizes minorities and women. She further charged that the history standards ignored such traditional historical figures as George Washington and Robert E. Lee in order to placate proponents of multiculturalism. Suddenly, *Education Week* reporter Karen Diegmueller (1995) notes, the rather academic discussion of standards burst onto the national scene:

Cheney's views won such exceptionally wide exposure because, as chairwoman of the National Endowment for the Humanities, she had lobbied for history standards, funded the project, and selected its leaders and many of the people on its 29-member board. Soon it became evident that the criticism was not about to subside—even though there were far more supporters than detractors. The U.S. Senate even weighed in, denouncing the history standards by a vote of 99 to 1. (p. 8)

To date, the history standards have not recovered from the negative public perception generated by Cheney's criticisms, even though a revised edition that attempted to address the criticisms was published in 1996 (National Center for History in the Schools [NCHS], 1996).

The language arts standards have also experienced strong opposition. The Standards Project for the English Language Arts (SPELA) was initially funded by the Fund for Improvement and Reform of Schools and Teaching (FIRST) of the U.S. Office of Educational Research and Improvement. SPELA was designed to be a three-year collaborative effort (beginning in September 1992) of the Center for the Study of Reading (CSR), the International Reading Association, and the National Council of Teachers of English. SPELA produced one complete draft of its standards, entitled *Incomplete Work of the Task Forces of the Standards Project for the English Language Arts*. This draft was to go through a number of iterations until a final document was produced. However, on March 18, 1994, the U.S. Department of Education notified SPELA that it would not continue funding for the project. According to NCTE, funding for the project was halted because of a number of "philosophical differences" between SPELA and the federal agencies. These differences included a disagreement over the inclusion of delivery standards, which was

supported by SPELA, and the lack of attention to a specific canon of children's literature, which was not supported by SPELA. However, the primary reason for cessation of funding appeared to be the federal government's assertion that SPELA was not attending to the basic task of identifying what students should know and be able to do in the English language arts. As noted by Janice Anderson, interim director of FIRST at the time the funding was halted, SPELA had not made "substantial progress toward meeting the objectives" of the project. The proposed standards, she stated, "are vague and often read as opinions and platitudes," focus too much on process rather than content, and lack "a coherent conceptual framework" ("NCTE, IRA Say," 1994, p. 4).

Problem 4: Different Levels of Generality

Another problem with the national documents that a school or district must address is the variance in the level of generality at which standards are stated. Even a cursory review of the standards generated by different groups reveals very different perspectives on the level of generality at which standards should be stated. For example, the *National Standards for Arts Education* (Consortium of National Arts Education Associations, 1994) provides the following as a standard:

- *Understanding the arts in relation to history and cultures*

In contrast, a document from *National Standards for United States History: Exploring the American Experience* (NCHS, 1994b) lists the following standard:

- *Students should understand the causes of the Civil War.*

The example from *National Standards for United States History* is obviously more specific than that from *National Standards for Arts Education*. In addition, the history document provides more detailed information for each of its standards than does the arts document. The degree to which standards are articulated in specific terms is critical because the level of specificity adopted by a school or district will affect the level of detail within the standards, the degree of comprehensiveness the standards aim for, and the number of standards created.

In summary, as efforts to develop standards have grown, the difficulties, often technical, sometimes political, also have grown. The apparent failure at the national level spawned the need for states to generate their own standards documents.

State Level Efforts

In addition to national documents that identify standards and benchmarks in various content areas, most states have identified standards and benchmarks or are in the process of identifying standards and benchmarks (Gandal, 1995a, 1995b). State efforts to create standards were given an impressive endorsement at the second Education Summit in Palisades, N.Y, in March 1996 when the state governors committed to designing standards and sharing conceptual and technical information regarding their efforts (National Governor's Association, 1996). These actions are consistent with the opinions of those educators who believe that it is at the state level that the standards movement will either succeed or fail. As education reporter Lynn Olson (1995a) notes:

The U.S. Constitution makes it clear: States bear the responsibility for educating their citizens. They decide how long students continue their education and how the schools are financed. They control what is taught, what is tested, which textbooks are used, and how teachers are trained.

Thus, despite all the talk about national education standards, it is the 50 individual states that ultimately will determine what students should know and be able to do. (p. 15)

It is probably accurate to say that most states would prefer not to simply adopt standards set by national organizations. For example, Fred Tempes, an associate superintendent in the California Department of Education explains, "I guess like most states we'd like to feel that we can set our own standards" (in Olson, 1995a, p. 15). Olson notes that 46 states have applied for federal grants under the Goals 2000: Educate America Act. Thirty-one states began work on identifying standards in 1991. As of April 1995, most of those states were still in the process of drafting or reviewing their standards.

In spite of these impressive findings, state efforts to set standards have been inconsistent. According to studies conducted by the American Federation of Teachers (AFT) (see Gandal, 1995a, 1996), there is both good news and bad news regarding state efforts to set standards. "The good news," the late AFT President Albert Shanker said, "is that the movement to upgrade academic standards has taken hold all across the country" (in Innerst, 1995, p. A4). The bad news is that the state-level attempts vary in terms of quality and level of effort. To date, the AFT has completed two studies of state efforts to construct standards. The first, entitled *Making Standards Matter. A 50-State Progress Report on Efforts To Raise Academic Standards,* was published in 1995 (see Gandal, 1995a). That initial study reported the following findings:

- Every state except Iowa is engaged in developing academic standards. Iowa has not set standards, opting for standards to be set by local schools and districts.

- Thirteen states have standards that are clear and specific enough to form the basis of core curriculum. The states with the clearest standards are California, Colorado, Georgia, and Virginia.

- Thirty-one states have or will have students' assessments linked to standards, but many of those standards are too vague.

- Seven states have taken steps to evaluate their standards against those of countries with high-achieving students (in Innerst, 1995, p. A4).

The second report, entitled *Making Standards Matter, 1996: An Annual 50-State Report on Efforts To Raise Academic Standards,* was published in 1996 (see Gandal, 1996). On the positive side, the report noted that a great deal of work had been done since the first report:

The tremendous amount of activity we've seen in the states over the past year is another strong indicator of the national commitment to raising academic standards. Over two-thirds of states have developed new or revised documents since we issued our report last year. Most of these states have come out with new documents in all four core subjects while some states have issued new standards in a few subjects. (p. 13)

However, the report concluded that state efforts are still far from acceptable. The report (see Gandal, 1996) noted the following:

- Forty-eight states are engaged in developing academic standards. (In addition to Iowa, since the publication of the 1995 report, Wyoming has decided against the construction of state standards.)

- Fifteen states have standards in all four core subject areas (i.e., English, history, mathematics, science) that are clear and well grounded in content.

- Forty-two states either have assessments or are in the process of developing assessments linked to their standards, but the standards are not strong enough in most of these states to provide a solid foundation for the assessments.

- Only 12 states have looked at what is expected of students in other countries, while developing their own standards, although more states recognize the need for internationally competitive standards.

The most damaging finding in both reports is that most state documents simply have weak standards. To illustrate, the 1996 report offers the following as an example of a strong mathematics standard: "The student will differentiate between area and perimeter and identify whether the application of the concept of perimeter or area is appropriate for a given situation" (Gandal, 1996, p. 16). Conversely, a weak mathematics standard from another state document is "Students should be able to represent and solve problems using geometric models" (Gandal, 1996, p. 16).

This lack of specificity in state documents has caused significant opposition to the standards movement.

Standards expert Matthew Gandal (1995b) explains that the 1992 "Common Core of Learning" standards in Virginia and the 1991 "Student Learning Outcomes" in Pennsylvania were so vague as to be judged as nonacademic by the constituents of those states. This perception led to the defeat of the entire reform package in those states and the redrafting of more specific standards in both states.

If we accept the findings of the AFT reports, then the support and guidance that can be expected from state-level documents is relatively limited. The vast majority of states have standards that are so vague that they will probably have to be reworked—or even totally rewritten—by schools and districts in those states. Even in the 15 states whose standards were judged to be specific enough, districts still most likely will have to supplement their state standards. For example, Colorado was judged by AFT to have standards that are specific enough to be used by schools and districts. However, the Colorado standards are stated at four levels: K–2, 3–5, 6–8, and 9–12. If a school or district in Colorado wishes to construct grade-level benchmarks (i.e., separate benchmarks for each grade level), it will have to extrapolate the 4 Colorado levels to 12 levels. Finally, most state documents are presented as "guidelines" to be used by local districts rather than as mandated standards that must be followed without alteration. Only three states will hold students accountable for meeting standards prior to high school graduation; fewer than half the states require or plan to require students to pass high school graduation exams linked to their standards, and only nine states will require students to pass graduation exams linked to their standards in all four core subjects (Gandal, 1996).

The standards documents that have been produced at the national and state levels are not always user friendly. The school or district wishing to design and implement a standards-based approach to schooling will more than likely have to augment and even rewrite the standards and benchmarks presented within those resources. While this can be a labor-intensive task, it provides schools and districts with the opportunity to tailor standards and benchmarks to their specific needs.

Teachers broadly support proposals to raise standards, which they expect to improve their students' academic performance.

Finding Solutions

The problems we have described may appear daunting. Yet, at every turn we find continued calls for academic standards. The polling firm Public Agenda has conducted a number of surveys on the issue over the last two years. They found that most Americans strongly support higher standards (Farkas et al., 1994). Teachers broadly support proposals to raise standards, which they expect to improve their students' academic performance (Johnson and Farkas, 1996). And a recent finding from Public Agenda indicates that students see value in standards as well, "Teenagers support the nationwide call for higher academic standards, which they think all students should have to meet" (Friedman and Duffett, 1997). So, while the nature of the difficulties inherent in describing clear and useful standards become more apparent, it is also apparent that support for this challenging work continues.

A Partial Solution

A number of states, districts, and schools that face the problems described above have taken advantage of a database of information developed at McREL. As part of its funding from the Office of Educational Research and Improvement, McREL has developed an extensive resource database that describes student knowledge and skills for all content areas. McREL has analyzed all the significant subject area documents across the various content areas and translated the information into a common format. The complete database is reported in the document *Content Knowledge: A Compendium of Standards and Benchmarks for K–12 Education* (Kendall and Marzano, in press). A previous edition of this report is available on the World Wide Web (**www.mcrel.org/standard.html**).

In all, the database describes 255 standards and their related benchmarks. These standards are organized into 14 major categories representing the following subject areas:

1. **Mathematics:** 9 standards, 226 benchmarks

2. **Science:** 16 standards, 265 benchmarks

3. **History.**
   K–4 History: 8 standards, 108 benchmarks
   U.S. History: 31 standards, 404 benchmarks
   World History: 46 standards, 722 benchmarks
   Historical Understanding: 2 standards,
      48 benchmarks

4. **Language Arts:** 8 standards, 274 benchmarks

5. **Geography:** 18 standards, 238 benchmarks

6. **Arts:**
   Dance: 6 standards, 62 benchmarks
   Music: 7 standards, 80 benchmarks
   Theatre: 6 standards, 72 benchmarks
   Visual Arts: 5 standards, 42 benchmarks
   Art Connections: 1 standard, 13 benchmarks

7. **Civics:** 29 standards, 427 benchmarks

8. **Economics:** 10 standards, 159 benchmarks

9. **Foreign Language:** 5 standards, 84 benchmarks

10. **Health:** 10 standards, 136 benchmarks

11. **Physical Education:** 5 standards, 105 benchmarks

12. **Behavioral Studies:** 4 standards, 100 benchmarks

13. **Technology:** 4 standards, 94 benchmarks

14. **Life Skills:**
    Thinking and Reasoning: 6 standards, 121 benchmarks
    Working with Others: 5 standards, 51 benchmarks
    Self-Regulation: 6 standards, 59 benchmarks
    Life Work: 7 standards, 69 benchmarks

These standards were constructed from the content of 112 documents. The documents represent a range of material, from nationally-funded standards documents, such as those from the National Council for History in the Schools, to state curriculum documents, such as the California Science Framework, to the work of privately funded groups, such as syllabus guidelines from the International Baccalaureate Organization.

How Can This Help?

The content of the McREL database has been developed in such a way that it could help schools, districts, and states address at least two of the significant problems described above: the problem of multiple documents and the problem of levels of generality. First, it provides an analysis of multiple documents, indicating what content descriptions were found in which of the many documents consulted. Thus, a school or district can be assured that all the content considered significant across all the relevant documents for a given subject area is represented in the database, providing a solid foundation from which to build content standards. Second, the database provides content described at consistent levels of generality across subject areas, and categorized according to basic distinctions accepted by many of the cognitive psychologists who study the structure of knowledge. Thus, a school or district working on standards would have a common model from which to determine the number of content standards appropriate for each subject area, and a common level of specificity that should aid in communication with everyone concerned—parents, teachers, and students.

More indirectly, the database can also help users concerning the other two problems described: standards that have generated or may generate controversy, and the problem regarding too much information in the standards.

The most serious controversies surrounding the development of standards could be said to focus on classroom activities, not strictly on the description of what students should know and be able to do. In the case of the language arts, for example, the early draft materials from NCTE/IRA provided no explicit standards, but offered instead numerous vignettes of the language arts classroom. It seems likely that this manner of presentation contributed heavily to concerns about vagueness in the standards. That is, the reader, rather than being provided with explicit descriptions of knowledge and skill, was required to infer from a description of classroom activities what knowledge and skills might be required of students who were successfully engaged in the activity. In the case of the history standards from the National Council for History in the Schools, much information also had to be inferred from reading student activities; and how these activities were described placed the effort under an unfavorable light. A panel convened to review the history standards determined most of the serious difficulty resided in the activities, which they faulted "for undermining principles of scholarship by asking leading questions or by inviting students to make easy moral judgments about historical questions that continue to be debated by scholars" (Council for Basic Education, 1995). Thus the approach, not the content described, was determined at base to have provoked the controversy.

The McREL database presents straightforward descriptions of knowledge and skill, rather than activities, and these descriptions are the result of reviewing as many documents as are considered to be significant for the subject they address. Using this as a source may provide some measure of security for those schools and districts undertaking to write standards, but who are leery of the controversy that has occurred at the national level.

Finally, there is little doubt more knowledge and skills have been identified in the national standards than can be addressed in the course of a student's K–12 education. The McREL database does provide the means for users to determine in how many different documents the same or similar student knowledge and skill is recognized as important. Unfortunately, this approach will not greatly reduce the amount of standards to be considered. At the present time, those who are undertaking the development of standards might wish to have their teachers and communities help them select from among these standards. This approach has several advantages. First, it engages individuals in the process of writing standards and helps make the rationale for standards more clear. Second, it surfaces any controversial issues, and allows for open discussion during the development of standards, rather than an acrimonious debate that begins once the standards have been published. Finally, it makes the final selection of content the responsibility of those who must take the greatest responsibility for teaching and learning. This may in fact be better for all concerned.

In summary, the task of developing standards is not an easy one. We have touched upon a few of the issues and suggested some possible solutions. As the problems become more clearly articulated, it is hoped that solutions will not be far to follow.

References

Aldridge, B. G., and Strassenburg, A. A., eds. *Scope, Sequence, and Coordination of National Science Education Content Standards: An Addendum to the Content Core Based on the 1994 Draft National Science Education Standards.* Arlington, Va.: National Science Teachers Association, 1995.

Brandt, R. "Overview: What To Do With Those New Standards." *Educational Leadership* 6(1995): 5.

Carnevale, A. P.; Gainer, L. J.; and Meltzer, A. S. *Workplace Basics: The Essential Skills Employers Want.* San Francisco: Jossey-Bass, 1990.

Center for Civic Education. *National Standards for Civics and Government.* Calabasas, Calif: CCE, 1994.

Consortium of National Arts Education Associations. *National Standards for Arts Education: What Every Young American Should Know and Be Able To Do in the Arts.* Reston, Va.: Music Educators National Conference, 1994.

Council for Basic Education. *Review Panels Find History Standards Worth Revising.* News release submitted for publication, October 11, 1995.

Diegmueller, K. "Running Out of Steam." *Struggling for Standards: An Education Week Special Report,* April 12, 1995.

Farkas, F.; Friedman, W.; Boese, J.; and Shaw, G. *First Things First: What Americans Expect From Public Schools.* New York: Public Agenda, 1994.

Finn, C. E., Jr. "The Biggest Reform of All." *Phi Delta Kappan* 8(1990): 584–92.

Friedman, W., and Duffett, A. *Getting By: What American Teenagers Really Think About Their Schools.* New York: Public Agenda, 1997.

Gandal, M. *Making Standards Matter: A 50-State Progress Report on Efforts To Raise Academic Standards.* Washington, D.C.: American Federation of Teachers, 1995a.

———. *Making Standards Matter, 1996: An Annual 50-State Report on Efforts To Raise Academic Standards.* Washington, D.C.: American Federation of Teachers, 1996.

———. "Not All Standards Are Created Equal." *Educational Leadership* 6 (1995b): 16–21.

Geography Education Standards Project. *Geography for Life: National Geography Standards.* Washington, D.C.: National Geographic Research and Exploration, 1994.

Innerst, C. "States Found Lacking on School Standards." *Washington Times,* July 27, 1995, p. A4.

Johnson, J., and Farkas, S. *Given the Circumstances: Teachers Talk About Public Education Today.* New York: Public Agenda, 1996.

Joint Committee on National Health Education Standards. *National Health Education Standards: Achieving Health Literacy,* Reston, Va.: Association for the Advancement of Health Education, 1995.

Kendall, J. S., and Marzano, R. J. *Content Knowledge: A Compendium of Standards and Benchmarks for K–12 Education.* Alexandria, Va.: Association for Supervision and Curriculum Development, 1996.

Marzano, R. J., and Kendall, J. S. *Designing Standards-Based Districts, Schools, and Classrooms.* Alexandria, Va.: Association for Supervision and Curriculum Development, 1996.

National Assessment of Educational Progress. *Framework for the 1994 National Assessment of Educational Progress Mathematics Assessment.* Washington, D.C.: NAEP, March 31, 1992.

National Association for Sport and Physical Education. *Moving into the Future: National Standards for Physical Education: A Guide to Content Assessment.* St. Louis: Mosby, 1995.

National Center for History in the Schools. *National Standards for History: Basic Edition.* Los Angeles: NCHS, 1996.

———. *National Standards for History for Grades K–4: Expanding Children's World in Time and Space.* Los Angeles, Calif.: NCHS, 1994a.

———. *National Standards for United States History: Exploring the American Experience.* Los Angeles, Calif.: NCHS, 1994b.

———. (1994c). *National Standards for World History: Exploring Paths to the Present.* Los Angeles, Calif: NCHS, 1994c.

National Commission on Excellence in Education. *A Nation at Risk: The Imperative for Educational Reform.* Washington, D.C.: U.S. Government Printing Office, 1983.

National Council for the Social Studies. *Expectations of Excellence: Curriculum Standards for Social Studies.* Washington, D.C.: NCSS, 1994.

National Council of Teachers of English and the International Reading Association. *Standards for the English Language Arts.* Urbana, Ill. and Newark, Del.: NCTE and IRA, 1996.

National Council of Teachers of Mathematics. *Curriculum and Evaluation Standards for School Mathematics.* Reston, Va.: NCTM, 1989.

National Council on Economic Education. *Content Statements for State Standards in Economics, K–12* (Draft). New York: NCEE, August 1996.

National Education Goals Panel. *The National Education Goals Report: Building a Nation of Learners.* Washington, D.C.: NEGP, 1991.

National Governors Association. *1996 National Education Summit Policy Statement.* Washington, D.C.: NGA, March 1996.

National Research Council. *National Science Education Standards.* Washington, D.C.: National Academy Press, 1996.

National Standards in Foreign Language Education Project. *Standards in Foreign Language Learning: Preparing for the 21st Century.* Lawrence, Kans.: Allen Press, 1996.

Olson, L. "Standards Times 50." *Struggling for Standards: An Education Week Special Report,* April 12, 1995a, pp. 14–22.

Pearsall, M. K., ed. *Scope, Sequence, and Coordination of Secondary School Science. Vol. 1. The Content Core: A Guide for Curriculum Designers.* Washington, D.C.: National Science Teachers Association, 1993.

Project 2061, American Association for the Advancement of Science. *Benchmarks for Science Literacy.* New York: Oxford University Press, 1993.

Ravitch, D. *National Standards in American Education: A Citizen's Guide.* Washington, D.C.: Brookings Institution, 1995.

Secretary's Commission on Achieving Necessary Skills (SCANS). *What Work Requires of Schools: A SCANS Report for America 2000.* Washington, D.C.: U.S. Department of Labor, 1991.

Shepard, L. *Setting Performance Standards for Student Achievement.* Stanford, Calif: National Academy of Education, Stanford University, 1993.

Standards Project for English Language Arts. *Incomplete Work of the Task Forces of the Standards Project for English Language Arts,* Urbana, Ill.: SPELA, no date.

Form at end of book

Assessment

To what extent will assessment promote student learning? What form or forms should assessment take for students to demonstrate their proficiency in meeting academic standards?

During the last decade, the terms *assessment* and *accountability* have become common in discussions about school reform and change. The question most parents are likely asking is, "How well does my child do in this class?" For teachers, the question is, "How will I hold students accountable for their learning and progress?" For school board members and others in the community, the question may be, "How are both students and teachers accountable to the community?" The answers are complex.

Readings 20, 21, and 22 present different perspectives on this broad issue. In Reading 20, Susan Andersen describes her classroom of students and the time taken away from instruction during the week(s) of mandated testing. Andersen wonders what the testing accomplishes.

Large-scale standardized tests have been criticized for not enabling students, teachers, and parents to view student progress over time. In Reading 21, Cheryl Kish and her colleagues argue for the use of portfolios to help assess individual student learning and to develop reflective thinking. They suggest that portfolios offer the possibility for positive growth as students think about their own work (self-evaluation) and decide what information (types of information and work exhibits) will be included in their portfolios.

With traditional assessment techniques (pencil-and-paper standardized tests) being criticized as insufficient and as "one-shot" assessments, the term *authentic assessment* has entered the education vocabulary. In Reading 22, James Terwilliger writes that there is little evidence to suggest that "authentic" assessment measures student learning. Terwilliger notes that the use of the term is misleading and denies the role of knowledge in determining what students know.

The Trouble with Testing

Susan R. Andersen

Susan R. Andersen is an early childhood consultant at the Iowa Department of Education and a member of the NAEYC Governing Board. She has been a teacher of Head Start, kindergarten, and primary children as well a teacher of adult learners in the field of early childhood.

In theory we give young children standardized tests so we can use the results to improve teaching methods. But most teachers will admit the tests do more to disrupt learning than to benefit teaching. As a practitioner, parent, or policymaker, you're familiar with the public pressure to "improve" test scores, and you may be able to cite your district's latest scores. But you might be unaware of just how much classroom time testing consumes, how frustrating testing is for teachers, and how emotionally trying it can be for young children and their families. These effects of standardized tests are not really documented; understanding them requires direct observation of the daily reality inside the classroom.

Observe, for example, my previous class of 28 second-graders, whose average age is seven years, three months. Among them are Dean, Robin, and Terri. (I'll say more about these three later.) By the time testing begins, the children and I have had about 30 days together. Our class is usually structured around learning teams, with desks pushed together in islands throughout the room. The

children are learning to question, listen, respond, and cooperate with each other.

But this week is different. We will be taking the mathematics and reading sections of the Iowa Tests of Basic Skills (ITBS). Instead of being in islands, the desks are separated individually; each child will work alone. For seven-year-olds this is not a trivial change. To compensate, I plan for morning snacks and double the length of the afternoon "self-selection" period, when the children can work on their own math and science projects. I want them to forget these tests.

Assessment avoids approaches that place children in artificial situations, impede the usual learning and developmental experiences in the classroom, or divert children from their natural learning processes. (NAEYC & NAECS/SDE 1991, 23)

The district has informed parents of the test dates and asked that the children arrive at school promptly with adequate rest. But the parents who read and understand this message are the ones who don't need to be told. Chances are, it's the parents who had little success at school themselves who haven't absorbed the message.

A Week of Tests

Monday

9:00 A.M. As the first day of testing begins, everyone is here but Dean, Robin, and Terri. I don't have to wait

Questions

The National Association for the Education of Young Children (NAEYC) has issued a position statement recommending that children not be required to participate in standardized test taking until after the third grade. This reading, which appeared in NAEYC's journal, gives reasons against standardized tests and reasons for other types of instruction and assessment. Evaluate your thinking about this issue: Should children eight years of age and younger be free from mandatory standardized testing?

Why or why not?

Why does age eight seem to be the "magic" age?

long for Robin, who runs in, breathless, a few minutes after nine o'clock. She is highly capable, well cared for, and far too pensive for her seven years. She has self-imposed standards of excellence and usually attains them.

A few minutes later Terri walks in. She is a child from a family whose current living conditions are called, in the jargon of school definitions, "doubling-up." She and her family recently arrived from out-of-state, have no home of their own, and have moved in with her uncle's family. Her records from previous schools never materialized; the family has obvious health needs and lacks both medical insurance and employment. Yet Terri's enthusiasm and maturity are high for her age. Her vocabulary includes such words as "unemployment," "welfare," "truck stops," and "migraines."

Twenty minutes later Dean is still absent. Dean overflows with personality and energy; he struggles to be the best in the class. Weighed against those assets, however, are insecurity and weak academic skills. Dean's family and living conditions are in flux. His personal needs and support systems vary with the day. When Dean enters the classroom, his manner and appearance usually tell me what his life has been like since I said good-bye to him the day before.

These three children are in no way unusual in a class of 28 in a middle-class neighborhood. As their teacher, I must shape the small number of school days we have together into learning experiences that respond to their needs. In my experience, the time we spend on this kind of testing is time that is worse than wasted—it is damaging. But the tests are required, so we begin.

By 9:30 A.M. I have explained the testing process and shown the children how to mark the ovals in the answer booklet. I've made sure the children have the correct booklets and have filled in the alphabetized ovals for all the letters of their name—last name, first name, plus more ovals to complete the line. It's a painstaking task.

How do I explain this use of time to the children? I continually encourage and praise them and say this is just one of the jobs we do at school. "Do your best," I tell them, "don't be worried." Time and again I go to a child's desk, listen to a question, and help the child consider the choices.

Dean finally arrives at 9:45 A.M., in the middle of the first test. I have him work quietly on some math puzzles that he enjoys rather than start a test section late and in confusion. He looks very tired.

Robin is smarter than the test. She asks all the logical questions for which there are no answers: Do they have this? Can they do that? Wouldn't this be true if . . .?

I tell her, "Yes, Robin, you are right to ask all those questions, but all we know is what they tell us here. What do you think?"

She marks an answer, and I agree. "That's what I would choose too. Good thinking." I walk away realizing that the test probably does not measure the real extent of Robin's higher-order thinking skills.

In theory we give young children standardized tests so we can use the results to improve teaching methods. But most teachers will admit the tests do more to disrupt learning than to benefit teaching.

Tuesday

9 A.M. Today Dean is on time. Terri is here. Robin is sick. We begin again. We've completed only one quarter of the test; the children have a long way to go. Today, because my class is so large, a Title I teacher is assisting me. Together we follow the drill: hand out the correct booklet, turn to the correct page, find the correct starting place, review how to blacken the ovals, and remind children of the test-taking pointers we covered yesterday. "If you're not sure," we tell them, "make your best guess. And when you're done, close your test book and read or write in your journal."

Five minutes after the test starts, Terri is finished, I go to her desk and ask if she tried to answer all the questions. "Yes," she said. "They were easy." "Just let me check to make sure you turned all the pages." Sure enough, she has filled in an oval for each question. At age seven she has learned that the smartest person is the first one done. If you don't know the answer, she reasons, why struggle? Just play the game. It's a logical approach, but this time her analysis has missed the mark, and her test score will fail to register her survival skills.

It's 9:45 A.M. Dean has wiggled for 20 minutes, sharpened his pencil, moved his desk, asked to go to the bathroom, lost his lunch ticket, and finally slammed his test book shut. He sighs loudly, feigning relief and accomplishment. I suspect what he really feels is frustration and insecurity.

At 12:30 P.M., Robin arrives. She knows we do not give tests in the afternoon. When I talk to Robin's mother by telephone, she suggests the girl is overly worried. We both understand, but neither of us knows how to help Robin cope with her high demands on herself and what she perceives to be our expectations.

Wednesday

9:20 A.M. Everyone is here. The tests are becoming routine. The children check their books, check the page, laugh at my jokes about ovals, and ask what the treat is for today. We have almost relaxed. Today there is another math test. Terri and Dean hate math. Robin is quite capable but works slowly, checking everything.

As we teachers pass among the desks, children tug our sleeves. "Is this one right?" Their faces beg for confirmation. We break the test rules, asking the children questions to help them think: "Can you tell me why you chose that answer? Well, because . . ." they begin—and often their eyes brighten and they erase their mark and choose the correct answer. My colleague and I exchange understanding expressions and go on, commiserating about our dilemma.

Once again Terri finishes early. I see her working with the white glue from her desk. With a small dab of glue on each page, she has glued her entire test booklet shut. It is hard not to laugh, imagining how the testing service will deal with this. How will their test appraise Terri's ingenious, mischievous mind?

Dean, meanwhile, has lost all confidence today; he spends most of his time trying to edge closer to John, the best math mind in the class, to copy his answers. Several times I ignore Dean, but finally our eyes meet and I tell him that he is capable by himself. I'm not sure he believes me.

What I want to say is, "Dean, your development and confidence are important to me. You have years to learn this material. I want to help you learn, not frustrate you to the point of giving up. I want you always to be learning, not to be discouraged."

At 10:15 A.M. it's time for recess. A welcome burst of energy—and the real tests of a young child's life: Is there a swing left? Who will play with me? Will I hit the ball? Will anyone make fun of me?

After recess I wash Martha's skinned knee and apply a bandage. We begin the tests again. The sting of Martha's knee probably won't affect her test score; what will affect it are the 10 times she stops working to check the bandage.

And so the week continues. On Thursday two students are out with the flu. Robin has to make up the sections of the test she missed. Terri says she has a migraine. Dean arrives late and says he might move again. I buy more treats to celebrate our collective endurance. We have spent the majority of this week on paper-and-pencil assessment, a process that goes against every principle of child development and appropriate practice I learned in college and graduate school. It feels very difficult to be a practitioner on these days.

As we teachers pass among the desks, children tug our sleeves. "Is this one right?" Their faces beg for confirmation. We break the test rules, asking the children questions to help them think:" Can you tell me why you chose that answer?" "Well, because . . ." they begin—and often their eyes brighten and they erase their mark and choose the correct answer. My colleague and I exchange understanding expressions and go on, commiserating about our dilemma.

The Aftermath

In a few weeks the test results will come back, and part two of this insanity will begin. My job then is to enter each child's scores as they fall above and below the line that represents average performance for second-graders. I sit on the floor plotting numbers and ask, Average for whom? For a homeless child, for the child who had no sleep because his dad had an all-night party, for the child who has outguessed the questions, or for the child whose knee hurt? How valid are these scores in determining appropriate instructional techniques in my classroom when they ignore such factors?

Perhaps I can compensate in my own class, but the influence of the test scores reaches farther than I am able. Terri's score will be sent to her next school as a measure of her ability. Dean's score will result in a whipping because his dad thinks Dean didn't try hard enough. And no matter how high her score is, it won't be good enough for Robin, who has been anxious about it for weeks. My school colleagues are anxious too. This single week of tests will affect placement and funding for our school's federal programs for the next school year.

To many adults—even so-called school reformers—one week of ITBS tests (and other tests like them) is only a minor inconvenience that might yield benefits. But during that week thousands of young children throughout the country will pay a real price in lost learning time and fractured confidence, and many will pay a further price at home. Assessment implies that at some time decisions will be made and some action will follow. But rarely do we interpret the scores to the children; frequently, not even to parents. For many parents their child's score does not measure just one day, or even a week, of their child's work; it mirrors the family's success, the parents' affluence, and the child's future.

And how should they know otherwise? Test scores are usually sent home with no explanation other than a computer statement that goes something like this: "Your child [*Name*] was given the Iowa Tests of Basic Skills. Her composite score is the best indicator of her overall achievement. Her score shows that she scored better than 3 percent of the pupils in Iowa and that 97 percent scored as well as or better. Her overall achievement appears to be low for her grade. The scores of one pupil are often compared with other pupils' scores. Generally, your child's scores are low when described in this way."

All children operate at different developmental levels in different skill areas throughout the year. They should not be so narrowly compared to each other. They should be observed and encouraged in their growth, their initiative, and their desire to continue to learn. Instead, by attaching percentage scores to children on the basis of a test, we label some seven-year-olds as failures. Some parents recognize the trends in learning rather than the labels, but more often the damage is much more personal and serious.

In reality the failure is ours. As a society we are failing to protect our children from unnecessary stress and unrealistic expectations. Sadly, most parents don't understand how absurd the blanket judgments we derive from standardized testing are and the significant negative effects on their children. Most educators believe they have no choice in the decision to give an increasing number of standardized tests. The tests are institutionalized; the scores drive too many school initiatives and curriculum decisions to stop using the tests.

For many parents their child's score does not measure just one day, or even a week, of their child's work; it mirrors the family's success, the parents' affluence, and the child's future. And how should they know otherwise? Test scores are usually sent home with no explanation other than a computer statement.

And, in fact, we're using more tests now than we used to. As teacher educator Vito Perrone pointed out in *A Letter to Teachers* (1991), the average high-school graduate in 1990 had taken approximately 19 standardized tests in his or her school career; the average graduate in 1950 had taken only three such tests (p. 129). It is no wonder professional organizations such as the National Association for the Education of Young Children, the National Council of Teachers of Mathematics, the National School Boards Association, the National Association of Elementary School Principals, and other groups independently have called for a moratorium on group standardized testing of young children before age eight. Instead, they suggest better ways to evaluate and observe young children as they learn.

For example, teachers could design more authentic demonstrations of a child's performance, interest, and development by collecting samples of the child's work over time.

Assessment demonstrates children's overall strengths and progress, what children can do, not just their wrong answers or what they cannot do or know. (NAEYC & NAECS/SDE 1991, 23)

Compiled into learning folios, these collections document the child's growth. Items selected by both the child and the teacher would demonstrate the child's progress as compared to his potential, which could take into account the home environment and other early learning experiences, factors ignored by the standardized tests.

The young child should be viewed in terms of "widely held expectations" for an age range. These expectations are generalizations about children's development

and learning. These frames of reference, based on research, knowledge, observations, and common sense, show common patterns of development over time (Nebraska Department of Education 1993).

Howard Gardner (1993) has identified the intelligences that don't easily emerge in a standardized test score. The seven intelligences are

- logical mathematics—the intelligence of numbers and reasoning,

- interpersonal—the intelligence of social understanding,

- musical intelligence—the intelligence of melody and rhythm,

- spatial intelligence—the intelligence of pictures and images,

- linguistic intelligence—the intelligence of words,

- bodily-kinesthetic—the intelligence of physical skill, and

- intrapersonal intelligence—the intelligence of self-knowledge.

These multiple intelligences are clear reminders of how young children demonstrate their interests and their skills in specific areas that aren't allowed to blossom or be acknowledged on a single test or day. Acknowledging the inherent talents of each person and encouraging these early interests is valuable to later developing life skills. This broader assessment approach recognizes potential and the ability to express one's learning in a variety of ways.

This kind of broad-based thinking allows for alternatives to document the progress of a child's learning, such as

- three-way conferencing among the parent, the teacher, and the child;

- recorded observations, videotapes, learning logs, and journals to document the questions, interests, and patterns of a developing learner;

- goal setting for the young child that includes support and commitment from the family and teacher and that has meaning for the child;

- demonstrations by children in learning centers and a demonstration of what learnings have taken place in a center; and

- a class demonstration of the completion of a project for parents or other learning partners.

These processes actually focus on the child's ability in a multidimensional way, and they include a relationship or interaction that generates a personal reaction to the work.

> **Sadly, most parents don't understand how absurd the blanket judgments we derive from standardized testing are or how significant the negative effects of testing on their children can be.**

The current process of early mass testing using standardized tests endangers learning and discourages children, teachers, and parents. So early in children's development, the potential is often dimmed and the process becomes intrusive.

What Are We Really Measuring When We Test Young Children? And Are the Findings Worth the Potential Damage?

As practitioners, as policy and program developers, and as parents we can continue to seek better ways to communicate the process of learning.

For the correct analogy for the mind is not a vessel that needs filling, but wood that needs igniting—no more—and then it motivates one towards originality and instills the desire for truth.

—Plutarch
On Listening

References

Gardner, H. 1993. *Multiple intelligences: The theory for practice.* New York: Basic.

National Association for the Education of Young Children (NAEYC) & National Association of Early Childhood Specialists in State Departments of Education (NAECS/SDE). 1991. Position statement. Guidelines for appropriate curriculum content and assessment in programs serving children ages 3 through 8. *Young Children* 46 (3): 21–38.

Nebraska Department of Education. 1993. *The primary program: Growing and learning in the heartland.* Lincoln: State of Nebraska.

Perrone, V. 1991. *A letter to teachers.* San Francisco: Jossey-Bass.

For Further Reading

Bredekamp, S., & C. Copple, eds. 1997. *Developmentally appropriate practice in early childhood programs.* Rev. ed. Washington, DC: NAEYC.

Bredekamp, S., & L. Shepard. 1989. How best to protect children from inappropriate school expectations, practices, and policies. *Young Children* 44 (3): 14–24.

Bredekamp, S., & T. Rosegrant, eds. 1992. *Reaching potentials: Appropriate curriculum and assessment for young children, volume I.* Washington, DC: NAEYC.

Bredekamp, S., & T. Rosegrant, eds. 1992. *Reaching potentials: Transforming early childhood curriculum and assessment, volume 2.* Washington, DC: NAEYC.

Cohen, D.L. 1990. Elementary principals issue standards for early childhood program quality. *Education Week* 9 (40): 14.

Gronlund, G. 1998. Portfolios as an assessment tool: Is collection of work enough? *Young Children* 53 (3): 4–10.

Kamii, C. 1990. *Achievement testing in the early grades: The games people play.* Washington, DC: NAEYC.

Katz, L., & S. Chard. 1989. *Engaging children's minds: The project approach.* Norwood, NJ: Ablex.

Meisels, S.J. 1987. Uses and abuses of developmental screening and school readiness testing. *Young Children* 42 (2): 4–6.

Meisels, S.J. 1989. High-stakes testing in kindergarten. *Educational Leadership* 46 (7): 16–22.

NAEYC. 1997. *Code of ethical conduct and statement of commitment. Guidelines for responsible behavior in early childhood education.* Washington, DC: Author. Brochure.

NAEYC. 1997. Position statement. Developmentally appropriate practice in early childhood programs serving children from birth through age 8. In *Developmentally appropriate practice in early childhood programs,* rev. ed., eds. S. Bredekamp & C. Copple, 3–30. Washington, DC: Author.

NAEYC. 1988. *Testing of young children: Concerns and cautions.* Washington, DC: Author. Brochure.

Shepard, L.A. 1989. Why we need better assessments. *Educational Leadership* 46 (7): 4–9.

Willer, B., & S. Bredekamp. 1990. Redefining readiness: An essential requisite for educational reform. *Young Children* 45 (5): 22–24.

Form at end of book

Portfolios in the Classroom:
A Vehicle for Developing Reflective Thinking

Cheryl K. Kish, Janet K. Sheehan, Karen B. Cole, L. Ruth Struyk, and Diane Kinder

Northern Illinois University

Introduction

What is the aim of education? Is it to arm our students with the skills required of 21st century citizens? Is it, as requested by Rosen (1988), "[to] . . . give students a process—a method for reaching conclusions and solving problems, [to] . . . allow them to become familiar with their own minds and hearts, [to] . . . give them the courage to engage in confrontation, and let them come to their own conclusions with integrity, individuality, and imagination" (p. 77). In other words, using Rosen's thoughts, is the aim of education to teach students how to think? Such a thinking "consists in turning" a subject over in the mind and giving it serious and consecutive consideration" (Dewey, 1933, p. 3). This kind of thinking, this better way of thinking, is *reflective thinking* (Farra, 1988).

Reflective thinking leads to creativity and the potential of releasing the human spirit. It moves one away from the primary concern of product to a concern with process. It is a thinking that investigates connections between what is known, what is read, and what is felt. It will arouse and guide curiosity while connecting experiences to a succession of ideas. Reflection is a process whereby we can promote meaningful learning.

Reflection and Learning

If reflection cultivates meaningful learning, what is the goal of that learning? Dewey's (1933) work would suggest that such learning aims at conclusions, has an end action in view, and takes one back to the real world. It is a learning that makes an intuitive grasp for something not directly perceived or for a new combination of things coming into existence out of semantic space. Such learning facilitates the aims of education. Reflective thought can result in a tangible product that allows one to assess whether learning, important learning, has taken place, "preserving it where it already exists, and changing looser methods of thought into stricter ones whenever possible" (Dewey, 1933, p. 78).

Reflective thought is seen by Brandom (1994) as the fourth dimension, a fourth "*r*" of teaching; one that goes beyond the content knowledge of "*r*eading, *r*iting, and *r*ithematic." A fourth "*r*" that is required of today's teachers—an "*r*" that is currently finding its way into teacher education programs around the country. This

Questions

Vermont and Kentucky are the only two states that have mandated the use of portfolios for assessing all students, K–12. What are the advantages of requiring teachers to work with students on developing portfolios?

What are the disadvantages of this form of assessment?

Should the use of portfolios as an assessment tool be mandatory or voluntary?

Why or why not?

fourth "r" investigates and defines a teacher's values and/or philosophy in the face of everyday instructional decisions and dilemmas. This fourth "r" provides professional knowledge that comes from both outside the teacher and from the teacher's own interpretations of her everyday experiences.

This move towards encouraging reflective thinking is occurring in teacher preparation programs, and subsequently in the classrooms of its graduates. Such an infusion of teachers in our nation's schools is helping to create classrooms that move away from providing students with merely predicable sets of skills, knowledge, and attitudes. These new classrooms are promoting learning by helping students discover strategies for monitoring and assessing their own learning efforts. In other words, teachers are helping their students become reflective thinkers. And by developing reflective thought, teachers are manifesting many positive educational outcomes: (a) Reflection reduces the tendency to be impulsive and improves general problem-solving skills, (b) Reflective thinking helps individuals analyze and deliberate issues, (c) Reflection enhances communication of differing perspectives, (d) Reflection promotes self-awareness of our psychological selves by forcing one to ask basic questions about herself.

These positive outcomes support meaningful learning which is both reflective and self-regulated (Branstord & Vye, 1989; Marzano, Brandt, & Hughes, 1988; Wittrock, 1991). Learning which, according to Herman (1992), is "to know something . . . not just to have received information but to have interpreted it and related it to other knowledge one already has" (p. 75).

Writing As a Vehicle

The problem is always fundamentally the same: given these children to be changed and this change to be made, how shall I proceed? Given this material for education, and this aim of education, what means and methods shall I use?

E. L. Thorndike, 1906, p. 143

How one proceeds is determined by one's educational goals. If a goal is to develop, encourage, and enhance reflective thinking, then how does one create an environment that allows students to reconstruct the events, emotions, and accomplishments of an experience and then, with that knowledge, increase their control over variables that affect learning (Ross, 1990)?

To answer that question, one might consider the following criteria: What methods empower my students; tell me enough about their growth, achievement, interests, and needs; connect what I'm teaching to what they are learning; and, fit well with regular classroom activities? It

is suggested that writing is an appropriate vehicle for accomplishing this intellectual work, encouraging this reflective thinking. Further, it is suggested that portfolios offer the ideal site for the nurturing of this intellectual self-consciousness. For portfolios offer a dynamic method of assessment, one that allows students a way to work on and document their efforts through reflection.

Reflection: The Role of Portfolios

Portfolios as an assessment device invites the student to tell the story of her work and in so doing help her become more reflective of her own practices. It is through the individual voice, the voice of a student made known in the portfolio, that legitimizes classroom experience and weds teaching to relevant instructional inquiry. It is the portfolio that provides the richest portrayal of student performance based upon multiple sources of evidence collected over time in authentic settings. It is the portfolio which nurtures reflective thought.

When we use portfolios, we are promoting active learning: a kind of learning that makes each student the prime stakeholder in her education. How does this happen? It happens because a portfolio demands that each student both select and justify her contents. Such high standards contribute to an intellectual self-consciousness that results in the scholarly ownership of their learning.

Why are portfolios such a powerful tool in developing a student's ability to do this "type" of learning—not just to absorb information but to learn to use it, to put it to work? The portfolio requires, actually creates, situations in which students must think about their own thinking, allowing them to monitor their progress, and through self-evaluation helps them take charge of their learning and encourage ownership, pride, and self-esteem. Such a tool fosters "wide-awake, careful, and thoughtful habits of thinking" (Dewey, 1933, p. 78). These careful habits of thinking are important outcomes of portfolios (Camp & Levine, 1991).

Using writing to encourage reflective thinking is a very effective method. For the use of writing in the context of a portfolio promotes a self-consciousness about the problem or issue being explored. It is this self-consciousness, this self knowledge, this understanding that enables our students to move beyond memorization and repetition to actual thought processes that come into play when one can demonstrate what one supposedly has learned. It is the recursiveness, this looping upon itself, this beginning understanding of what is meant and where one is going that allows a "consecutive ordering [of thought] in such a way that each [thought] determines the next as its proper outcome, while each outcome in turn leans back on, or refers to, its predecessors" (Dewey, 1933, p. 4).

This recursiveness, this cognitive element of reflection, enables our students to make order out of incongruity and dissonance and is in sharp contrast to the linear procedures so often promoted in our nation's classrooms. Such self-monitoring reflection, allows for the reshaping and elaborating of goals and central ideas and then the powerful presentation of these goals and ideas in writing. Such an outcome clearly underscores that not only is reflection valued as an aid to writing, but writing is valued as an aid to reflection (Murray, 1978; Nystrand & Wiederspiel, 1977; Wason, 1980).

Essential Features of Portfolios

Although portfolios are flexible enough to accommodate much more than just written expression, a portfolio system is a natural complement for the writing classroom. This harmony occurs because a portfolio system can reward the critical elements of writing practice: writing in which the writer questions deeply and gets lost; discussion with peers and teacher; feedback from others; and extensive revision (Belanoff & Dickson, 1991). By examining the usage and benefits of the writing portfolio, critical features of portfolio systems can be identified that are relevant to broader applications of portfolios.

A portfolio can be defined then as a record of learning that focuses on the student's work and her/his reflection on that work (National Education Association, 1993). This emerging model of portfolios describes the following five critical features of the portfolio. The first tour of these, as described by Camp and Levine (1991) are: (a) multiple samples of writing are collected over a number of occasions, (b) there is variety in the kinds of writing or purposes for writing that are represented, (c) the process of writing is emphasized through editing, revising and rewriting and (d) there is evidence of reflection on individual pieces or on one's change as a writer across time (Camp & Levine, 1991). A further element of portfolios that results in many positive benefits is stressing student ownership of the portfolio (National Education Association, 1993). This causes students to feel empowered that their voice will be heard, and encourages the kind of active learning where students want to improve and share their writings in their portfolios (Mills-Courts & Amiran, 1991). Although all five of these elements are important features of portfolio assessment, the reflective element has been described as "the most important aspect of the portfolio process" (Camp & Levine, p. 203). Reflective writings allow the greatest opportunity for student growth, as well as provide important information to guide instruction (Camp & Levine). Similarly, other educators have recently cited the importance of reflection in the portfolio process (Anson, 1994; Arter, 1992; Buschman, 1993; Fairchild, 1993; Herbert, 1992; Mills-Courts & Amiran, 1991; Taylor, 1991).

Using portfolios in the classroom can help the kind of reflexive thinking that causes one to understand, analyze, and evaluate one's assumptions in order to act upon them (Mills-Courts & Amiran, 1991). In other words portfolios can aid in developing the critical thinking and problem-solving skills that are the foundation for good decision-making in all facets of our lives. Three aspects of reflection that can be enhanced through the use of portfolios in the classroom are explored here: the cognitive, the socio-emotional, and the moral elements of reflection.

Cognitive Element of Reflection

When students develop the ability to synthesize information gained from the analytic and evaluative processes to enhance their meaningful understanding of the subject, they are engaging in cognitive reflection. Research tells us that it is important to create opportunities for students to reflect about their thinking in order to determine why they learn or fail to learn (Flavell, 1979; Sternberg, 1984). Cognitive reflection is also a key factor in helping students develop self-regulated learning. As a learner progresses from being assisted by others to a self-assisted state, the learner needs to determine what skills they have acquired and what they have yet to acquire to progress in a specific context. As a first step in this diagnostic process, the learner needs to be able to reflect upon his/her progress in a meaningful way. Portfolios can serve as a scaffolding technique to help the learner make the transition from being dependent on others for direction in his/her writings to becoming an independent writer.

This development is exemplified in an elementary school portfolio program which can be adapted to the high school level. The teachers facilitated independent writing by asking guiding questions that caused the students to reflect upon their learning. Typical questions included "What do you know about numbers now that you didn't know in September?", "What would you like your mom or dad to understand about your portfolio?", or "What is unique about your portfolio?" (Herbert, 1992). This was done to help students reflect upon their learning, in order to heighten their awareness and commitment to a critical assessment of their learning.

A similar but more extensive method of scaffolding meaningful reflective practices through the use of portfolios was conducted in the Pittsburgh Arts PROPEL program. This program was conducted for high-school students in the areas of the visual arts, music, and imaginative writing. For approximately four months, teachers modeled the use of reflective questioning, allowed students to orally reflect upon each other's writing, and required short contemplative critiques on their individual pieces, before allowing students to reflect upon their body of work. With this structured guidance, the students were able to determine what processes and strategies they used in their writing and to evaluate their individual pieces and their change as a writer (Camp & Levine, 1991). In this way, the learners progressed to a self-assisted state in evaluating their portfolios.

Cognitive reflection was also evident in the portfolios of the New York City Writing Project. Junior-high students were required to include a letter explaining any changes the student saw in their reading, writing, and learning attitudes or strategies. A teacher stressed the importance of the reflective, self-assessment letters in the portfolio process when she said "They were significant for my students because they allowed them to reflect on their own growth and learning over the course of the school year" (Camp & Levine, 1991, p. 203). These two projects underscored the importance of student reflection in the learning process. The positive outcomes of student reflections from these projects were determining: what the student feels she has done well, what the student's interests, goals, and values in writing are, and what the student's strategies and processes for writing are, together with her understanding and awareness of them, (Camp & Levine). If learners can engage in each of these activities, then learning has been facilitated. The evaluative role of the learning process has been placed with the person most in touch with the learner's ability, achievement, and progress, the learner herself.

Socio-emotional Element of Reflection

The benefits of reflecting on one's work across time are not limited to cognitive growth. This reflection on one's own work, as it develops across time, can foster positive socio-emotional growth as well. The socio-emotional element of reflection allows examining socio-cultural influences and factors that influence personality development.

Part of the rationale for developing a classroom portfolio system is that it can foster high self-esteem (National Education Association, 1993). By re-examining attribution theory one can see how this would occur. According to attribution theory, one of the positive outcomes of attributing one's successes to her own ability and effort is the development of a positive self-concept (Weiner, 1984). The apparent benefit of witnessing one's progress over time then is to develop positive attributions of learning to oneself, which is later translated into higher self-esteem and positive socio-emotional growth. For instance, a teacher who implemented a portfolio system discovered that the confidence of her class grew as they saw their improvement over time. Even her most recalcitrant

writer began to write and share his writing, since the portfolio process documented his successes rather than his failures (Frazier & Paulson, 1992).

A developing sense of awareness of one's maturity as a writer, or as a person can also be fostered through the implementation of portfolio assessment. This was manifested in the New York City Writing Project by the writings of a student to his teacher in which he reflected upon his development in his writings and concluded "I feel I have changed in my writing because now I concentrate on real life more than the fantasy world. . . . I guess my mind is maturing. . . . I know that my mind and writing abilities will develop more and I will have an open mind about things" (Camp & Levine, 1991, p. 205). The reflection on his writings enabled him to connect the change in his writings with his maturation as a person and even to project how he expects to develop in the future.

Another aspect of socio-emotional growth can occur when portfolios allow teachers/learners to uncover sources of subconscious cultural learning. Murphy (1994) points out that much subconscious cultural-based learning takes place in the learning of language. For instance, the type of dialogue used in the home may subconsciously influence the person's writing style. If the student's work does not meet the teacher's expectations, then reflective questions about the writings can aid in reconciling this conflict by uncovering systematic patterns in the writing. Murphy suggests that students could be asked to compare and contrast different pieces of writing in their portfolios to trace rhetorical patterns in the writing. These reflective questions could then serve the function of helping students and teachers to be aware of the subconscious cultural learning that is occurring.

Moral Element of Reflection

Reflective practices can also be instrumental in cultivating the guiding questions of one's belief structure. This moral element of reflection facilitates the questioning of ethical assumptions that guide one's actions. Portfolio systems can he implemented to encourage moral reflection and the subsequent development of one's personal belief structure. Further, they can encourage the valuing of multiple interpersonal and social perspectives to obtain a richer and fuller vision of the world. As expressed by Mills-Courts and Amiran (1991), "If students are to integrate their learning experiences into a focused whole, we need to develop their ability to reflect upon their own thinking—not just as college students but as lifetime learners, as citizens of the world." It has been proposed that teaching can promote this kind of personal growth and reflection by having learners reflect on their current knowledge and alternative viewpoints to deepen that knowledge (Belenky,

Clinchy, Goldberger, & Tarule, 1986). We argue that portfolio implementation provides one medium whereby the element of moral reflection can be developed.

Self-reflection in the portfolio allows the student to develop a sense of how the writing connects with his/her past writings. From this, the writer can discern what patterns or themes have developed in her writing. Subsequently, the student can begin to acknowledge and question his/her view of the world. This can be critically important for young adolescents "who are attempting to make sense of the world and their place in it, to establish habits of mind" (Camp & Levine, 1991, p. 203).

Portfolios can also advance the ability to empathize with alternative perspectives. When portfolios include evaluations from the teacher or peers, as well as from oneself, the student is forced to acknowledge and reconcile these multiple perspectives. This advantage was evident for David, who shared his literacy portfolio with his classmates. Each reader made comments on the portfolio and these comments helped foster his developing sense of values. David had just come to this new school after being expelled from his previous school. Referring to the student comments of his portfolios David said "I thought nobody likes me, and nobody wanted to be with me. But after I put my portfolio together, I found people do like me and want me to be around them. They want me to do good . . ." (Hansen, 1992, p. 68).

Summary

Implementing portfolio assessment in a manner which encourages reflective thinking has many potential benefits. Portfolios can cultivate that better way of thinking that consists of ". . . turning a subject over in the mind and giving it serious and consecutive consideration" (Dewey, 1933, p. 3), reflective thinking. It is this reflective thinking that can nurture a positive growth process in all aspects of our lives. Portfolios can empower students to enhance their cognitive, socio-emotional, and moral development. This comes about not from the collection of works, but from the way in which the portfolio assessment process is implemented. Critical features of the implementation of the portfolios that endow the portfolio process with this power are the structuring of the portfolios to depict changes across time, the encouragement of student reflections, the opportunity for self-evaluations, and the emphasis on student ownership of the portfolios. Therefore, as portfolio systems are developed to serve many purposes, it is important to strive to retain these critical features.

One challenge will undoubtedly be developing ways to maintain the integrity of the concept of portfolios to promote individual growth, when the portfolio is serving school-, district-, or state-wide accountability needs. In

these instances, the primary goal will be on obtaining reliable and valid achievement data. This goal is very compatible with a standardization of the portfolio assessment process. Yet, will a standardized system in which students turn in required pieces of writing all done with the same number of rewrites retain the critical features of the portfolio to promote positive growth? This is the challenge in the future of portfolio assessment.

References

Anson, C. M. (1994). Portfolios for teachers: Writing our way to reflective practice. In L. Black, D. A. Daiker, J. Sommers, & G. Stygall (Eds.), *New directions in portfolio assessment* (pp. 185–200). Portsmouth, NH: Boynton-Cook.

Arter, J.A. (1992, April). *Portfolios in practice: What is a portfolio?* Paper presented at the annual meeting of the American Educational Research Association, San Francisco, CA.

Belanoff, P., & Dickson, M. (Eds.). (1991). Portfolios: Process and product. Portsmouth, NH: Boynton-Cook.

Belenky, M. F., Clinchy, B.M., Goldberger, N. R., & Tarule, J. M. (1986). *Women's ways of knowing: The development of self, voice, and mind.* New York: Basic Books.

Brandom, L. (1994). Straight to the heart: Using reflective writing to develop relational teachers. *Current Issues in Middle Level Education, 3*(2), 67–76.

Bransford, J. D., & Vye, N. (1989). A perspective on cognitive research and its implications in instruction. In L. B. Resnick & L. E. Klopfer (Eds.), *Toward the thinking curriculum: Current cognitive research* (pp. 117–140). Alexandria, VA: ASCD.

Buschman, L. (1993). Taking an integrated approach. *Learning, 21,* 22–25.

Camp, R., & Levine, D. (1991). Portfolios evolving: background and variations in sixth- through twelfth-grade classrooms. In P. Belanoff & M. Dickson (Eds.), *Portfolios: Process and product* (pp. 194–205). Portsmouth, NH: Boynton-Cook.

Dewey, J. (1933). *How we think: A restatement of the relation of reflective thinking to the education process.* Chicago, IL: D.C. Heath.

Fairchild, R. (1993, March–April). *Going beyond assessment: Turning portfolios into tools for student reflection.* Paper presented at the annual meeting of the Conference on College Composition and Communication, San Diego, CA.

Farra, H. (1988). The reflective thought process: John Dewey revisited. *Journal of Creative Behavior.* 1, 1–8.

Flavell, J. H. (1979). Metacognition and cognitive monitoring: A new area of cognitive-development inquiry. *American Psychologist, 34,* 905–911.

Frazier, D. M. & Paulson, F. L. (1992). How portfolios motivate reluctant writers. *Educational Leadership, 49,* 62–65.

Graham, S., & Harris, K. (1986). Components analysis of cognitive strategy instruction: Effects on learning disabled students' compositions and self-efficacy. *Journal of Educational Psychology, 81,* 353–361.

Hansen, J. (1992). Literacy portfolios: Helping students know themselves. *Educational Leadership, 49,* 66–68.

Herbert, E. A. (1992). Portfolios invite reflection—from students and staff. *Educational Leadership, 49,* 58–61.

Herman, J. (1992). What research tells us about good assessment. *Educational Leadership, 49*(8), 74–78.

Marzano, R., Brandt, R., & Hughes, D. I. (1988). *Dimensions of thinking: A framework for curriculum and instruction.* Alexandria, VA: ASCD.

Mills-Court, K, & Amiran, M. R. (1991). Metacognition and the use of portfolios. In P. Belanoff & M. Dickson (Eds.), *Portfolios: Process and product* (pp. 101–112). Portsmouth, NH: Boynton-Cook.

Murphy, S. (1994). Writing portfolios in K–12 schools: Implications for linguistically diverse students. In L. Black, D. A. Daiker, J. Sommers, & G. Stygall (Eds.), *New directions in portfolio assessment* (pp. 140–156). Portsmouth, NH: Boynton-Cook.

Murray, D. M. (1978). Internal revision: A process of discovery. In D. R. Cooper & L. Odell (Eds.), Research on composing: Points of departure (pp. 85–103). Urbana, IL:

National Council of Teachers of English. National Education Association. (1993). Student portfolios. Author.

Nystrand, M., & Wiederspiel, M. (1977). Case study of a personal journal: Notes toward an epistemology of writing. In M. Nystrand (Ed.), *Language as a way of knowing: A book of reading* (pp. 140–149). Toronto: The Ontario Institute for Studies in Education.

Rosen, J. (1988). Problem-solving and reflective thought: John Dewey, Linda Flower, Richard Young. *Journal of Teaching Writing, 6* (1), 69–78.

Ross, D. D. (1990). Programmatic structures for the preparation of reflective teachers. In R. T. Clift, W. R. Houston, & M. C. Pugach (Eds.), *Encouraging reflective practice in education* (pp. 97–118). New York: Teachers College Press.

Schon, D. (1987). *Educating a reflective practitioner.* San Francisco: Jossey-Bass Publishers.

Schunk, D., & Swartz, C. (1993). Goals and progress feedback: Effects on self-efficacy and writing achievement. *Contemporary Educational Psychology, 18,* 337–354.

Sternberg, R. (Ed.), (1984). *Mechanisms of cognitive development.* New York: Freeman.

Taylor P. (1991) *In the process: A visual arts portfolio assessment pilot project.* California Art Education Association, Carmichael, CA.

Thorndike, E. L. (1906). *The principles of Teaching.* New York: A.G. Seiler.

Wason, P. (1980). Specific thoughts on the writing process. In L. Gregg & E. Steinberg (Eds.), Cognitive processes in writing (pp. 129–137). Hillsdale, NJ: Erlbaum.

Weiner, B. (1984). Principles for a theory of student motivation and their application within an attributional framework. In R. Ames & C. Ames (Ed.), *Research on motivation in education* (Vol. 1). Orlando, FL: Academic Press.

Wilson, S. M., Shulman, L. S., & Richert, A. E. (1987). 150 different ways of knowing: Representations of knowledge in teaching. In J. Calderhead (Ed.), *Exploring teachers' thinking* (pp. 104–124). London: Cassell.

Wittrock, M. C. (1991). Testing and recent research in cognition. In M. C. Wittrock & E. L. Bakers (Eds.), *Testing and cognition.* Englewood Clifts, NJ: Prentice Hall.

Form at end of book

Semantics, Psychometrics, and Assessment Reform:
A Close Look at "Authentic" Assessments

James Terwilliger

School reform advocates have argued that "authentic" classroom assessments are complex performances or exhibitions that "are designed to be truly representative of performance in the field." The use of "authentic" implies that such assessments are superior to more conventional assessments. However, proponents of "authentic" assessment rarely present data, evidential or consequential, in support of the validity of "authentic" assessments. Further, as typically conceived, "authenticity" denigrates the importance of knowledge and basic skills as legitimate educational outcomes despite substantial evidence to the contrary. It is suggested that "authentic" be discontinued in future scholarly discussions of classroom assessment.

It is obvious to even the most casual reader of the literature on educational assessment that the field is currently undergoing a fundamental and profound transformation. The traditional concepts and methodologies associated with assessment are being questioned by a variety of critics including school reform advocates, subject matter experts, cognitive theorists, and others. In general, advocates for change recommend the assessments of achievement should be designed to reflect more precisely complex "real-life" performances and problems than is possible with short-answer and choice-response questions that characterize many teacher-made tests.

The purpose of this article is to raise question about the claims that are frequently made by advocates of assessment reform. My critique focuses on the work of Wiggins (1989a, 1989b, 1993), who first introduced the concept of "authentic" assessment and who is one of the most influential critics of traditional assessment approaches. However, it is clear that the notion of "authenticity" has widespread appeal. A computer search of the ERIC database reveals 96 journal articles or papers published since 1989 with the phrase "authentic assessment" in the title. Several journals have devoted special issues to the topic, e.g., *Educational Leadership* (December 1996/January 1997), *Journal of Secondary Gifted Education* (vol. 6, no. 1), and *Middle School Journal* (vol. 25, no. 2). Darling-Hammond and her colleagues at Teachers College have produced a book (Darling-Hammond, Ancess, & Falk, 1995) and numerous technical reports on the use of "authentic assessment" in the New York schools.

Questions

This reading examines the use of what is often called "authentic" assessment (for example, portfolio assessment) and calls such assessment into question. What are the main arguments against authentic assessment?

Is Terwilliger correct in stating that assessing students' learning of knowledge is not furthered by the use of authentic assessment?

Why or why not?

I wish to make it clear at the outset that I do not oppose some of the ideas that have been put forth by advocates of "authentic" assessment. In fact, I agree that assessment practices are in need of reform. However, I believe that, as is often the case, the rhetoric of the reformers is misleading and largely unsupported by data. (This point was made several years ago by Beck (1991) but seems to have been ignored.) I fear that there is a danger that perfectly useful and appropriate assessment methods will be discarded in a rush to adopt a variety of other techniques of unknown psychometric and educational quality. I believe that alternative assessment procedures should be adopted in combination with more traditional forms of assessment as evidence of the educational and psychometric value of such alternatives becomes available.

Word Magic and Assessment Reform

The *American Heritage Dictionary* gives the following definitions of "authentic":

1. a. Worthy of trust, reliance, or belief: *authentic records.*
b. Having an undisputed origin: genuine. 2. Law. Executed with due process of law: *an authentic deed.*

Synonyms are listed as "real," "genuine," and "authoritative." Obviously, terms like these have a decidedly positive connotation. Therefore, objects or products to which these terms are applied are likely to be viewed as more desirable or of better quality than objects or products that are not so described. That is why these terms appear so frequently in commercials and advertisements in the popular media, e.g., statements such as "Coke is the *real* thing!," "*Genuine* factory auto parts," and "*Authentic* French cuisine." A bakery chain in the Twin Cities has recently introduced Renaissance breads with the slogan, "Authentic handmade breads in the European tradition."

It seems that the word "authentic" has an almost mystical power. Phrases such as "authentic instruction," "authentic performance," and "authentic outcomes" are appearing with increasing frequency in the educational literature. (One can only speculate about forms of instruction, performance, and outcomes that might be labeled "inauthentic.") One of the more memorable titles in the Teachers College series is "An Authentic Journey: Teachers' Emergent Understandings About Authentic Assessment and Practice" (Einbender & Wood, 1995).

A variety of books with titles such as *Authentic Assessment in Action* (Darling-Hammond et al., 1995) and *Assessment of Authentic Performance in School Mathematics* (1992) have been published. Lesh and Lamon, the editors of the latter book, provide the following interesting definition:

Stated simply, authentic mathematical activities are those that involve: (i) real mathematics, (ii) realistic situations,

(iii) questions or issues that might actually occur in a real-life situation, and (iv) realistic tools and resources. (p. 18)

There are two problems with this definition. First, as previously noted, words like "real," "realistic," and "real-life" are synonymous with the word "authentic." Therefore, the definition is circular. Second, and more fundamental, what constitutes "realistic" or "real-life" situations and "realistic" tools and resources are frequently open to debate. What appears to be "realistic" to one individual often seems to be "unrealistic" to another. One way to "objectively" define "real-life" questions and situations would be to construct a database that could be employed in defining the likelihood that a student would encounter specific questions, problems, and the like in nonschool settings. Lacking such a database, test designers typically rely on individual (or, perhaps, team) judgments of what is "realistic."

Educational assessment is a complex process that is built on a variety of assumptions about the purposes of education along with a set of data-gathering procedures that need to be judged against a series of both practical and technical standards. The use of labels that impute special status to a specific set of data collection procedures only serves to obscure fundamental assessment questions that must be addressed. For example, questions concerning the validity of assessment techniques help to focus discussion on relevant data instead of arguments about "authenticity." Therefore, terms like "authentic," "genuine," and "real-life" should be reserved for advertising copy and avoided in scholarly discussions of educational assessment.

Origins of "Authentic" Tests

The term "authentic" was first introduced in reference to tests by Wiggins (1989b) in an article in *Educational Leadership,* a journal for school administrators and general educators. Wiggins defined "authentic" tests in terms of complex performances or exhibitions in which a student completes a report or makes a public presentation following an extended period of work on an out-of-class assignment. Wiggins presents the example shown in Figure 1.

Wiggins concludes his discussion of "authentic" tests as follows:

In sum, authentic tests have four basic characteristics in common. First, they are designed to be truly representative of performance in the field; only then are the problems of scoring reliability and logistics of testing considered. Second, far greater attention is paid to the teaching and learning of the *criteria* to be used in the assessment. Third, self-assessment plays a much greater role than in conventional testing. And fourth, the students are often expected to present their work and defend themselves publicly and orally to ensure that their apparent mastery is genuine. (p. 45)

An Oral History Project for Ninth-Graders

To the Student:

You must complete an oral history based on interviews and written sources and then present your findings orally in class. The choice of subject matter is up to you. Some examples of possible topics include: your family, running a small business, substance abuse, a labor union, teenage parents, and recent immigrants.

Create three workable hypotheses based on your preliminary investigations and four questions you will ask to test out each hypothesis.

Criteria for Evaluation of Oral History Project

To the Teacher:

Did student investigate three hypotheses?

Did student describe at least one change over time?

Did student demonstrate that he or she had done background research?

Were the four people selected for the interviews appropriate sources?

Did student prepare at least four questions in advance, related to each hypothesis?

Were those questions leading or biased?

Were follow-up questions asked where possible, based on answers?

Did student note important differences between "fact" and "opinion" in answers?

Did student use evidence to prove the ultimate best hypothesis?

Did student exhibit organization in writing and presentation to class?

Figure 1. An example of a test of performance. Courtesy of Albin Moser, Hope High School, Providence, RI. To obtain a thorough account of a performance-based history course, including the lessons used and pitfalls encountered, write to Dave Kobrin, Brown University, Education Department, Providence, RI 02912. (From Wiggins, 1989b, p. 44.)

It is instructive to examine the example Wiggins gives in light of the four characteristics he claims all "authentic" tests share. First, what "field" is represented in the oral history project? Because the choice of topic is left to the student, the "field" must be history with special emphasis on techniques employed by historians who employ "first-person" sources in their research. In fact, this approach is hardly "truly representative of performance in the field" if the "field" is more broadly defined as history because the great majority of historians rely on written rather than "first-person" sources in their work.

Second, it is not clear that the criteria for evaluation of the project were shared with the students. (In fact, the example strongly suggests that the criteria were for the teacher only.) Therefore, how could they have been "taught and learned"? Even if the criteria were shared with the students in advance, what exactly would a teacher expect them to learn from them? Most students would use the criteria as a checklist to make certain they had satisfied the teacher's demands before turning their projects in for evaluation by the teacher! Because many of these criteria are very specific to the particular project, they appear to have limited value as general learning outcomes.

As an aside, it is not clear from the criteria presented exactly how they are to be employed in evaluating the projects. Because most of the questions posed can readily be answered "yes" or "no," it would be possible to devise a simple checklist. Obviously, a more elaborate scoring system could also be designed, but the example provides no clues if that is the case. As is the case in all examples he gives in his writings, Wiggins provides no data regarding the reliability of scoring (or the amount of time devoted to scoring) the "authentic" tasks he recommends. The lack of supporting data is a reflection of the secondary role Wiggins gives to such issues in his reference to "scoring reliability and logistics of testing" in the above quote.

Third, there is no indication that self-assessment is involved in the oral history project.

Finally, it is clear that the oral history project does involve an oral presentation to the class. Presumably, the oral presentation may also be followed by a discussion during which the presenter would have to answer questions and defend his or her work.

"Authenticity" and Validity

Several issues are highlighted through the detailed comparison of the oral history example with the criteria for "authentic" tests given by Wiggins. The same example and criteria for "authenticity" were presented in a follow-up article (1989a) that appeared in the *Phi Delta Kappan*. First, it is not entirely clear what is meant by the phrase, "designed to be truly representative of performance in the field." What exactly is the "field" in this example? Who decides what is "truly representative" of the field? This raises questions regarding test *validity*. In his follow-up article, Wiggins's only reference to validity of "authentic" tests is the comment, "Far greater attention is paid throughout to the test's 'face' and 'ecological' validity" (1989a, p. 712). To focus on face validity is to concentrate only on the surface features of an assessment. To do so misses the point that the validity of an assessment device is fundamentally linked to how well the device reflects an underlying construct, e.g., analytical reasoning ability.

Messick (1994) has discussed at length issues associated with the validation of performance assessments. He cites the classic treatment of performance test by Fitzpatrick and Morrison (1971) in which they state, "there is no absolute distinction between performance tests and other classes of tests" (p. 238). Using this as a point of departure, Messick states

Hence, performance assessments must be evaluated by the same validity criteria, both evidential and consequential, as are other assessments. Indeed, such basic assessment issues as validity, reliability, comparability, and fairness need to be uniformly addressed for all assessments because they are not just measurement principles, they are *social values* that have meaning and force outside of measurement wherever evaluative judgments and decisions are made. (p. 13)

With regard to special claims of "authenticity," Messick notes

The portrayal of performance assessments as *authentic* and *direct* has all the earmarks of a validity claim but with little or no evidential grounding. That is, if authenticity is important to consider when evaluating the consequences of assessment for student achievement, it constitutes a tacit validity standard, as does the closely related concept of directness of assessment. We need to address what the labels authentic and direct might mean in validity terms. We also need to determine what kinds of evidence might legitimize both their use as validity standards and their nefarious implication that other forms of assessment are not only indirect, but inauthentic. (p. 14)

As previously noted, Wiggins presents *no* validity data, evidential or consequential, in any of his writings on "authentic" assessment.

Assessment and Educational Philosophy

A theme that runs through conceptions of "authentic" testing is an emphasis on performances that are designed to assess "higher order" outcomes. Wiggins (1989b, p. 45) lists several characteristics of "authentic" tests. Tests that are "authentic" should include tasks that are contextualized and complex, involve a student's own research, emphasize *depth* more than breadth, and involve somewhat "ill-structured" problems. He specifically disavows any interest in "atomized tasks," corresponding to "isolated outcomes," "mere recall," and "plug-in skills." Such pejorative terms make it clear that Wiggins has little respect for the assessment of knowledge or basic skills.

Wiggins (1993, pp. 222–225) gives examples of a variety of "roles and situations through which students can perform with knowledge." He argues that such roles could serve as "templates" for better test design because, "These roles and situational challenges are common to professional life" (p. 222). Wiggins claims it is a "logical fallacy" to argue that students must be given "drills" and "tests concerning their mastery of drills" before requiring performance in professional roles and situations. "Drill testing" is a means to an end, and "it is certainly not to be confused with the important performance itself" (p. 222).

Wiggins ignores the possibility that most "roles and situational challenges common to professional life" involve an extensive knowledge base. Individuals who lack the knowledge base have little or no chance of performing successfully in the "real-life" roles that he describes. For example, an historian typically specializes in a particular time period and geographical region for his or her research, e.g., Colonial America during the period 1650–1770. In order to make a useful contribution to the literature on this topic, the historian must first become familiar with a vast amount of work previously published by other historians working on this and related topics.

Knowledge and Expertise

The fundamental role played by knowledge in "real-life" is well documented in the extensive body of work on the nature of expertise. Chi, Glaser, and Farr (1988) have edited a series of papers that summarize much of the work in this field. In their overview of this work, Glaser and Chi list several "key characteristics" of the performance of experts. The first characteristic they cite is that expertise generally is restricted to specific domains of performance and does not transfer from one domain to another. They state

The obvious reason for the excellence of experts is that they have a good deal of domain knowledge. This is easily demonstrated; for example, in medical diagnosis, expert physicians have more differentiations of common diseases into disease variants (Johnson et al., 1981). Likewise, in examining taxi drivers' knowledge of routes, Chase (1983) found that expert drivers can generate a far greater number of secondary routes (i.e., lesser known streets) than novice drivers. (1988, p. xvii)

Knowledge and Literacy

Wiggins's emphasis on roles "common to professional life" reflects a very narrow view of educational outcomes. Hirsch (1987) is critical of attempts to dismiss knowledge in favor of more lofty educational goals. He argues that the denigration of "mere facts" by advocates of instruction in "higher order" skills creates a false dichotomy.

The polarization of educationists into facts-people versus skills-people has no basis in reason. Facts and skills are inseparable. There is no insurmountable reason why those who advocate the teaching of higher order skills and those who advocate the teaching of common traditional content should not join forces.

No philosophical or practical barrier prevents them from doing so, and all who consider mature literacy to be a paramount aim of education will wish them to do so. (1987, p. 133)

Proponents of educational reform who stress "critical thinking" and similar "higher order" thinking skills should consider Hirsch's advice seriously when planning classroom instruction and assessment.

Conclusions

The promotion of "authentic" assessment, however well intentioned, is flawed in several respects. First, "authentic" is misleading and confusing. The term inappropriately implies that some assessment approaches are superior to others because they employ tasks that are more "genuine" or "real." This claim is based largely on an appeal to face validity, a concept that has been abandoned by modern psychometric theorists. Second, it is a mistake to deny the role of knowledge in the assessment of educational outcomes. To do so ignores a substantial body of theory and ample empirical evidence that supports the central role of knowledge in many domains of performance.

References

Beck, M. D. (1991, April). *"Authentic assessment" for large-scale accountability purposes: Balancing the rhetoric.* Paper presented at annual meeting of American Educational Research Association, Chicago.

Chi, M., Glaser, R., & Farr, M. (Eds.). (1988). *The nature of expertise.* Hillsdale, NJ: Lawrence Erlbaum Associates.

Darling-Hammond, L., Ancess, J., & Falk, B. (1995). *Authentic assessment in action: Studies of schools and students at work.* New York: Teachers College Press.

Einbender, L., & Wood, D. (1995). *An authentic journey: Teachers' emergent understandings about authentic assessment and practice.* New York: Columbia University, Teachers College National Center for Restructuring Education, Schools, and Teaching.

Fitzpatrick, R., & Morrison, E. (1971). Performance and product evaluation. In R. L. Thorndike (Ed.), *Educational measurement* (2nd ed., pp. 237–270) New York: American Council on Education/Macmillan.

Hirsch, E. D. (1987). *Cultural literacy: What every American needs to know.* New York: Houghton-Mifflin Co.

Lesh, R., & Lamon, S. (Eds.). (1992). *Assessment of authentic performance in school mathematics.* Washington, DC: AAAS Press.

Messick, S. (1994). The interplay of evidence and consequences in the validation of performance assessment. *Education Researcher,* 23(2), 13–23.

Wiggins, G. (1989a). A true test: Toward more authentic and equitable assessment. *Phi Delta Kappan,* 20, 703–713.

Wiggins, G. (1989b). Teaching to the (authentic) test. *Educational Leadership,* 46, 41–47.

Wiggins, G. (1993). *Assessing student performance.* San Francisco: Jossey-Bass Publishers.

Form at end of book

WiseGuide Wrap-Up

Currently, a key topic for educators and policy makers at all levels is standards and assessment. There are multiple perspectives and no simple answers. Some believe that detailed standards should list the content knowledge that students must master and that students should be required to pass a statewide standardized test based on those standards. Others hold that education is a state or local district responsibility, that standards should be flexible to meet students' needs, and that assessment should reflect the criteria determined by the state or local jurisdiction. Explore the issues related to high-stakes testing currently underway in several states, including your own state. What are some standards and assessment issues now being discussed in your state? Nationally?

R.E.A.L. Sites

This list provides a print preview of typical **Coursewise** R.E.A.L. sites. (There are over 100 such sites at the **Courselinks™** site.) The danger in printing URLs is that web sites can change overnight. As we went to press, these sites were functional using the URLs provided. If you come across one that isn't, please let us know via email to: webmaster@coursewise.com. Use your Passport to access the most current list of R.E.A.L. sites at the **Courselinks** site.

Site name: Mid-Continent Regional Education Laboratory
URL: http://www.mcrel.org/
Why is it R.E.A.L.? McREL is, according to the journal *Educational Leadership*, in the forefront of work on content standards. This site provides links to lesson plans, curriculum resources, and activities for teachers. The links are easy to find and are organized by content area (for example, the arts, foreign languages, social sciences). The site also provides lists of resources for further information, including the names, addresses, phone numbers, and electronic addresses for the various content area organizations (for example, National Council of Teachers of English).
Key topic: content standards
Try this: Choose one of the McREL microsites. Provide a summary of the plan or program discussed at the site, and your opinions of its merit.

Site name: State Curriculum Frameworks and Contents Standards
URL: http://www.ed.gov/offices/OERI/statecur/
Why is it R.E.A.L.? Developed by the U.S. Department of Education, Office of Research and Improvement (OERI), this site lists the content standards in all of the states that have adopted content standards. It is updated as states adopt and/or revise content standards.
Key topics: content standards, states
Try this: Visit the OERI home page, and make note of resources that you find useful as a student, or those that you will find useful as a teacher.

Site name: U.S. Department of Education
URL: http://www.ed.gov/
Why is it R.E.A.L.? You can find the latest information on standards and assessment at this site, including the priorities of the administration and the Goals 2000 documents.
Key topics: standards, Goals 2000
Try this: Review the Education Headlines. Are there issues or developments that you were not aware of? Investigate articles of interest to you.

section 4 | Curricular Issues

Learning Objectives

By studying curricular issues, students will:

- Examine current developments and research findings related to brain-based research as it influences curriculum decisions.

- Examine current developments and research findings related to uses of multiple intelligences as it influences curriculum decisions.

- Suggest ways to incorporate these findings when developing a curriculum unit (topic) for a particular grade level or discipline content area.

In the past several years, two developments—new findings from brain research and the creation of the theory of multiple intelligences—have revolutionized curricular issues. These new findings have had a major impact on the way we view learning and intelligence.

New brain research reveals that the brain's capacity to reshape itself in response to experience—learning—is lifelong. Brain research indicates that learning creates new neural pathways. Just as establishing pathways in a wilderness area makes it easier for a traveller to get from one place to another, so it is easier for further learning to occur when neural pathways are being refined and added to rather than created in the first place. The challenge for educators today is to develop learning environments and instructional practices that enhance the brain's capacity to reshape itself.

In addition to discovering that intelligence is not fixed and unchanging, we as a society have also come to recognize that humans are intelligent in as many ways as are valued in one or more cultures. Teachers have come to see that "traditional" schooling put too much emphasis on some kinds of intelligence (for example, linguistic and logical) and too little emphasis on other kinds of intelligences (for example, musical, interpersonal).

Both of these areas—brain research and multiple intelligences—have had a major impact on the educational curriculum and on how that curriculum is taught. While brain research continues and the number of identified intelligences expands, our understanding of the practice of teaching must remain fluid. It is no longer accurate to believe that we know all of the curriculum to be taught and how to teach that curriculum. There is no end in sight for the expansion of knowledge and for the incorporation of that knowledge into effective teaching.

Brain-Based Learning Research

Questions

Reading 23. Based on what is currently known about how the brain works, what changes in school organization and structure would be most valuable in allowing students to "act on learning?"

Reading 24. Sousa suggests several actions that principals may take when reforming their schools to help students learn. From brain-based research, what are some actions teachers may decide to implement to promote student learning? Of these suggested teacher actions, which do you think are likely to be most effective and why?

How can brain-based research help teachers plan and implement the teaching of important content, concepts, and skills?

In recent years, researchers have focused on studying how students learn so that they can provide classroom teachers with specific suggestions for helping students to learn more effectively. In some instances, teachers have to modify their teaching styles and schools need to change their organizational structures and practices to accommodate research findings and suggestions. As researchers learn more about the teaching and learning processes, it is likely that students will become more effective learners and that teachers will become more effective teachers.

Cognitive Science and Its Implications for Education

Knowing the difference between a duet and trio requires far less mental power than judging which group has superior talent. Similarly, asking a 10-year-old to find the sum of two digits will cause him less mental strain than having him explain the purpose of addition. Whether recognizing a fact, carrying out a skill, or making complex judgments, our brains provide us with amazing powers.

Gary D. Kruse

Gary D. Kruse is assistant principal of Northwest High School in Grand Island, Nebr.

A much clearer understanding of the brain's functions and processes has been developed during the last several decades. This growing body of knowledge has far-reaching implications for educational methods and practices. The brain is the result of thousands of years of human evolution. Only recently, largely due to advanced technology, have we begun to unravel the mind's secrets at the molecular, cellular, and functional level.

The Architecture of the Brain

The basic working units of the brain are 100 billion specialized nerve cells (neurons), each capable of making up to 50,000 connections as meaning is detected. It is this ability to dis-criminate, register, store, and retrieve meaning that is the essence of all human learning. Neurons communicate or make connections through the use of chemical messengers called neuro-transmitters. The process takes the form of electrochemical impulses traveling from one neuron to another by crossing a minute gap called the synapse. This electrochemical "dance" between neurons using chemical messengers is believed to give rise to our power to derive or evoke meaning (Sylwester, 1995).

The earliest structure of the brain, the brain stem, appears to be an extension of our spinal chord. The brain stem contributes to our general alertness and serves as an early warning system to the rest of the brain regarding incoming sensory information. Hence, all learning initially begins at a sensory level of cognitive processing. Meaning and understanding are the result of further cognitive functions within the brain (Ornstein and Thompson, 1984).

Located atop the brain stem lies the limbic system. This system provides the chemicals that influence focus, attention, and concentration. The thalamus, located near the limbic system, is the "gateway valve" for the flow of all information into the brain. The hippocampus, a part of the system, serves as a way station for the temporary storage of information. Short-term memory may reside within this structure.

Questions

Based on what is currently known about how the brain works, what changes in school organization and structure would be most valuable in allowing students to "act on learning?"

The largest part of the brain is the cerebrum. It is divided into two hemispheres that are connected by the largest band of neurons found in the brain, the corpus callosum. Its role is to act as a communication "bridge" between hemispheres, which work in concert to make sense out of incoming information. Each hemisphere contributes various forms of thinking to derive meaning.

This lateralization of cognitive processing by hemisphere gives us the ability to think both divergently and convergently. It allows us to approach complexities in life from an intuitive as well as a logical manner. The hemispheres of the cerebrum process information from both a "parts-to-whole" and "whole-to-parts" perspective, allowing us to conceive a holistic as well as a detailed pattern of thought regarding an object, event, or relationship (Ornstein and Thompson, 1984).

Covering the cerebrum is the cortex, which houses two-thirds of all neurons in the brain. It is within this thin layer composed of billions of columns of neurons that genuine learning occurs (Suzuki, 1994).

The cortex is divided into lobes, each lobe carrying out a variety of functions. Researchers have found neurons of similar function grouped together within these lobes. At the rear of the brain lies the visual processing area; within this area are about 100,000 neurons whose purpose is to work to identify facial features such as the height of a hairline or exact distance between the eyes on a facial image (Ackerman, 1994). These "face cells" help us recognize a face as that of a friend or foe, brother or sister.

Temporal lobes contain a number of critical attributes for learning. An area in the left temporal lobe the size of a silver dollar is responsible for receiving all spoken words and forwarding these sounds for further processing to determine semantic meaning. This area discriminates between just 44 "sound bits" that comprise the entire English Language. An area of similar size in the right temporal lobe helps process spatial information for meaning. It is also in the temporal lobes that researchers have found evidence of permanent episodic memory (Ornstein and Thompson, 1984; Damasio and Damasio, 1992).

Frontal lobes of the cortex serve as our center for thought. It is here that such purposeful actions as planning or deciding occur. Neurons found throughout the cortex help to complete the construction of understanding. Alphabet letter symbols, for example, strung together in the temporal lobe to create words are forwarded onto associative fields in the parietal lobes to become sentences, paragraphs and, eventually, a story. These associative fields take in previously processed information and aid in developing conceptual understanding (Damasio and Damasio, 1992).

Some Notions Regarding Human Learning

Human learning is a direct result of the brain's associative properties and memory systems, the origins of which are currently being investigated by scientists. The ability, however, of one neuron to communicate with another places these associative mechanisms at the heart of all human learning. Though complex, we are moving closer toward the realization that a biological basis exists for learning. The implications of this fact for education are awesome (Kandel and Hawkins, 1992).

Researchers describe the brain as an extremely dynamic organ. It appears that it is rarely at rest and constantly searches for meaning. Moreover, the organ grows as meaning is attached and new synaptic connections are laid down. Hemispheres of the cerebrum provide their owner with a number of different perspectives when interpreting information for meaning. Besides helping to decipher the world outside us, the brain also appears to have the capability to go off on its own to evoke new ideas (Suzuki, 1994).

[The brain] is rarely at rest and constantly searches for meaning.

It is obvious this organ of learning is by no means the passive repository for skills and facts it was once thought to be. Current evidence would suggest the following regarding cognitive processing:

1. The brain is our learning organ.

2. The brain constantly searches for meaning.

3. The brain is a dynamic processor of information.

4. We can enhance or inhibit the operation of the brain.

5. Learning is a "sociocognitive act" tying social interaction, cognitive processing, and language together in an interactive manner.

6. Multi-sensory activities that embed skills and facts into natural experiences appear to enhance the brain's search for meaning.

7. A school day in which "connectiveness" exists between concepts taught enhances the brain's search for meaning.

8. The pace of instruction appears to influence the brain's search for meaning.

9. Information delivered within the student's context, tied to his or her prior understanding, and moving

from a concrete to abstract levels of processing appears to enhance the brain's search for the meaning.

10. To learn (beyond a perceptual level) requires the student to "act on the learning." To act means involvement.

A Most Immodest Proposal

Educational methods and practices have traditionally treated the brain as a passive repository. Knowledge has been transmitted by subject-area specialists inside a self-contained classroom setting. Current practices promote passive learning through a heavy reliance on students listening, reading, and practicing in isolation. The school day is composed of small increments of time (e.g., 50 to 90-minute periods) in which a subject specialist delivers discrete skills and memorizable facts period by period. In assembly-line fashion, students move from subject to subject, rarely encountering a conceptual tie or relationship (Gardner, 1991; Brooks and Brooks, 1993).

Both traditional instruction and student evaluation have become more a measure of the ability to recognize and recall than a genuine understanding of the concepts.

Both traditional instruction and student evaluation have become more a measure of the ability to recognize and recall than a genuine understanding of the concepts. Under the current scheme, curricula are viewed vertically (K–12). No consideration is given to what knowledge and concepts are being taught across the day, week, or semester. No ties or connections exist for the student to attach between subject areas.

This arrangement is built on the false notion that human learning is a linear progression within the mind, a notion that cognitive researchers dispute. They point out that knowledge is constructed by the brain through situational and experiential encounters influenced to a large degree by pace, context, connectiveness, prior understanding, and one's ability or freedom to act on the learning. The traditional vertical view of curriculum has resulted in a system of education driven by a textbook and taught at a rapid pace, causing many students difficulty in cognitively processing information (Brooks and Brooks, 1993).

Many characteristics of our schools disagree with the findings of cognitive research. The isolation as well as fragmentation of knowledge neither complements nor enhances the associative powers of the human mind. The current methods of transmitting knowledge may eliminate the "whole to parts" processing ability of the cerebrum, thereby eliminating the larger picture or understanding for the student. A heavy reliance on the spoken or printed word effectively shuts down other sensory input available to the brain in its search for meaning. At times the message sent to youngsters today is that one's ability to recognize and recall (remember) is of far more value than understanding or applying a concept to life.

Finally, the practice of delivering information out of context, then assuming the student will be able to transfer it to changing life situations, may be totally unrealistic. Information taught out of context is neither meaningful nor relevant to most young people, causing them serious problems in attempting to process it. This common form of instruction could be the major reason we find such inordinate amounts of rote practice occurring in the current school setting.

To move schools toward a greater sensitivity in cognitive processing, we should adopt new views of time, curriculum, learning, and the role of teachers. This will require major shifts on the part of the educational community (Hart, 1983; Kruse and Kruse, 1995).

Our view of time needs to change dramatically. The Carnegie unit equates "seat time" with learning by awarding students credit for successfully completing coursework. For most of the 20th century we have been locked into a view that the school day should be composed of standard increments of time. Common sense, as well as research, should tell us otherwise. Genuine learning occurs at different rates and to different degrees for each student. The best judges of "how fast" or "how much" are the student and the teacher.

The traditional role of teachers must also change. Teachers should be trained and organized into teams composed of various grade levels or content specialties. The need to create a coherent school day in which the student's mind encounters conceptual ties and connections throughout, necessitates dialogue on a daily basis between subject area specialists. Integration can be two teachers doing something together—however, integration can be a much fuller and richer act, involving an entire team of specialists making conceptual connections as they appear in real life. This type of organization requires a complete change from the traditional "department," which is a working unit originally designed to search for truth, not teach youngsters (Kruse, 1994).

Curriculum should be viewed across the school day. Constant dialogue between team members should occur to make the curriculum coherent. Activities designed by the team embedding essential facts and skills into natural experiences will be a major team responsibility. Finally, the future school day should place utmost value on developing student understanding through honoring student questions, allowing students to work cooperatively, and encouraging student interaction in order to initiate a full array of cognitive functions (Kruse and Zulkoski, 1997).

Conclusion

Understanding the ability of the mind to attach novel information to already stored understandings has major implications for current instructional practices, setting, and the manner in which we organize teachers. A greater coherency is needed within the school day to tap into the associative powers of the mind. To accomplish this a new view of time, curriculum, learning, and teacher role will be necessary. Greater authenticity toward knowledge and its delivery is essential to provide relevance and meaning.

> **Understanding the ability of the mind to attach novel information to already stored understandings has major implications for current instructional practices . . .**

To achieve this a much higher degree of collegiality by teachers will be called for in the future, implying a completely different product than has been stamped out over the past century by training institutions. Perhaps the most critical factor being suggested by cognitive research is that of the brain's potential to learn. It appears, barring major insults, this organ's potential to learn is limitless if educational practices and methods "complement, not complicate" its search for meaning.

References

Ackerman, S. J. "Face Facts, How Does the Circuitry of Our Brain Allow Us To Recognize Faces?" *Brainwork—The Neuroscience Newsletter,* November/December 1994.

Arwood, E. *Pragmatism, Theory and Application.* London: Aspen, 1983.

Brooks, J. G., and Brooks, M. G. *In Search of Understanding. The Case for Constructivist Classrooms.* Alexandria, Va.: ASCD, 1993.

Caine, R. N., and Caine, G. C. *Making Connections: Teaching and the Human Brain.* Menlo Park, Calif.: Addison Wesley Longman, 1994.

Damasio, A. R., and Damasio, H. "Brain and Language." *Scientific American,* September 1992.

Gardner, H. *The Unschooled Mind: How Children Think and How Schools Should Teach.* New York: Basic Books, 1991.

Goldman-Rakic, P. S. "Working Memory and the Mind." *Scientific American,* September 1992.

Hart, L. *Human Brain and Human Learning.* New York: Longman, 1983.

Kandel, E. R., and Hawkins, R. D. "The Biological Basis of Learning and Individuality." *Scientific American,* September 1992.

Kotulak, R. "Unraveling the Mysteries of the Brain." (A series of articles) *Chicago Tribune,* April 1993.

Kruse, C. A., and Kruse, G. D. "The Master Schedule: Improving the Quality of Education." *NASSP Bulletin,* May 1995.

Kruse, G. D. "Thinking, Learning, and Public Schools: Preparing for Life." *NASSP Bulletin,* September 1994.

Kruse, G. D., and Zulkoski, M. "The Northwest Experience: A Lesser Road Traveled." *NASSP Bulletin,* December 1997.

LeDoux, J. "Emotion, Memory, and the Brain." *Scientific American,* 1994.

Orastein, R., and Thompson, R. F. *The Amazing Brain.* Boston, Mass.: Houghton-Mifflin, 1984.

Suzuki, J. *The Brain.* (A five-part television series) Discovery Channel, 1994.

Sylwester, R. *A Celebration of Neurons: An Educators Guide to the Human Brain.* Alexandria, Va.: ASCD, 1995.

Form at end of book

Brain Research Can Help Principals Reform Secondary Schools

There is no panacea that will make teaching and learning a perfect process —and that includes brain research. It is a long leap from a research finding to changing schools and practice because of that finding. We need to seek out and evaluate the research that seems to be sufficiently reliable to enhance our practice.

David A. Sousa

David A. Sousa is an educational consultant and former superintendent of the New Providence (N.J.) Public Schools. He is author of NASSP's How the Brain Learns. *Readers may continue the dialogue on the Internet at DavidSNJ@aol.com.*

In the past few years, more educators have become interested in brain research and its potential applications to educational practice. Signs of this increased awareness are everywhere. Staff development programs are devoting more time to this area; more books about the brain are available; brain-compatible teaching units are sprouting up; and the journals of most major educational organizations have devoted special issues to the topic.

Educators now recognize that there is a rapidly growing research base in cognitive science. Sophisticated medical instruments, such as functional MRIs and PET scans, produce new three-dimensional maps of the human brain in action. These maps reveal which parts of the brain are involved in performing various activities, including learning. The growing volume of case studies of individuals recovering from brain injuries and disease gives us amazing new insights into how the brain develops, ages, learns, and remembers.

We are now in the midst of an unprecedented revolution of knowledge about the human brain, including how it collects, processes, and interprets information. Never before have we known more about human learning. Never before have we had the potential for being so successful with more students. That's the good news. The bad news is that this valuable information is not getting to the educational practitioner fast enough.

We are now in the midst of an unprecedented revolution of knowledge about the human brain, including how it collects, processes, and interprets information.

As neuroscience reveals more about the brain, we now need to reconsider our practice. Teachers enter classrooms every day trying to teach the students of the 1990s with a knowledge base about learning that has not changed since the 1960s. Principals, in their roles as instructional leaders, must decide how this research can help reform the instructional component of secondary schools.

What Makes Today's Students Different?

We often hear teachers remark that students are much different today in the way they learn. They seem to have a shorter attention span and bore easily. Why is that? I believe there are changes occurring in the environment of learners that alter the ways they approach the learning process.

First, the rapidly changing multimedia-based culture and the stresses that result from the ever-increasing pace of living are changing what the developing brain learns from the world. Children have become accustomed to these rapid sensory and emotional changes, and respond by engaging in all types of activities of short duration at home and at the mall. By acclimating itself to these changes, the brain responds more readily to the unique and different.

Second, school is but one of many factors influencing today's youth. They are wrestling with the need to be different while under pressure to conform. They must develop and deal with relationships, identify peer groups, and respond to religious influences. Add to this mix the changes in family patterns and lifestyles, as well as the effects of diet, drugs, and sleep deprivation, and we can realize how very different the environment of today's young person is from that of just 15 years ago.

Schools and teaching, however, have changed very little. No doubt secondary principals will point to technology as a major leap forward. But frankly, the aging computers in many schools provide little if any of the options that students can get with the more powerful computers many of them have access to at home.

In too many high school classrooms, lecturing continues to be the main method of instruction as teachers struggle to cover the overcrowded curriculum. The overhead projector is often the most advanced technology available. Students comment that school is a dull, nonengaging environment that is much less interesting than what is available outside school. They have a difficult time focusing for extended periods, are easily distracted, and see little novelty and relevancy in what they are learning.

Rather than decrying the changing brain and culture, principals need to adjust schools to accommodate these changes. Now that we have a more scientifically based understanding about today's "novel" brain and how it learns, we must rethink what we do in classrooms and schools.

Rather than decrying the changing brain and culture, principals need to adjust schools to accommodate these changes.

Here are some of the emerging topics from the research that relate to the teaching/learning process and some suggestions that secondary principals should view as opportunities to reform instruction.

Understanding Emotions in Learning

How a person "feels" about a learning situation determines the amount of attention he or she devotes to it. Emotions interact with reason to support or inhibit learning. Students need to feel an emotional connection to their work, their peers, and their teachers. For an increasing number of students, school is a place where making emotional connections is more important than anything else.

How a person "feels" about a learning situation determines the amount of attention he or she devotes to it.

To be successful learners and productive citizens, students need to know how to use their emotions intelligently. Most teacher-training classes have told prospective secondary teachers to focus on reason and to avoid emotions in their lessons. Yet, students must feel physically safe and emotionally secure in their schools and classrooms *before* they can process the enormous amount of information we give them.

What Principals Can Do

- Keep your school free of weapons and violence.

- Make sure your teachers are knowledgeable about how emotions consistently affect attention and learning.

- Work with teachers to promote emotional security in the classroom by establishing a positive climate that encourages students to take risks. Students must sense that the teacher wants to help them be right rather than catch them being wrong.

- Discuss with your staff ways to teach students about their emotions. Look for opportunities to teach about such topics as controlling impulses, delaying gratification, expressing feelings, managing relationships, and reducing stress. Students should recognize they can manage their emotions for greater productivity, and can develop emotional skills for greater success in life.

- Establish an emotional climate that makes your school a place where people want to come to work. Remember that teachers have emotions, too. Be sure to reward appropriate risk taking.

Sensory Engagement during Learning

The cognitive research reaffirms strongly that we learn best when we are actively involved in interesting and challenging situations, and when we "talk" about the learning. Talking activates the brain's frontal lobe, which is necessary for understanding, meaning, and memory. Yet, in too many secondary schools students sit quietly and passively for long stretches in rooms with little visual stimulation, primarily listening to teachers talk.

What Principals Can Do

- Provide the technology and materials needed to make schools engaging and interesting places. Teachers need to use a multi-sensory approach consistently so that students are actively involved in their learning.

- Encourage teachers to make classrooms visually appealing places where learners are teachers, and teachers are learners.

- Remind teachers that whoever explains, learns. At appropriate intervals, students should be standing up, moving about (there's 15 percent more blood in the brain when we stand), and discussing with each other what they are learning while they are learning it. This social interaction is also emotionally stimulating and enhances the learning process. Be sure to make clear that you support this type of activity and recognize its contribution to learning.

Adolescents' Biological Rhythms and Sleep

Our daily biological rhythms vary with age. Studies at the Brown University Sleep Research Laboratory and the Minnesota Regional Sleep Disorder Center show that the rhythms responsible for overall intellectual performance start about an hour later in the day for an adolescent than for an adult. Because of this shift in rhythms, teenagers are sleepier in the morning and tend to stay up later at night. They also tend to perform better in problem solving and memory tasks later in the day rather than earlier.

Student sleepiness earlier in the day limits their motivation to learn and affects their academic performance, In contrast, these students go to after-school jobs at a time when they are more alert and more productive. Thus, the circadian shifts may lead students to disaffection with school and a preference for their after-school jobs.

Adequate sleep is also vital to the memory storage process, especially for young learners. The encoding of information into the long-term memory sites occurs during sleep, more specifically, during the rapid-eye movement (REM) stage. This is a slow process and can flow more easily when the brain is not preoccupied with external stimuli.

Most teenagers need about nine hours of sleep each night but many are not getting nearly that amount. There are several factors responsible for eroding sleep time. In the morning, high schools start earlier, teens spend more time grooming, and some travel long distances to school. At the end of the day, there are athletic and social events, part-time jobs, and homework. Add to this the shift in their body clocks that tends to keep them up later, and the average sleep time is more like five to six hours.

This sleep deprivation not only disturbs the memory storage process but can lead to other problems as well. Students nod off in class and become irritable. Worse, their decreased alertness due to fatigue can lead to accidents both in and out of school.

> . . . teenagers are sleepier in the morning and tend to stay up later at night. They also tend to perform better in problem solving and memory tasks later in the day. . . .

What Principals Can Do

- Look at what and when in the school day you ask students to perform certain tasks, such as taking standardized tests.

- Consider realigning opening times and course schedules more closely with the students' biological rhythms to increase the chances of successful learning. Some Minnesota school districts are now experimenting with later starting times for their high schools. No doubt this requires communities to make some difficult adjustments. The districts that have switched to later high school start times, however, report a more relaxed atmosphere in which students are attentive and interested in learning.

- Remind students of the importance of sleep to their mental and physical health, and encourage them to reexamine their daily activities to provide for adequate sleep.

Reformatting the Learning Period for Maximum Retention

Principals and teachers need to consider reformatting the lesson period so it addresses the expectations of the novel brain. For example, humor is an excellent way to get focus. The normal brain responds to laughter by releasing endorphins, the body's natural "feel-good" chemicals.

Timing in the lesson is crucial. Teachers need to know about the primacy-recency effect—the phenomenon whereby people tend to remember best that which comes first in a learning segment, and remember second best that which comes last. And the percentage of remembering time increases as the learning episode shortens, and decreases as the lesson time lengthens.

Since attention span for most secondary students runs about 20 minutes, they are likely to retain more if the 40-minute period is taught in two 20-minute segments, with a short break in between. Teach the new material first when students are more apt to remember it, and do a closure activity last. In block scheduling, an 80-minute period can be a blessing or a disaster, depending on how the time is used. A block containing four 20-minute segments will be much more productive than one continuous lesson.

Retention is also likely to be greater if teachers work harder at helping students find meaning (relevancy) in the learning. Too often students ask, "Why do I need to know this?"—a sure sign that meaning has been lost. Teachers should be certain to include some statement or activity aimed at making the learning relevant to today's students.

Journal writing can be a very effective strategy to enhance meaning and increase retention. It can be done in nearly all grade levels and subject areas, and is particularly effective when done as a closure activity. Students keep a different journal for each class or subject area. At the end of the lesson, they write down what they learned, how the learning relates to what they already know, and how they can use this information or skill in the future.

Teachers may be reluctant to use this technique because they believe it takes up too much class time while adding more papers for them to evaluate. However, this strategy takes just three to five minutes, two or three times a week. The teacher only spot-checks journals periodically. The substantial gain in student understanding and retention will be well worth the small amount of time invested.

What Principals Can Do

- Explain the difference between humor and sarcasm. Research findings confirm that a person's emotional state greatly influences what they recall during a learning episode. Humor, on the other hand, often recalls positive experiences, like acceptance or success. Conversely, teacher's sarcasm causes students to recall unpleasant experiences, like rejection or failure.

- Ensure the staff thoroughly understands the primacy-recency effect so they can use it effectively in their classrooms.

- Use departmental meetings for reviewing curriculum guides to ensure they include activities to promote relevancy.

- Encourage journal writing across all curriculum areas and grade levels. Suggest that teachers keep journals of their changing practices. Keep your own journal to monitor school and staff progress.

Keeping Rote Learning to a Minimum

Although the number of neurons in our brain declines as we age, our ability to learn, remember, and recall depends largely on the number of connections between neurons. The stability and permanence of these connections depend on the nature of the thinking process, and the type and degree of rehearsal that occurred during the learning episode.

Brain scans show that using higher order thinking skills engages the brain's frontal lobe. This engagement helps learners make connections between past and new learning, creates new pathways, strengthens existing pathways, and increases the likelihood that the new learning will be consolidated and stored for future retrieval. Rote learning, of course, can also lead to permanent storage, but students soon realize they can use rote learning to carry information just long enough to take a test and then discard it.

Many teachers recognize the need to do more activities that require elaborate thinking rather than just rote learning. They admit that students demonstrate a much greater depth of understanding when they use higher levels of thinking. They also admit, however, that there are barriers to using this approach regularly because it takes more time. Examples of the barriers they cite are the pressures to cover an ever-expanding curriculum and the tyranny of quick-answer testing of all types.

Brain scans show that using higher order thinking skills engages the brain's frontal lobe.

What Principals Can Do

- Reassess your school's curriculum and testing procedures. These barriers will not be overcome easily, but you can work with your teachers to reach a compromise.

- Encourage teachers to engage the novel brain with challenging activities that require elaborate thinking.

- Facilitate the development of alternative assessment strategies.

Maintaining Ongoing Staff Development

Science is revealing new research findings about the human brain nearly every week. Some of these findings bear directly on the teaching/learning process, and it is up to educators to determine their usefulness. We have to learn much more about these scientific endeavors. We should read the appropriate research and engage in conversations among ourselves and with the scientific community. When we understand the science involved, we are more likely to devise strategies and techniques that translate this new research into effective classroom practice.

What Principals Can Do

- Provide frequent opportunities for teachers to discuss how their classroom practices relate to the research.

- Invite scientists in your community along with your school's science teachers to educate the rest of the staff on the structure and functions of the human brain.

- Develop and maintain an ongoing staff development program that will help teachers update their knowledge base.

There is, of course, no panacea that will make teaching and learning a perfect process—and that includes brain research. It is a long leap from a research finding to changing schools and practice because of that finding. We need to seek out and evaluate the research that seems to be sufficiently reliable to enhance our practice. These are exciting times for our profession, and principals can play a leading role in bringing this excitement to their staff and schools.

Useful Resources

Caine, Renate, and Caine, Geoffrey. *Making Connections: Teaching and the Human Brain*. Alexandria, Va.: Association for Supervision and Curriculum Development, 1991.

Goleman, Daniel. *Emotional Intelligence*. New York: Bantam Books, 1995.

"How a Child's Brain Develops." *Time*, February 3, 1997.

Hyerle, David. *Visual Tools for Constructing Knowledge*. Alexandria, Va.: Association for Supervision and Curriculum Development, 1996.

Jensen, Eric. *The Learning Brain*. Del Mar, Calif.: Turning Point Publishing, 1995.

Sousa, David. *How the Brain Learns*. Reston, Va.: National Association of Secondary School Principals, 1995.

Sylwester, Robert. *A Celebration of Neurons: An Educator's Guide to the Human Brain*. Alexandria, Va: Association for Supervision and Curriculum Development, 1995.

Form at end of book

Multiple Intelligences

As teachers make curricular and instructional decisions, to what extent should they consider students' development of their individual multiple intelligences in selecting active learning activities?

The traditional view of intelligence, which has long governed curriculum delivery, has been challenged recently as being too narrow and as excluding a number of students who do not do well on traditional measures of intelligence. The theory that has been most successful in supplanting the traditional view of intelligence is that of multiple intelligences, proposed by Howard Gardner approximately fifteen years ago. Recent brain research tends to bolster Gardner's theory: The elements that constitute intelligence are complex and are not limited to a single entity. For example, brain research has confirmed that our musical, language, and kinesthetic abilities work somewhat independently.

One of the many valuable contributions of multiple intelligences theory is that intelligence is now viewed as being in the plural. As a result, students who are smart in unconventional ways can be valued for the ways in which they are intelligent.

Another valuable contribution of multiple intelligences theory is that teachers increasingly realize that there are many ways to teach any concept and that many different ways should be used to promote student learning.

The First Seven . . . and the Eighth:
A Conversation with Howard Gardner

Human intelligence continues to intrigue psychologists, neurologists, and educators. What is it? Can we measure it? How do we nurture it?

Kathy Checkley

Howard Gardner *is Professor of Education at Harvard Graduate School of Education and author of, among other books,* The Unschooled Mind: How Children Think and How Schools Should Teach *(1991). He can be reached at Roy B. Larsen Hall, 2nd Floor, Appian Way, Harvard Graduate School of Education, Cambridge, MA 02138.* **Kathy Checkley** *is a staff writer for* Update *and has assisted in the development of ASCD's new CD-ROM,* Exploring Our Multiple Intelligences, *and pilot online project on multiple intelligences.*

Howard Gardner's theory of multiple intelligences, described in Frames of Mind *(1985), sparked a revolution of sorts in classrooms around the world, a mutiny against the notion that human beings have a single, fixed intelligence. The fervor with which educators embraced his premise that we have multiple intelligences surprised Gardner himself. "It obviously spoke to some sense that people had that kids weren't all the same and that the tests we had only skimmed the surface about the differences among kids," Gardner said.*

Here Gardner brings us up-to-date on his current thinking on intelligence, how children learn, and how they should be taught.

How do you define intelligence?

Intelligence refers to the human ability to solve problems or to make something that is valued in one or more cultures. As long as we can find a culture that values an ability to solve a problem or create a product in a particular way, then I would strongly consider whether that ability should be considered an intelligence.

First, though, that ability must meet other criteria: Is there a particular representation in the brain for the ability? Are there populations that are especially good or especially impaired in an intelligence? And, can an evolutionary history of the intelligence be seen in animals other than human beings?

I defined seven intelligences (see box, p. 177) in the early 1980s because those intelligences all fit the criteria. A decade later when I revisited the task, I found at least one more ability that clearly deserved to be called an intelligence.

That would be the naturalist intelligence. What led you to consider adding this to our collection of intelligences?

Somebody asked me to explain the achievements of the great biologists, the ones who had real mastery of taxonomy, who understood about different species, who could recognize patterns in nature and classify objects. I realized that to explain that kind of

Questions

Howard Gardner opines that multiple intelligences are not synonymous with learning styles. How are multiple intelligences and learning styles similar or different?

ability, I would have to manipulate the other intelligences in ways that weren't appropriate.

So I began to think about whether the capacity to classify nature might be a separate intelligence. The naturalist ability passed with flying colors. Here are a couple of reasons: First, it's an ability we need to survive as human beings. We need, for example, to know which animals to hunt and which to run away from. Second, this ability isn't restricted to human beings. Other animals need to have a naturalist intelligence to survive. Finally, the big selling point is that brain evidence supports the existence of the naturalist intelligence. There are certain parts of the brain particularly dedicated to the recognition and the naming of what are called "natural" things.

How do you describe the naturalist intelligence to those of us who aren't psychologists?

The naturalist intelligence refers to the ability to classify plants, minerals, and animals, including rocks and grass and all variety of flora and fauna. The ability to recognize cultural artifacts like cars or sneakers may also depend on the naturalist intelligence.

Now, everybody can do this to a certain extent—we can all recognize dogs, cats, trees. But, some people from an early age are extremely good at recognizing and classifying artifacts. For example, we all know kids who, at age 3 or 4, are better at recognizing dinosaurs than most adults.

Darwin is probably the most famous example of a naturalist because he saw so deeply into the nature of living things.

Are there any other abilities you're considering calling intelligences?

Well, there may be an existential intelligence that refers to the human inclination to ask very basic questions about existence. Who are we? Where do we come from? What's it all about? Why do we die? We might say that existential intelligence allows us to know the invisible, outside world. The only reason I haven't given a seal of approval to the existential intelligence is that I don't think we have good brain evidence yet on its existence in the nervous system—one of the criteria for an intelligence.

You have said that the theory of multiple intelligences may be best understood when we know what it critiques. What do you mean?

The standard view of intelligence is that intelligence is something you are born with; you have only a certain amount of it; you cannot do much about how much of that intelligence you have; and tests exist that can tell you how smart you are. The theory of multiple intelligences challenges that view. It asks, instead, "Given what we know about the brain, evolution, and the differences in cultures, what are the sets of human abilities we all share?"

My analysis suggested that rather than one or two intelligences, all human beings have several (eight) intelligences. What makes life interesting, however, is that we don't have the same strength in each intelligence area, and we don't have the same amalgam of intelligences. Just as we look different from one another and have different kinds of personalities, we also have different kinds of minds.

This premise has very serious educational implications. If we treat everybody as if they are the same, we're catering to one profile of intelligence, the language-logic profile. It's great if you have that profile, but it's not great for the vast majority of human beings who do not have that particular profile of intelligence.

Can you explain more fully how the theory of multiple intelligences challenges what has become known as IQ?

The theory challenges the entire notion of IQ. The IQ test was developed about a century ago as a way to determine who would have trouble in school. The test measures linguistic ability, logical-mathematical ability, and, occasionally, spatial ability.

What the intelligence test does not do is inform us about our other intelligences; it also doesn't look at other virtues like creativity or civic mindedness, or whether a person is moral or ethical.

We don't do much IQ testing anymore, but the shadow of IQ tests is still with us because the SAT—arguably the most potent examination in the world—is basically the same kind of disembodied language-logic instrument.

The truth is, I don't believe there is such a general thing as scholastic aptitude. Even so, I don't think that the SAT will fade until colleges indicate that they'd rather have students who know how to use their minds well—students who may or may not be good test takers, but who are serious, inquisitive, and know how to probe and problem-solve. That is really what college professors want. I believe.

Can we strengthen our intelligences? If so, how?

We can all get better at each of the intelligences, although some people will improve in an intelligence area more readily than others, either because biology gave them a better brain for that intelligence or because their culture gave them a better teacher.

School matters, but only insofar as it yields something that can be used once students leave school.

Teachers have to help students use their combination of intelligences to be successful in school, to help them learn whatever it is they want to learn, as well as what the teachers and society believe they have to learn.

Now, I'm not arguing that kids shouldn't learn the literacies. Of course they should learn the literacies. Nor am I arguing that kids shouldn't learn the disciplines. I'm a tremendous champion of the disciplines. What I argue against is the notion that there's only one way to learn how to read, only one way to learn how to compute, only one way to learn about biology. I think that such contentions are nonsense.

It's equally nonsensical to say that everything should be taught seven or eight ways. That's not the point of the MI theory. The point is to realize that any topic of importance, from any discipline, can be taught in more than one way. There are things people need to know, and educators have to be extraordinarily imaginative and persistent in helping students understand things better.

A popular activity among those who are first exploring multiple intelligences is to construct their own intellectual profile. It's thought that when teachers go through the process of creating such a profile, they're more likely to recognize and appreciate the intellectual strengths of their students. What is your view on this kind of activity?

My own studies have shown that people love to do this. Kids like to do it, adults like to do it. And, as an activity, I think it's perfectly harmless.

I get concerned, though, when people think that determining your intellectual profile—or that of someone else—is an end in itself.

You have to use the profile to understand the ways in which you seem to learn easily. And, from there, determine how to use those strengths to help you become more successful in other endeavors. Then, the profile becomes a way for you to understand yourself better, and you can use that understanding to catapult yourself to a better level of understanding or to a higher level of skill.

How has your understanding of the multiple intelligences influenced how you teach?

My own teaching has changed slowly as a result of multiple intelligences because I'm teaching graduate students psychological theory and there are only so many ways I can do that. I am more open to group work and to student projects of various sorts, but even if I wanted to be an "MI professor" of graduate students, I still have a certain moral obligation to prepare them for a world in which they will have to write scholarly articles and prepare theses.

Where I've changed much more, I believe, is at the workplace. I direct research projects and work with all kinds of people. Probably 10 to 15 years ago, I would have tried to find people who were just like me to work with me on these projects.

I've really changed my attitude a lot on that score. Now I think much more in terms of what people are good at and in putting together teams of people whose varying strengths complement one another.

How should thoughtful educators implement the theory of multiple intelligences?

Although there is no single MI route, it's very important that a teacher take individual differences among kids very seriously. You cannot be a good MI teacher if you don't want to know each child and try to gear how you teach and how you evaluate to that particular child. The bottom line is a deep interest in children and how their minds are different from one another, and in helping them use their minds well.

Now, kids can be great informants for teachers. For example, a teacher might say, "Look, Benjamin, this obviously isn't working. Should we try using a picture?" If Benjamin gets excited about that approach, that's a pretty good clue to the teacher about what could work.

The theory of multiple intelligences, in and of itself, is not going to solve anything in our society, but linking the multiple intelligences with a curriculum focused on understanding is an extremely powerful intellectual undertaking.

When I talk about understanding, I mean that students can take ideas they learn in school, or anywhere for that matter, and apply those appropriately in new situations. We know people truly understand something when they can represent the knowledge in more than one way. We have to put understanding up front in school. Once we have that goal, multiple intelligences can be a terrific handmaiden because understandings involve a mix of mental representations, entailing different intelligences.

People often say that what they remember most about school are those learning experiences that were linked to real life. How does the theory of multiple intelligences help connect learning to the world outside the classroom?

The theory of multiple intelligences wasn't based on school work or on tests. Instead, what I did was look at the world and ask, What are the things that people do in the world? What does it mean to be a surgeon? What does it mean to be a politician? What does it mean to be an artist or a sculptor? What abilities do you need to do those things? My theory, then, came from the things that are valued in the world.

So when a school values multiple intelligences, the relationship to what's valued in the world is patent. If you cannot easily relate this activity to something that's valued

The Intelligences, in Gardner's Words

- Linguistic intelligence is the capacity to use language, your native language, and perhaps other languages, to express what's on your mind and to understand other people. Poets really specialize in linguistic intelligence, but any kind of writer, orator, speaker, lawyer, or a person for whom language is an important stock in trade highlights linguistic intelligence.

- People with a highly developed logical-mathematical intelligence understand the underlying principles of some kind of a causal system, the way a scientist or a logician does; or can manipulate numbers, quantities, and operations, the way a mathematician does.

- Spatial intelligence refers to the ability to represent the spatial world internally in your mind—the way a sailor or airplane pilot navigates the large spatial world, or the way a chess player or sculptor represents a more circumscribed spatial world. Spatial intelligence can be used in the arts or in the sciences. If you are spatially intelligent and oriented toward the arts, you are more likely to become a painter or a sculptor or an architect than, say, a musician or a writer. Similarly, certain sciences like anatomy or topology emphasize spatial intelligence.

- Bodily kinesthetic intelligence is the capacity to use your whole body or parts of your body—your hand, your fingers, your arms—to solve a problem, make something, or put on some kind of production. The most evident examples are people in athletics or the performing arts, particularly dance or acting.

- Musical intelligence is the capacity to think in music, to be able to hear patterns, recognize them, remember them, and perhaps manipulate them. People who have a strong musical intelligence don't just remember music easily—they can't get it out of their minds, it's so omnipresent. Now, some people will say, "Yes, music is important, but it's a talent, not an intelligence," and I say, "Fine, let's call it a talent." But, then we have to leave the word *intelligent* out of *all* discussions of human abilities. You know, Mozart was damned smart!

- Interpersonal intelligence is understanding other people, it's an ability we all need, but is at a premium if you are a teacher, clinician, salesperson, or politician. Anybody who deals with other people has to be skilled in the interpersonal sphere.

- Intrapersonal intelligence refers to having an understanding of yourself, of knowing who you are, what you can do, what you want to do, how you react to things, which things to avoid, and which things to gravitate toward. We are drawn to people who have a good understanding of themselves because those people tend not to screw up. They tend to know what they can do. They tend to know what they can't do. And they tend to know where to go if they need help.

- Naturalist intelligence designates the human ability to discriminate among living things (plants, animals) as well as sensitivity to other features of the natural world (clouds, rock configurations). This ability was clearly of value in our evolutionary past as hunters, gatherers, and farmers; it continues to be central in such roles as botanist or chef. I also speculate that much of our consumer society exploits the naturalist intelligences, which can be mobilized in the discrimination among cars, sneakers, kinds of makeup, and the like. The kind of pattern recognition valued in certain of the sciences may also draw upon naturalist intelligence.

---

in the world, the school has probably lost the core idea of multiple intelligences, which is that these intelligences evolved to help people do things that matter in the real world.

School matters, but only insofar as it yields something that can be used once students leave school.

How can teachers be guided by multiple intelligences when creating assessment tools?

We need to develop assessments that are much more representative of what human beings are going to have to do to survive in this society. For example, I value literacy, but my measure of literacy should not be whether you can answer a multiple-choice question that asks you to select the best meaning of a paragraph. Instead, I'd rather have you read the paragraph and list four questions you have about the paragraph and figure out how you would answer those questions. Or, if I want to know how you can write, let me give you a stem and see whether you can write about that topic, or let me ask you to write an editorial in response to something you read in the newspaper or observed on the street.

The current emphasis on performance assessment is well supported by the theory of multiple intelligences. Indeed, you could not really be an advocate of multiple intelligences if you didn't have some dissatisfaction with the current testing because it's so focused on short-answer, linguistic, or logical kinds of items.

MI theory is very congenial to an approach that says: one, let's not look at things through the filter of a short-answer test. Let's look directly at the performance that we value, whether it's a linguistic, logical, aesthetic, or social performance; and, two, let's never pin our assessment of understanding on just one particular measure, but let's always allow students to show their understanding in a variety of ways.

You have identified several myths about the theory of multiple intelligences. Can you describe some of those myths?

One myth that I personally find irritating is that an intelligence is the same as a learning style. Learning styles are claims about ways in which individuals purportedly approach everything they do. If you are planful, you are supposed to be planful about everything. If you are logical-sequential, you are supposed to be logical-sequential about everything. My own research and observations suggest that that's a dubious assumption. But whether or not that's true, learning styles are very different from multiple intelligences.

Multiple intelligences claims that we respond, individually, in different ways to different kinds of content, such as language or music or other people. This is very different from the notion of learning style.

You can say that a child is a visual learner, but that's not a multiple intelligences way of talking about things. What I would say is, "Here is a child who very easily represents things spatially, and we can draw upon that strength if need be when we want to teach the child something new."

Another widely believed myth is that, because we have seven or eight intelligences, we should create seven or eight tests to measure students' strengths in each of those areas. That is a perversion of the theory. It's re-creating the sin of the single intelligence quotient and just multiplying it by a larger number. I'm personally against assessment of intelligences unless such a measurement is used for a very specific learning purpose—we want to help a child understand her history or his mathematics better and, therefore, want to see what might be good entry points for that particular child.

What experiences led you to the study of human intelligence?

It's hard for me to pick out a single moment, but I can see a couple of snapshots. When I was in high school, my uncle gave me a textbook in psychology. I'd never actually heard of psychology before. This textbook helped me understand color blindness. I'm color blind, and I became fascinated by the existence of plates that illustrated what color blindness was. I could actually explain why I couldn't see colors.

As long as you can lose one ability while others are spared, you cannot just have a single intelligence.

Another time when I was studying the Reformation, I read a book by Erik Erikson called *Young Man Luther* (1958).[1] I was fascinated by the psychological motivation of Luther to attack the Catholic Church. That fascination influenced my decision to go into psychology.

The most important influence was actually learning about brain damage and what could happen to people when they had strokes. When a person has a stroke, a certain part of the brain gets injured, and that injury can tell you what that part of the brain does. Individuals who lose their musical abilities can still talk. People who lose their linguistic ability still might be able to sing. That understanding not only brought me into the whole world of brain study, but it was really the seed that led ultimately to the theory of multiple intelligences. As long as you can lose one ability while others are spared, you cannot just have a single intelligence. You have to have several intelligences.

Note

1. See Erik Erikson, *Young Man Luther* (New York: W.W. Norton, 1958).

Form at end of book

Variations on a Theme:
How Teachers Interpret MI Theory

Teachers are planning projects, lessons, assessments, apprenticeships, and interdisciplinary curriculums around the intelligences theory. Like intelligence itself, the adaptations exhibit infinite variety.

Linda Campbell

Linda Campbell is Professor of Graduate Education Program at Antioch University Seattle, and author of Teaching and Learning Through MI, *published by Allyn and Bacon 1996 and 1999 and* Questions Answered: MI School Programs & Their Results *(in press) with ASCD. She can be reached at 2326 6th Ave., Antioch University Seattle, Seattle, WA 98121 or email lindacam@premier1.net.*

In Eeva Reeder's math classes at Mountlake Terrace High School in Edmonds, Washington, students learn algebra kinesthetically. When studying how to graph equations, they head for the school's courtyard. There they identify X and Y coordinates in the lines of the large, square, cement blocks that form the pavement. They then plot themselves as points on the large cement axes. Reeder maintains that when her students physically pretend to be graphs, they learn more about equations in a single class session than they do in a month of textbook study.

On the Tulalip Indian reservation in Marysville, Washington, elementary school students spend their mornings rotating through learning stations. For example, to learn about photosynthesis, students might act out the process at one station, read about it at another station, and at others, sing about photosynthesis, chart its processes, discuss plant and human life cycles, and finally, reflect on events that have transformed their lives, just as chloroplasts transform the life cycle of plants.

Meanwhile, in Pittsburgh, middle school arts teachers organize their curriculums around major student projects that emphasize both process and product. In music, creative writing, dance, and visual arts classes, students perform tasks that actual artists, musicians, and writers undertake. In a visual arts class, for example, students may work in portraiture for several weeks, learn how to work with different media, study portraits of recognized artists, and, ultimately, create, display, and reflect upon a final work, using all the principles and skills they have acquired.

Curricular Adaptations

What do these three scenarios have in common? They are all curricular interpretations of Howard Gardner's theory of multiple intelligences. As such, they share one of its central tenets: a school is responsible for helping all students discover and develop their talents or strengths. In doing this, the school not only awakens children's joy in learning but also fuels the persistence and effort necessary for mastering skills and information and for being inventive.

Questions

Campbell suggests five ways of adapting curriculum using multiple intelligences theory. Are these five curricular adaptations feasible for the classes you will teach?

Are there other curricular adaptations you might make in your teaching?

What are they, and how are they appropriate for your instruction?

The article "Variations on a Theme: How Teachers Interpret MI Theory" is reprinted by permission of the author.

Since Gardner first published *Frames of Mind: The Theory of Multiple Intelligences* in 1983, educators began applying his theory in their classrooms. Just as Gardner maintains that each person has a unique cognitive profile, so too have educators shown that there is no single preferred multiple intelligences model. Individual teachers and entire schools have implemented the theory, making it the basis of their mission statements and curriculums. But they have done it in diverse, and sometimes conflicting ways.

In the course of my university teaching, my staff development work, and my research for *Teaching and Learning Through Multiple Intelligences* (1996), I have discovered scores of approaches to multiple intelligences. Some teachers interpret the theory as an instructional process that provides numerous entry points into lesson content. Some say it suggests we need to develop each student's talents early in life. Others dedicate equal time to the arts each day. Many teachers use multiple intelligences to integrate curriculum, to organize classroom learning stations, or to teach students self-directed learning skills through project-based curriculum. Still others establish apprenticeship programs with community experts to teach students real-world skills. None of these adaptations is more correct than any other. Teachers apply the theory in the way they consider most appropriate for their students, school, and community.

Following are descriptions of five of the many multiple intelligences curricular formats currently being used: multiple intelligence-based lesson designs, interdisciplinary curriculums, student projects, assessments, and apprenticeships. All are guided in large part by students' talents, strengths, and interests.

1. Lesson Designs

Many teachers use the multiple intelligences as entry points into lesson content. As our first example showed, Reeder teaches algebra and geometry kinesthetically. Students who have trouble understanding math through paper-and-pencil exercises often grasp concepts easily when they build models or role-play math formulas.

Other teachers attempt to engage all eight intelligences in their lessons. Sharon Thetford, a multiage intermediate teacher at Tulalip Elementary School, sets up eight learning stations that her students rotate through each day. While such lesson planning is admittedly daunting at first, many teachers report that thinking in multiple modes quickly becomes second nature.

To begin lesson planning, teachers should reflect on a concept that they want to teach and identify the intelligences that seem most appropriate for communicating the content. The "instructional menus" shown on p. 183 offer some ideas for expanding pedagogical repertoires and quickly infusing variety into lessons.

Many teachers ask students to select the ways they would like to learn. Others use the menus for homework, rotating through the eight menus over eight weeks. For example, a teacher may ask students to do their homework musically for the first week. The students then share their musical reviews in class. The following week, the teacher repeats the process with a different menu. For the ninth week, the teacher may encourage students to use their favorite homework strategies. In this way, all students confront their weaknesses and engage their strengths.

Although the multiple intelligences theory provides an effective instructional framework, teachers should avoid using it as a rigid pedagogical formula. One teacher who attempted to teach all content through all eight modes each day admitted that he occasionally had to tack on activities. Even students complained that some lessons were "really stretching it." Instructional methods should be appropriate for the content.

There may be as many models of multiple intelligences teaching as there are teachers!

This is not to say that a teacher should consistently avoid an intelligence because it is out of his or her comfort zone. Instead, teachers should team up with colleagues so that they can increase both their own and their students' educational options.

Teachers at Wheeler Elementary School in Louisville, Kentucky, plan and teach in teams based on their intelligence strengths. Each teacher assumes responsibility for two intelligences and contributes to his or her grade level curriculum accordingly. Students then rotate from classroom to classroom, learning from three or four teachers for each unit of study. When interviewed, students have said they appreciate the hands-on nature of their learning and each teacher's enthusiasm.

2. Interdisciplinary Curriculums

Many elementary educators have embraced multiple intelligences teaching, but high school teachers can just as easily adopt the theory. In fact, because high schools typically offer liberal arts programs, most *already* feature a comprehensive multiple intelligences curriculum. Students can quickly identify experts in specific intelligences by the subjects they teach!

Rather than totally reworking the curriculum, secondary educators need only adapt it to highlight various intelligences. For some schools this means adding a stronger arts program; for some teachers, it means adding learning stations in their classrooms or bringing in community experts in various disciplines to mentor their students.

Some secondary teachers have capitalized on their school's multiple intelligences programs by coordinating schoolwide interdisciplinary units. Although interdisciplinary instruction is popular, here is one provison: Gardner is careful to remind educators that the core disciplines continue to offer the most sophisticated knowledge accrued over centuries. Before thinking in interdisciplinary terms, we must first possess the knowledge of the individual disciplines.

Seattle's International Focus

An inner-city Seattle high school piloted a schoolwide multiple intelligences week on international awareness. Teachers continued to teach within their own disciplines, but all created lessons with an international focus. Literature faculty introduced short stories from the cultures of their students. Business education teachers focused on international trade issues, thereby complementing math instructors' lessons on foreign stock exchanges. Social studies teachers compared diverse forms of government and surveyed civil rights issues. Physical education teachers taught games from around the world, while health teachers conducted a unit on infectious diseases. Art and music educators engaged students in a variety of visual media and ethnomusicology. And in science classes, students studied local and global environmental issues.

The Seattle teachers became so excited over their unit plans that they invited parents to attend their classes, scheduling the classes in the late afternoon and evening for the parents' convenience. The week was a huge success: the students appreciated the cohesive curricular focus, and hundreds of parents—including immigrant parents—attended.

Montana's Use of the Arts

Montana's Framework for Aesthetic Literacy (Montana Office of Public Instruction 1994) is another approach to interdisciplinary, multiple intelligences-based curriculums. This K–12 English and language arts curriculum is taught through the visual and performing arts. Because the teachers prefer the inquiry approach over structuring curriculums thematically, they begin each unit by posing a thought-provoking, open-ended question to guide students in their studies. They might ask questions like:

What is beauty? Who determines the standards for what is beautiful?

How do we use imagination to explain our world?

How do the arts reflect their cultures?

How does balance work? Why is it important?

To seek answers, students might attend a play or a symphony, see a film, or tour a museum. They make discoveries, draw connections, construct knowledge, and seek meaning and resolution on their own.

The Montana framework suggests a three-step curricular approach. First, students are immersed in an artistic experience. Second, they study essential English and language arts concepts while also practicing diverse thinking and communication skills. Finally, they generate their own products and answers to the unit's focus question. Through this curricular sequence, students use their multiple intelligences to acquire literacy skills and to reflect on relevant and worthwhile questions.

3. Student Projects

Some educators use the theory of multiple intelligences to promote self-directed learning. They prepare students for their adult lives by teaching them how to initiate and manage complex projects. Students learn to ask researchable questions; to identify varied resources; to create realistic time lines; and to initiate, implement, and bring closure to a learning activity. Regardless of the disciplinary focus, these projects typically draw on numerous intelligences.

Even primary-age children can learn how to execute projects. With teacher guidance, students at Project Spectrum—Howard Gardner's lab school at Harvard—study local birds and their nesting habits. They design and build bird houses and then observe whether their designs successfully meet the needs of the birds or whether modifications are required.

Middle school students in the small town of Lakewood, Washington, learn biology concepts by solving a mock crime. They conduct investigations, gather and study evidence, and suggest hypotheses they must support. Once they solve the crime, they analyze the problem-solving approaches that led to the correct answer.

Some teachers encourage students to identify their own topics to pursue for classroom projects. For example, high school students in Palo Alto, California, wanted to recommend to the city how it might use a property in a redevelopment area. They did this by presenting videotape documentaries to the city council.

High school students in Ithaca, New York, became interested in cancer therapies after a classmate was diagnosed with leukemia. The students undertook research projects, interviewed medical personnel, and visited hospitals to understand the disease and identify traditional and nontraditional healing approaches.

Projects such as these typically span two weeks to two months. Some teachers include three or more projects in a year-long curriculum, claiming that in this way, students can cover more information in greater depth than they could with conventional classroom approaches.

Project Guidelines

Because the skills of managing one's own learning must be explicitly taught, one elementary teacher (Campbell 1994) created the following project guidelines to teach his students how to conduct projects.

1. State your goal. (Example: I want to understand how optical illusions work.)

2. Put your goal into the form of a question. (Example: What are optical illusions and why do they fool our eyes?)

3. List at least three sources of information you will use. (For example, library books, eye doctors, prints of M.C. Escher's work, the art teacher.)

4. Describe the steps you will use to achieve your goal. (Find books on optical illusions and read those books, look up optical illusion in the encyclopedia, look at Escher's work.)

5. List at least five main concepts or ideas you want to research. (Example: What are optical illusions? How is the human eye tricked?)

6. List at least three methods you will use to present your project. (Example: Construct a model of how the human eye works. Hand out a sheet of optical illusions for class members to keep. Have the class try to make some.)

7. Organize the project into a time line. (Week 1: Read sources of information. Interview adults. Week 2: Look at a variety of optical illusions. Make diagram of eye.)

8. Decide how you will evaluate your project. (Examples: Practice in front of an adult and get his or her feedback. Practice in front of two friends. Fill out a self-evaluation form. Read the teacher's evaluation.)

By working through these project guidelines, students naturally engage several intelligences. In the project on optical illusions, most students used seven of the eight intelligences. Perhaps more important, by initiating and completing projects of their choice, they acquired valuable autonomous learning skills.

4. Assessments

To show what they've learned from their projects and other coursework, students should be asked to do more than fill in blanks and supply short answers to specific questions. They should demonstrate their higher-order thinking skills, generalize what they learn, provide examples, connect the content to their personal experiences, and apply their knowledge to new situations.

When appropriate, students may even select the way they will demonstrate what they've learned. Some teachers have used multiple intelligences menus as assessment options. The teacher specifies criteria for quality work, knowledge, and skills, but leaves students free to use flow charts, role plays, original songs, or other approaches.

Teachers at Eleanor Roosevelt Elementary School in Vancouver, Washington, have developed approaches that involve both parents and students in assessment. Students individually evaluate the skills and knowledge they have acquired and include their assessments in their portfolios. They also work in groups to assess one another's projects and evaluate their courses and teachers. Parents participate in a number of ways: by setting goals and assessing with their children, by reviewing student videotapes, by evaluating courses, and by writing informal comments during their visits to the classroom. Such diverse tools and increased participation yield more comprehensive pictures of student progress while giving students and their parents a stronger voice in schooling.

5. Apprenticeships

Gardner suggests that schools personalize their programs for students by offering them apprenticeships during the elementary and secondary school years. The apprenticeships he recommends would not track students into careers at an early age. Instead, they would contribute to a well-rounded liberal arts education and consume approximately one-third of students' schooling experience. Ideally, each student would participate in three apprenticeships: one in an art form or craft, one in an academic area, and a third in a physical discipline such as dance or sports. Students would have input into which apprenticeships they pursued.

Through such apprenticeships, students are learning something frequently lost in today's fast-paced society: that one gains mastery of a valued skill gradually, with effort and discipline over time. Once students achieve competence in the disciplines they are studying, they experiment with their own approaches and creative extensions.

Apprenticeship programs may be offered as part of the regular school curriculum or as extracurricular enrichment opportunities.

At the Key School in Indianapolis—the first multiple intelligences school in the U.S.—teachers, parents, or community members mentor students in 17 crafts or disciplines—each one called a "pod." Each student attends a pod of his or her choice four times a week to work on

Multiple Intelligences Menus

Linguistic Menu

Use storytelling to explain _____.
Conduct a debate on _____.
Write a poem, myth, legend, short play, or news article about
_____.
Create a talk show radio program
   about _____.
Conduct an interview of _____
   on _____.

Logical-Mathematical Menu

Translate a _____ into a mathematical
   formula.
Design and conduct an experiment
   on _____.
Make up syllogisms to demonstrate _____.
Make up analogies to explain _____.
Describe the patterns or symmetry in _____.
Others of your choice _____.

Bodily-Kinesthetic Menu

Create a movement or sequence of movements to explain

_____.
Make task or puzzle cards for _____.
Build or construct a _____.
Plan and attend a field trip that will _____.
Bring hands-on materials to demonstrate

_____.

Visual Menu

Chart, map, cluster, or graph _____.
Create a slide show, videotape, or photo album
   of _____.
Create a piece of art that demonstrates

_____.
Invent a board or card game to demonstrate

_____.
Illustrate, draw, paint, sketch, or sculpt _____.

Musical Menu

Give a presentation with appropriate musical accompaniment
   on _____.
Sing a rap or song that explains _____.
Indicate the rhythmical patterns in _____.
Explain how the music of a song is similar
   to _____.
Make an instrument and use it to demonstrate

_____.

Interpersonal Menu

Conduct a meeting to address _____.
Intentionally use _____ social skills
   to learn about _____.
Participate in a service project to _____.
Teach someone about _____.
Practice giving and receiving feedback
   on _____.
Use technology to _____.

Intrapersonal Menu

Describe qualities you possess that will help you successfully
   complete _____.
Set and pursue a goal to _____.
Describe one of your personal values
   about _____.
Write a journal entry on _____.
Assess your own work in _____.

Naturalist Menu

Create observation notebooks of _____.
Describe changes in the local or global environment

_____.
Care for pets, wildlife, gardens, or parks

_____.
Use binoculars, telescopes, microscopes, or magnifiers
   to _____.
Draw or photograph natural objects _____.

---

material related to one or more intelligences. Because each pod is open to any student in the school, children of varying ages participate in each of them.

Pod topics include architecture, cooking, and gardening, as well as themes called Sing and Song, Logowriter, Imagine Indianapolis (city planning), and Young Astronauts. In addition to the in-school experiences, a local museum offers Key students apprenticeships in shipbuilding, journalism, animation, or weather monitoring.

Programs such as this offer students powerful opportunities to work with older students or adults who

have achieved competence in a discipline or craft. And when they are immersed in real-world tasks, students begin to see where their efforts may lead.

No Prescriptions

These five curricular approaches—multiple intelligence-based lesson designs, interdisciplinary curriculums, student projects, assessments, and apprenticeships—represent only a handful of adaptations of Gardner's theory of intelligence. In actuality, there may be as many models of multiple intelligences teaching as there are teachers! Educators, it appears, readily embrace the theory because it affirms what they already know and do.

Multiple intelligences does not demand an overhaul of a curriculum; it merely provides a framework for enhancing instruction and a language to describe one's efforts. Unlike most educational reforms, it is not prescriptive. Its broad view of human abilities does not dictate how and what to teach. Rather, it gives teachers a complex mental model from which to construct curriculum and improve themselves as educators.

References

Campbell, B. (1994). *The Multiple Intelligences Handbook: Lesson Plans and More.* Stanwood, Wash.: Campbell and Associates, Inc.

Campbell, L., B. Campbell, and D. Dickinson. (1996). *Teaching and Learning Through Multiple Intelligences.* Needham Heights, Mass.: Allyn and Bacon (college division of Simon and Schuster).

Gardner, H. (1983). *Frames of Mind: The Theory of Multiple Intelligences.* New York: Basic Books.

Montana Office of Public Instruction. (1994). *Framework for Aesthetic Literacy: Montana Arts and English Curriculum.* Helena, Mont.: Author.

Form at end of book

Integrating Learning Styles and Multiple Intelligences

What does it mean to express kinesthetic intelligence in an interpersonal way? Integrating styles and intelligences can help children learn in many ways—not just in the areas of their strengths.

Harvey Silver, Richard Strong, and Matthew Perini

Harvey Silver is President, Richard Strong is Vice President, and Matthew Perini is Director of Publishing at Silver Strong & Associates, Inc., Aspen Corporate Park, 1480 Route 9 North, Woodbridge, NJ 07095 (e-mail: silver_strong@msn.com)

In the 20th century, two great theories have been put forward in an attempt to interpret human differences and to design educational models around these differences. Learning-style theory has its roots in the psychoanalytic community; multiple intelligences theory is the fruit of cognitive science and reflects an effort to rethink the theory of measurable intelligence embodied in intelligence testing.

Both, in fact, combine insights from biology, anthropology, psychology, medical case studies, and an examination of art and culture. But learning styles emphasize the different ways people think and feel as they solve problems, create products, and interact. The theory of multiple intelligences is an effort to understand how cultures and disciplines shape human potential. Though both theories claim that dominant ideologies of intelligence inhibit our understanding of human differences, learning styles are concerned with differences in the *process* of learning, whereas multiple intelligences center on the *content* and *products* of learning. Until now, neither theory has had much to do with the other.

Howard Gardner (1993) spells out the difference between the theories this way:

In MI theory, I begin with a human organism that responds (or fails to respond) to different kinds of *contents* in the world. . . . Those who speak of learning styles are searching for approaches that ought to characterize *all* contents (p. 45).

We believe that the integration of learning styles and multiple intelligence theory may minimize their respective limitations and enhance their strengths, and we provide some practical suggestions for teachers to successfully integrate and apply learning styles and multiple intelligence theory in the classroom.

Learning Styles

Learning-style theory begins with Carl Jung (1927), who noted major differences in the way people perceived (sensation versus intuition), the way they made decisions (logical

Multiple intelligence theory is concerned with differences in the *process* of learning, whereas learning-styles theory centers on the *content* and *products* of learning.

H. Silver, R. Strong, and M. Perini (1997), "Integrating Learning Styles and Multiple Intelligences," *Educational Leadership*, v55, n1, 22–27. Reprinted with permission of the Association for Supervision and Curriculum Development. Copyright © 1997 by ASCD. All rights reserved.

thinking versus imaginative feelings), and how active or reflective they were while interacting (extroversion versus introversion). Isabel Myers and Katherine Briggs (1977), who created the Myers-Briggs Type Indicator and founded the Association of Psychological Type, applied Jung's work and influenced a generation of researchers trying to understand specific differences in human learning. Key researchers in this area include Anthony Gregorc (1985), Kathleen Butler (1984), Bernice McCarthy (1982), and Harvey Silver and J. Robert Hanson (1995). Although learning-style theorists interpret the personality in various ways, nearly all models have two things in common:

- *A focus on process.* Learning-style models tend to concern themselves with the process of learning: how individuals absorb information, think about information, and evaluate the results.

- *An emphasis on personality.* Learning-style theorists generally believe that learning is the result of a personal, individualized act of thought and feeling.

Most learning-style theorists have settled on four basic styles. Our own model, for instance, describes the following four styles:

- *The Mastery style learner* absorbs information concretely; processes information sequentially, in a step-by-step manner; and judges the value of learning in terms of its clarity and practicality.

- *The Understanding style learner* focuses more on ideas and abstractions; learns through a process of questioning, reasoning, and testing; and evaluates learning by standards of logic and the use of evidence.

- *The Self-Expressive style learner* looks for images implied in learning; uses feelings and emotions to construct new ideas and products; and judges the learning process according to its originality, aesthetics, and capacity to surprise or delight.

- *The Interpersonal style learner,*[1] like the Mastery learner, focuses on concrete, palpable information; prefers to learn socially; and judges learning in terms of its potential use in helping others.

Learning styles are not fixed throughout life, but develop as a person learns and grows. Our approximate breakdown of the percentages of people with strengths in each style is as follows: Mastery, 35 percent; Understanding, 18 percent; Self-Expressive, 12 percent; and Interpersonal, 35 percent (Silver and Strong 1997).

Most learning-style advocates would agree that all individuals develop and practice a mixture of styles as they live and learn. Most people's styles flex and adapt to various contexts, though to differing degrees. In fact,

most people seek a sense of wholeness by practicing all four styles to some degree. Educators should help students discover their unique profiles, as well as a balance of styles.

Strengths and Limitations of a Learning-Style Model

The following are some *strengths* of learning-style models:

- They tend to focus on how different individuals process information across many content areas.

- They recognize the role of cognitive and affective processes in learning and, therefore, can significantly deepen our insights into issues related to motivation.

- They tend to emphasize thought as a vital component of learning, thereby avoiding reliance on basic and lower-level learning activities.

Learning-styles models have a couple of limitations. First, they may fail to recognize how styles vary in different content areas and disciplines.

Second, these models are sometimes less sensitive than they should be to the effects of context on learning. Emerging from a tradition that viewed style as relatively permanent, many learning-style advocates advised altering learning environments to match or challenge a learner's style. Either way, learning-style models have largely left unanswered the question of how context and purpose affect learning.

Multiple Intelligence Theory

Fourteen years after the publication of *Frames of Mind* (Gardner 1983), the clarity and comprehensiveness of Howard Gardner's design continue to dazzle the educational community. Who could have expected that a reconsideration of the word *intelligence* would profoundly affect the way we see ourselves and our students?

Gardner describes seven intelligences; linguistic, logical-mathematical, spatial, musical, bodily-kinesthetic, interpersonal, and intrapersonal.[2] The distinctions among these intelligences are supported by studies in child development, cognitive skills under conditions of brain damage, psychometrics, changes in cognition across history and within different cultures, and psychological transfer and generalization.

Thus, Gardner's model is backed by a rich research base that combines physiology, anthropology, and personal and cultural history. This theoretical depth is sadly lacking in most learning-style models. Moreover, Gardner's seven intelligences are not abstract concepts, but are recognizable through common life experiences. We all intuitively understand the difference between musical and linguistic, or spatial and mathematical intelligences, for example. We all show different levels of aptitude in various content areas. In all cases, we know that no individual is universally intelligent; certain fields of knowledge engage or elude everyone. Gardner has taken this intuitive knowledge of human experience and shown us in a lucid, persuasive, and well-researched manner how it is true.

Yet, there are two gaps in multiple intelligence theory that limit its application to learning. First, the theory has grown out of cognitive science—a discipline that has not yet asked itself why we have a field called cognitive science, but not one called affective science. Learning-style theory, on the other hand, has deep roots in psychoanalysis. Learning-style theorists, therefore, give psychological *affect* and individual personality central roles in understanding differences in learning.

Learning styles are not fixed throughout life, but develop as a person learns and grows.

Multiple intelligence theory looks where style does not: It focuses on the content of learning and its relation to the disciplines. Such a focus, however, means that it does not deal with the individualized process of learning. This is the second limitation of multiple intelligence theory, and it becomes clear if we consider variations within a particular intelligence.

Are conductors, performers, composers, and musical critics all using the same musical intelligence? What of the differing linguistic intelligences of a master of free verse like William Carlos Williams and a giant of literary criticism like Harold Bloom? How similar are the bodily-kinesthetic intelligences of dancers Martha Graham and Gene Kelly or football players Emmitt Smith and golfer Tiger Woods? How can we explain the difference in the spatial intelligences of Picasso and Monet—both masters of modern art?

Most of us would likely agree that different types of intelligence are at work in these individuals. Perhaps one day, Gardner's work on the "jagged profile" of combined intelligences or, perhaps, his insistence on the importance of context will produce a new understanding of intelligence. But at the moment, Gardner's work does not provide adequate guidelines for dealing with these distinctions. Most of us, however, already have a way of explaining individual differences between Monet and Picasso, Martha Graham and Gene Kelly, or between different students in our classrooms: We refer to these individuals as having distinct *styles.*

Of course, as Gardner would insist, radically different histories and contexts go a long way in explaining distinctions between Monet and Picasso, for example. But

how are teachers to respond to this explanation? As all teachers know, we must ultimately consider differences at the individual level. Learning styles, with their emphasis on differences in individual thought and feeling, are the tools we need to describe and teach to these differences.

We all intuitively understand the difference between musical and linguistic, or spatial and mathematical intelligences.

Best of all, learning styles' emphasis on the individual learning process and Gardner's content-oriented model of multiple intelligences are surprisingly complementary. Without multiple intelligence theory, style is rather abstract, and it generally undervalues context. Without learning styles, multiple intelligence theory proves unable to describe different processes of thought and feeling. Each theory responds to the weaknesses of the other; together, they form an integrated picture of intelligence and difference.

Integrating Learning Styles and Multiple Intelligences

In integrating these major theories of knowledge, we moved through three steps. First, we attempted to describe, for each of Gardner's intelligences, a set of four learning processes or abilities, one for each of the four learning styles. For linguistic intelligence, for example, the *Mastery* style represents the ability to use language to describe events and sequence activities; the *Interpersonal* style, the ability to use language to build trust and rapport; the *Understanding* style, the ability to develop logical arguments and use rhetoric; and the *Self-expressive* style, the ability to use metaphoric and expressive language.

Next, we listed samples of vocations that people are likely to choose, given particular intelligence and learning-style profiles. Working in this way, we devised a model that linked the process-centered approach of learning styles and the content and product-driven multiple intelligence theory. [See Figure 1.]

Figure 2 shows how you might construct a classroom display of information about intelligences, styles, and possible vocations. Consider kinesthetic intelligence and the difference between a Tiger Woods and a Gene Kelly: People who excel in this intelligence, with an *Understanding* style, might be professional athletes (like Tiger Woods), dance critics, or sports analysts; people with a *Self-expressive* style might be sculptors, choreographers, dancers (like Gene Kelly), actors, mimes, or puppeteers.

The following outline shows how we categorized abilities and sample vocations for the seven intelligences, by learning style:

Figure 1 Sample "kinesthetic" vocations by style.

Mastery	Interpersonal
The ability to use the body and tools to take effective action or to construct or repair *Mechanic, Trainer, Contractor, Craftsperson, Tool and Dye Maker*	The ability to use the body to build rapport, to console or persuade, and to support others *Coach, Counselor, Salesperson, Trainer*

Kinesthetic

Understanding	Self-Expressive
The ability to plan strategically or to critique the actions of the body *Physical Educator, Sports Analyst, Professional Athlete, Dance Critic*	The ability to appreciate the aesthetics of the body and to use those values to create new forms of expression *Sculptor, Choreographer, Actor, Dancer, Mime, Puppeteer*

Linguistic

Mastery: The ability to use language to describe events and sequence activities (*journalist, technical writer, administrator, contractor*)

Interpersonal: The ability to use language to build trust and rapport (*salesperson, counselor, clergyperson, therapist*)

Understanding: The ability to develop logical arguments and use rhetoric (*lawyer, professor, orator, philosopher*)

Self-expressive: The ability to use metaphoric and expressive language (*playwright, poet, advertising copywriter, novelist*)

Logical-Mathematical

Mastery: The ability to use numbers to compute, describe, and document (*accountant, bookkeeper, statistician*)

Interpersonal: The ability to apply mathematics in personal and daily life (*tradesperson, homemaker*)

Understanding: The ability to use mathematical concepts to make conjectures, establish proofs, and apply mathematics and data to construct arguments (*logician, computer programmer, scientist, quantitative problem solver*)

Self-expressive: The ability to be sensitive to the patterns, symmetry, logic, and aesthetics of mathematics and to solve problems in design and modeling (*composer, engineer, inventor, designer, qualitative problem solver*)

Spatial

Mastery: The ability to perceive and represent the visual-spatial world accurately (*illustrator, artists, guide, photographer*)

Figure 2. Student choice: Assessment products by intelligence and style.

Linguistic

Mastery
- Write an article
- Put together a magazine
- Develop a plan
- Develop a newscast
- Describe a complex procedure/object

Interpersonal
- Write a letter
- Make a pitch
- Conduct an interview
- Counsel a fictional character or a friend

Understanding
- Make/defend a decision
- Advance a theory
- Interpret a text
- Explain an artifact

Self-Expressive
- Write a play
- Develop a plan to direct
- Spin a tale
- Develop an advertising campaign

Interpersonal: The ability to arrange color, line, shape, form, and space to meet the needs of others (*interior decorator, painter, clothing designer, weaver, builder*)

Understanding: The ability to interpret and graphically represent visual or spatial ideas (*architect, iconographer, computer graphics designer, art critic*)

Self-expressive: The ability to transform visual or spatial ideas into imaginative and expressive creations (*artist, inventor, model builder, cinematographer*)

Bodily-Kinesthetic

Mastery: The ability to use the body and tools to take effective action or to construct or repair (*mechanic, trainer, contractor, craftsperson, tool and dye maker*)

Interpersonal: The ability to use the body to build rapport, to console and persuade, and to support others (*coach, counselor, salesperson, trainer*)

Understanding: The ability to plan strategically or to critique the actions of the body (*physical educator, sports analyst, professional athlete, dance critic*)

Self-expressive: The ability to appreciate the aesthetics of the body and to use those values to create new forms of expression (*sculptor, choreographer, actor, dancer, mime, puppeteer*)

Musical

Mastery: The ability to understand and develop musical technique (*technician, music teacher, instrument maker*)

Interpersonal: The ability to respond emotionally to music and to work together to use music to meet the needs of others (*choral, band, and orchestral performer or conductor; public relations director in music*)

Understanding: The ability to interpret musical forms and ideas (*music critic, aficionado, music collector*)

Self-expressive: The ability to create imaginative and expressive performances and compositions (*composer, conductor, individual/small-group performer*)

How similar are the kinesthetic intellegences of Martha Graham and Gene Kelly, or Emmitt Smith and Tiger Woods?

Interpersonal

Mastery: The ability to organize people and to communicate clearly what needs to be done (*administrator, manager, politician*)

Interpersonal: The ability to use empathy to help others and to solve problems (*social worker, doctor, nurse, therapist, teacher*)

Understanding: The ability to discriminate and interpret among different kinds of interpersonal clues (*sociologist, psychologist, psychotherapist, professor of psychology or sociology*)

Self-expressive: The ability to influence and inspire others to work toward a common goal (*consultant, charismatic leader, politician, evangelist*)

Intrapersonal

Mastery: The ability to assess one's own strengths, weaknesses, talents, and interests and use them to set goals (*planner, small business owner*)

Interpersonal: The ability to use understanding of oneself to be of service to others (*counselor, social worker*)

Understanding: The ability to form and develop concepts and theories based on an examination of oneself (*psychologist*)

Self-expressive: The ability to reflect on one's inner moods, intuitions, and temperament and to use them to create or express a personal vision (*artist, religious leader, writer*)

As the final step in constructing the intelligence-learning style menus, we collected descriptions of products that a person with strengths in each intelligence and style might create. For example, in the linguistic intelligence domain, a person with the *Mastery* style might write an article, put a magazine together, develop a newscast, or describe a complex procedure. By contrast, a person with a *Self-expressive* style might write a play, spin a tale, or develop an advertising campaign (see fig. 2). In the kinesthetic intelligence domain, a person with an *Understanding* style might choreograph a concept or teach a physical education concept; a person with a *Self-expressive* style might create a diorama or act out emotional states or concepts. A class display of such lists might accompany charts like the sample shown in Figure 2.

How to Use the Integrated Intelligence Menus

Several years ago, Grant Wiggins reminded us that we can't teach everything. It is also quite obvious that we can't use every teaching method nor every form of assessment. Here are some ways to use the Integrated Intelligence Menus—particularly for performance assessment—without trying to do everything at once.

1. *Use the menus as a compass.* Keep a running record of the styles and intelligences you use regularly and of those you avoid. When a particular form of assessment doesn't work, offer the student another choice from another part of the menu.

2. *Focus on one intelligence at a time.* Offer your students a choice in one of the four styles, or urge them to do two assessments: one from a style they like and one from a style they would normally avoid.

3. *Build on student interest.* When students conduct research, either individually or in groups, show them the menus and allow them to choose the product or approach that appeals to them. They should choose the best product for communicating their understanding of the topic or text. Students thus discover not only the meaning of quality, but also something about the nature of their own interests, concerns, styles, and intelligences.

In developing assessments, teachers must devise their own standards and expectations. But we can judge the model itself by two powerful standards:

- Does it help us develop every student's capacity to learn what we believe all students need to know?

- Does it help each student discover and develop his or her unique abilities and interests?

In conjunction, both multiple intelligences and learning styles can work together to form a powerful and integrated model of human intelligence and learning—a model that respects and celebrates diversity and provides us with the tools to meet high standards.

Notes

1. The term *interpersonal style* overlaps with Gardner's *interpersonal intelligence.* In Gardner's model, interpersonal intelligence is a category related to the content and products of knowledge. In our learning-style model, the interpersonal style refers to a way of processing knowledge.
2. Gardner has recently introduced an eighth intelligence—*naturalist.* Although our integrated intelligence menus can easily accommodate this new category, we have chosen to work only with the classic seven intelligences.

References

Briggs, K. C., and I. B. Myers. (1977). *Myers-Briggs Type Indicator.* Palo Alto, Calif.: Consulting Psychologists Press.

Butler, K. (1984). *Learning and Teaching Style in Theory and Practice.* Columbia, Conn.: The Learner's Dimension.

Gardner, H. (1983). *Frames of Mind: The Theory of Multiple Intelligences.* New York: Basic Books.

———. (1993). *Multiple Intelligences: The Theory of Practice.* New York: Basic Books.

Gregorc, A. (1985). *Inside Styles: Beyond the Basics.* Maynard, Mass.: Gabriel Systems, Inc.

Jung, C. (1927). *The Theory of Psychological Type.* Princeton, N.J.: Princeton University Press.

McCarthy, B. (1982). *The 4Mat System.* Arlington Heights, Ill.: Excel Publishing Co.

Silver, H. F., and J. R. Hanson. (1995). *Learning Styles and Strategies.* Woodbridge, N.J.: The Thoughtful Education Press.

Silver, H. F., and R. W. Strong. (1997). *Monographs for Learning Style Models and Profiles.* (Unpublished research).

Form at end of book

WiseGuide Wrap-Up

Research from fields outside of education has been, and still is, transforming how curriculum is taught. For example, brain research has led to increased emphasis on students and less emphasis on textbooks. For years, educators and psychologists believed that intelligence was fixed. This belief led to such practices as ability grouping and tracking in high schools. The theory of multiple intelligences has revolutionized, and is still revolutionizing, these practices.

As more information from brain research becomes available, educators must remain committed to the idea of changing their teaching methods and practices to effectively teach all students.

R.E.A.L. Sites

This list provides a print preview of typical **Coursewise** R.E.A.L. sites. (There are over 100 such sites at the **Courselinks™** site.) The danger in printing URLs is that web sites can change overnight. As we went to press, these sites were functional using the URLs provided. If you come across one that isn't, please let us know via email to: webmaster@coursewise.com. Use your Passport to access the most current list of R.E.A.L. sites at the **Courselinks** site.

Site name: Mix and Match

URL: http://www.jsmf.org/articles&papers/EDWEEK1-96.html

Why is it R.E.A.L.? This article, originally published in *Education Week* and part of the James S. McDonnell Foundation site, includes descriptions of classrooms using the most recent brain research to guide how subject matter is taught.

Key topic: brain-based teaching

Try this: Visit the home page of the James S. McDonnell Foundation. What is the purpose of this foundation?

Site name: The Brainstore

URL: http://www.thebrainstore.com/

Why is it R.E.A.L.? This site provides a list of resources for teachers to use to learn about brain-based learning, as well as resources for translating that knowledge into instruction.

Key topic: brain-based teaching

Try this: Browse the online catalog as though you were an elementary school teacher. Which products would you find useful? Would your selections change if you were working with older learners?

Site name: Multiple Intelligence Development Assessment Scales

URL: http://www.ange/fire.com/oh/themidas/index.html

Why is it R.E.A.L.? This site provides information about assessing the intelligences of students.

Key topic: multiple intelligences

Try this: Specifically, what are the "multiple intelligences"? Do you think you know where you fit in?

section 5 | Meeting the Needs of Students

Learning Objectives

By studying the issues related to meeting students' needs, students will:

- Recognize classrooms that have students with diverse abilities, interests, and backgrounds, and develop ways to provide students with opportunities to learn to their maximum.

- Consider ways to include students with special needs in general education classroom activities as appropriate.

- Seek information about a range of teaching strategies and, if possible, use these strategies in classrooms during the semester.

Students entering classrooms today are diverse and come from various background experiences. Teachers are being challenged to meet the needs of each learner and to provide each student with an opportunity to learn. They need to regularly adjust daily learning activities to meet the needs of all of the learners in a classroom. For example, in a class studying the Civil War, one group of students may need to review the previous lesson for important content, concepts, and skills, while another group may be working independently or in cooperative groups in learning centers, while still another group may be gathering additional data about the Civil War. The teacher will need to work with these students individually and in a group setting. Those experiences take thoughtful planning and implementation. It goes without saying that planning for classroom assessment is also integral to planning to meet student needs. The ideal is that students with various abilities and interests will experience the joy of learning.

In the past, female and male students received different information and treatment in classrooms. It behooves teachers to be aware of gender when calling on students for response, asking students to help in the classrooms, assigning seats, and so forth. Teachers often unconsciously favor one gender over the other. Over the years, teachers have noted that females attack learning in mathematics in ways that differ from males. To what extent are these gender differences also noted in other discipline content areas?

Classrooms today are more diverse than in previous years. In some schools, well over half of the classes have students from various ethnic, racial, and cultural backgrounds. Their educational backgrounds, traditions, values, and attitudes offer exciting possibilities for learning, but at the same time, present challenges for teachers, students, and the educational community. Indications are that during the twenty-first century, children of color will make up the majority of students in most classrooms.

Students with Special Needs

Questions

Reading 28. How would you explain the different perceptions of philosophy and beliefs that parents, teachers, and administrators hold regarding the inclusion of students with special needs in general education classrooms? What are some likely processes that could be used to bring the thinking of these three groups together?

Reading 29. What practical and realistic adjustments would you make in your classroom curriculum and instructional practices for students with special needs assigned to your classes?

Reading 30. If bilingual education were removed from the political agenda, how could schools respond to helping non-English-speaking students reach proficiency in English so as to be full and active participants in United States society?

Reading 31. Assume that several students in your class have been identified as "gifted." How could you modify or enhance your curriculum and classroom activities to meet the needs of those students? Write your philosophy about education for gifted and talented learners, and share your philosophy with classmates.

Reading 32. Going beyond the suggestions VanTassel-Baska presents in her reading, what are some other practices schools could adopt that focus on the development of all students? How could these practices be implemented?

How should teachers plan to ensure that all students have opportunities to learn and achieve their potential?

Since the passage of Public Law 94-142 and subsequent changes that require that special needs students be educated in the least restrictive environment, schools and teachers have worked to meet these requirements by including, as much as possible, students with special needs in regular classroom activities. Attitudes and perspectives regarding inclusion vary and are addressed in Reading 28 by Vidovich and Lombard and in Reading 29 by Gary M. Chesley and Paul D. Calaluce.

Students whose native language is other than English are a growing group entering elementary, middle, and secondary schools today. Classrooms often have students who speak a variety of languages—Spanish, Thai, Ukrainian, Yiddish, and so forth. Helping these students learn English and academic content is no easy task, as Richard Rothstein describes in Reading 30.

Talented and gifted students are an often-neglected group. In Readings 31 and 32, both John F. Feldhusen and Joyce VanTassel-Baska argue that such students need to be challenged intellectually in school and elsewhere to develop their gifts and talents to the maximum.

Parents', Teachers', and Administrators' Perceptions of the Process of Inclusion

Daniel Vidovich and Thomas P. Lombard

A survey was conducted in three Pennsylvania school districts (Fayette County) for purposes of determining parents', teachers', and administrators' perceptions of the inclusion process. When 10 item questionnaires developed by the co-author (Lombardi, 1994a) were used, administrators scored in the most supportive range (87%), followed by parents (76%), and then teachers (67%). There was little difference among the three school district ratings. An item analysis revealed that half the teachers have mixed feelings about teaching students with disabilities in their classes. Two thirds of the teachers have not attended any training sessions designed to promote responsible inclusion. Almost all the parents are willing to serve on home-school teams to encourage inclusion. However, few of the parents have attended recent meetings which discussed education and training for students with disabilities.

Inclusion is a philosophical belief leading to a restructuring process in education occurring across the country. It supports educating every student with a disability in the school, and when appropriate, the class that student would have attended had he or she not had a disability (Lombardi, 1994b). It is a natural growth of the concepts of normalization, mainstreaming, and least restrictive environments.

Recently, the Pennsylvania Department of Education (Pennsylvania School Board Association, 1994) revised their guidelines to define specially designed instruction for students with special needs. These guidelines include adaptations or modifications to the general education curriculum, instruction, and environment to accommodate individual needs. The guidelines require Pennsylvania school districts to institute Instructional Support Teams by 1995. These teams will include administrators, teachers and parents when possible. Their function will be to recommend strategies to be implemented so students with disabilities will have greater opportunity to be educated in regular classroom environments. According to Chalfant and Van Dusen Pysh (1989), it is important that school support teams receive a real commitment from all the faculty, administrators, and parents if they are to be effective. In an effort to determine the relative commitment to an inclusion philosophy, a survey was

---

Questions

How would you explain the different perceptions of philosophy and beliefs that parents, teachers, and administrators hold regarding the inclusion of students with special needs in general education classrooms?

What are some likely processes that could be used to bring the thinking of these three groups together?

---

conducted in three Fayette County Pennsylvania School Districts. These districts were chosen not only because of convenience for data collection but also because a great number of students in these districts are in the mild range of disabilities: As such, they are likely candidates for successful integration in regular classes if appropriate supports are in place.

Method

Using checklists developed by the coauthor (Tables 1, 2, and 3), three school districts in Fayette County, Pennsylvania, were surveyed to determine parents', teachers' and administrators' perceptions and commitment to an inclusion philosophy. For analysis, these school districts will be referred to as District A, B, and C.

Each school district has approximately 350 students per grade or a total of approximately 4000 students in each of the three districts. There are approximately 250 teachers in each school district. Using a random sample, twenty teachers from each district were surveyed for a total of sixty teachers. These included all teachers with no differentiation between special and regular teachers. Twelve parents from each district were surveyed for a total of thirty six parents. These were parents of students identified as receiving special education services. Eighteen administrators were surveyed, six from each district. Checklists had been developed for each group to reflect different activities generally associated with their position and the inclusion movement and philosophy. The coauthor used his training, literature review and experiences, especially from serving on the West Virginia Department of Education Integrated Education Committee, to develop each of the checklists. Colleagues reviewed and made suggestions for construct validity and reliability. Once all the checklists were received, a comparison was made for group as well as any district differences. In addition, an item analysis was conducted to determine each groups' relative support, concerns and readiness for inclusion. Scores are presented in Tables 1, 2 and 3.

Results

Districts

There was very little difference between the three districts on combined overall scores for inclusion. The number of affirmative answers from District A was 7.7 (77%), District B was 7.6 (76%) and District C was 7.3 (73%). The number of no answers was District A, 2.3 (23%), District B, 2.4 (24%) and District C, 2.7 (27%). As noted previously, these school districts are similar in terms of school populations. Bordering each other, they also have a similar social and economic base.

Parents

All parents of District A had their children with disabilities attending their home school. District B had the majority of their children at their home school with ten out of twelve children. School District C had seven out of twelve children. The exact numbers are presented in Table 1. Several parents wrote comments on their survey that they desired their child to be at school with their friends rather than a separate or different school. Most parents answered the second question in a positive manner noting they would take their child with a disability to the same social functions they would had he or she not had a disability. All three groups of parents expect their disabled students to follow home rules and regulations as well as complete home chores as children without a disability according to answers on questions three and four. The majority of parents agreed on question five that they encouraged their children to participate in social and recreational events with age appropriate nondisabled children. In fact, several parents proudly wrote on their survey their son or daughter was a star on their respective sport team. Although the majority of parents encourage their children to participate in their own Individualized Education Program development, several parents commented they did not know what an I.E.P. was. This finding may be of special concern to the school districts. According to the ratings of question seven, parents basically feel it is important to discipline their children with disabilities as they would other children. Parents were not as positive with question eight as they were with earlier questions. It may be quite difficult for parents who cared for their disabled children all their lives to encourage them to live on their own independently. Some parents wrote they didn't think their child could live on his or her own as an adult. Parents from all three districts lack background information and support as indicated in the question nine ratings. Very few parents have attended recent meetings which discussed the education and training of children with their child's disability. Assuming this may be representational, school districts throughout Pennsylvania and perhaps the country are going to have to provide more and better training to parents of students with disabilities. Lastly and perhaps of greatest importance, answers to question ten clearly indicate that parents are willing to serve on home-school teams to encourage appropriate placement of their children with disabilities into responsible inclusion programs.

Table 1 — Parents' Perceptions of Responsible Inclusion

From School Districts A, B, and C

Inclusion Advocate   *10 Undecided*   *7 + 6 Supporter*   *9 + 8 Status quo*   *5 + lower*

Questions	Response Yes			Response No		
	A	B	C	A	B	C
1. Does your child with a disability attend the same school he would have attended without a disability?	12	10	7	0	2	5
2. Do you take your child with a disability to the same social functions you would have if she did not have a disability?	10	11	9	2	1	3
3. Are your rules and regulations at home the same for your child with a disability as for your other children? If only child, are they the same for her as if she did not have a handicap?	11	10	11	1	2	1
4. Does your child with a disability have specific chores and home responsibilities you expect him to complete?	11	11	9	1	1	3
5. Do you encourage your child with a disability to participate in social and recreational events with age appropriate children without disabilities?	10	9	10	2	3	2
6. If capable, do you encourage your child to actively participate in the development of goals and objectives of her IEP?	11	10	10	1	2	2
7. Do you discipline your child with a disability the same as you would had he not had a disability?	10	9	9	2	3	3
8. As your child with a disability gets older, would you allow her to live independent from you?	8	6	9	4	6	3
9. Have you attended any recent meetings which discussed the education and training of children with your child's disability?	4	2	3	8	10	9
10. Are you willing to serve on a home-school team to encourage appropriate placement of children with disabilities in responsible inclusion programs?	11	12	10	1	0	2
	A	B	C	A	B	C
Totals	98	90	88	22	30	32
Scores	8.2	7.5	7.3	1.8	2.5	2.7

Teachers

It seems relatively clear from the ratings in question one that many teachers are tentative about the inclusion of students with disabilities into regular classrooms. In fact half of the teachers surveyed in District C indicated an unwillingness to have students with disabilities in their classes. These numbers can be seen in Table 2. Written comments indicated the special students would be disruptive and would not benefit from such a move. However it does appear from answers to question two that teachers from District A and B are supportive of modifications to meet diverse needs and rates of learning while District C is somewhat undecided. Teachers from all three districts according to answers from question three and four are open to suggestions and modifications to their teaching and classroom management as well as for sharing these responsibilities with other professionals. This information is important since almost all the approaches and options for integrating students with special needs into regular classrooms require degrees of collaboration and consultation (Research Triangle Institute, 1993). For question five, teachers noted that if students achieved the goals from their I.E.P.s, they considered they were successful. Nineteen teachers felt they could not expect the same suc-

Table 2   **Teachers' Perceptions of Responsible Inclusion**

From School Districts A, B, and C

Questions	Yes			No		
	A	B	C	A	B	C
1. Are you willing to have age appropriate students with disabilities in your class?	14	12	10	6	8	10
2. Do you modify your curriculum, methods and materials to meet the diverse needs and rates of learning in your class?	18	15	14	2	5	6
3. Are you open to suggestions and modifications in your teaching and classroom management?	18	18	15	2	2	5
4. Are you willing to share your teaching responsibilities and classroom management with other professionals?	17	17	16	3	3	4
5. Are your expectations for students with disabilities to be successful the same as they are for other students?	13	14	14	7	6	6
6. Do you call on and praises students with disabilities as much as you do other students in your class?	20	20	19	0	0	1
7. Do you promote and use heterogeneous grouping?	18	18	18	2	2	2
8. Do you promote and use peer tutoring?	14	12	14	6	8	6
9. Do you promote and use adaptive technology (e.g. expanded keyboards) and customized software (e.g., Tutor Tech)?	2	5	5	18	15	15
10. Have you attended any training sessions designed to promote responsible inclusion?	6	6	4	14	14	16

cess criteria for students with special needs as they expect from other students. Teachers, almost without exception, call and praise students with disabilities as much as they do other students according to results from question six. Relative to question seven, teachers appear to be advocates of heterogeneous groupings in their classrooms. Several commented they generally group higher level students to work with lower level students. However there was somewhat less support on question eight for peer tutoring. According to Brinkley (94) peer tutoring is one of the practices which is critical to successfully integrating students with disabilities. It would appear that the majority of teachers in all three school districts commented they are unable to promote and use adaptive technology, such as expanded keyboards or customized software, because they lack funds to purchase the equipment. Therefore readers are cautioned not to overreact to the low scores rated in question number nine. Teachers may be willing to better use technology but first it must be made available. Lastly, the three school districts have not provided sufficient training for teachers designed to promote responsible in-

clusion. School district A and B had six out of twenty teachers who had training and District C was worse with only four out of twenty teachers. Several teachers wrote on their survey they are willing to attend training sessions on their own time if training was made available.

Administrators

As can be seen in Table 3, the administrators surveyed indicated their schools do have a mission statement supportive of an inclusion philosophy according to ratings received on question one of their survey. This is paramount if responsible inclusion is being considered (Wieck, 1993). Answers from question two are varied among the three school districts with one, two, and three negative comments regarding students with disabilities attending their home schools. Several administrators wrote comments stating in 1995-96 all disabled students would be attending their home schools against their wishes. These comments seem to indicate either one of two factors. Some administrators are less supportive of inclusion or they do not feel home school placement is necessary to

Table 3 — Administrators' Perceptions of Responsible Inclusion

From School Districts A, B, and C

Questions	Yes			No		
	A	B	C	A	B	C
1. Does your school have a mission statement which encourages a responsible inclusion philosophy? (e.g., All students can learn and individual differences are respected.)	4	6	4	2	0	2
2. Would all the students with disabilities in your school attend your school if they were not disabled?	4	5	3	2	1	3
3. Do you encourage your regular teachers to accept students with disabilities in their classes?	6	6	6	0	0	0
4. Do you allow time and flexible scheduling so special and regular teachers can consult and collaborate?	2	1	3	4	5	3
5. Do you recommend students with disabilities for placement base upon needs rather than categorical labels?	6	6	6	0	0	0
6. Do you have a plan for promoting social integration with nondisabled classmates such as school dances, clubs, athletic events, etc.?	5	6	6	1	0	0
7. Do you have a plan for promoting physical integration with nondisabled classmates such as home room assignments, lunch schedules, locker locations, etc.?	6	6	6	0	0	0
8. Do you expect students with disabilities who have IEPs to be as successful in reaching their goals as nondisabled students in reaching their goals?	6	4	5	0	2	1
9. Are related services such as speech and physical therapy brought to the student in his home school programs as opposed to bringing the student to the service?	5	6	6	1	0	0
10. Do you encourage parents of students with disabilities to become active members in general school organizations such as the Parent Teacher Association?	4	6	5	2	0	1

maintain an inclusion philosophy. All eighteen administrators agreed on question three, they encourage their regular teachers to accept students with disabilities in their classes. On the other hand, administrators in all three school districts had a problem with finding time for flexible scheduling so special and regular teachers could consult and collaborate. Comments regarding question four indicate time is a problem with most teachers getting together before school, during lunch, preparation periods or even during an activity bell schedule. According to Lombardi (1994a) administrators must build in time for team planning and problem solving.

All administrators agreed on recommending students with disabilities for placement based upon need rather than categorized labels under question five. Pennsylvania has a generic special education classification system as compared to some of the other states, such as West Virginia, which still require specific categorical labels for special education identification and eligibility. Almost all the administrators agreed with question six for pro-

moting social integration with nondisabled classmates such as dances, clubs, athletic events and other school activities. The administrators agreed on question seven that they do have plans for promoting physical integration of students with disabilities in such areas as locker assignments, homeroom locations and lunch schedules. In fact three of the administrators indicated it was a top priority. Unfortunately not all of the administrators felt on question eight that students with disabilities who have an IEP will be as successful in reaching their goals as nondisabled students. Goals formulated for Individualized Education Programs should be realistic and obtainable. All but one of the administrators indicated on question nine that supportive services such as speech therapy were brought to the student as opposed to bringing the student to the service. The administrators had mixed views on question ten which asked if they encourage parents of students with disabilities to become active members of general school organizations such as the Parent Teachers Association. School District B administrators all agreed they encourage parents to join. Administrators in School District C agreed in five of the six surveys; administrators in District A in four of the six surveys. It should be noted that some of the schools in Fayette County do not have Parent Teacher Associations and this may account for the slight differences noted among the Districts.

Comparison

Noted previously, there was very little difference in ratings between School Districts A, B, and C. Fayette County is the second poorest county in Pennsylvania and this probably has a relationship to degree of equipment and technology available in the schools and to the teachers. The use of technology can be of assistance in personalizing education and assisting students with disabilities in regular classroom situations (Lombardi, 92). The administrators had the highest rating as inclusion supporters with School District A, B, and C scores of 8, 8.6, and 8.3. Parents scored next highest with scores of 8, 7.5, and 7.3 putting them in the supportive and upper undecided range. Teachers had the lowest scores in all three school districts with scores of 7, 6.8, and 6.4 indicating a more pronounced rating in the undecided category regarding their perceptions of inclusion as a philosophy and program design. These scores are based on a maximum of 10 points, one for each of the ten questions.

Discussion

Responsible inclusion has more to do with a philosophy and belief than placement of all students in general classrooms and programs (Lombardi, 94a). Determining how parents, teachers and administrators perceive inclusion would appear to be an important first step in this process. This survey seems to indicate that teachers who will be directly involved in educating students with disabilities in regular classes are still somewhat more skeptical than parents. This is consistent with an earlier study reported by the coauthor (Lombardi, 94b). Reasons continue to be time, support, and lack of training. Administrators are more positive but need to address and remedy the concerns of teachers and parents. Both teachers and parents welcome opportunities for training regarding responsible inclusion and this is a very positive finding from this study. Since the three districts under study had similar needs, they should be able to combine their resources as they proceed to implement inclusion plans.

References

Brinkley, J. H. (1993). On line, *Front Line 2*, (1), p. 3.
Chalfant, J. C. & Pysh, M. V. (1989). Teacher assistance teams: Five descriptive studies on 96 teams., *RASE*, 10(6), 49–58.
Lombardi, T. P. (1992). *Learning strategies for problem learners*, Bloomington. Indiana: Phi Delta Kappa Educational Foundation, Fastback 345.
Lombardi, T. P. (1994a). *Responsible inclusion: Restructuring education and training for students with disabilities.* Bloomington, Indiana: Phi Delta Kappa Educational Foundation, Fastback 373.
Lombardi, T. P., Nuzzo, D. L., Kennedy, K. D. & Foshay, J. (1994b). Perceptions of parents, teachers, and students regarding an integrated education inclusion program. *High School Journal*, 77 (4), 315–321.
Pennsylvania School Board Association (1994). *Information Legislative Service 32* (3), 5–6.
Research Triangle Institute (1993). *Educational programs and program options for integrating students with disabilities: A decision tool.* Longmont, CO.: Sopris West, Inc.
Wieck, C. (1993). The only label that counts is a person's name. *Front Line 1* (3), p. 12.

Form at end of book

The Deception of Inclusion

Gary M. Chesley and Paul D. Calaluce, Jr.

Gary M. Chesley, EdD, Assistant Superintendent, and Paul D. Calaluce, Jr., Director of Pupil Personnel Services, Cheshire Public Schools, 29 Main St., Cheshire, CT 06410.

Our national obsession with the inclusion of special education students into the mainstream is analogous to the description of a liberal as an individual who frantically throws 200 feet of rope to a drowning swimmer struggling only 100 feet from the shore. This liberal throws the rope in the conviction that he is saving another. Then he scampers frantically down the beach, seeking other souls to save, before he pulls the original dying victim to safety. His good intentions are misguided and provide us with a lesson about how schools treat individuals with disabilities.

Today, far too many special needs children are drowning. They are being short-changed in the name of socialization. We are truly reliving the myth of the "Emperor's New Clothes." Everyone is afraid to state the obvious. Full inclusion for all is a myth that exists in the hearts of its supporters—those who have lost sight of practical reality. Harsh words perhaps, but they express a sentiment that needs to be addressed so that we may best prepare students with disabilities to become successful participants in our society. Once again the educational pendulum has taken a good idea to the extreme.

Inclusionists argue that children with disabilities make the greatest gains when they are completely educated, *included,* in general education classes. Although there is a good deal of evidence that supports the argument that social gains can be made by students with disabilities in full inclusionary programs, the professional literature is devoid of documentation in support of the argument that full inclusionary programs improve the cognitive development of students with disabilities.

Inclusionists also contend that through cooperative planning, students with disabilities receive lessons that are modified to meet their specific needs while remaining fully involved in general education classes. On the surface this contention seems instructionally plausible and the politically correct philosophical stance for a school system to take. For those of us who walk through the halls of our nation's schools, it is clear that this strategy is flawed for several fundamental reasons.

The instructional coordination required in many of these cases sets up situations where the left hand cannot know what the right hand is doing. It is extremely difficult for a principal to provide all of the staff generally involved in supporting a fully mainstreamed child with the time necessary to adjust and to

From "The Deception of Inclusion" by G. M. Chesley and P. D. Calaluce, Jr., 1997, *Mental Retardation,* volume 35, no. 6, pp. 488–490. Copyright by the AAMR.

Questions

What practical and realistic adjustments would you make in your classroom curriculum and instructional practices for students with special needs assigned to your classes?

enhance curricular experiences for one child. As a result, too much planning is done "on the fly" and without a timely effort to assess the value of the modifications. In reality, many students with disabilities go through their educational career with a paraprofessional assisting them in class after class. Recently, a parent complained that her son, who had severe handicaps, had received less than an A in his English class. She contended that the boy's B+ was a result of the paraprofessional not following completely the classroom teacher's direction. What is the student actually learning in such a case, and does anyone really care?

Equally problematic is the general education curriculum's lack of focus on functional and vocational skills. Curricular demands as early as first grade do not match the educational needs of many students with disabilities. Even with an infinite amount of planning, the educational interests of some students with disabilities cannot be met through modifications to the general education curriculum. Meanwhile, the performance of special education students on state-mandated performance instruments, such as Connecticut's CAPT (Connecticut Academic Performance Test), are a siren call for many to criticize the overall performance of our schools. These results, in reality, indicate the need for more aggressive and intensive remediation for our lowest achievers. Sufficient remediation is not likely to occur when a special needs student is fully included with peers who are zooming ahead academically.

Many students who have handicaps graduate from high school without the skills required to be successful in the adult world. These skills cannot, and should not, be the main focus of the general education curriculum. Classroom modifications are becoming so intrusive that many special needs students are, in the end, responsible for just a small sampling of the curriculum requirements that their peers take for granted; and this is precisely where the educational establishment is blinded at the sight of the emperor's new clothes. Too often, we feel warm and fuzzy at the mere presence of a child with disabilities mainstreamed in a regular classroom. Mom and Dad are pacified and "a program is in place"; but warm and fuzzy does not necessarily translate into academic results. When headlines scream out that high school graduates do not demonstrate basic academic skills, it is too often the special education students who are not making the grade. These young people have not acquired the cognitive skills needed to be competitive in our society nor the functional and vocational skills required for independent living. Parents tend to accept this reality only when their child is approaching graduation and the safety net of public education is about to be removed. Recently, the parents of a child who has been totally included for his entire school career petitioned a school district for an out-of-state residential placement for the student's senior year. When

asked why they were requesting a program diametrically opposed to that for which they had advocated throughout the previous 10 years, their stunning response was that the child (in the end) was not prepared for the adult world.

Another fundamental requirement of a full inclusionary program is the commitment of a regular education teacher with the expertise and the perseverance to modify instruction appropriately for one, two, three or more students in a single classroom setting. In theory, all teachers provide differentiated instruction that recognizes learning styles and modalities appropriate to all students. Teaching that recognizes the needs of learners who have disabilities is sound instruction for all children. That is the theory we all know. In reality, even our best trained and most willing teachers have difficulty meeting the diverse needs of their heterogeneously grouped classes, let alone the special requirements of students with moderate to severe disabilities. *"I have twenty-five children in my second grade class, and you can't expect me to take on more students with special needs,"* has become the oft-heard plea in school after school. This sentiment carries some grain of truth to even the most hard-core supporters of inclusion and clearly illustrates one of the legitimate road blocks to a full inclusionary program. It is inconceivable to imagine a third-grade teacher being asked to focus an entire curriculum on life skills and functional academics. Yet, it is precisely this type of program that is required by many students with severe disabilities. Yasutake and Lerner (1996) reported that 41.9% of regular educators feel that inclusion is not workable, regardless of the level of support provided, with only 4.6% responding very positively about the academic results of inclusion.

It is very disconcerting to attend a Planning and Placement Team meeting where loving parents insist that all services recommended for their child be implemented within the regular classroom. Services, such as speech and occupational therapy, are tightly focused and require a special approach and setting to maximize their effectiveness. These services, and others like them, are not delivered productively in the general education classroom. It is also common practice for independent evaluators, experts from the world outside the public schools, to recommend individual one-to-one instruction to remediate learning and language difficulties; however, these services too belong as a supplement to regular instruction.

In addition, parental demands for inclusion are often unrealistic, and at times absurd. Recently, the parent of a student with almost total intellectual and language impairment insisted that her son be included in a high school French class. Other parents of a child with multiple disabilities, including mental retardation and chronic health problems, demanded that she attend a week-long outdoor nature excursion while hooked to a life support device rather than the alternative educational experience planned for general education students not participating. The parent was making this demand on purely philosophical grounds, dismissing the fact that the field trip would be dangerous and educationally incomprehensible to the student.

Today's public schools are a microcosm of the communities that they serve. We have the opportunity to use a public school experience to teach children with disabilities the many cognitive and social skills needed for assimilation into the community. The socialization gains are important but need to be placed within a valid educational context. Proponents of inclusion assume that through mainstreaming skills will be assimilated as they are taught in the regular classroom. A better solution is to work intensively on skill development and remediation first in a more intensive setting, with the goal being to mainstream children incrementally when they can best benefit from being included. Students with disabilities should be educated to the maximum extent possible with peers who do not have disabilities, but they should not be asked to sacrifice cognitive and vocational preparation for social interaction.

The original guiding philosophy of P.L. 94–142 acknowledged that students with disabilities require individually designed educational plans that offer the child a blend of specialized instruction in different settings. A continuum of service options *and* integrated social experiences in mainstream classes was the vision in this legislation. We should return to that philosophy. Local schools should develop a practical litmus test that guides the placement of children with disabilities. Issues such as planning time, the preparation and commitment of teachers, the acceptance of the child's peer group, how and where services are best delivered, and a clear identification of targeted skills should guide the placement process. Quite simply, we need to ask whether the classroom teacher can achieve the best academic results for the identified child.

Teachers and parents of special education students must look carefully and forthrightly at the real needs of our children and recommend the programs and learning environments that will best prepare them for academic as well as social success as adults. We must remove the emperor's cloak of inclusion and substitute it with a warm woolen coat, one that will provide the practical academic foundation to serve children well for years to come.

Reference

Yasutake, D., & Lerner, J. (1996). Teachers' perceptions of inclusion for students with disabilities: A survey of general and special educators. *Learning Disabilities: A Multidisciplinary Journal, 7*(1), 1–7.

Form at end of book

Bilingual Education:
The Controversy

Our commonly held notion of how earlier generations of immigrants were educated—often used as the chief argument in support of English immersion—is a myth, Mr. Rothstein reveals.

Richard Rothstein

Richard Rothstein is a research associate of the Economic Policy Institute, Washington, D.C. This article is adapted from a chapter in his book, The Way We Were? *(Century Foundation Press, 1998), and is reprinted with permission from the Twentieth Century Fund/Century Foundation, New York, N.Y. The book is available from the Brookings Institution, 1775 Massachusetts Ave. N.W., Washington, DC 20036; ph. 800/275-1447. © 1998, Twentieth Century Fund/Century Foundation.*

Bilingual education, a preferred strategy for the last 20 years, aims to teach academic subjects to immigrant children in their native languages (most often Spanish), while slowly and simultaneously adding English instruction.[1] In theory, the children don't fall behind in other subjects while they are learning English. When they are fluent in English, they can then "transition" to English instruction in academic subjects at the grade level of their peers. Further, the theory goes, teaching immigrants in their native language values their family and community culture and reinforces their sense of self-worth, thus making their academic success more likely.

In contrast, bilingual education's critics tell the following, quite different, story. In the early 20th century, public schools assimilated immigrants to American culture and imparted workplace skills essential for upward mobility. Children were immersed in English instruction and, when forced to "sink or swim," they swam. Today, however, separatist (usually Hispanic) community leaders and their liberal supporters, opposed to assimilation, want Spanish instruction to preserve native culture and traditions. This is especially dangerous because the proximity of Mexico and the possibility of returning home give today's immigrants the option of "keeping a foot in both camps"—an option not available to previous immigrants who were forced to assimilate. Today's attempt to preserve immigrants' native languages and cultures will not only balkanize the American melting pot but hurt the children upon whom bilingual education is imposed because their failure to learn English well will leave them unprepared for the workplace. Bilingual education supporters may claim that it aims to teach English, but high dropout rates for immigrant children and low rates of transition to full English instruction prove that, even if educators' intentions are genuine, the program is a failure.

The English First Foundation, a lobbying group bent on abolishing bilingual education, states that most Americans "have ancestors who learned English the same way: in classrooms where English was the only language used for all learning activities."[2] According to 1996 Republican Presidential nominee Bob Dole, the teaching of English to immigrants is what "we have done . . . since our founding to speed the melting pot. . . . We must stop the practice of multilingual education as a means of instilling ethnic pride, or as a therapy for low self-esteem, or out of elitist guilt over a culture built on the traditions of the West."[3]

Speaker of the House Newt Gingrich chimed in as well:

If people had wanted to remain immersed in their old culture, they could have done so without coming to America. . . . Bilingualism keeps people actively tied to their old language and habits and maximizes the cost of the transition to becoming American. . . . The only viable alternative for the American underclass is American civilization. Without English as a common language, there is no such civilization.[4]

This viewpoint has commonsense appeal, but it has little foundation in reality.

Bilingual Education: The History

Despite proximity to their homeland, Mexican Americans are no more likely to reverse migrate than were Europeans in the early 20th century. One-third of the immigrants who came here between 1908 and 1924 eventually abandoned America and returned home.[5]

What's more, the immigrants who remained did not succeed in school by learning English. During the last great wave of immigration, from 1880 to 1915, very few Americans succeeded in school, immigrants least of all. By 1930, it was still the case that half of all American 14- to 17-year-olds either didn't make it to high school or dropped out before graduating. The median number of school years completed was 10.

Far from succeeding by immersing themselves in English, immigrant groups did much worse than the native-born, and some immigrant groups did much worse than others. The poorest performers were Italians. According to a 1911 federal immigration commission report, in Boston, Chicago, and New York, 80% of native white children in the seventh grade stayed in school another year, but only 58% of Southern Italian children, 62% of Polish children, and 74% of Russian Jewish children did so. Of those who made it to eighth grade, 58% of the native whites went on to high school, but only 23% of the Southern Italians did so. In New York, 54% of native-born eighth-graders made it to ninth grade, but only 34% of foreign-born eighth-graders did so.[6]

A later study showed that the lack of success of immigrants relative to the native-born continued into high school. In 1931, only 11% of the Italian students who entered high school graduated (compared to an estimated graduation rate of over 40% for all students). This was a much bigger native/immigrant gap than we have today.

While we have no achievement tests from that earlier period by which to evaluate relative student performance, I.Q. tests were administered frequently. Test after test in the 1920s found that Italian immigrant students had an average I.Q. of about 85, compared to an average for native-born students of about 102. The poor academic achievement of these Italian Americans led to high rates of "retardation"—that is, being held back and not promoted (this was the origin of the pejorative use of the term "retarded").

A survey of New York City's retarded students (liberally defined so that a child had to be 9 years old to be considered retarded in the first grade, 10 years old in the second grade, and so on), found that 19% of native-born students, were retarded in 1908, compared to 36% of Italian students. The federal immigration commission found that the retardation rate of children of non-English-speaking immigrants was about 60% higher than that of children of immigrants from English-speaking countries.[7] The challenge of educating Italian immigrant children was so severe that New York established its first special education classes to confront it. A 1921 survey disclosed that half of all (what we now call) "learning disabled" special education children in New York schools had Italian-born fathers.[8]

As these data show—and as is the case today—some groups did better than others, both for cultural reasons and because of the influence of other socioeconomic factors on student achievement. If Italian children did worse, Eastern European Jewish children did better. This is not surprising in light of what we now know about the powerful influence of background characteristics on academic success. In 1910, 32% of Southern Italian adult males in American cities were unskilled manual laborers, but only one-half of 1% of Russian Jewish males were unskilled. Thirty-four percent of the Jews were merchants, while only 13% of the Italians were. In New York City, the average annual income of a Russian Jewish head-of-household in 1910 was $813; a Southern Italian head-of-household averaged $688.[9]

But even with these relative economic advantages, the notion that Jewish immigrant children assimilated through sink-or-swim English-only education is a nostalgic and dangerous myth. In 1910, there were 191,000 Jewish children in the New York City schools; only 6,000 were in high school, and the overwhelming majority of these students dropped out before graduating. As the Jewish writer Irving Howe put it, after reviewing New York school documents describing the difficulties of "Americanizing" immigrant children from 1910 to 1914,

"To read the reports of the school superintendents is to grow impatient with later sentimentalists who would have us suppose that all or most Jewish children burned with zeal for the life of the mind."[10] There may have been relatively more such students among the Jewish immigrants than in other immigrant communities, Howe noted, but they were still a minority.

Immersing immigrants in an English-language school program has been effective—usually by the third generation. On the whole, immigrant children spoke their native language; members of the second generation (immigrants' native-born children) were bilingual, but not sufficiently fluent in English to excel in school; members of the third generation were fluent in English and began to acquire college educations. For some groups (e.g., Greek Americans), the pattern more often took four generations; for others (e.g., Eastern European Jews), many in the second generation may have entered college.

This history is not a mere curiosity, because those who advocate against bilingual education today often claim that we know how to educate immigrant children because we've done it before. However, if we've never successfully educated the first or even second generation of children from peasant or unskilled immigrant families, we are dealing with an unprecedented task, and history can't guide us.

Today's Hispanics are not the first to seek bilingual assimilation.

To understand the uniqueness of our current challenge, compare the enormous—by contemporary standards—dropout rate of New York City Jewish students in 1910 with that of Mexican students in the Los Angeles school district today. Like New York in 1910, Los Angeles now is burdened with a rising tide of immigrants. In 1996, there were 103,000 Hispanic students in grades 9–12 in Los Angeles (out of the city's total K–12 Hispanic population of 390,000). Hispanic high school students were about 26% of the total Hispanic student population in Los Angeles in 1996,[11] compared to 3% for Jews in New York in 1910 (only 6,000 high school students out of 191,000 total Jewish enrollment). In Los Angeles today, 74% of Mexican-born youths between the ages of 15 and 17 are still in high school; 88% of Hispanic youths from other countries are still in attendance.[12] More than 70% of Hispanic immigrants who came to the United States prior to their sophomore year actually complete high school (compared to a 94% high school completion rate for whites and a 92% rate for blacks).[13] English immersion programs for Jews early in this century (and certainly similar programs for Italians) cannot teach us anything that would help improve on today's immigrant achievement or school completion, much of which may be attributable to bilingual education programs, even if imperfectly administered.

If the notion is misleading that English immersion led previous generations of immigrants to academic success, so too is the claim that bilingual education repudiates the assimilationist approach of previous immigrants. In reality, today's Hispanics are not the first to seek bicultural assimilation. Some 19th- and early 20th-century European immigrants also fought for and won the right to bilingual education in the public schools.[14] Native-language instruction was absent from 1920 until the mid-1960s only because a fierce anti-German (and then anti-immigrant) reaction after World War I succeeded in banishing it from American classrooms. Even foreign-language instruction for native-born students was banned in most places. If Chicago's Bismarck Hotel found it necessary to rename itself the "Mark Twain," it should not be surprising that bilingual education programs were also abolished.

Before World War I, immigrant groups often pressed public schools to teach children in their native language. The success of these groups depended more on whether adult immigrant activists had political power than on a pedagogical consensus. The immigrants' objective, as it is today, was to preserve a fragment of ethnic identity in children for whom the pull of American culture seemed dangerously irresistible. In this, they were supported by many influential educators. William Harris, the school superintendent in St. Louis and later U.S. commissioner of education, argued for bilingual education in the 1870s, stating that "national memories and aspirations, family traditions, customs and habits, moral and religious observances cannot be suddenly removed or changed without disastrously weakening the personality." Harris established the first "kindergarten" in America, taught solely in German, to give immigrant students a head start in the St. Louis schools.[15]

Nineteenth-century immigrant parents were often split over the desirability of bilingual education, as immigrant parents are split today. Many recognized that children were more likely to succeed if schools' use of the native language validated the culture of the home. But others felt that their children's education would be furthered if they learned in English only.

The first bilingual public school in New York City was established in 1837 to prepare German-speaking children for eventual participation in regular English schools. The initial rule was that children could remain in German-language instruction only for 12 months, after which they would transfer to a regular school. But the

German teacher resisted this rule, believing that, before transferring, the children needed more than the limited English fluency they had acquired after a year of German instruction. The record is unclear about how often the rule was stretched.

Many immigrant children, not just Germans, did not attend school at all if they could not have classes in their native language. In his 1840 address to the New York legislature, Gov. William Seward (later Lincoln's secretary of state) explained that the importance of attracting immigrants to school—and of keeping them there—motivated his advocacy of expanded native-language instruction: "I do not hesitate to recommend the establishment of schools in which [immigrant children] may be instructed by teachers speaking the same language with themselves." Only by so doing, Gov. Seward insisted, could we "qualify . . . [them] for the high responsibilities of citizenship."

Buoyed by Seward's endorsement, Italian parents in New York city demanded a native-language school as well, and in 1843 the Public School Society established a committee to determine whether one should be established. The committee recommended against an Italian-language school, claiming the Italian community was itself divided. "Information has been obtained," the committee stated, "that the more intelligent class of Italians do not desire such a school, and that, like most [but not, apparently, all] of the better class of Germans, they would prefer that those of their countrymen who come here with good intentions should be Americanized as speedily as possible."[16]

Bilingual education, though sometimes controversial, was found nationwide. In Pennsylvania, German Lutheran churches established parochial schools when public schools would not teach in German; in 1838, Pennsylvania law converted these German schools to public schools. Then, in 1852, a state public school regulation specified that "if any considerable number of Germans desire to have their children instructed in their own language, their wishes should be gratified."[17]

In 1866, succumbing to pressure from politically powerful German immigrants, the Chicago Board of Education decided to establish a German-language school in each area of the city where 150 parents asked for it. By 1892 the board had hired 242 German-language teachers to teach 35,000 German-speaking children, one-fourth of Chicago's total public school enrollment. In 1870, a public school established in Denver, Colorado, was taught entirely in German. An 1872 Oregon law permitted German-language public schools to be established in Portland whenever 100 voters petitioned for such a school. Maryland, Iowa, Indiana, Kentucky, Ohio, and Minnesota also had bilingual education laws, either statewide or applying only to cities with large immigrant populations. In Nebraska, enabling legislation for bilingual education was enacted for the benefit of German immigrant children as late as 1913.[18]

There was considerable variation in how these programs arranged what we now call the "transition" to English. In St. Louis, Harris' system introduced English gradually, beginning in the first grade. The 1888 report of the Missouri supervisor of public instruction stated that "in some districts the schools are taught in German for a certain number of months and then in English, while in others German is used part of the day and English the rest. Some of the teachers are barely able to speak the English language." Ohio's 1870 rules provided that the lower grades in German-language public schools should be bilingual (half the instructional time in grades 1 through 4 could be in German), but in grades 5 through 8 native-language instruction had to be reduced to one hour a day. Baltimore permitted public schools in the upper grades to teach art and music in German only, but geography, history, and science had to be taught in both English and German. In some midwestern communities, there was resistance to any English instruction: an 1846 Wisconsin law insisted that public schools in Milwaukee must at least teach English (as a foreign language) as one academic subject.[19]

While Germans were most effective in demanding public support for native-language instruction, others were also successful. In Texas in the late 19th century, there were seven Czech-language schools supported by the state school fund. In California, a desire by the majority to segregate Chinese children seemed to play more of a role than demands by the Chinese community for separate education. San Francisco established a Chinese-language school in 1885; the city later established segregated Indian, Mongolian, and Japanese schools.[20]

Support for bilingual education was rarely unanimous or consistent.

San Francisco's German, Italian, and French immigrants, on the other hand, were taught in their native languages in regular public schools. Here, bilingual education was a strategy designed to lure immigrant children into public schools from parochial schools where they learned no English at all. According to San Francisco's school superintendent in 1871, only if offered native-language instruction could immigrant children be brought into public schools, where, "under the care of American teachers," they could be "molded in the true form of American citizenship."[21]

Support for bilingual education was rarely unanimous or consistent. In San Francisco, the election of an "anti-immigrant" Republican school board majority in 1873 led to the abolition of schools in which French and German had been the primary languages of instruction and to the firing of all French- and German-speaking teachers. After protests by the immigrant community, bilingual schools were reestablished in 1874. In 1877, the California legislature enacted a prohibition of bilingual education, but the governor declined to sign it. William Harris' bilingual system in St. Louis was dismantled in 1888, after redistricting split the German vote and the Irish won a school board majority.[22]

In 1889, Republican Gov. William Hoard of Wisconsin sponsored legislation to ban primary-language instruction in public and private schools, claiming the support of German immigrant parents. The *Milwaukee Sentinel* published a front-page story about "a German in Sheboygan County . . . who sent his children away to school in order that they might learn English." The father, reported the *Sentinel*, complained that "in the public schools of the town, German teachers, who . . . did not know English . . . had been employed . . . , [and] he felt it essential to the welfare of his children, who expected to remain citizens of this country, to know English."[23]

But both the newspaper and Wisconsin's Republican politicians had misjudged the immigrants' sentiments. In response to the anti-bilingual law, enraged German Americans (who had previously supported Republican candidates) mobilized to turn the statehouse over to Democrats and to convert the state's 7-to-2 Republican majority in Congress to a Democratic majority of 8-to-1. The Democrats promptly repealed the anti-bilingual education law.

An almost identical series of events took place in Illinois, where formerly Republican German American voters mobilized in both East St. Louis and Chicago to elect a liberal Democrat, Peter Altgeld, governor in 1890, largely because of his bilingual school language policy. These upheavals in two previously safe Republican states played an important role in the election of Democrat Grover Cleveland as President in 1892. Nonetheless, the controversy continued, and in 1893 the *Chicago Tribune* began a new campaign against German-language instruction. In a compromise later that year, German instruction was abolished in the primary grades but retained in the upper grades, while Chicago's mayor promised German Americans a veto over future school board appointments to ensure that erosion of primary-language instruction would not continue.[24]

But these controversies ended with World War I. Six months after the armistice, the Ohio legislature, spurred by Gov. James Cox, who was to be the Democratic Presidential candidate in 1920, banned all German from the state's elementary schools. The language posed "a distinct menace to Americanism," Cox insisted. The *New York Times* editorialized in 1919 that, although some parents "want German to be taught [because it] pleases their pride . . . , it does not do their children any good." Within the following year, 15 states in which native-language instruction had flourished adopted laws requiring that all teaching be in English. By 1923, 35 states had done so.[25] Only when Nebraska went so far as to ban native-language instruction in parochial as well as public schools did the Supreme Court, in 1923, strike down an English-only law.[26]

During the next 30 years, bilingual instruction had its ups and downs, even where English was not the native language. In 1950, Louisiana first required English, not French, to be the language of public school instruction. In the Southwest, where teaching in Spanish had long been common, the practice continued in some places and was abolished in others. Tucson established a bilingual teaching program in 1923, and Burbank established one in 1931. New Mexico operated bilingual schools throughout most of the 20th century, up until the 1950s. The state even required the teaching of Spanish to English-speaking children in elementary school. But in 1918, Texas made teaching in Spanish a crime, and, while the law was not consistently enforced (especially along the Mexican border), as recently as 1973 a Texas teacher was indicted for not teaching history in English.[27] In the same year, Texas reversed itself and adopted bilingual education as its strategy.

When bilingual education began to reemerge in the 1970s—spurred by a Supreme Court finding that schools without special provisions for educating language-minority children were not providing equal education—the nation's memory of these precedents had been erased. Today many Americans blithely repeat the myth that, until the recent emergence of separatist minority activists and their liberal supporters, the nation had always immersed its immigrant children in nothing but English and this method had proved its effectiveness.

Bilingual Education: Mixed Evidence

This mixed history, however, does not prove that bilingual education is effective, any more so than English immersion or intense English-language instruction. To an unbiased layperson, the arguments of both advocates and opponents of bilingual education seem to make sense. On the one hand, it's reasonable to insist that children who don't speak English continue their education in a language they understand in history, literature, math, and science, while they learn English. It's also reasonable to expect, however, that this might make it too tempting to defer English-language instruction. Moreover, the best way to do something difficult—e.g., making the transition to English—is simply to do it without delay. It makes sense to acknowledge that children may adapt better to school if the school's culture is not in conflict with that of the home. But some immigrant parents may be more intent on preserving native culture for their children than are the children themselves.

Modern research findings on bilingual education are mixed. As with all educational research, it is so difficult to control for complex background factors that affect academic outcomes that no single study is ultimately satisfying. Bilingual education advocates point to case studies of primary-language programs in Calexico, California; Rock Point, Arizona; Santa Fe, New Mexico; New Haven, Connecticut; and elsewhere that show that children advance further in both English and other academic subjects when native-language instruction is used and the transition to English is very gradual. Opponents point to case studies in Redwood City and Berkeley, California; in Fairfax, Virginia; and elsewhere that prove that immersion in English or rapid and intensive English instruction is most effective.[28] Overall, the conflicting evidence from these case studies does not suggest that abolition of bilingual education or even the substitution of parental choice for pedagogical expertise in determining whether bilingual approaches should be used would improve things much.

The problem is especially complex because not only economic factors but also generational variation apparently affects the achievement of immigrant youths. In 1936, the principal of a high school in New York City that enrolled large numbers of Italian immigrants wrote:

The problem of juvenile delinquency . . . baffles all the forces of organized society. . . . The highest rate of delinquency is characteristic of immigrant communities. . . . The delinquent is usually the American-born child of foreign-born parents, not the immigrant himself. Delinquency, then, is fundamentally a second-generation problem. This intensifies the responsibility of the school.[29]

The same is true today. The challenge now facing immigrant educators is that academic achievement for second-generation Hispanic and Asian children is often below that of children who arrive in the U.S. as immigrants themselves.[30] Many of these children of the second generation seem to speak English, but they are fully fluent in neither English nor their home language. Many of their parents, frustrated that their own ambition has not been transmitted to their children, may become convinced that only English immersion will set their children straight, while others seek bilingual solutions to prevent the corruption of American culture from dampening their children's ambition.

In the absence of persuasive evidence, the issue has become politicized. In a country as large as ours, with as varied experience, there is virtually no limit to the anecdotes and symbols that can be invoked as substitutes for evidence.

Opponents of bilingual education promote Hispanic parents to the media when they claim they want their children to learn English without bilingual support; the clear implication is that only liberal ideologues and separatists support native-language instruction. These claims, like those circulated by the *Milwaukee Sentinel* a century ago, may not reflect the feelings of most parents. And the technology of teaching a new language to immigrant children is complex; both bilingual education advocates and opponents claim their goal is full English literacy as rapidly as possible. But there's no reason to expect that politicized parent groups are the best judges of language acquisition research.

There are also successful adult immigrants who brag of their English fluency, acquired either with or without bilingual education. As always, such anecdotal evidence should be treated with caution. Richard Rodriguez' autobiography, *Hunger of Memory,* describes his successful education in an English-only environment. But Rodriguez, unlike most immigrants, was raised in a predominantly English-speaking neighborhood and was the only Spanish speaker in his class.[31] His experience may be relevant for some immigrants, but not relevant for many others.

Whichever method is, in fact, more effective for most immigrant children, there will be many for whom the other method worked well. It may be the case that immigrant children's social and economic background characteristics should affect the pedagogy chosen. Even if some Russian Jewish immigrants did not require bilingual education to graduate from high school, perhaps Italians would have progressed more rapidly if they'd had access to bilingual instruction. Today, the fact that some (though not all) Asian immigrants seem to progress rapidly in school without native-language support provides no relevant evidence about whether this model can work well for Mexican or Caribbean children, especially those low on the ladder of socioeconomic status and those whose parents have little education. Nor does it tell us much about what the best pedagogy would be for Asians who generally do less well in school, such as Hmong, Laotian, and Cambodian children.[32]

It is certain, however, that the American "melting pot" has never been endangered by pluralist efforts to preserve native languages and cultures. Bilingual instruction has *never* interfered with the powerful assimilationist influences that overwhelm all children whose parents migrate here. And this is equally true of Spanish-speaking children today.

After the last 20 years of bilingual education throughout America, Spanish-speaking children continue to assimilate. From 1972 to 1995, despite rapidly accelerating immigration (more Hispanic youths are first-generation immigrants today than 20 years ago), the Hispanic high school completion rate has crept upward (from 66% to 70%). Hispanic high school graduates who enroll in college jumped from 45% to 54% (for non-Hispanic whites, it's now 64%). And the number of Hispanic high school graduates who subsequently complete four years of college jumped from 11% to 16% (for non-Hispanic whites, it's now 34%).[33] A study of the five-county area surrounding Los Angeles, the most immigrant-affected community in the nation, found that from 1980 to 1990, the share of U.S.-born Hispanics in professional occupations grew from 7% to 9%, the share in executive positions grew from 7% to 10%, and the share in other administrative and technical jobs grew from 24% to 26%.[34] Overall, 55% of U.S.-born Hispanics are in occupations for which a good education is a necessity, in an area where bilingual education has been practiced for the last generation.

Perhaps we can do better. Perhaps we would do better with less bilingual education. But perhaps not. All we can say for sure is that the data reveal no apparent crisis, and the system for immigrant education with which we've been muddling through, with all its problems, does not seem to be in a state of collapse.

The best thing that could happen to the bilingual education debate would be to remove it from the political realm. Sound-bite pedagogy is no cure for the complex interaction of social, economic, and instructional factors that determine the outcomes of contemporary American schools.

Notes

1. Technically, "bilingual education" refers to all programs designed to give any support to non-English-speaking children, including programs whose main focus is immersion in English-speaking classrooms. In public debate, however, the term generally refers to only one such program, "transitional bilingual education (TBE)," in which native-language instruction in academic subjects is given to non-English speakers. In this article, I use the term in its nontechnical sense to refer only to "TBE" programs.
2. Web site, English First Foundation: http://englishfirst.org.
3. Mark Pitsch, "Dole Takes Aim at 'Elitist' History Standards," *Education Week,* 13 September 1995, p. 18.
4. Newt Gingrich, *To Reach America* (New York: HarperCollins, 1995), pp. 161–62.
5. Irving Howe, *World of Our Fathers* (New York: Simon and Schuster, 1983), p. 58.
6. Michael R. Olneck and Marvin Lazerson, "The School Achievement of Immigrant Children: 1900–1930," *History of Education Quarterly,* Winter 1974, pp. 453–82, Tables 3, 5, 6.
7. David K. Cohen, "Immigrants and the Schools," *Review of Educational Research,* vol. 40, 1970, pp. 13–27.
8. Seymour B. Sarason and John Doris, *Educational Handicap, Public Policy, and Social History* (New York: Free Press, 1979), pp. 155–56, 340–51.
9. Olneck and Lazerson, Tables 11 and 12.
10. Howe, pp. 277–78.
11. *Fall 1995 Preliminary Ethnic Survey* (Los Angeles: Information Technology Division, Los Angeles Unified School District, Publication No. 124, 1996).
12. Georges Vernez and Allan Abrahamse, *How Immigrants Fare in U.S. Education* (Santa Monica, Calif.: RAND Corporation, 1996), Table 3.2.
13. These figures are not strictly comparable; estimates are based on data in Vernez and Abrahamse, Table 4.2, and in National Center for Education Statistics, *Dropout Rates in the United States: 1995* (Washington, D.C.: Office of Educational Research and Improvement, U.S. Department of Education, NCES 97–473, 1997), Table 9.
14. Native-language instruction in public schools was also common in the Southwest, particularly in Texas, New Mexico, and Arizona, which were formerly part of Mexico and whose native populations, not their immigrants, were originally Spanish-speaking Mexicans. It was also common in Louisiana, where French-language public schools were established well after the Louisiana Purchase to preserve native French culture.
15. Diego Castellanos, *The Best of Two Worlds: Bilingual-Bicultural Education in the United States* (Trenton: New Jersey State Department of Education, CN 500, 1983), pp. 23–25.
16. Sarason and Doris, pp. 180–81, 194.
17. Heinz Kloss, *The American Bilingual Tradition* (Rowley, Mass.: Newbury House, 1977), pp. 149–50.
18. Ibid., pp. 61, 86, 180; Castellanos, p. 19; and Mary J. Herrick, *The Chicago Schools: A Social and Political History* (Beverly Hills, Calif.: Sage, 1971), p. 61.
19. Kloss, pp. 69, 86, 158–59, 190; and Castellanos, pp. 24–25.
20. Kloss, pp. 177–78, 184.
21. Castellanos, p. 23; and Paul E. Peterson, *The Politics of School Reform, 1870–1940* (Chicago: University of Chicago Press, 1985), p. 55.
22. Peterson, pp. 55–56; Castellanos, p. 25; and James Crawford, *Bilingual Education: History, Politics, Theory, and Practice* (Trenton, N.J.: Crane Publishing Company, 1989), p. 22.
23. "The School Question," *Milwaukee Sentinel,* 27 November 1889.
24. Herrick, p. 61; Kloss, p. 89; Peterson, pp. 10, 58; William F. Whyte, "The Bennett Law Campaign in Wisconsin," *Wisconsin Magazine of History,* vol. 10, 1927, pp. 363–90; and Bernard Mehl, "Educational Criticism: Past and Present," *Progressive Education,* March 1953, p. 154.
25. Crawford, pp. 23–24; and David Tyack, "Constructing Difference: Historical Reflections on Schooling and Social Diversity," *Teachers College Record,* Fall 1993, p. 15.
26. *Meyer* v. *Nebraska,* 262 US 390 (1923).
27. Castellanos, pp. 43, 49; Crawford, p. 26; and idem. *Hold Your Tongue* (Reading, Mass.: Addison-Wesley, 1992), p. 72.
28. See, for example, Rudolph Troike, "Research Evidence for the Effectiveness of Bilingual Education," *NABE Journal,* vol. 3, 1978, pp. 13–24; *The Bilingual Education Handbook: Designing Instruction for LEP Students* (Sacramento: California Department of Education, 1990), p. 13; Iris Rotberg, "Some Legal and Research Considerations in Establishing Federal Bilingual Policy in Bilingual Education," *Harvard Educational Review,* May 1982, pp. 158–59; and Rosalie Pedalino Porter, *Forked Tongue: The Politics of Bilingual Education* (New York: Basic Books, 1990), p. 141.

29. Leonard Covello, "A High School and Its Immigrant Community—A Challenge and an Opportunity," *Journal of Educational Sociology,* February 1936, p. 334.

30. Ruben G. Rumbaut, "The New Californians: Research Findings on the Educational Progress of Immigrant Children," in idem and Wayne Cornelius, eds., *California's Immigrant Children: Theory, Research, and Implications for Educational Policy* (San Diego: Center for U.S.-Mexican Studies, University of California, 1995).

31. For a discussion of Rodriguez as prototype, see Stephen D. Krashen, *Under Attack: The Case Against Bilingual Education* (Culver City, Calif.: Language Education Associates, 1996), p. 19.

32. Rumbaut, Table 2.6.

33. *Dropout Rates in the United States: 1995,* Table A-37; and National Center for Education Statistics, *The Condition of Education 1997* (Washington, D.C.: U.S. Department of Education, NCES 97–388, 1997), Indicators 8, 22.

34. Gregory Rodriguez, *The Emerging Latino Middle Class* (Malibu, Calif.: Pepperdine University Institute for Public Policy, 1996), Figure 22.

FRAME the DEBATE

Form at end of book

Programs for the Gifted Few or Talent Development for the Many?

Students at all ages and grade levels are entitled to challenging and appropriate instruction if they are to develop their talents fully, Mr. Feldhusen points out.

John F. Feldhusen

John F. Feldhusen is the Robert B. Kane Distinguished Professor of Education, Purdue University, West Lafayette, Ind.

The gifted education movement grew out of the pioneering research of Lewis Terman and Lita Hollingworth and took flight after the launch of Sputnik in 1957. The momentum continued to build with the subsequent publication of the Marland Report in 1972, which documented neglect of the gifted in American schools.[1] With small-scale financial support from the federal government and larger support from most state governments, educational programs were developed in nearly all the states. Elementary programs favored the pull-out enrichment model, while secondary programs favored the use of special classes.[2]

Supporters of the development of programs included a number of organizations: the National Association for Gifted Children, the Talented and Gifted (TAG) Division of the Council for Exceptional Children, and state associations for the gifted, as well as a host of individuals, among them James Gallagher, E. Paul Torrance, A. Harry Passow, Abraham Tannenbaum, Paul Witty, Barbara Clark, Joseph Renzulli, Irving Sato, Dorothy Sisk, Julian Stanley, and Joyce VanTassel-Baska, who led the field with their research and expertise in developing procedures for identifying and educating gifted children. The magnitude of growth in gifted education is documented in *National Excellence: A Case for Developing America's Talent*, a 1993 report from the U.S. Department of Education.[3]

Strong attacks on the emerging field came in 1985 with the publication of two books: *Keeping Track: How Schools Structure Inequality,* by Jeannie Oakes, which criticized the grouping practices of American schools; and *Educating the Ablest: Programs and Promising Practices,* by June Cox, Neil Daniels, and Bruce Boston, which rendered a negative evaluation of the vapid pullout enrichment programs that the authors characterized as having seen their day.[4] In 1988 Paul Chapman took both the intelligence and the achievement testing movements to task for having come to dominate school practice to the advantage of the Nordic population and the disadvantage of black, Hispanic, and low-income youths.[5]

Paul Kingston and Lionel Lewis in *The High-Status Track,* an edited volume published in 1990, presented the views of 13 scholars who indicted the secondary- and college-level institutions in the U.S. that have risen to

Questions

Assume that several students in your class have been identified as "gifted." How could you modify or enhance your curriculum and classroom activities to meet the needs of those students?

Write your philosophy about education for gifted and talented learners, and share your philosophy with classmates.

elite status with clearly excellent academic programs but, as the authors see it, restrictive admission policies that systematically block many minority and low-income youths from enrolling. Graduates of these elite schools move into career tracks that practically ensure the attainment of high-level professional positions, while young people who do not attend such institutions rarely attain equal professional status. "These schools," they write, "are socially elite, largely enrolling offspring of the upper-middle and upper classes. Moreover, their graduates are prepared for privilege and enjoy disproportionate access to high-status occupations."[6]

In *The Manufactured Crisis,* their 1995 defense of American schools, David Berliner and Bruce Biddle also attacked gifted programs as elitist and biased. They wrote:

Despite their seductive appeal, and despite their frequent promotion by privileged Americans, enrichment programs are not the way to improve American education. There is no evidence that they accomplish the goals claimed for them, and they tend to weaken some of the most impressive traditional strengths of America's schools.[7]

Berliner and Biddle are wrong in asserting that no evidence exists that gifted programs accomplish their goals. Indeed, there is much evidence that they do. However, by focusing programs on the elite few, programs for the gifted probably do little to improve schools overall.

It is clear that the programs are under severe attack. However, in *Dumbing Down Our Kids,* Charles Sykes says that it is the children who suffer when gifted programs come under attack and disappear.[8] And Ellen Winner has argued in her recent book, *Gifted Children: Myths and Realities,* that no society can afford to ignore its most gifted members and that all must give serious thought to how best to nurture and educate talent.[9] Thus the goal for all of us must be to *find ways to develop the talents and special aptitudes of as many young people as possible,* while recognizing the special needs of highly talented youths for learning experiences at a level and pace appropriate to their abilities.

Categorizing and Labeling

It is immoral to identify a large majority of the nation's young people as "ungifted," which implies that they are devoid of talent, and it is equally immoral to provide no or inappropriate educational services to precocious youths who are ready for high-level, fast-paced, in-depth instruction. We do the former when we carry out an elaborate process with tests and rating scales that results in the labeling of approximately 5% of the school populations as "gifted," thereby indirectly labeling the rest as "ungifted." We do the latter when we insist that precocious youths be placed in heterogeneous or inclusive classrooms that pay no attention to their educational needs, a point argued in a 1993 research report.[10] That report, based on classroom observations throughout the U.S. and on an extensive survey of classroom practices, concluded that most gifted and talented children receive little or no instruction appropriate to their levels of readiness, even though most states and the federal government have set up offices and provided funding to local school districts for special programs and services for academically gifted youth.

The original Marland Report advocated services for precocious youths in six areas: general giftedness, leadership, creativity, psychomotor abilities, academic talent, and artistic talent. But schools have focused almost entirely on general giftedness. Identification schemes promulgated by Alexina Baldwin and Jay Wooster in 1977 and by others later showed school personnel how to crunch numbers from I.Q. tests, achievement tests, and rating scales to derive a single index of overall ability, rank the index numbers, and draw a cutoff above which a child is declared "gifted."[11] A national study in 1982 showed how arbitrary and potentially fraught with error and psychometric ignorance this type of generic identification process can be.[12]

After having been identified through an elaborate process of seeking the "truly gifted," a child is admitted to one of the ubiquitous pullout enrichment programs. Tuesday and Friday mornings at 10, Jane, Tom, Mary, and Bob leave their classroom and go to the "GT room" for instruction in higher-level thinking skills, for work on independent projects, for field trips, and so on. Research published in 1991 showed that worthwhile learning did occur in these settings, but it was never demonstrated that children not identified as "gifted" would not also have profited from the activities.[13] Moreover, critics have found a lot wrong with the approach, declaring that the pullout/enrichment model should be replaced with increasingly more specialized and challenging academic services geared to children's levels of precocity.[14] Subsequent research by James Kulik suggested that special groupings of high-ability youths in particular academic areas do lead to higher academic achievement.[15]

But it is now 1998. While the pullout/enrichment model is still in widespread use, countervailing forces—the inclusion movement, the promotion of detracking, heterogeneous grouping by age and grade level, and the serving of precocious youngsters in regular classrooms—grew in strength in the late 1980s and 1990s, inspired by Jeannie Oakes' work and by Robert Slavin's work with cooperative learning.[16] Thus many precocious and highly talented young people get no specialized instruction whatsoever, and the goals and practices of existing programs are often ineffectual for them.

The residual effect of all these years of failing to meet the special needs of precocious youth is, paradoxically, a continuing pressure in the public schools to degroup, de-track, and group heterogeneously, often disregarding any signs that some children are so advanced that regular classroom instruction is of little value to them. These children are expected to cool it, teach others who are less able, and socialize. In rapidly increasing numbers, such children are fleeing to private schools if their families can afford them, to the state-supported residential schools for precocious youths now operating in 11 states, to early college admission, to dual enrollment in college and public schools, to summer and Saturday programs at colleges and universities, to home schooling, to magnet schools, and to charter schools. It should also be noted that, in defiance of the faddish inclusion movement, some public school districts continue to offer special schools or special full-time classes for gifted and talented youths. These schools and classes can be extremely beneficial for highly talented youths, especially those who are academically talented.

Talent Orientation

Traditionally, programs for the gifted have focused only on those who are deemed "generally gifted" or are "academically gifted." Instead, I believe children exhibit a wide diversity of talents in the vocational/technical area, in the academic disciplines, in the arts, and in the personal and social domains. In identifying the talents of our young people, we should make use of tests, rating scales, auditions, and classroom observations by teachers. Moreover, while we should be concerned with nurturing the talents of all young people at all levels of ability, we need to pay special attention to those who are very highly talented and often neglected in school. All young people need challenging learning experiences, and we can provide them only when we know the nature and level of their talents. Elsewhere, I have spelled out procedures that schools can use in talent identification and development in education (TIDE),[17] and a number of schools are already accomplishing these tasks well.

Once students have been identified, schools can provide learning experiences that encompass a wide variety of areas. My colleagues and I have conducted research that suggests that precocious youths typically have strong talents in three or four areas.[18] We don't know much yet about less-able youngsters, but two projects carried out by Kenneth Seeley in 1984 and Kenneth McCluskey and others in 1995 give us clues that talent strengths can be identified and used to draw underachievers, school dropouts, and delinquents back into the mainstream of education.[19]

My colleagues and I have developed a framework for meeting the needs of young people with diverse talents throughout the K–12 grade spectrum. All young people need recognition as legitimate human beings, and this we visualize as the base of a pyramid, a foundation on which all else is built. A wide variety of learning experiences can then be seen as rays extending vertically upward from this base, with the length of each varying according to an individual student's talents and interests. Thus the longest rays would be nearest the center and represent relatively strong talents. From this variety of learning experiences students can derive increasing understanding of their own talents and capabilities, and from that understanding they can build a personal commitment to develop their talents. Using this model, school counselors are assigned the task of helping all students gain acceptance in some appropriate groups, while the coordinator of gifted programs and services (with the new title of "talent development specialist") would have the task of identifying, with the help of teachers, students' specific strengths and aptitudes and organizing as many activities, classes, and services as possible to serve the needs of youths with special talents.

The TIDE Alternative

Talents are capabilities in specific domains of aptitude. Some young people are very highly talented academically, artistically, in technical areas, or in interpersonal activities, while others have moderate or low levels of these special talents. Academic talents (e.g., mathematics, social studies, writing, science, literature) show themselves in classroom learning and on standardized achievement tests. Artistic talents are revealed in art classes, competitions, and performances. The technical areas of talent include computers, industrial technology, home arts, agriculture, nursing, and so on, and high levels of performance in these areas, both inside and outside of school, are evidence of such talent strengths. Finally, the interpersonal talents include special ability in leadership, teaching, counseling, care giving, and so on. Indeed, we agree heartily with Howard Gardner, who has said, "It is clear that many talents, if not intelligences, are overlooked nowadays; individuals with these talents are the chief casualties of the single-minded, single-funneled approach to the mind."[20]

We were thrilled theoretically and practically when we first saw Françoys Gagné's model of talent development, suggesting the direction of the development of human abilities is from broad, general aptitudes toward increasingly specific talents.[21] Gagné has pursued a career-oriented, programmatic line of research, establishing the nature and development of human talents.

Our own research at Purdue University and with many public schools, hundreds of teachers, and thousands of young people convinces us that there is an urgent need in all schools to help students at all levels of achievement and ability to identify their special aptitudes and talents.

All schools also need to provide instruction, services, activities, and guidance to help students optimize the development of their talents.[22] Many talents can be identified through testing, but observation and ratings of students in real, challenging learning activities are the ideal ways to discover and nurture students' domain-specific talents.

We must broaden our conception of human talents beyond the narrow academic focus that now prevails in schools. The assessment of talents is both an "inter-student" process of finding those with high levels of talent and an "intra-student" process of helping each student find his or her own talent strengths. We must recognize that talent identification is a long-term process that depends on a wide variety of tests and challenging learning experiences in which teachers and others provide feedback that helps students come to understand the nature of their own talents and to commit themselves to their long-range development.

It is undesirable to identify some students as "gifted" and the rest as "ungifted." All students at all ages have relative talent strengths, and schools should help students identify and understand their own special abilities. Those whose talents are at levels exceptionally higher than those of their peers should have access to instructional resources and activities that are commensurate with their talents. The one-size-fits-all mentality that is at least partly an outgrowth of the inclusion movement reflects a mistaken view of human development. Highly talented young people suffer boredom and negative peer pressure in heterogeneous classrooms.[23] Students at all ages and grade levels are entitled to challenging and appropriate instruction if they are to develop their talents fully.

Notes

1. Sidney Marland, *Education of the Gifted and Talented: Report to the Congress of the United States by the U.S. Commissioner of Education* (Washington, D.C.: U.S. Government Printing Office, 1972).

2. Joseph Renzulli, *The Enrichment Triad Model: A Guide for Developing Defensible Programs for the Gifted* (Mansfield Center, Conn.: Creative Learning Press, 1977); June Cox, Neil Daniels, and Bruce Boston, *Educating Able Learners: Programs and Promising Practices* (Austin: University of Texas Press, 1985); S. M. Moon, John F. Feldhusen, and Deborah R. Dillon, "Long-Term Effects of an Enrichment Program Based on the Purdue Three-Stage Model," *Gifted Child Quarterly*, vol. 38, 1994, pp. 38–48; and John F. Feldhusen, Steve M. Hoover, and Michael F. Sayler, *Identifying and Educating Gifted Students at the Secondary Level* (Monroe, N.Y.: Trillium Press, 1990).

3. U.S. Department of Education, *National Excellence: A Case for Developing America's Talent* (Washington, D.C.: U.S. Government Printing Office, 1993).

4. Jeannie C. Oakes, *Keeping Track: How Schools Structure Inequality* (New Haven, Conn.: Yale University Press, 1985); and Cox, Daniels, and Boston, op. cit.

5. Paul D. Chapman, *Schools as Sorters: Lewis M. Terman, Applied Psychology and the Intelligence Testing Movement* (New York: New York University Press, 1988).

6. Paul W. Kingston and Lionel S. Lewis, *The High Status Track* (Albany, N.Y.: State University of New York Press, 1990), p. xi.

7. David C. Berliner and Bruce J. Biddle, *The Manufactured Crisis* (New York: Addison-Wesley, 1995), p. 211.

8. Charles J. Sykes, *Dumbing Down Our Kids* (New York: St. Martin's Press, 1995).

9. Ellen Winner, *Gifted Children: Myths and Realities* (New York: Basic Books, 1996).

10. Karen L. Westberg, Francis X. Archambault, Jr., and Scott W. Brown, "A Survey of Classroom Practices with Third- and Fourth-Grade Students in the United States," *Gifted Education International*, vol. 12, 1997, pp. 29–33.

11. Alexina Baldwin and Jay Wooster, *Baldwin Identification Matrix for the Identification of Gifted and Talented Students* (Buffalo, N.Y.: DOK Publishers, 1977).

12. E. Susan Richert, James J. Alvino, and Robert C. McDonnel, *National Report on Identification: Assessment and Recommendations for Comprehensive Identification of Gifted and Talented Youth* (Sewell, N.J.: Educational Improvement Center-South, 1982).

13. Vicki Vaughn, John F. Feldhusen, and J. William Asher, "Meta-analyses and Review of Research on Pull-out Programs in Gifted Education," *Gifted Child Quarterly*, vol. 35, 1991, pp. 92–98.

14. Cox, Daniels, and Boston, op. cit.; and F. P. Belcastro, "Elementary Pull-out Programs for the Intellectually Gifted—Boon or Bane?," *Roeper Review*, vol. 9, 1987, pp. 208–12.

15. James A. Kulik, *An Analysis of the Research on Ability: Historical and Contemporary Perspectives* (Storrs, Conn.: National Research Center on the Gifted and Talented, 1992).

16. Oakes, op. cit.; and Robert E. Slavin, *Cooperative Learning: Theory, Research, and Practice* (Englewood Cliffs, N.J.: Prentice-Hall, 1990).

17. John F. Feldhusen, *Talent Identification and Development in Education*, 2nd ed. (Sarasota, Fla.: Center for Creative Learning, 1995).

18. Ibid.; and John F. Feldhusen, Betty J. Wood, and David Yuu Dai, "Gifted Students' Perception of Their Talents," *Gifted and Talented International*, in press.

19. Kenneth Seeley, "Perspectives on Adolescent Giftedness and Delinquency," *Journal for the Education of the Gifted*, vol. 8, 1984, pp. 59–72; and Kenneth W. McCluskey et al., *Lost Prizes, Talent Development, and Problem Solving with At-Risk Students* (Sarasota, Fla.: Center for Creative Learning, 1995).

20. Howard Gardner, "If Teaching Had Looked Beyond the Classroom: The Development and Education of Intelligence," *Innotech Journal*, vol. 16, 1992, p. 31.

21. Françoys Gagné, "From Giftedness to Talent: A Development Model and Its Impact on the Language of the Field," *Roeper Review*, vol. 18, 1995, pp. 103–11.

22. John F. Feldhusen, "How to Identify and Develop Special Talents," *Educational Leadership*, February 1996, pp. 66–69.

23. James Gallagher, Christine Harradine, and Mary Ruth Coleman, "Challenge or Boredom? Gifted Students on Their Learning," *Roeper Review*, vol. 19, 1997, pp. 132–36.

Form at end of book

The Development of Academic Talent:
A Mandate for Educational Best Practice

The case could be made that all of education should be about talent development, a view of schooling that focuses on the optimal, not the minimal, development of each student, Ms. VanTassel-Baska suggests.

Joyce VanTassel-Baska

Joyce VanTassel-Baska is the Jody and Layton Smith Professor of Education at the College of William and Mary, Williamsburg, Va., where she also directs a center for gifted education.

The earliest Western concepts of talent focused on what today we might call identification: observing and judging performance in specific domains valued by a society. This view has not changed very much since the days of ancient Greece. What has changed is that we have researched various constructs related to talent, such as giftedness, creativity, and motivation; our society has enlarged the domains of value to include more academic and nonacademic areas of learning; and our ways of observing talent have become more refined through testing specific aptitudes and general reasoning abilities. A monolithic view of giftedness simply as high intelligence has been displaced in favor of a multifaceted view of talents and abilities. That view continues to be extended and amplified in many ways.

In recent years there has also been a shift toward an emphasis on *talent development* as the central metaphor for gifted education. This contemporary trend might be traced to the publication of Howard Gardner's *Frames of Mind,* a work that excited the imaginations of many educators and inspired them to think about applying Gardner's ideas about multiple intelligences to classroom contexts and curricula.[1] Another precipitating event was the publication of *National Excellence: A Case for Developing America's Talent,* a report that pointed out schooling practices that inhibit the development of America's talented youths.[2] These two events in education have spawned many editorials, articles, and reactions from general educators and educators of the gifted; both groups see the trend in highly positive ways.[3]

Yet it is clear that the shift toward thinking about education as a talent development enterprise did not originate with Gardner or the national report. The work of Julian Stanley and his colleagues in the 1970s, for example, provided a major emphasis on precocious talent in specific academic areas.[4] A. Harry Passow's work with Project Talent in the 1960s also focused the field on looking for talent to emerge in students through classroom-based approaches. Calvin Taylor in the 1960s and 1970s developed the "multiple talent totem poles," providing a theoretical and research base for the popular program Talents Unlimited, recommended for use with most learners.

Questions

Going beyond the suggestions VanTassel-Baska presents in her reading, what are some other practices schools could adopt that focus on the development of all students?

How could these practices be implemented?

VanTassel-Baska, J. (1998), "The Development of Academic Talent: A Mandate for Educational Best Practice," *Phi Delta Kappan,* 79(10) 760–763.

The case could be made that all of education should be about talent development, a view of schooling that focuses on the optimal, not the minimal, development of each student. Based on such an idea, many educational institutions have reformed their practice using talent development ideas. Whole schools have been founded and many others have been reorganized around the talent development concept as it applies to all learners.[5]

The more specialized talent search model for finding precocious talent identifies and serves more than 200,000 students per year through four national searches. Talent development efforts in the arts, especially through private lessons and tutorials, continue to thrive.[6] And parents, as the engineers of their own children's talent development processes, are becoming ever more discerning about appropriate opportunities at given stages of development.

High-Level Talent Development

Many researchers in the past 20 years have focused sharply on the processes of talent development that matter the most in producing high-level talent in various domains. Benjamin Bloom contributed important insights about the relationship between talent development in the academic domain and talent development in the arts and in sports, noting that the processes were virtually the same.[7] Key variables in the external environment that he cited included supportive parents or surrogates; excellent teaching in the talent area; special experiences, including competitions that served both to motivate and to encourage the next stage of the development of talent; and motivational encouragement to pursue the talent development process. Bloom also noted the importance of internal variables in the process, such as willingness to practice and train, strong interest in and commitment to the talent area, and the ability to learn rapidly and well.

More recently, Mihaly Csikszentmihalyi, Kevin Rathunde, and Samuel Whalen have studied the talent development process in adolescence.[8] Their findings contribute greatly to our understanding of talent development that is based as much on connative elements, such as intrinsic motivation and optimal experience, as on a strictly cognitive model. These researchers noted two personality variables that are important to the process of talent development: concentration and openness to experience. They also found that there was a strong need for the identification of talent in a culturally valued area in order for optimal development to occur. Moreover, talented adolescents need both support and challenge from their families and their teachers.

Just as Bloom and Csikszentmihalyi and his colleagues have documented certain insights about talent development by studying world-class contemporary performers in various fields and talented adolescents on the verge of high-level achievement, 75 years of research exists on the talent development processes of eminent individuals in various fields, cultures, and eras. Catherine Cox's landmark work documented the roles of intelligence, family support, and personal perseverance as critical variables in the lives of 300 eminent personalities.[9] Other work on eminent personalities has focused on themes of adversity, creative productivity, and hard work.[10] It would appear that eminent individuals across fields have exhibited common characteristics and behaviors that may have accounted for their greatness. What emerges from this literature that is particularly compelling is the strong sense of the interplay of internal and external variables that affected the process.

Some research contributions on talent development at the presecondary level has been studies of prodigies.[11] These young people show advanced development at the level of an expert adult, as in the cases of music and chess prodigies. For prodigies, the ages of 10 to 13 are critical in accessing formal modes of advanced development in a field through mentors, models, contests, and apprenticeships.[12]

Another line of research has focused strongly on interventions for precocious youths. The talent search projects at Johns Hopkins, Duke, Denver, and Northwestern Universities have all conducted intensive research on the benefits of acceleration in various forms. Studies show that gifted students who undertook accelerated coursework as preteens continue to benefit years later, when they choose more prestigious schools, take on more challenging coursework, and show strong motivation for pursuing further education and productive career paths.[13] Recent evidence also suggests that students benefit not only from acceleration of academic coursework but also from acceleration of choices based on vocational interests and predispositions.[14] Perhaps the greatest contribution of the research from these projects is the demonstration that chronological age is not the most relevant determinant for readiness to learn certain kinds of knowledge, that talented students are capable of learning advanced material at a substantially faster rate than their agemates, and that this capacity is in evidence from a very early age.[15]

A Model for Schools

The talent search projects provide a viable model for schools to emulate, incorporating all the necessary elements to help programs support a focus on talent development. Three elements are critical. First is a flexible philosophy with regard to age and grade placement. The program must be founded on a belief that able students can handle much more at earlier ages than is usually thought possible and that it is more important to find their challenge levels than to pay attention to age or grade considerations.

Second, there must be a commitment to use tests to improve curriculum and instruction. The purpose of tests is not to pigeonhole students but rather to indicate their readiness for advanced and challenging work. The careful use of diagnostic/prescriptive approaches ensures that students are neither bored nor frustrated by the level of work.[16] Furthermore, there must be a tight relationship between what is tested and the instruction that follows in order to facilitate higher-level understanding of important concepts.

The third critical element is a strong support structure for teachers and administrators. The setting out of specific procedures for program development and implementation ensures that those conducting the program have sufficient guidance to guarantee effectiveness.

It is also not incidental that extended-year programs are used to implement this talent development model. Summer programs, Saturday programs, and after-school programs have proliferated in the past 20 years in order to provide appropriate learning experiences for students in grades 5 through 12.[17] Many of these extended-year models are creative and flexible in their scheduling and effectively use shorter time frames for basic work and longer time frames for more challenging learning opportunities, not unlike the recent recommendations emanating from the U.S. Department of Education's *Prisoners of Time* study.[18]

Also central to the success of the talent development model is the use of instructors who are knowledgeable in their disciplines and committed to the proposition that able students can learn more in a shorter period of time than our traditional models of education have suggested.[19]

Finally, the talent development model includes ongoing research to continue the effectiveness of the approach.

It is notable that many elements of the talent search and development model overlap with practices promoted by the current reform agenda:

- using tests as diagnostic tools to help place students in the curriculum;

- using high curriculum standards to set appropriately high levels of challenge for each student;

- assessing learning in nontraditional ways that capture the maximum capacity of students to perform;

- emphasizing core domains of learning;

- using action research coupled with longitudinal approaches; and

- establishing meaningful collaboration between universities and K–12 education.

Social Support for Talent Development

Contrary to popular belief, talented individuals do not make it on their own. Not only is the process of talent development lengthy and rigorous, but the need for support from others is crucial for ultimate success. One important source structure is the family.[20] Research continues to attest to the strong role that parents play in advancing a child's educational aspirations and opportunities. Parents fulfill the role of support in a variety of ways, including direct teaching.[21] Virtually all the talent development literature resounds with the importance of parents as nurturers, encouragers, and even direct facilitators of all educational experiences for their children. Pablo Casals' mother, who gave up her home life to travel with her son so that he could study cello with the best teacher in Barcelona, represents the prototypical self-sacrifice described in much of the talent development literature.

The development of a first-rate talent must be a high priority in families, but even when the child's talent is at a lower level the family must still provide the support and challenge necessary for development. Troubled families also contribute in important ways to the process. Robert Albert found families of creative individuals to have a "wobble" effect—the parents were somewhat removed emotionally from the children, thus allowing a child's creative energy to be self-directed rather than parent-supervised.[22] Moreover, the absence of parents through death or divorce appears to catalyze some talented individuals to develop their capacities to very high levels.

Mentors appear to affect talent development in a profoundly positive way.[23] Mentors may be seen as emotional supports as well as sources of cognitive stimulation for talented individuals. In fact, the more emotional connections established through socioeconomic background, ethnic background, or gender, the more efficacious the match may be. The mentor can be a family member, a teacher, or someone deliberately sought out to provide an important boost to the talent development process at a crucial stage.

Crystallizing experiences also have a role to play in talent development. Gardner's notion of such experiences emphasizes that moment when an individual is able to discern that a powerful experience represents a direction to take and a commitment to a lifelong pattern of work.[24] Other researchers have recognized the crucial role of real-world apprenticeship experiences in solidifying the talent development process.[25]

The Internal World of the Individual

If academic talent is to thrive, then we must also be concerned about the internal life of individuals, the habits of mind they develop, the lifestyles they adopt, and the values they hold about work and education. The literature on talent development clearly elucidates the individual's own responsibilities for developing talent.[26] Thus we must nurture in students a strong sense of self-discipline and of the importance of owning and asserting their own talent.

Implications for Schools

What can schools do to assist in the overall talent development enterprise? It would appear that there is much that could be done. The movement for national content standards encourages schools to focus on higher-level concepts, skills, and ideas. Adopting the talent search model is a second way of bringing about a focus on talent development. Purposeful testing, high-powered curriculum and instruction from knowledgeable teachers, efficient use of time, and rigorous assessment of learning combine to create a coherent approach to meaningful learning. This model raises the role of school administrators to architects and engineers rather than merely managers, and it also assumes that teachers can motivate students to perform at levels well beyond more typical age and grade placements.

A third way to enable talent development to take hold in schools would be to change the values that pervade schools as social institutions. In the current grip of egalitarian mania, when equal outcomes—not equal opportunities—are stressed, the values associated with talent development often receive limited attention. Schools must recognize that their first obligation is to teach students not only how to learn but also what is important to know. Schools must show that they value excellence. One way to do so is to honor talent in multiple domains.[27] For example, schools need to consider pep rallies for National Merit finalists and award-winning musicians as well as for football and basketball players.

Another way that schools could demonstrate a commitment to academic excellence would be to institute the College Board Advanced Placement (AP) program in all disciplines (26 are available), with courses articulated up to the AP level for promising students in grades 5–12. The AP program provides college-level coursework for students in high school and can function as a design-down model for more rigorous curriculum experiences during the elementary and middle school years. All talented learners should have the option of taking at least three AP courses during their secondary school experience.

Schools also need to be able to take a flexible approach to curriculum and scheduling. Students should have access to advanced curriculum at whatever age readiness can be demonstrated.[28] Time should be regarded as a variable that can be manipulated in whatever ways will promote advanced learning for all students.

The development of academic talent is an important part of any education reform agenda. The talent development model has the power to mobilize American education at elementary and secondary levels to move beyond limited and ineffective gifted programs and the mediocrity that grips so many of our schools. It has the appeal to mobilize parents to support it. After all, shouldn't all of education today be in the business of developing talent at whatever levels possible? The tool kit is open and awaits only strong intentions matched to skillful use by conscientious practitioners.

Notes

1. Howard Gardner, *Frames of Mind: The Theory of Multiple Intelligences* (New York: Basic Books, 1983).
2. *National Excellence: A Case for Developing America's Talent* (Washington, D.C.: U.S. Department of Education, 1993).
3. Donald J. Treffinger and John F. Feldhusen, "Talent Recognition and Development: Successor to Gifted Education," *Journal for the Education of the Gifted,* vol. 19, 1996, pp. 181–93.
4. Julian Stanley, Daniel Keating, and Lynn Fox, *Mathematical Talent: Discovery, Description, and Development* (Baltimore: Johns Hopkins University Press, 1974).
5. Howard Gardner, *Multiple Intelligences: The Theory in Practice* (New York: Basic Books, 1993).
6. Gilbert Clark and Enid Zimmerman, "What Do We Know About Artistically Talented Students and Their Teachers?," *Journal of Art and Design Education,* vol. 13, 1994, pp. 275–86.
7. Benjamin S. Bloom, *Developing Talent in Young People* (New York: Ballantine Books, 1985).
8. Mihaly Csikszentmihalyi, Kevin Rathunde, and Samuel Whalen, *Talented Teenagers: The Roots of Success and Failure* (New York: Cambridge University Press, 1993).
9. Catherine M. Cox, *The Early Mental Traits of Three Hundred Mental Geniuses* (Stanford, Calif.: Stanford University Press, 1926).
10. Robert S. Albert, "Observations and Suggestions Regarding Giftedness, Familial Influences, and the Achievement of Eminence," *Gifted Child Quarterly,* vol. 22, 1978, pp. 201–11; Mildred Goertzel, Victor Goertzel, and Ted Goertzel, *Three Hundred Eminent Personalities* (San Francisco: Jossey-Bass, 1978); Dean K. Simonton, *Greatness: Who Makes History and Why* (New York: Guilford, 1994); and R. Ochse, *Before the Gates of Excellence: The Determinants of Creative Genius* (New York: Cambridge University Press, 1990).
11. David Feldman, *Nature's Gambit* (New York: Basic Books, 1986).
12. David Feldman, "Intelligences, Symbol Systems, Skills, Domains, and Fields: A Sketch of a Developmental Theory of Intelligence," in Hilda C. Roselli and Gary A. Maclaughlin, eds., *Proceedings from the Bush Symposium on Intelligence: Theory into Practice, Blueprinting for the Future* (Tampa: University of South Florida, 1992), pp. 78–99.
13. Julian C. Stanley, "Varieties of Intellectual Talent," *Journal of Creative Behavior,* vol. 31, 1997, pp. 93–119; Linda E. Brody and Camilla P. Benbow, "Accelerative Strategies: How Effective Are They for the Gifted?," *Gifted Child Quarterly,* vol. 3, 1987, pp. 105–10; and Marie A. Swiatek and Camilla P. Benbow, "Ten-Year Longitudinal Follow-up of Ability-Matched Accelerated and Unaccelerated Gifted Students," *Journal of Educational Psychology,* vol. 83, 1991, pp. 528–38.

14. David Lubinski and Camilla P. Benbow, "The Study of Mathematically Precocious Youth: The First Three Decades of a Planned 50-Year Study of Intellectual Talent," in Rena F. Subotnik and Karen D. Arnold, eds., *Beyond Terman: Contemporary Longitudinal Studies of Giftedness and Talent* (Norwood, N.J.: Ablex, 1994), pp. 255–81.

15. Joyce VanTassel-Baska and Paula Olszewski, *Patterns of Influence on Gifted Learners: The Home, the Self, and the School* (New York: Teachers College Press, 1989); and Nancy M. Robinson et al., "The Structure of Abilities in Math-Precocious Young Children: Gender Similarities and Differences," *Journal of Educational Psychology,* vol. 88, 1996, pp. 341–52.

16. Anne Lupkowski and Susan E. Assouline, *Jane and Johnny Love Math: Recognizing and Encouraging Mathematical Talent in Elementary Students* (Unionville, N.Y.: Royal Fireworks Press, 1992).

17. Nicholas Colangelo and Gary A. Davis, eds., *Handbook of Gifted Education,* 2nd ed. (Boston: Allyn and Bacon, 1997).

18. National Education Commission on Time and Learning, *Prisoners of Time* (Washington, D.C.: U.S. Department of Education, 1995).

19. Joyce VanTassel-Baska, ed., *Excellence in Educating the Gifted and Talented Learner* (Denver: Love Publishing, 1998).

20. Bloom, op. cit.

21. Kathleen V. Hoover-Dempsey and Howard M. Sandler, "Parental Involvement in Children's Education: Why Does It Make a Difference?," *Teachers College Record,* vol. 97, 1995, pp. 310–31.

22. Robert S. Albert, "Family Positions and the Attainment of Eminence: A Study of Special Family Positions and Special Family Experiences," *Gifted Child Quarterly,* vol. 24, 1980, pp. 87–95.

23. Mary K. Pleiss and John F. Feldhusen, "Mentors, Role Models, and Heroes in the Lives of Gifted Children," *Educational Psychologist,* vol. 30, 1995, pp. 159–69.

24. Joseph Walters and Howard Gardner, "The Crystallizing Experience: Discovering an Intellectual Gift," in Robert J. Sternberg and Janet E. Davidson, eds., *Conceptions of Giftedness* (New York: Cambridge University Press, 1986), pp. 306–31.

25. Joseph S. Renzulli, *The Enrichment Triad Model: A Guide for Developing Defensible Programs for the Gifted and Talented* (Mansfield Center, Conn.: Creative Learning Press, 1977); and John F. Feldhusen and Margaret E. Kolloff, "An Approach to Career Education for the Gifted," *Roeper Review,* vol. 2, 1979, pp. 13–17.

26. Ochse, op. cit.

27. John F. Feldhusen, "A Call for Overhaul: Gifted Education Overlooks Talent," *School Administrator,* April 1995, pp. 10–11.

28. Swiatek and Benbow, op. cit.; and Brody and Benbow, op. cit.

Form at end of book

Gender and Multicultural Issues

Questions

Reading 33. In the past, culture has been defined by some as being deficient in some way. Write a definition of culture using positive descriptive terms. How will your definition of culture help you to promote positive learning experiences?

Reading 34. Why is the development and implementation of a culturally relevant pedagogy important for today's learners? How will you likely develop and use curriculum content and teaching/learning activities to have a culturally relevant classroom?

Reading 35. How are critical media and other literacies linked to multicultural learning for students in various disciplines and at various grade levels? What type of learning activities that address these issues are you likely to plan for your classes? Outline the beginning of such activities, and share it with classmates. To what extent, if any, is the development of multiple literacies likely to promote effective citizenship skills?

Reading 36. Why do you think that girls and boys in primary grades use different strategies to solve mathematical problems? How might these differences influence the way girls and boys are taught mathematics?

How has recognition of multicultural and gender issues impacted the curriculum and classroom instruction?

As classrooms become more culturally diverse and pluralistic, teachers need to know and understand the cultures of their students. When acquiring information about student backgrounds and characteristics, teachers must be careful that existing or new stereotypes are not reinforced. In Reading 33, Cornell Thomas and others suggest that teachers should look for and discuss similarities rather than differences.

The in-depth conversation with Gloria Ladson-Billings in Reading 34 describes "culturally relevant pedagogy" applicable to language arts. Many of these pedagogies are applicable to other content disciplines as well. In Reading 35, Douglas Kellner argues for the need to develop several literacies to help students be effective and contributing citizens in the coming years.

Finally, attention needs to be given to gender-different teaching/learning styles. These differences are noted in students' thinking about mathematics and other content areas. In Reading 36, Elizabeth Fennema and colleagues describe their longitudinal study of students learning mathematics in grades 1–3. The implications of this study extend beyond mathematical learning in these primary grades.

Culture Defined:
A Twenty-First Century Perspective

Widening our perceptions of students rather than accepting stereotypes can open doors to learning for students and teachers alike.

Cornell Thomas

Cornell Thomas, Ed.D., is a professor and chair of the Educational Foundation and Administration Department in the School of Education, Texas Christian University, Fort Worth, Texas.

To educate as the practice of freedom is a way of teaching that anyone can learn. That learning process comes easiest to those of us who teach who also believe that there is an aspect of our vocation that is sacred; who believe that our work is not merely to share information but to share in the intellectual and spiritual growth of our students. To teach in a manner that respects and cares for the souls of our students is essential if we are to provide the necessary conditions where learning can most deeply and intimately begin. . . . Such teachers approach students with the will and desire to respond to our unique beings, even if the situation does not allow the full emergence of a relationship based on mutual recognition. Yet the possibility of such recognition is always present.

—*bell hooks,* Teaching to Transgress[1]

Hooks' notions of education, so eloquently expressed in this quote, speak to the heart-felt beliefs of many educators. This quote certainly speaks to mine as I consider the education of our young students. In particular, students in poor urban school environments seem to occupy my thoughts most in this area. Hooks reinforces for me the belief that most students come to school with existing knowledge; that most students come to school with the abilities and desire to learn; and that most students, when allowed to, can make needed connections for the process of internalized learning to occur.

Reality seems to demonstrate a different set of beliefs. Results from test scores, college entrance figures, dropout rates, and prison statistics seem to point a lack of student success in many schools. These results seem to counter my beliefs about most students. These data seem to indicate that many students lack prior or existing knowledge; do not come to school with the abilities and desire to learn; and do not possess the ability to make needed connections for the process of internalized learning to occur. A closer look at the data tells us that students from poor urban schools fare worse than others in these areas.

A conflict seems to exist between beliefs and currently perceived reality in this discussion. The question then is: why does this conflict exist? If most students really can learn, why don't they? If we still believe that most students can learn, what must happen to make this premise a reality? The following discussion may prove beneficial as educators attempt to find answers to these perplexing questions.

Questions

In the past, culture has been defined by some as being deficient in some way. Write a definition of culture using positive descriptive terms.

How will your definition of culture help you to promote positive learning experiences?

If most students really can learn, why don't they? If we still believe that most students can learn, what must happen to make this premise a reality?

"Culture Defined: A Twenty-First Century Perspective" by Cornell Thomas, *Educational Horizons,* 1998, v76, n3, pp. 122–126. Reprinted with permission.

Doing the Right Thing?

Ladies and gentleman, welcome back to the beginning of this new school year. We have before us some great challenges. Our superintendent has mandated new reading and math programs for our growing numbers of low-achieving students in the district. Both systems emphasize breaking down components into minute pieces of information and connecting them until, at some point along the continuum, we create some level of comprehension worth celebrating. Due to our changing demographics over the past two years, both programs will be a part of our curriculum. Yes, we will have a very interesting school year for sure.

We have another issue that continues to challenge our level of success. However, I think we have a solution that will work for this one. We all understand that as our demographics change, so must we. We must look at different ways of teaching to reach these new faces impacting our professional lives. Now, last year we studied African-American culture. Due to these studies, we know that African-Americans are successful in the fields of sports and entertainment. In both of these fields, rhythm seems to play a dominant role. Therefore rhythm and the incorporation of rhythmic patterns in our teaching, for those classes designated for African-American students, will be very important. We also know that, due primarily to somewhat unstructured early life experiences, single-parent homes, and struggles against racial injustice, most of these students are culturally and economically deprived. A modified, less challenging curriculum is needed. These students are, we must remember, "at risk."

These and other facts have informed us of needed curriculum changes. We will de-emphasize science and health so we can concentrate more on the basics. We will celebrate African-American heritage month for the first time with two planned events. The first event will enlighten our students about some of the great African-Americans in history. The second event will focus on the many inventions of African-Americans. To raise the levels of self-esteem among our African-American students, the district has allocated funds for our school to begin an intramural sports program along with an African-American music teacher to start a gospel choir. These funds are in addition to allocations previously provided for our existing extracurricular academic programs.

Now we must turn our attention to another cultural group that is growing in this school. Our Hispanic population is growing rather quickly. In order to meet their needs we will follow the same methods of study and planning employed to address our African-American concerns. Our goal is to study the culture of every group of students that reach at least 5 percent of the school's student body. Through this multicultural approach to the study of their traditions and norms, we can make them more successful students at Ronald Reagan Elementary School.[2]

Some may view this scenario as an exaggeration when talking about what occurs in schools. They would argue that very few organizations overgeneralize groups of peo-ple to this degree. Others would say that the images created by this scenario are real and exist in today's schools. Arguments would attempt to show how practices of identification and justification often create similar unfortunate results. I agree with them. In schools the process of becoming knowledgeable about and familiar with a group of people often ends with simplistic labels being placed on students. Justification practices typically end up creating rationales for lowering the predicted levels of student growth. Do we identify groups of people in ways that help us see value in difference, or do identification processes cause us to consider difference measured against some standard, typically resulting in classifying some individuals as having less value? In other words, don't these conceptual divisions between theory and practice, belief and action, fact and value, and statements and intent pose perceptual barriers toward student, teacher, and school success? The answers to these concerns can often be found in how we approach the issue of culture.

At issue, it seems, is the significance that people in power try to place on others within the society.

This article attempts to address an issue that often poses perceptual barriers as teachers work toward helping students reach higher levels of social and academic success in our public urban schools. An attempt will be made to show the detrimental effects of cultural ideology most commonly practiced in schools. I will then make efforts to reinforce a way of looking at culture that moves away from overgeneralization and discriminatory practices, which are often the *result* of the surface-level multiculturalism training—the study of customs and traditions of ethnic groups devoid of any social, political, and historical context—teachers so often receive. The approach proposed here will hopefully help illustrate the importance of developing relationships by using different cultural perspectives and also the power of this process when working with students. Perhaps discussions such as this one can assist those helping to better prepare teachers to develop more positive, fun, energized, and successful teaching and learning environments.

Culture

Descriptions and definitions of culture abound. Tylor defines culture as "that complex whole that includes knowledge, belief, art, morals, law, custom, and many other capabilities and habits acquired by man as a member of society."[3] Bullivant's view of culture is quite different from Tylor's. Bullivant believes that culture "embodies strategies by which social groups maximize their perceived advantage relative to other groups. . . . [Culture] contains not only survival instructions but also often an elaborate justification for their type and purpose."[4] In the second definition it seems that the purpose of classifying groups of people into "cultures" is to support lowered expectations for some individuals while providing advantages for others. Actions such as these are at times purposeful. Most of the time, however, they emerge from a continual barrage of subliminal messages that reinforce such ideology.

Banks states that culture is "an essential aspect of all people, and consists of the behavior patterns, symbols, institutions, values and other components of society."[5] At issue, it seems, is the significance that people in power try to place on others within the society. Bullivant's notions of justification can be seen historically as individuals have attempted to define themselves and gain power within a society using group norms. Terms such as "high culture" and "cultural deprivation" are employed. Success is often defined in ways that are more easily attainable for one group than others. In schools, testing practices and teaching procedures favor one set of life experiences over other ways, making the transition from home to school more difficult for some students. The types of decisions made and actions taken, based on this premise, help to maintain the tiered society that has always existed in this country, among others.

Representations of people based on cultural justifications help to form our way of thinking and living in a society of multiple perspectives. In some ways this need for justification stifles our desire to know and our need to bring meaning to this phenomenon called life. Our desire for power based on cultural norming slows the process of learning—of understanding—and seeing knowledge and truth right in front of us. Arrogance becomes a major barrier in all that we attempt to do.

Sonia Nieto says that culture includes "the ever-changing values, traditions, social and political relationships, and world view shared by a group of people bound together by a combination of factors that can include a common history, geographic location, language, social class, and/or religion."[6] Nieto's notion of culture as *ever changing* is supported when looking at our evolving society and how these transformative activities impact the way we make sense of and successfully navigate life experiences. My own work also supports these thoughts:

Our country, for example, has moved from an agrarian to an industrialized nation and now into an age in which change is recognized on an almost daily basis. The age of technology has created a superhighway carrying us where no person has gone before at the blink of an eye.[7]

The civil rights movement of the '50s and '60s helped to open doors once closed to women and some people of color. These doors to education, representation, higher-paying employment, and more access to travel have provided experiences that many individuals had never considered before. Experiences such as these also cause individuals to reconsider previously held beliefs and standards of living. This represents just two examples of how, as society evolves, so do knowledge, customs, habits of thinking, art, language . . . culture.

Implications for Teachers

So how would this concept of culture as ever changing influence what we do in our classrooms? Would the results of such activities positively affect teaching and learning environments in our urban schools? How would the movement toward creating a community of learners who value differences in schools be enhanced?

Traditional methods of cultural identification often cause us to frame the way people live their lives. The process causes groups of people to be placed in boxes, with virtually immovable walls. Our need to explain everything, including human characteristics, causes us to limit what we see; forces us to see the world with blinders on; and creates an environment that prevents acceptance of more individuals. This way of seeing the world has proved to be disastrous in many classrooms and schools, especially those in urban school settings.

This approach is explained by definitions of culture, such as Bullivant's, that describe the vilification of underrepresented people by those in control. A society in which differences are seen as problematic and of lesser value becomes the norm. This way of viewing culture attempts to identify differences as problems or "pathologies" in people and leads to institutionalized practices that keep "others" from sharing in the life experiences many in this society enjoy. They become practices that build walls of ignorance and self-doubt on one side and of ignorance and self-centeredness on the other, fueled by flames of misinformation.

These same issues can be found in many of our schools. Institutional practices based on overgeneralized definitions of culture have helped to create tiered educational systems. Expectations of students based on learned, stereotyped definitions of culture also become pathological processes. Instead of looking at how we attempt to educate, we place blame for our lack of success on children, their parents, and poverty. These practices must stop.

If we really want to see more students achieve higher levels of academic and social success, we must move away from this deficit-model approach. One step includes considering other notions of culture. We must begin to realize that it is not the experiences, or lack thereof, students bring to the classroom that pose our greatest challenges; it is how we perceive and value these experiences as potential connectors for new learning and what we do with them as a starting point for more teaching and learning to take place. We must help teachers begin to see these experiences of students as valid and valuable connectors to bridge the gap between what students *already know* and what we want them to learn. These connectors, which we have for so long refused to acknowledge, are needed for more successful learning opportunities to become normal, everyday occurrences in all classrooms.

Concluding Thoughts

We must work to prepare and support teachers in ways that help them to see the impact of a changing society on generalized cultural practices. It is the fluidity of "culture" that we need to understand. . . .

Any hope of affecting that future in more positive directions depends on how well we understand, teach about, internalize, and make use of contemporary cultural change.[8]

Teachers who internalize this way of thinking are better able to see the value of enjoying change and the different ways people live their lives.

Teachers begin to view difference without automatically weighing its value based on simply personal ways of thinking. We allow students to explore, challenge, think of what might be, of what one might become despite current situations. This premise can become a powerful tool for teachers attempting to prepare students for successful interpersonal experiences with individuals different from themselves.[9]

Instead of looking at how we attempt to educate, we place blame for our lack of success on children, their parents, and poverty. These practices must stop.

Embracing this type of cultural ideology helps to widen perceptions of people. The blinders are discarded and a new world can be seen. When considering the cultural backgrounds of students, we must keep in mind that although generalizations can be made, they can lead us off course in developing the types of relationships needed for successful classrooms.

As I have said so many times before; if we really want our students to learn, if we really care and want to become successful teachers, then instead of just teaching from some skills-based set of cultural competencies, we must emphasize the need to get to know students and allow students to get to know us.

Notes

1. bell hooks, *Teaching to Transgress: Education as the Practice of Freedom* (New York: Routledge, 1994).
2. Cornell Thomas, *Educational Equality and Excellence: Perceptual Barriers to the Dream* (Duncanville, Texas: Nellnetta, 1996).
3. Edward Tylor, *Primitive Culture* (New York: Harper, 1958).
4. Brian Bullivant, *Pluralism: Cultural Maintenance and Evolution* (Avon, England: Multilingual Matters Ltd., 1984).
5. James Banks, *Teaching Strategies for Ethnic Studies* (Boston: Allyn and Bacon, 1991).
6. Sonia Nieto, *Affirming Diversity: The Sociopolitical Context of Multicultural Education* (New York: Longman, 1992).
7. Thomas, *Educational Equality.*
8. Priscilla Walton, "The Complexities of a Multicultural Nation: What Will Multiculturalism Mean in the Year 2050?" *Multicultural Education* 5 (Fall 1997): 1.
9. Thomas, *Educational Equality.*

Form at end of book

Focus on Research:
A Conversation with Gloria Ladson-Billings

What does it mean to develop a culturally relevant pedagogy? How might we think about community in our teaching? In this interview, Gloria Ladson-Billings explores the implications of these and other questions for language arts teachers.

Arlette Ingram Willis and Karla C. Lewis

Arlette Willis is an Assistant Professor at the University of Illinois at Urbana-Champaign.

Karla C. Lewis is a graduate student in Educational Policy Studies at the University of Illinois at Urbana-Champaign.

Gloria Ladson-Billings is an Associate Professor in the department of Curriculum and Instruction at the University of Wisconsin at Madison. In 1996, she received the American Educational Research Association's Palmer O. Johnson Award for her outstanding article "Toward a Theory of Culturally Relevant Pedagogy," in the *American Education Research Journal.* Ladson-Billings' research focuses on preparing preservice educators to successfully teach in a diverse society and on improving the achievement of culturally diverse students. Her work adds significantly to the literature on educational pedagogy, multicultural education, and classroom instruction. From her research, she has developed a theory of culturally relevant pedagogy that is applicable to all classroom settings. Ladson-Billings' research illuminates the needs of teachers to become more culturally aware, sensitive, respectful, and responsive to cultural differences. We [*Language Arts* (LA)] interviewed her during the summer of 1997 about the applicability of her theory to the teaching of language arts.

LA: Good morning, Gloria. Can you tell me a little bit about how you decided to study African American students and academic success?

Gloria: Basically, I was after a kind of paradigm shift because the literature is replete with information about students—Black students' failure. In fact, if you just go through a computer search and punch in the descriptor, "Black Education," and you inevitably come up with a cross-reference that says things like, "see 'Culturally Disadvantaged,'" or "see 'At Risk.'" So even when you're not looking for those kinds of things, they're so ingrained in the public mind and in the literature that to try to break away from deficit models is a very difficult thing to do. That's really what I wanted to do. I wanted to stop asking the question, "What's wrong?" and begin to ask the question, "What's right?" as a way for us to begin to build on the literature and begin to better prepare teachers for success with our children.

LA: In your work, you have developed the notions of culturally relevant pedagogy and culturally relevant teaching. Can you describe what these terms mean to you?

Questions

Why is the development and implementation of a culturally relevant pedagogy important for today's learners?

How will you likely develop and use curriculum content and teaching/learning activities to have a culturally relevant classroom?

Gloria: In the study I conducted in California, I worked with eight teachers and I don't think any of them would use this terminology. Maybe they would now, since its been out there for a while, but this is not how they identify themselves. I needed a way to describe what I was seeing among these teachers. There are three things that are common to all eight of these teachers. The first is that they are focused on academic achievement. Some of them are quite warm, others are a little more cool, in their demeanor, but their real focus is academic achievement. That came across loud and clear. The second thing that we saw with these teachers was a focus on what I called the students' cultural competence. And by that I mean that the teachers allow the students to be *who they are,* so the kids come with what some may call dialect—I like to think of it as a different language. The teachers don't spend time trying to rid them of that language. Rather, they try to help kids understand where the language is appropriate and how it translates. Those are terms that get used by these teachers. They don't correct the kids. They say, "Well, this is how you translate that into a standard form." What my colleague, Mary Louise Gomez, calls "American edited English," rather than the notion of standard English.

It's particularly important when we think about the education of African American males, because of the salience of their culture. African American male culture is so powerful, not just among African American males. It's marketable; everyone wants to be like Mike [Jordan]. You know, you can't go anywhere without, encountering African American male culture, even in a town like Madison, Wisconsin that is largely European-American. You will see little White boys dressed a particular way, taking on Black cultural forms. Cultural competence is really important and these teachers figured out that you have to marry that, if you will, with academic achievement. The third thing among the teachers that really makes them stand out is what I call the socio-political consciousness. It's not enough to individually be an academic achiever and be culturally competent, you also have to have a greater sense of community and be in a position to critique your own education. If you just have those first two, what you get is a lot of what I see on the college campus: kids who are smart and well-grounded, but who turn around and blame other kids who don't make it. You get folks saying, "Well, I made it! What's wrong with you," adopting a "blaming the victim" mentality. What these teachers really focus on is, "Look, we're in a system, and you've got to understand how the system works, the ways in which it is unfair, the ways in which it advantages some and disadvantages others so that you develop a broader sense of community—because what we really need you for, in terms of your own citizenship, is to build a strong community." Those are the three broad ideals that ground this area.

LA: How are you using the term "community"?

Gloria: Well, it's multiple communities. But, given that I work with elementary teachers in a school community that was economically depressed, had been ravaged by drugs, and had little or no tax base, the teachers were, indeed, focused on the local community. There are certain instances in the data that show how they help kids connect with the larger communities, communities grounded by their culture. I did the research for the book *The Dreamkeepers: Successful Teachers of African American Children* (1994) in California. Most Californians, not all, but most Californians came from somewhere else. The kids have connections in places like Louisiana, Texas, Mississippi, and Oklahoma. They helped the kids understand: that's part of your community, too. Then, they also helped them understand the notion of the global culture. More specifically, one teacher whose class I was in was talking to the kids about Nelson Mandela. He had been released from prison and was in the States. He had come to Oakland, and kids had gone with their families to hear him speak. After the presentation, there was this long discussion about "What is the connection between Nelson Mandela and you?" The kids' first reaction was, "He is black." The teacher really pushed them, asking, "Well, there are lots of black people. How are you connected to this one?" The kids, then, began to talk about struggles for liberation and the idea that there is a broader global community and that what Nelson Mandela did was not just for the good of Black South Africa. It was for the good of the country, yes, because it was an unjust country, but it was also for the good of the continent. Finally, they surmised that it will be for the good of the world to realize that struggles for justice continue.

LA: What points about culturally relevant teaching do you wish you could get across more clearly to teachers?

Gloria: Well, those three things, I think, are the important ones. I always start with academic achievement, although I think of them like a three-legged stool: if you pull one out, then you don't have what I'm calling culturally relevant teaching. I always foreground academic achievement because I think that gets lost somewhere when people talk about multicultural education or teaching the "at risk." There's all this stuff about being nice. "Oh, I'm so nice to my kids. I treat my kids so sweetly. I love my kids." Well, that's good, but your job and the reason you're picking up a paycheck is that the kids are supposed to be learning something. I really don't want to move off that important focus.

LA: What are some of the virtues or qualities you believe are important for a teacher to have in order to be a successful teacher of minority children?

Gloria: What I've been working on the last maybe fifteen years, if you count my work at Santa Clara and at Stanford before coming here, is helping teachers understand that they have a culture. In almost every place I've been, most of the preservice and inservice people that I've worked with, have been European-American monolingual women, whose culture, to them, is invisible. They tend to believe that culture is that thing "all you other nice people have." There's this notion of discrete artifacts that are other people's culture. But if you were to turn around and say to those people, "Tell me something about your culture," they're likely to say, "Well, you know, I don't have any culture. I'm just an American." Someone saying they're *just an American* really says *you're* not; it says that the kids are not. But, I'm an American too.

Of course, it's taken me forty-some years to figure that out, because no one ever related to me in that way. The major thing that I think people who are going to teach kids, any kids—not just kids different from themselves, but particularly if they're teaching kids who are different from themselves culturally, racially, ethnically, linguistically—is to understand that they, themselves, are cultural beings. What that understanding will do is help them understand that the kinds of decisions they make, the way they think, the way they see the world, is culturally mediated. For example, I've seen some teachers use wonderful multicultural literature—read from it, share it with the kids, and not have a clue as to what they're reading, not really understand the ideas that are being conveyed. Now, that doesn't make them bad people. What it does, though, is it points out to me that they haven't recognized their own cultural grounding in a way to say, "Gee, I may not really understand this." One of the major things I think is important for teachers to be successful, is not to decide, "Oh, I've gotta go out and study these fifteen cultures." Human beings group themselves in infinite varieties. You will never learn all the cultures there are to learn. But if you learn your own, it's one of the things that I think will help you understand that culture functions in particular ways. And so, while you may not know all the subtleties and nuances of culture, you can recognize its operation. That's one of the reasons people almost always ask, "Do you think Black teachers have to teach Black kids?" No, because I've seen Black teachers be incredibly successful with White kids. Lisa Delpit talks about the Black woman who goes up and teaches the kids in Alaska. Now, what's going on there? Well, this is a person who understands herself as a cultural being, knows that they see the world in a particular way, not the *only* way. Often, what I confront with my students is this belief that their way in the world is the *right* way. Now, everybody else's way is okay, but it's not really the *right* way. There's only *one* way to think about justice. There's only *one* way to think about equality or democracy. And yet, there are a lot of ways in which people explicate notions of justice or freedom, and democracy.

LA: How do the language arts, especially reading and writing, fit in with your vision of culturally relevant teaching?

Gloria: I would probably use the term literacy as opposed to language arts because I think it's a little bit broader. I think there are ways to be literate and not have achieved all the skills you need in reading or writing, for example. I think of language arts as a special case of literacy. I don't think teachers can be effective in anybody's paradigm if they don't promote literacy and help kids to be able to communicate effectively; to be able to read, as Paulo Freire (1985) would say, "the world and the word." Because language is so powerful, one of the things that I think teachers have to really be aware of is that, when they help kids develop literacy skills, they do help kids become empowered. The frustrations that I see with kids in classrooms is that they have ideas, they want to express themselves in particular ways, and because they don't have specific reading and writing skills, they're cut off. They end up being disruptive or withdrawn or any number of things that we see as socially deviant. Yet, if we could find ways in which to tap into these kids' skills to motivate them and encourage them, you'd see a very different kid. I think language arts is really key to this end.

I also think it's important to remember the role that literacy played in the liberation and freedom struggles of Black people in this country. People often mention Freire, and I have in this interview, but before Freire, there was Septima Clark. She understood that people have to have a purpose for reading. You just can't give them a book with the alphabet in it and expect them to be excited about that. She also understood that language is deeply tied to people's sense of who they are. Right now, we're moving into this real push for mathematics. Bob Moses talks about mathematics as part of the second civil rights struggle. But literacy was part of the first civil rights struggle. We had to get people to read so that they could register to vote. We understood that, but also tied into that first civil rights struggle was a kind of disjuncture among the civil rights leadership, people like Martin Luther King, who was incredibly eloquent. This is a man with a Ph.D., talking to disenfranchised farmers who had no formal schooling; how does a Martin Luther King make sense to a farmer? We have a cultural worker, like Septima Clark, who sets up citizenship schools for people like Fannie Lou Hamer and Esau Jenkins, people who fanned out across the South to say, "You know what? This preacher man is gonna come here, and he's gonna be using some big words, but that only means X, Y, and Z." They were really the conduits through which the civil rights struggle was made powerful for people who ordinarily wouldn't have any access to that language. Language is so incredible, so powerful, that I don't think you can think about calling yourself culturally relevant if you have not considered the power of language.

LA: You have given our readers some examples of culturally relevant literacy teaching in the work of Septima Clark, but how about for the everyday teacher? What might culturally relevant literacy teaching look like in the everyday elementary classroom?

Gloria: I saw a teacher—I actually saw this video of a teacher. What she does in her class is just incredible. She starts off her year with her kids—I think she has fourth graders—and she asks all the kids to go home and get a story. This one little kid said, "I don't have a story." She said, "Honey, if you have lived, you have got a story." She sends the kids home to get these stories from parents, grandparents, aunties, neighbors, and friends. Then, she gets all these stories back and she develops the curriculum from the stories. There are spelling words, for example, all over the place. One spelling word she had on the list was emancipated. This kid jumped up and said, "That was from my story!" because he had talked to his grandfather. Here you have a fourth grader not doing short and long vowels, but using powerful language. She had found a way to take the stories that belonged to the kids in the community and make it part of "official knowledge," as Michael Apple would say. The other thing that I saw on the video was a grandmother who came and she read Sharon Bell Mathis's *The Hundred Penny Box* (1986). At the end of the story, she said, "You know what? This could have been my story." Then, she told a story about her grandmother. These are examples of having the literacy sort of come up out of the textbook; up out of children's literature, up out of the classroom; these are things that you see in a culturally relevant classroom. Literacy that's not boxed-in or confined. Classrooms where kids get an opportunity to see literacy practices all over the place. The advantage that I think the language arts has is that, not only do people "do literacy," a good literacy teacher continues to show them how they use it, and they certainly have these opportunities to create it.

LA: Some people have suggested that your notion of culturally relevant teaching is "just good teaching." Could you say a little bit about how you respond to this statement?

Gloria: Well, my knee-jerk response is, "Right. It is just good teaching!" But I have a follow-up response or question, and that is, "How come so little of it is going on in the classrooms with children who look like me?" If it's just good teaching, why are we having such difficulty making it happen? I specifically call it "culturally relevant." I haven't called it African-centered, although certainly there are elements of African-centeredness that you could see there, because I am convinced that, if we teach our kids in ways that respect who they are, that have intellectual and academic integrity, and help develop in them a sort of critical consciousness, it doesn't matter so much if the kids in the classroom are Latina/Latino, Asian, European, Native, or African American. Now that's a lot of skills that teachers have to have to be able to do this, but it's not as if they have to reinvent themselves. I've juxtaposed culturally relevant teaching to something I called assimilationist teaching. That's really a political statement. When I see assimilationist teachers, I typically see people who are not "bad teachers." They're going through the motions; they're doing things that they probably were taught to do in education schools, or that they saw themselves when they were students. Their view of what they're doing, the preconceptions that reinforce what they're doing are such that they believe: "there are only so many people who can be successful anyway; there are only so many slots of opportunity out there; and the cream rises to the top." I'm using all these cliches, but they believe that some kids are destined to fail. What's frightening to me is that these beliefs are starting to appear at lower and lower grade levels. I'm not talking about the calculus teacher who says, "Look, only ten percent of these folks are going to go on." I'm talking about the kindergarten teacher who responds to kids coming in on day one in a way that says, "You haven't come knowing your alphabet, knowing all your colors and shapes. You haven't come reading." Then, treats kids as if they don't deserve to be taught to read! Maybe the early childhood people won't like me for this, but to me, kindergarten is where you just start. You have to start somewhere. We've developed a whole mindset that if you don't already come with the skills, if you don't already come with the knowledge, you don't deserve to be taught them. It doesn't bother me for people to say "That's just good teaching." I just want to see more of it and I want to see it happen in those places where people don't make it happen.

LA: Your writing is focused more on preservice teacher education than on inservice teaching; however, in talking about teaching, I'm reminded of a quote from one of your articles. You wrote, "Culturally relevant teaching uses the students' culture to empower students to be able to critically examine educational content and process and ask what role they have in creating a truly democratic and multicultural society." Would you talk about how that fits with what you have just said about literacy teaching?

Gloria: I should probably give a more concrete example. One of my teachers was frustrated because her kids seemed to be so down on their own community. These kids are ten, eleven, and twelve years old, who come to school in a community in which, the streets are not clean, there are abandoned buildings, there are guys hanging out on the corner accosting people to see if they want to buy some drugs, and there are drive-by shootings. Yet, not ten minutes away, there are beautiful, pristine communities that don't look like this at all. They're separated, but they're not isolated. If they want to go to a full-service supermarket, where the meat and produce are fresh, they leave their community. They can see these things, like nicer parks in the adjacent communities. As a consequence, you have kids who are very negative about their community, saying, "I just wanna get out of this place. I can't stand this place!" The teacher was sort of frightened that this is being reinforced if the kids don't see anything of value in their own community. She began a huge community study, at first by pleading with the people at the historical society to let her into an archive that was off-limits to the public so that she could get some historical photos of the community over the years. The kids began doing oral histories, interviewing people who were long-term residents of the community. They also began to study and understand that the geographic location of the community was strategic and that all kinds of things contributed to the community being in the shape it was, including some unscrupulous real estate deals that forced people out, so that more houses were packed into smaller spaces. All through this study, what you have are kids writing letters to city council people, reading about the history of the community, and talking to people as they try to understand the changes in their community. Its current state didn't just happen—people weren't just lazy, but several social forces had come together to create the current situation. Now, the teacher said, "You can do like some people and pack up and move away. Or, you can be a part of bringing this community back to what it once was and what I believe its future will be." This kind of use of literacy skills is what I am referring to. Clearly, the kids had to be articulate enough, had to be literate enough, do enough writing and speaking to accomplish something. Then the teacher realized that she couldn't just have this sort of amorphous optimism; "Well, we're gonna fix the community." She had to focus them in on a project. Next, they took on this burned-out strip mall that was a haven for drug dealers and prostitutes and drunks. The kids got all of the information about what the strip mall had been, saw the transcripts of the county, and learned that the county had basically given up on it. Finally, they developed a proposal; they had an architect in and reconfigured what

it could be. She just kept pushing until ultimately the kids were at the city council meeting. They got on the agenda and made this presentation. This is important for kids and its important for that community. Whether or not it will ever come to be, who can say? Importantly, they weren't dismissed nor was it just a community interest story for local TV. They presented their proposal before the regular city council meeting and the city council members took what they had to say seriously. This is what I mean about becoming citizens.

Citizenship is not just about going to vote and not breaking laws. That's certainly some basic stuff you want people to do. But to function as a citizen, you've got to do a lot more. There's a whole series of civic behaviors that teachers have to take on if they want the kids to be able to do this.

LA: You've noted in several of your publications that the student populations are growing ever diverse, while teacher populations are predominantly Euro-American females. What do teachers need to know explicitly that would help them deal with cultural differences that exist in their classrooms?

Gloria: That kind of goes back to my earlier response about knowing one's own culture. What if we were in America, where all children were White and the teacher was from Thailand? Would there be any expectation for the children to become Thai? I don't think so. Yet, there is a not-so-subtle expectation that the children are to become like the teacher. The teacher never questions his or her cultural assumptions, never questions the way in which he or she does things.

I'm actually reading a novel right now by Frank Chin, called *Donald Duk* (1991). His reaction to the celebration of Chinese New Year captures this idea. He says, "Here we go with this Chinese New Year's stuff. I hate to hear about this stuff." Why does he hate to hear about it? Because it's a kind of essentialized, discrete characterization that, "Oh, all Chinese people do X, Y, Z." It's a very flat and monolithic picture of the culture.

What do teachers need to do? They need to do what they would do if they were working with kids who they see as equal-status kids. There's this expectation that middle-class teachers in middle-class schools are going to encounter their kids, their kids' communities, their kids' parents and those people who are important to them in all kinds of settings. That is *not* the expectation in most urban classrooms. The expectation is that kids will come to school and, if I encounter your parent, it will be in some formal setting like the school conference, back-to-school night, maybe some presentation. Do I expect to see your parent walking up and down the street? No, because we don't walk up and down the same street. But the teachers who were part of this study made it a point to walk up and down the same streets. How do they do this? Some teachers will just pick a particular Sunday that they will go to your church. No big fanfare. They don't go up to kids and say, "I'm coming to your church on Sunday." You just look up and here is Miss Devereaux sitting in the church. "Oh! There's my teacher!" So this visible presence in the community sends a signal, I think, to both the kids and their parents that says, "I'm invested here." All of the African American teachers got their hair done in that community. They'd look for hairdressers there. Anybody who knows anything about our culture knows that, if you want to know what's going on in the community, you either show up at the beauty shop or the barber shop, because people are talking about some heavy stuff there. This insertion of oneself into the community is important.

LA: Can culturally relevant pedagogy exist in a framework that is applicable to all students?

Gloria: If you think about those three main things: that people focus on academic achievement, that they want kids to be comfortable being who they are, that they value what the kids bring with them and help develop and maintain it; not just say, "Oh, it's okay that you speak that way, but not here." I mean, that won't help the kids develop it. And we want kids to be socially and culturally aware, critically conscious. I can't imagine that anyone would say, "I don't want that for my kid." It tends to be more subtle for middle-class kids. Case in point: I've been in classrooms where kids get their papers back from teacher tests. I've seen kids of color who didn't do well on a test basically ball up the test or just throw it in their backpack, end of story. I've seen White, middle-class kids that didn't do as well as they expected—they might have done okay, but didn't do as they hoped—and they will argue this point. I mean, go on and on about why they're right. Now, part of that is a sense of personal empowerment, that: "I have the right to do this." Somewhere they've got this sort of critical consciousness, if you will, maybe sort of more egocentric. I can't imagine any parent not wanting this thing to happen for their kids.

On another level, there are some preconceptions that I think all teachers have. One has to do with how they see themselves and others. We've got some decent literature that suggests that teacher status gets tied to the status of the kids. Among the teachers in my study, none saw themselves as low status because they didn't see the kids as low status. A teacher's conception of his/her self and others is powerful. The second preconception that these teachers have, has to do with this whole issue of social relations. How do we organize ourselves in the classroom? What the culturally relevant teachers do is say, "Look, we're a community. We're all going to work towards a sense of being a community." There are certain rules or norms in a community, and communities tend not to be competitive.

What many current African American scholars benefitted from were classrooms that had a kind of "sponsored mobility." If you look neat enough, clean enough, your hair was combed, your mother signed all the forms, she showed up at PTA meetings, she baked the cookies; you were worth the time and investment. That "sponsored mobility" then created a kind of tension for you because it sets you in opposition to the kids who didn't meet that, whatever that criterion is. It's kind of what Signitia Fordham's (1986) work talks about with this "acting White" phenomenon. It's not just the kids internalizing more of this "acting White," it's the way in which schools and teachers reward kids for certain criteria that may have nothing to do with their academic achievement. I mean, ultimately, they become achievers because they get all this support. The way in which the teachers in my study construct the social relations in the classroom differs. They say, "Look, we are a community." Some of them use the term "community" and some use the term "family," others use the term "team." There's always this sense that there is a collective. For example, one teacher in the study, Mrs. Harris, might say: "Who was fighting outside? I know it wasn't anybody from this room! Was it someone from *this* room?" It's never letting the individual hang out there on his/her own. It's always saying we have a responsibility to act in a certain way, because of who we are!

Miss Devereaux, another one of the teachers in my study, did something that I thought was just incredible. The room across the hall, for whatever reason, was assigned by the administrator for gifted kids. He had put all the kids who were identified as gifted at the fourth and fifth grade level, in one room. And there were about ten of them. Then, he filled the room with these sort of potentially gifteds. This was now the GATE classroom: *Gifted and Talented Education*. It had a little plaque that Miss Williams placed by the door. The kids in Miss Devereaux's classroom didn't understand what it meant. They said, "What is G A T E? What is that?" Off the top of her head, Miss Devereaux replied, "Oh, gifted and talented education." The kids said, "If they're gifted and talented, if they're GATE, then what are we?" In a split second, Miss Devereaux went and got a piece of paper and started writing something. She went out and taped it next to her name, on the wall. It said, "Better Than GATE." She said, "I don't care who they are over there. Whoever they are, we're better!" She had this conception of we're always a group—one person's success is a group's success. By the same token, someone's individual failure also reflects on the group. Thus, Mrs. Harris' statement, "I know nobody in our class was out there fighting," is saying, "we can not behave that way." The sense of social relations, is very powerful.

Finally, the teachers have different conceptions of knowledge. What is worth studying? How can we critique what we study? This is a very poor school district in which these people have a lot of out-of-date stuff, or didn't have any stuff. Not having the materials is never an excuse for these teachers. Now don't get me wrong; I'm not advocating that anybody should just take out-of-date, bad information. But if you put me in a forced-choice situation and said, "Good curriculum or good pedagogy," I'm going to vote for good pedagogy because a good curriculum cannot teach itself.

LA: You have made it clear that educators need to become more informed about the needs of African American students. You have written that it is important to address "not simply *what* and how successful teachers of African American students achieve success, but also *why* they do it." What do you see as some of the unique needs of African American students, and why do you think some teachers are more successful than others?

Gloria: Well, I think you're fooling yourself if you don't recognize that race still matters. I mean, the President is now on a big campaign to address it. On the one hand, the polls indicate White Americans think it's no big deal, but it is a consuming issue for African Americans; not out of a sense of need, nor out of a sense that we can't function, because we certainly function. We go to work everyday, we do what we have to do to raise our families. But we're never permitted to forget it. We're never allowed to move away from it, both implicitly and explicitly. I think that teachers have to recognize that, in racially stratified society, kids are coping with that burden. The kids know that the difference exists and I think that, by trying to ignore it, trying to pretend that it doesn't exist, we only make school that much more unreal for kids. It's not a real thing; it's just something they have to do.

This question of "*why?*" in my quote, not knowing just "*what?* and how?*" but *why* they do it, I think is important. One of the things that I think the research has done for me is move me away from looking for magical answers, it's moved me away from the "right" technique, away from the notion that, "If you just teach reading this way, it's going to do it." I don't believe any of that. That's probably not what this readership wants to hear, but I believe that successful teaching is grounded in beliefs and values that teachers have about the educability of learners. If you believe the kids can learn, if you are committed to having that come to pass, you're going to try everything! You might start out with whole language, but if you find a kid that's not getting it, then you're gonna say, "Hey, let me pull this basal out and see if I can break this down for this

kid. Let me grapple with it." I'm going to do whatever I can because I believe the kid can learn and it's my job to ensure that this happens.

I've gotten almost fixated with the notion of not just what we do or what people do, but what meanings we make of what people do. The example I've been using with teachers during inservice activities is that, in the morning, during the school year, in my household, it is chaotic. If the people from Child Protective Services came you'd see a news article, "Professor Arrested." My daughter is terrible about getting up because she's terrible about going to bed. She's the first kid that the bus picks up. Getting her to school is a chore, we get there by the skin of our teeth. You know what's interesting? Going to a White, middle-class school, they don't count tardies; it's not an issue. She has no tardies listed, but she's always sort of getting there by the skin of her teeth, papers flying everywhere, hanging out the backpack, some piece of a breakfast—if I was able to get that organized—in her hand, a bagel or a piece of toast or what have you. No one would dare say, "Here comes Jessica. Her parents don't value education. Look at her coming in here late all the time. The child hasn't had any breakfast." No one would say that stuff because of who they perceive me to be. I would argue that, at the same moment on the other side of this town, in a more working-class community, the very same things can be transpiring: a kid coming in late, papers all over the place, may or may not have had breakfast, may have breakfast in her hand. However, the meaning of that would be: "These people just don't value education. You know, they're not organized; they don't know." I'm trying to get people to understand the meanings that they are making. There's this whole sense that some kids are entitled and that there's no excuse for not giving them the very best, while other kids are not entitled.

LA: In your recent article (Ladson-Billings, 1994) you wrote, "To some teachers, simultaneously dealing with the flood of new materials and modified instructional approaches seems like an overwhelming task" (p. 24). I would guess that there are many teachers of African American students who may wish to become more culturally attuned and adopt a more culturally relevant teaching position, but find the task daunting. What can inservice teachers do to address inequalities, how do they change, and what must they change to make their classrooms more culturally relevant?

Gloria: Part of this is a kind of systemic problem that teachers are always having to grapple with. I would suggest that if people are really serious about their teaching, they're changing all the time anyway. This question is kind of like, "How do you eat an elephant?" My response is, "One bite at a time." There's no way you're going to get that whole elephant in your mouth. The task becomes to figure out, "Where do you want to start?" I started out as a secondary school teacher, teaching seventh and eighth graders U.S. History and World Cultures, along with teaching English, because, in middle school you never get the luxury of teaching just one thing. I became intrigued by the fact that so many kids couldn't read and I didn't know what to do. I couldn't teach them to read. I wasn't prepared in that way to understand the theories behind learning to read. I went back to school. I actually started a masters degree in the Psychology of Reading, at Temple University. I was just so frustrated with kids who I knew were smart kids, but the text stood between them and their ability to achieve.

My advice to teachers, is to not figure out, "How am I going to change my whole curriculum?" Instead, teachers need to decide: "What is the thing that I'm going to focus on? Where am I going to begin to improve?" One of the teachers in my study, Ann Lewis, is a good example of a teacher undergoing change. Ann was really at a crisis point in her career, probably described as nearing burnout. Her principal offered her a scholarship to the Bay Area Writing Project. When she came back she was a changed woman. She got so into writing and intellectual engagement with what it means to be a writer that she changed her writing in the classroom. She got so excited about that one year, but the next year it was about literature. Every year she was looking for new and different things to do. I think that's what makes teaching exciting, that you can make these changes and not that you get overwhelmed by just doing everything. Its important that you become more deliberate in the kinds of changes you want to make.

LA: You've participated on national standard panels. How might English language arts national standards be applied to transform schools in meaningful ways for traditionally under-served students?

Gloria: This is a hard question because you have to understand that I believe that the standards are a fiction. My participation in the standards is much more a political statement. You can't get in the game unless you talk the standards language. Therefore, part of my participation is ensuring that some aspect of the standards incorporates issues that I think are important. I don't believe that the standards by themselves are going to do anything. The standards appease a public that is concerned that somehow our schools are not meeting the mark. I don't think they will transform schools in which kids are underserved because it's not just having a standard, it's having the means to the standard.

The standards say you should do X, Y, and Z. If you have the curriculum resources, if you have the equipment,

if you even have the facilities, your ability to participate is different from people who don't. I want to give you an example of why it's really troublesome to set the standards, particularly the way in which local districts and municipalities are creating their own. In Wisconsin, in fourth grade social studies, the focus is on the State. One of the things we get into is the importance of the prairie in the development of the state, agriculturally and geographically. I wouldn't argue with anybody that that is an important thing to know about Wisconsin. My daughter went to an elementary school that was right next to a prairie restoration project. All year they went out in the prairie, they wrote prairie poems, and each kid picked his or her own spot. As the seasons changed, they would go back out and look at the prairie and draw and make these phenology journals. They had science, language arts, and social studies prairie-themed projects. I work with kids on the other side of town, fourth graders who I think are equally smart if not smarter than the kids in this school. Their school is right next to a bakery, not a neighborhood bakery, a big, old factory-type bakery. Their teachers did take them to the prairie. They had to order a bus. They went out to the prairie. They had a tour guide; he explained the environment. They had seeds. The kids would throw some seeds and help bring the prairie back because of all the development. However, their understanding of the prairie is going to be primarily a vicarious one. They'll read *Little House on the Prairie* (Wilder, 1975) just like my daughter. Now, who's going to really meet and/or exceed the standard? The kids in my daughter's class! Through no fault of their own, the kids in the working-class community, where the standard doesn't conform to their opportunities to learn, are disadvantaged. These are the things that worry me about this hope of creating a national standard. It suggests a very static picture of the curriculum. It doesn't take into account what I see as understanding how learning takes place.

I think you really have to be careful in the delineation of the standards. I think the proliferation of the standards are at a point where teachers are going to be so overwhelmed that they're going to actually be kind of paralyzed by the whole process. How can you know; unless the textbook publishers, who are not above any of this, create a text that says, "We have all the standards covered? Then, we retreat from real intellectual activity, to a much more scripted, predictable, stiff activity in which the kids just cover the material and we say, "We've met the standards."

LA: What is your current research focus?

Gloria: I have a zillion things in the pot. I was hoping to devote this summer to analyzing data I've gathered on novice teachers. People have commented that, in my previous work, all of the teachers in the study are experienced teachers. The least amount of experience of any of the teachers in my study is twelve years. I made a point of doing a project that looks at novice teachers who have gone through a special program we have called "Teaching for Diversity." I want to find out if it makes any difference to have a preparation program that raises these kinds of questions on these issues. Another project that Mary Louise Gomez and I are doing is called, "Teachers Helping Teachers." We are in a large school of mostly working-class families. Some homeless children attend this school. We have ten K–1 teachers that we're looking at. We want to understand how they are helping to develop the literacy practices of students in their classrooms and how they can learn from each other. One of the things that's been really interesting in this particular project is that nine of the ten teachers have more of a literature base and whole language approach to the teaching of literacy because that's what's prescribed in the curriculum. But, one of the teachers is very traditional, teaching the kids sound symbol recognition, phonics, these kinds of things. She's always been kind of marginalized in this school because she does these things. Basically, the assignment is for them to share with each other. One assignment was to bring in an example of some work that the kids are doing in the classrooms. This teacher brought in letters that her kids had written after they had seen a local production of *Peter Rabbit*. Their assignment was to write to Peter and to give him advice. She passed the letters around for others to see. The student letters were just fabulous. They were imaginative and kids were using really important large vocabulary, but you could see the spelling errors were there also. One of teachers asked, "Did they copy this?" She said, "No, you can see all the letters are different." Another teacher asked, "Do you help them do all of this?" She said, "No, this is what's expected." What they are seeing, is that something of value that must be happening in the traditional teachers' classroom because her kids can perform differently.

In this study, another thing we've asked the teachers to do is to identify for us those students who are struggling, that is, those students about whose literacy development they are most concerned. By and large, they have identified African American children. However, the traditional teacher selected a White boy. I think people were surprised because they knew the child. She said, "He isn't even coming close to his potential." I think all these teachers are pretty good teachers, and certainly have the kids' interest at heart. But, for teachers to all have this list of kids that they're concerned about, and for all of them to be African Americans, and not have others, causes you to ask yourself, "What's going on here?" That's something that I want to push teachers to at least be able to interrogate; to ask, "If it turns out that all the African American children are failing, what's going on?"

LA: Do you have any closing words?

Gloria: I want people to have some optimism, to recognize that I didn't do this kind of work to hold these teachers up and say, "All of the rest of you are terrible." I kind of did it to say this was in the realm of possibility, and so we need to think differently about what we're doing. It probably sounds preachy, but I guess I just want people to realize that they can do something, they can make a difference. One of the things that frustrates me in inservice situations is that we often talk about wonderful notions of what can happen in classrooms, and then I hear teachers say, "Well, we can't do that." Part of it is the total sense of not having any power. I guess I'm really trying to help teachers understand that they do have some power and they have to exercise that power. It may not be welcomed, and it may not be smooth-sailing if they do it, but I think, with their own integrity and sense of self-efficacy, they have to be able to look themselves in the mirror each morning and say, "I'm going out here and I'm going to do the very best that I can because it's the right thing to do."

LA: Thank you.

References

Chin, F. (1991). *Donald Duk*. Minneapolis, MN: Coffee House.

Fordham, S. & Ogbu, J. (1986). Black students' school success: Coping with the "Burden of 'acting white.' " *Urban Review, 18*(3), 176–206.

Freire, P. (1985). *The politics of education: Culture, power, and liberation*. South Hadley, Massachusetts: Bergin and Harvey.

Ladson-Billings, G. (1991). *The dreamkeepers: Successful teachers of African American children*. San Francisco: Jossey-Bass.

Ladson-Billings, G. (1994). What we can learn from multicultural educational research. *Educational Leadership*, May, 22–26.

Mathis, S. B. (1986). *The hundred penny box*. New York: Puffin Books.

Wilder, L. I. (1975). *Little house on the prairie*. New York: Perennial Library.

Form at end of book

Multiple Literacies and Critical Pedagogy in a Multicultural Society

Douglas Kellner

Douglas Kellner holds the George Kneller Chair in Philosophy of Education at University of California at Los Angeles, Los Angeles, CA 90095. His primary areas of scholarship are philosophy of education, cultural studies, and new technologies.

We are in the midst of one of the most dramatic technological revolutions in history, changing everything from the ways that we work, to the ways that we communicate with each other, to how we spend our leisure time. This technological revolution, centering on information technology, is often interpreted as the beginning of a knowledge society, and ascribes education a central role in every aspect of life. This Great Transformation poses tremendous challenges to education to rethink its basic tenets, to deploy the new technologies in creative and productive ways, and to restructure education in the light of the metamorphosis we are now undergoing.

At the same time that we are going through a technological revolution, important demographic and sociopolitical changes are occurring in the United States and the rest of the world. Emigration patterns have brought an explosion of new peoples into the United States in recent decades and the country is now more racially and ethnically diverse, more multicultural, than ever before. This creates the challenge of providing people from diverse races, classes, and

backgrounds with the tools to enable them to succeed and participate in an ever more complex world. Critical pedagogy considers how schooling can strengthen democracy, create a more egalitarian and just society, and promote a process of progressive social change.

In this essay, I argue that we need multiple literacies for our multicultural society, that we need to develop new literacies to meet the challenge of new technologies, and that other literacies of diverse sorts—including an even more fundamental importance for print literacy—are of crucial importance in restructuring education for a high-tech society. My argument is that education today needs to foster a variety of literacies to empower students and to make education relevant to the demands of the present and future. I assume that new technologies are altering every aspect of our society; and that we need to understand and make use of them both to understand and transform our world.

I first discuss how critical pedagogy can promote multicultural education and sensitivity to cultural difference, and then focus on the importance of developing media literacy to engage critically the wealth of media materials that currently inundate us. Media literacy involves teaching the skills that will empower citizens and students to become sensitive to the politics of representations

Questions

How are critical media and other literacies linked to multicultural learning for students in various disciplines and at various grade levels

What type of learning activities that address these issues are you likely to plan for your class? Outline the beginning of such activities, and share it with calssmates.

To what extent, if any, is the development of multiple literacies likely to promote effective citizenship skills?

of race, ethnicity, gender, sexuality, class, and other cultural differences. Next, I discuss the need to cultivate a wide range of types of critical literacies to deal with the exigencies of the cultural and technological revolution in which we are currently involved, ranging from computer literacy to multimedia literacy to new forms of cultural literacy. Such concerns are part of a critical pedagogy that summons educators, students, and citizens to rethink established curricula and teaching strategies to meet the challenge of empowering individuals to participate democratically in our increasingly multicultural and technological society.

Multiculturalism and Media Pedagogy

A number of educators and theorists recognize the ubiquity of media culture in contemporary society, the growing trends toward multicultural education, and the need for media literacy that addresses the issue of multicultural difference.[1] There is an expanding recognition that media representations help construct our images and understanding of the world and that education must meet the dual challenges of teaching media literacy in a multicultural society and sensitizing students and publics to the inequities and injustices of a society based on gender, race, and class inequalities and discrimination. Recent critical studies analyze the role of mainstream media in exacerbating these inequalities and suggest ways that media education and the production of alternative media can promote a healthy multiculturalism of diversity and more robust democracy. They thus confront some of the most serious difficulties and problems that face us as educators and citizens as we move toward the twenty-first century.

A recent collection edited by Diane Carson and Lester D. Friedman, *Shared Differences,* demonstrates how media of cultural representation such as film, video, and photography can be used to promote multicultural education. The text opens with a statement by Carson that a sense of urgency concerning America's increasingly multicultural society drove her and Friedman to investigate how multicultural education can help us invigorate education for the contemporary era:

A teacher's inclusion of multicultural pedagogy and an active engagement with diverse ethnic, racial, and national issues is critical to America's social well-being. . . . We must put our beliefs into practice, aware that the defining characteristics and enabling understanding of ethnic, racial, and national groups can and ought to be taught. Teachers must acknowledge uniqueness and difference as they also applaud similarity, for the strength of small communities and also society at large derives from celebrating our diversity (*SD,* p. ix).

Carson expands her pitch for multicultural education as a response to deal creatively with growing diversity,

which facilitates "strategies for sharing, understanding, and enjoying" our proliferating cultural multiplicities and differences (*SD,* p. x). She urges developing pedagogic practices that will promote multicultural understanding, that will empower students, and that will strengthen education. Carson's and Friedman's dual project is to argue that the issues of multiculturalism are central to academic disciplines from literature to anthropology, and that media pedagogy can serve to promote the goals of multicultural education and critical media literacy. They accordingly assemble a broad array of studies by teachers who use media technology to promote multiculturalism in a number of disciplines in two- and four-year colleges. Each of their fourteen contributors outlines course goals, discusses how they use media and media education to promote these goals, and analyzes course experiences. Each also presents the syllabus used in the course to provide practical models of how to organize courses in multicultural education and media pedagogy.

The result is a very useful collection of models of practical criticism that will enable teachers in various fields to use media education to promote goals internal to their discipline. On the whole, the collection advances the social goals of making teachers and students sensitive to the politics of representation, to how media audiences' images of race, gender, sexuality, and cultural differences are in part generated by cultural representations, and to how negative stereotyping presents harmful cultural images. This book stresses the need for a diversity of representations to capture the cultural wealth of contemporary America. Teachers can gain insight into how media can serve their pedagogical goals and how they can both use media to promote multicultural education and to use this material to teach media literacy as well.

Following Carson's Preface and overview of the project, the collection opens with an essay by coeditor Friedman, "Struggling for America's Soul: A Search for Some Common Ground in the Multicultural Debate." Friedman notes the current conflicts over multiculturalism in American society and the debates over multicultural education in the academic world. In this contentious and conflicted terrain, he suggests, we must seek common ground, to articulate what unites as well as divides us, and come to appreciate our commonalities as well as our differences. In fact, the rancor in some of the education wars over curricula, pedagogy, and education in general are part and parcel of broader cultural wars between competing groups and ideologies fighting over the future of U.S. society and culture. Since educational debates are often intimately connected with political struggles, it is necessary to articulate clearly the different positions within the debates and, if possible and appropriate, to seek a common ground for consensus.

Indeed, I have long believed that there is no necessary conflict between traditional and multicultural education, that the educational process is strengthened with the incorporation of voices, viewpoints, and perspectives excluded from traditional canons, and that multicultural curricula, deployed wisely, can improve many academic courses. Friedman attempts to articulate some principles that would enable multicultural education to enrich rather than replace the traditional curriculum and that would provide a common ground for both traditionalists and multiculturalists to rethink education. Reaching a common and higher ground in the debates over education requires, in Friedman's view, acknowledging that while knowledge is constructed and transmitted from specific locations, "knowledgeable, well-trained teachers can generate discussions about cultures other than their own" (*SD,* p. 3). For Friedman this entails accepting that multicultural curricula need not "be taught only, or even primarily, to members of ethnic minorities," nor that "one monocultural approach (e.g. Eurocentrism) [be replaced] with another monocultural methodology (e.g. Afrocentrism)" (*SD,* p. 3).

If multicultural education is to promote genuine diversity and expand the curriculum, it is important both for groups excluded from mainstream education to learn about their own heritage and for dominant groups to explore the experiences and voices of minority and excluded groups. Moreover, as Friedman stresses, while it is important and useful to study cultures and voices excluded from traditional canons, dead white European male authors may have as much of importance to teach all students as excluded representatives of minority groups whom multiculturalists want, often with good reason, to include in the curriculum. Thus, Friedman convincingly argues that "Western culture, despite its myriad faults, remains a crucial influence on American political, intellectual and social thought and, as such, should play an important role in classrooms" (*SD,* p. 3).

In reality, few advocates of multicultural education call for jettisoning the traditional canon and altogether replacing the classics with new multicultural fare. Genuine multicultural education requires expanding, not contracting, the curriculum, broadening and enriching it, not impoverishing it. It also involves, as Friedman stresses, including white ethnic groups in the multicultural spectrum and searching out those common values and ideals that cut across racial and cultural boundaries. Thus, multicultural education can both help us understand our history and culture, and can move toward producing a more diverse and inclusive democratic society.

Shared Differences suggests how multicultural education can be used to enrich the subject matter of many traditional disciplines, ranging from literature to anthropology. In addition, traditional disciplines and texts can themselves be taken as the topic of critical scrutiny and inquiry, and can thus be used to promote the pedagogical goals of developing sensitivity to cultural difference. The emphasis in the reader is on using a medley of media material to present aspects and effects of the politics of representation from a variety of perspectives. Thus, an anthropologist discusses how media culture can be used to teach ethnography and cultural critique that is sensitive to cultural representation and difference (Michael M. J. Fischer); writing teachers present a course dedicated to writing about literature and various forms of popular media which helps make students aware of the forms of cultural rhetoric and difference (Margaret Himley and Delia C. Temes); an English professor (Linda Dittmar) discusses how the English curriculum can be transformed by the addition of film and media culture; a public health professor (Clarence Spigner) discusses how negative media representations can contribute to problems of health and social well-being; and historian Carlos E. Cortes discusses how media education can contribute to better historical understanding and sociopolitical sensitivity.

These studies provide a variety of arguments for the importance of including media texts in the curriculum and for using and studying the media to advance the aims of a variety of pedagogic practices. The teaching of writing, for example, as Himley and Temes stress, is enhanced by engaging students in analyzing cultural rhetoric and difference in various domains of social discourses. Print journalism, film, television, photographic images, advertising, and political rhetoric are all forms of writing, all cultural texts that influence how we see the world, and the practice of critically dissecting these writings helps us to see how all of these cultural forms represent different modes of writing with their own biases and perspectives. Attending to the representation of difference within the broader field of society and culture can enable students to avoid manipulation by cultural rhetorics and to empower students to find their own voices within the cacophony of competing and conflicting discourses of the present age. Critically dissecting cultural materials also empowers students to reflect upon their own commonalities and differences, and to respect their differences from others, while becoming critical of those who would suppress differences or present some differences (such as race, gender, and class) negatively, stereotypically, and pejoratively.

The authors in *Shared Differences* thus present arguments legitimating the use of media materials in a number of disciplines to promote both traditional pedagogic goals (the transmission of knowledge, the cultivation of reading and writing skills, the mastering of fields and disciplines), as well as to contribute to the production of a more diverse democratic polity that appreciates and affirms differences between ethnic, racial, and cultural groups. On the other hand, many of the teachers who are using multicultural media as a tool to promote their own disciplines downplay the importance of cultivating media literacy as an important tool in developing students' critical and analytical skills. One needs to be aware that each media technology (film, video, photography, multimedia, and so on) have their own biases, their own formal codes and rules; and that the ways in which the media themselves construct and communicate meaning needs to be an explicit focus of awareness and analysis.[2]

Moreover, media culture constructs models of multicultural difference, privileging some groups while denigrating others. Grasping the construction of difference and hierarchy in media texts requires learning how they are constructed, how they communicate and metacommunicate, and how they influence their audiences. Textual and semiotic analysis of media artifacts helps to reveal their codes and conventions, their values and ideologies, and thus their meanings and messages.[3] In particular, critical cultural studies should analyze representations of class, gender, race, ethnicity, sexual preference, and other identity markers in the texts of media culture, as well as attending to national, regional, and other cultural differences, how they are articulated in cultural representations, and how these differences among audiences create different readings and receptions of cultural texts.

On the whole, the contributions to *Shared Differences* focus on using media to promote multicultural education and downplay theorizing and developing the skills of media literacy. Most of the contributors focus on the politics of positive or negative representations and do not present more complex methods of gaining media literacy, or articulate more general principles or models. Although many of the practical course curricula and syllabi present materials for developing media literacy, this topic is not overtly theorized and is merely mentioned in passing. In the next section, therefore, I will engage a series of books published over the past decade that contribute to developing a critical pedagogy of media literacy. My argument for developing such skills as part of standard educational training is that the media themselves are a form of cultural pedagogy and thus must be countered by a critical media pedagogy that dissects how media communicate and affect their audiences and how students and citizens can gain skills to critically analyze the media.

Media Literacy and the Challenges of Contemporary Education

While *Shared Differences* focuses on multicultural media pedagogy as a response to the need to develop multicultural education and understanding, a large number of books on media literacy over the past decade start from the premise of the ubiquity of media culture in contemporary society and produce a more general argument for critical media literacy as a response to media bombardment. "Media literacy" involves a knowledge of how media work, how they construct meanings, how they serve as a form of cultural pedagogy, and how they function in everyday life. A media-literate person is skillful in analyzing media codes and conventions, criticizing media stereotypes, values, and ideologies, and thus reading media critically. Media literacy thus empowers people to use media intelligently, to discriminate and evaluate media content, to dissect media forms critically, and to investigate media effects and uses.

A critical media literacy is necessary because media culture strongly influences our view of the world; it imparts knowledge of geography, technology, the environment, political and social events, how the economy works, and related topics in our society and the world at large. Media entertainment is also a form of cultural pedagogy, teaching dominant values, ways of thought and behavior, style and fashion, and providing resources for constituting individual identities.[4] The media are both crucial sources of knowledge and information, and sources of entertainment and leisure activity. They are our storytellers and entertainers, and are especially influential since we are often not aware that media narratives and spectacles themselves are a form of education, imparting cultural knowledge, values, and shaping how we see and live our social worlds.

Consequently, media literacy is an important part of multicultural education because many people's conceptions of gender, sexuality, race, ethnicity, and class are constituted in part by the media. More than this, the media are often important in determining how people view social groups and reality; conceive of gender roles of masculinity and femininity; and distinguish between good and bad, right and wrong. Because the media shape attitudes and behavior, provide role models, influence conceptions of proper and improper conduct, and provide crucial cultural and political information, they are an important form of pedagogy and socialization.

Sometimes "the media" are lumped into one homogeneous category, but it is important to discern that there are many media of communication and forms of cultural pedagogy, ranging from print media such as books, newspapers, and magazines to film, radio, television, popular music, photography, advertising, and many other multimedia cultural forms, including video games, computer culture, CD-ROMs, and the like. A media-literate person thus needs to be able to read, understand, evaluate, discriminate, and criticize different kinds of media materials, and ultimately, as I shall suggest below, produce media artifacts, in order to use media as means of expression and communication. Media literacy thus requires traditional print literacy skills as well as visual literacy, aural literacy, and the ability to analyze narratives, spectacles, and a wide range of cultural forms. Media literacy involves reading images critically, interpreting sounds, and seeing how media texts produce meaning in a multiplicity of ways.[5] Since media are a central part of our cultural experience from childhood to the grave, training in media literacy should begin early in life and continue into adulthood, as new technologies are constantly creating new media and as new genres, technical innovations, aesthetic forms, and conventions are constantly emerging.

Len Masterman has been associated with helping inaugurate a media literacy movement and his book *Teaching the Media* is frequently cited in the literature on the topic as a key text.[6] Masterman makes the case that the ubiquity of the media in transmitting knowledge requires educators from primary schools and beyond to impart critical knowledge of how the media work to construct meaning. Yet Masterman's focus is on "delineation of a number of general principles for teaching across the media" and he does not really develop a concept or practical pedagogy of media literacy in his book, which engages specific media and forms of media culture.[7] Rather, drawing heavily on British cultural studies, he provides a comprehensive overview of media education, discussing such topics as media institutions, text and rhetoric, ideology, audiences, and approaches to media education.

Masterman's text provides a useful general introduction to teaching the media, though his British-oriented approach might provide blocks to using his book in a North American setting.[8] Moreover, while a general media literacy may be of some use in transmitting general ideas and principles, one needs to develop a media literacy that is sensitive to the differences among the specific media, engaging students in critically analyzing and dissecting a wide range of media materials, including such disparate phenomena as TV news, rock music, action-adventure film, advertising, and multimedia web sites. Hence, the principle of difference should not only be part of a multicultural education making students sensitive to social and cultural difference; one should also see how different media construct their materials in different ways. One also needs to construct different forms of media literacy according to the age, interests, needs, and capacities of specific students. Obviously, teaching media literacy in kindergarten through the elementary grades is going to involve different strategies and pedagogy than teaching media literacy to high school, college, or adult audiences.

Contributions toward a critical pedagogy of difference are found in recent contributions to expanding media literacy by scholars influenced by poststructuralist theory. Allan Luke and Carmen Luke, for example, have pointed to the usefulness of poststructuralist thought in rethinking education under contemporary conditions.[9] Carmen Luke has shown how difference is often occluded in mainstream media culture and how cultural studies in the classroom can generate alternative readings and critically valorize difference.[10] In turn, Allan Luke has shown how a poststructuralist-inspired discourse analysis can help dissect the construction of difference in cultural texts and be an important instrument in a critical pedagogy.[11] The Lukes and others have also argued how the proliferation of new media require new pedagogies and forms of multiliteracy—a theme that I take up in later sections of this essay.[12]

Although we are moving into an increasingly global media culture, critical media pedagogy should draw from media and cultural material familiar to students in different countries and parts of the world. In the 1990s, for instance, a series of books have been published in the United States dealing with various dimensions of media literacy and education and using North American media material. Similarly, earlier cultural studies and models of media literacy often engaged material from English and Australian contexts that were not always accessible to individuals in the North American context. Today there is a burgeoning tradition of cultural studies engaging material from a variety of cultures, ranging from the United States to Taiwan, in what might be seen as the globalization of cultural studies. Thus, whereas John Fiske's earlier works primarily dealt with the English and Australian materials and the contexts in which he was himself living, teaching, and researching, his more recent books focus on North American media culture and contexts, reflecting his new domicile.[13] Henry Giroux, Peter McLaren, and others have linked cultural studies with critical pedagogy and systematically elaborated theoretical principles and models, while carrying out practical studies of contemporary media culture.[14] In all of these cases, the issue of multiculturalism and the analysis of gender, race, and class in terms of the politics of representation and audience reception are stressed. Similar emphases are also found in the cultural studies of Grossberg, Kellner and Ryan, Kellner, and a number of other works in North American cultural studies.[15]

Other noteworthy attempts to develop a critical pedagogy focusing on cultivating media literacy and multicultural education include the work of James Schwoch, Mimi White, and Susan Reilly who recognize that the media are a form of pedagogy that constructs social knowledge and requires critical dissection of its mode of teaching.[16] The authors demonstrate how media images, discourse, symbols, and narratives constitute social meanings and subjectivities. Critically scrutinizing the dominant forms of media culture, the authors develop a critical pedagogy of representation that dissects the values, meanings, and ideologies constructed in media texts. Combining analyses of news, information, and entertainment, the authors see "media as perpetual pedagogy" and provide critical insights into the sort of pedagogy provided by mainstream media while providing a counterpedagogy of their own.

In the same critical spirit, David Sholle and Stan Denski discuss media education and the (re)production of culture, critically analyzing the social production of knowledge through mass media of communication and proclaiming the need for a critical pedagogy that criticizes its limitations, distortions, and biases.[17] The authors stress the importance of building bridges across disciplines, using theory to connect media education with the empowerment of students and the promotion of radical democracy. Combining the critical theory of the Frankfurt school with British cultural studies, feminism, and postmodern theory, Sholle and Denski call for contextualizing education within the framework of its functions in U.S. society, and they connect critical pedagogy and media education with transformative practice and the goal of producing a more democratic society.

In addition, Sholle, Susan Reilly, Peter McLaren, and Rhonda Hammer have published a co-authored text, *Rethinking Media Literacy,* which provides theoretical models of critical media literacy and practical studies that exemplify the project.[18] They attempt to develop the literacies that will help make possible more critical cultural analysis and awareness, as well as the empowerment of students and citizens. In particular, Hammer indicates how student video projects can empower students to learn the conventions and techniques of media production and use the media to advance their own aims.[19] Whereas film production involves heavy capital investment, expensive technology, and thus restricts access, video production is more accessible to students, easier to use, and enables a broad spectrum of students actually to produce media texts, providing alternative modes of expression and communication. Video technology thus provides access to a large number of voices excluded from cultural production and expression, materializing the multicultural dream of democratic culture as a dialogue of a rainbow of voices, visions, ideas, and experiences.

The books that I have discussed all address the issue of promoting multiculturalism and media literacy on a university level. They are geared for the most part to college undergraduate and even graduate teaching and thus are on a fairly high level of sophistication. Yet one could argue that multicultural and media literacy should be taught at all stages of education, that it is extremely important to begin teaching multiculturalism and media literacy at early levels. Moreover, I would suggest that media material can be especially valuable in teaching multiculturalism and positive social values to young children and teenagers, in view of the important role of media culture in their lives. There are in-

deed associations, groups, and texts that are oriented toward teaching multicultural education and media literacy to students in the K–12 range.[20] Surveying this vastly expanding material goes beyond the limits of this study, and here I merely want to mention the scope of importance of teaching media literacy and multiculturalism on all levels from kindergarten through graduate school and beyond. We live in a world of media and new technologies, and our social world is increasingly multicultural, providing new opportunities to enjoy richness and diversity, but also producing new social conflicts and problems.

It is the challenge of education and educators to devise strategies to teach media literacy while using media materials to contribute to advancing multicultural education. For, against McLuhan who claims that the younger generation are naturally media literate, I would argue that developing critical media literacy requires cultivating explicit strategies of cultural pedagogy and models of media education.[21] Media literacy involves making unconscious and prereflective understanding conscious and reflective, drawing on people's learned abilities to interact with media. All people in a media culture such as ours are media literate, they are able to read and interpret the multitude of cultural forms with which they daily interact, but their media literacy is often unconscious and unreflective, requiring the cultivation of cognitive skills of analysis, interpretation, and critique. Moreover, as many students and teachers of media literacy have discovered, most individuals who cultivate media literacy competencies actually reach new levels of media enjoyment due to their abilities to apply critical skills that disclose new dimensions, connections, and meanings.

Yet within educational circles, there is a debate over what constitutes the field of media pedagogy, with different agendas and programs. A traditionalist "protectionist" approach would attempt to "inoculate" young people against the effects of media addiction and manipulation by cultivating a taste for book literacy, high culture, and the values of truth, beauty, and justice, and by denigrating all forms of media and computer culture. Neil Postman in his books *Amusing Ourselves to Death* and *Technopolis* exemplifies this approach.[22] A "media literacy" movement, by contrast, attempts to teach students to read, analyze, and decode media texts, in a fashion parallel to the cultivation of print literacy. Media arts education in turn teaches students to appreciate the aesthetic qualities of media and to use various media technologies as tools of self-expression and creation. Critical media literacy, as I would advocate it, builds on these approaches, analyzing media culture as products of social production and struggle, and teaching students to be critical of media representations and discourses, but also stressing the importance of learning to use the media as modes of self-expression and social activism.

Critical media literacy not only teaches students to learn from media, to resist media manipulation, and to empower themselves vis-à-vis the media, but it is concerned with developing skills that will empower citizens and that will make them more motivated and competent participants in social life. Critical media literacy is thus tied to the project of radical democracy and concerned with developing skills that will enhance democratization and participation. Critical media literacy takes a comprehensive approach that teaches critical skills and how to use media as instruments of social change. The technologies of communication are becoming more and more accessible to young people and average citizens, and they should be used to promote education, democratic self-expression, and social progress. Thus, the same technologies that could threaten the end of participatory democracy, by transforming politics into media spectacles and the battle of images, and by turning spectators into cultural zombies, could also be used to help invigorate democratic debate and participation.[23]

Indeed, teaching critical media literacy should be a participatory, collaborative project. Students are often more media savvy, knowledgeable, and immersed in media culture than their teachers and thus can contribute to the educational process through sharing their ideas, perceptions, and insights. On the other hand, critical discussion, debate, and analysis should be encouraged with teachers bringing to bear their critical perspectives on student readings of media material. Teaching critical media literacy encounters some obstacles that must be engaged. Because media culture is often part and parcel of students' identity and most powerful cultural experience, teachers must be sensitive in criticizing artifacts and perceptions that students hold dear, yet an atmosphere of critical respect for difference *and* inquiry into the nature and effects of media culture should be encouraged.

Another challenge in developing critical media pedagogy results from the fact that in a sense it is not a pedagogy in the traditional sense with firmly established principles, a canon of texts, and tried-and-true teaching procedures. Critical media pedagogy is in its infancy, it is just beginning to produce results, and is thus more open and experimental than established print-oriented pedagogy. Moreover, the material of media culture is so polymorphous, multivalent, and polysemic that it requires sensitivity to different readings, interpretations, and perceptions of the media's complex images, scenes, narratives, meanings, and messages. Media culture is as complex and challenging to decipher critically as book culture.

I have so far downplayed hostility toward media education and the media themselves. Educational traditionalists conceive of literacy in more limited print-media paradigms and, as I suggested above, often adopt a "pro-

tectionist" approach when they address the issue of the media at all, warning students against corruption, or urging that they limit media use to "educational" materials. Yet many teachers at all levels from kindergarten to the university have discovered that media material, judiciously used, can be valuable in a variety of instructional tasks, helping to make complex subject matter accessible and engaging. Obviously, media cannot substitute for print material and classroom teaching, and should be seen as a supplement to traditional materials rather than a magic panacea for the failures of traditional education. Moreover, as I argue in the next section, traditional print literacy and competencies are more important than ever in our new high-tech societies.

It is also highly instructive, I would argue, to teach students at all levels to critically engage popular media materials, including the most familiar film, television, music, and other forms of media culture. Yet, here one needs to avoid an uncritical media populism, of the sort that is emerging within certain sectors of British and North American cultural studies. In a review of *Rethinking Media Literacy,* for instance, Jon Lewis attacked what he saw as the overly critical postures of the contributors to this volume, arguing: "If the point of a critical media literacy is to meet students halfway—to begin to take seriously what *they* take seriously, to read what *they* read, to watch what *they* watch—teachers *must* learn to love pop culture."[24] Note the authoritarian injunction that "teachers *must* learn to love popular culture" followed by an attack on more critical approaches to media literacy.

Teaching critical media literacy, however, involves occupation of a site above the dichotomy of fan or censor. One can teach how media culture provides significant statements or insights about the social world, positive visions of gender, race, and class, or complex aesthetic structures and practices, thus putting a positive spin on how it can provide significant contributions to education. Yet one should also indicate how media culture can promote sexism, racism, ethnocentrism, homophobia, and other forms of prejudice, as well as misinformation, problematic ideologies, and questionable values. A more dialectical approach to media literacy engages students' interests and concerns, and should, as I suggested above, involve a collaborative approach between teachers and students since students are deeply absorbed in media culture and may know more about some of its artifacts and domains than their teachers. Consequently, they should be encouraged to speak, discuss, and intervene in the teaching/learning process. This is not to say that media literacy training should romanticize student views that may be superficial, mistaken, uninformed, and full of various problematical biases. Yet exercises in media literacy can often productively involve intense student participation in a mutual learning process where both teachers and students together learn media literacy skills and competencies.

It is also probably a mistake to attempt to institute a top-down program of media literacy imposed from above on teachers, with fixed texts, curricula, and prescribed materials. Diverse teachers and students will have very different interests and concerns, and will naturally emphasize different subject matter and choose examples relevant to their own and their students' interests. Courses in critical media literacy should thus be flexible enough to enable teachers and students to constitute their own curricula to engage material and topics of current concern, and to address their own interests. Moreover (and crucially) educators should discern that we are in the midst of one of the most intense technological revolutions in history and must learn to adapt new computer technologies to education, as I suggest in the following section, and this requires the development of new multiple literacies.

New Technologies, Multiple Literacies, and Postmodern Pedagogy: The New Frontier

The studies on multicultural education and critical media literacy that I have examined up to this point neglect to interrogate computer culture and the ways that the Internet and new computer technologies and cultural forms are dramatically transforming the circulation of information, images, and various modes of culture. I want to argue that students should learn new forms of computer literacy that involve both how to use the computer to do research and gather information, as well as to perceive it as a cultural terrain that contains texts, spectacles, games, and new interactive multimedia. Moreover, computer culture is a discursive and political location in which students can intervene, engaging in discussion groups and collaborative research projects, creating their web sites, and producing new multi-media for cultural dissemination. Computer culture enables individuals to participate actively in the production of culture, ranging from discussing public issues to creating their own cultural forms. However, to take part in this culture requires not only accelerated forms of traditional modes of print literacy that are often restricted to the growing elite of students who are privileged to attend adequate and superior public and private schools, but new forms of literacy as well, thus posing significant challenges to education.

It is indeed a salient fact of the present age that computer culture is proliferating and so we have to begin teaching computer literacy from an early age. Computer literacy, however, itself needs to be theorized. Often the term is synonymous with the technical ability to use computers, to master existing programs, and maybe engage in

some programming oneself. I want to recommend expanding the conception of computer literacy from using computer programs and hardware to developing, in addition, more sophisticated abilities in traditional reading and writing, as well as the capability to dissect critically cultural forms taught as part of critical media literacy and new forms of multiple literacy. Thus, on this conception, genuine computer literacy involves not just technical knowledge and skills, but refined reading, writing, and communicating abilities that involve heightened capacities for critically analyzing, interpreting, and processing print, image, sound, and multimedia material. Computer literacy involves intensified abilities to read, to scan texts and information, to put together in meaningful patterns mosaics of information, to construct meanings and significance, to contextualize and evaluate, and to discuss and articulate one's own views.

Thus, in my expanded conception, computer literacy involves technical and creative abilities concerning developing basic typing skills, using computer programs, accessing information, and using computer technologies for a variety of purposes ranging from verbal communication to artistic expression. There are ever more overlaps between media and computer culture as audio and video material becomes part of the Internet, as CD-ROM and multimedia develop, and as new technologies become part and parcel of the home, school, and workplace. Therefore, the skills of decoding images, sounds, and spectacles learned in critical media literacy training can also be valuable as part of computer literacy as well. Furthermore, print literacy takes on increasing importance in the computer world as one needs to scrutinize critically and scroll through tremendous amounts of information, putting new emphasis on developing reading and writing abilities. Indeed, Internet discussion groups, chat rooms, email, and various related forums require writing skills in which a new emphasis on the importance of clarity and precision is emerging as communications proliferate. In this context of information saturation, it becomes an ethical imperative not to contribute to cultural and information overload, and to communicate concisely one's thoughts and feelings.

In a certain sense, computers are becoming the technological equivalent of Hegel's Absolute Idea, able to absorb everything into its form and medium. Computers are now not only repositories of text and print-based data, but also contain a wealth of images, multimedia sights and sounds, and interactive environments that, like the broadcast media, are themselves a form of education that require a critical pedagogy of electronic, digitized culture and communication. From this conception, computer literacy is something like Hegelian synthesis of print and visual literacy, technical skills, and media literacies, brought together at a new and higher stage. While Postman and others produce a simplistic Manichean dichotomy between print and visual literacy, we need to learn to think dialectically, to read text and image, to decipher sight and sound, and to develop forms of computer literacy adequate to meet the exigencies of an increasingly high tech society.

Thus, a postmodern pedagogy requires developing critical forms of print, media, and computer literacy, all of crucial importance in the new technoculture of the present and fast-approaching future.[25] Whereas modern pedagogy tended to be specialized, fragmented, and differentiated, and was focused on print culture, a postmodern pedagogy involves developing multiple literacies and critically analyzing, dissecting, and engaging a multiplicity of cultural forms, some of which are the products of new technologies and require developing new literacies to engage the new cultural forms and media. In fact, contemporary culture is marked by a proliferation of cultural machines that generate a panoply of print, sound, environmental, and diverse aesthetic artifacts within which we wander, trying to make our way through this forest of symbols. This requires the development of a new multimedia literacy that is able to scan, interact with, traverse, and organize new multimedia educational environments.[26] Multimedia literacy involves not just reading, but interacting: clicking to move from one field to another if one is involved in a hypertext environment such as one finds on web sites or CD-ROMs; capturing, saving, and downloading material relevant to one's own projects; and perhaps responding verbally or adding one's own material if it is a site that invites this kind of participation.

In addition to the linear cognitive skills needed for traditionally reading print material, multimedia literacy requires the ability to read hypertexts that are often multidimensional, requiring the connecting of images, graphics, texts, and sometimes audio-video material. It also involves making connections between the complex and multilayered cyberworld and its connection with the real world. Moreover, as Carmen Luke reminds us, "Since all meaning is situated relationally—that is, connected and cross-referenced to other media and genres, and to related meanings in other cultural contexts—a critical literacy relies on broad-based notions of intertextuality."[27]

Thus, one must learn to read multimedia forms that are themselves overlapping and interrelated, switching from text to graphics to video to audio, decoding in turn sight, sound, and text. In a global information environment, this also may involve switching from sites from one country to another, requiring contextual understanding and literacy that is able to read and interact with people and sites from different cultures. As Carmen Luke puts it:

[N]ew [forms of] virtual communication are emerging, which require an intertextual understanding of how meanings shift

across media, genres, and cultural frames of reference. Whether one "visits" the Louvre online, joins an international newsgroup of parents of Downs Syndrome children, or visits the www site of an agricultural college in Kenya, cross-cultural understanding and "netiquette" is increasingly crucial for participating effectively in global communications.[28]

Thus, multimedia literacy should be contextual; it requires thematizing the background and power relations of cultural forms (including analysis of the political economy of the media and technology, of how corporate organizations control production and dissemination, and how oppositional and alternative media and uses are possible[29]) as well as the context and power relations of the specific media use in question (for example, the differences between television watching in the classroom, at home with one's family, with one's friends or alone; or the difference between computer use for research, data organization, email, or playing games). Multimedia literacy also envisages new modes of collaborative work on research projects or web sites, new forms of student/teacher participation and interaction, and new pedagogical uses for the new technologies which may appear exotic in the present, but which will become increasingly commonplace in the future and will force a rethinking of education.

And so we need to begin learning how to read and deploy these new multimedia environments and interact with these fascinating and seductive cultural forms whose massive impact on our lives we have only begun to understand. Education should teach how to read and interact with this new computer and multimedia environment as part of new forms of multiple literacy. Such an effort would be part of a new critical pedagogy that attempts to empower individuals so that they can analyze and criticize the emerging technoculture, as well as participate in its cultural forums and sites.

In addition to the critical media literacy, print literacy, computer literacy, and multimedia literacy discussed above, multiple literacies involve cultural literacy, social literacy, and ecoliteracy. Since a multicultural society is the context of education in the contemporary moment, new forms of social interaction and cultural awareness are needed that appreciate differences, multiplicity, and diversity. Therefore, expanded social and cultural literacy is needed that appreciates the cultural heritages, histories, and contributions of a diversity of groups. Thus, whereas one can agree with E. D. Hirsch that we need to be literate in our shared cultural heritage, we also need to become culturally literate in cultures that have been hitherto invisible, as Henry Louis Gates and his colleagues have been arguing in their proposals for multicultural education.[30]

Social literacy should also be taught throughout the educational system, ranging from a focus on how to relate and get along with a variety of individuals, how to negotiate differences, how to resolve conflicts, and how to communicate and socially interact in a diversity of situations. Social literacy also involves ethical training in values and norms, and delineating proper and improper individual and social behavior. It also requires knowledge of contemporary societies and thus overlaps with social and natural science training. Indeed, given the tremendous role of science and technology in the contemporary world, the threats to the environment, and the need to preserve and enhance the natural as well as social and cultural worlds, it is scandalous how illiterate the entire society is concerning science, nature, and even our own bodies. An ecoliteracy should thus appropriately teach competency in interpreting and interacting with our natural environment, ranging from our own body to natural habitats like forests and deserts.

The challenge for education today is thus to promote multiple literacies to empower students and citizens to use new technologies to enhance their lives and to create a better culture and society based on respect for multicultural difference and the fuller democratic participation of individuals and groups largely excluded from wealth and power in the previous modern society. A positive postmodernity would thus involve creation of a more egalitarian and democratic society in which more individuals and groups were empowered to participate. The great danger facing us, of course, is that the new technologies will increase the current inequalities based on class, gender, and racial divisions. So far, the privileged groups have had more immediate access to new technologies. It is therefore a challenge of education today to provide access to new technologies and to the literacies needed for competence in order to overcome some of the divisions and inequalities that have plagued contemporary societies during the entire modern age.

Yet, there is also the danger that youth will become totally immersed in a new world of high-tech experience and lose their social connectedness and ability to communicate interpersonally and relate concretely to other people. Statistics suggest that more and more sectors of youth are able to access cyberspace and that college students with Internet accounts are spending as much as four hours a day in the new realm of technological experience.[31] The media have been generating a moral panic concerning allegedly growing dangers in cyberspace, with lurid stories of young boys and girls lured into dangerous sex or running away from home, endless accounts of how pornography on the Internet is proliferating, engendering calls for increasing control, censorship, and surveillance of communication—usually by politicians who are computer illiterate. The solution, however, is not to ban access to new technologies, but to teach students and citizens how to use these technologies so that they can be employed for productive and creative rather than problematic ends.

To be sure, there are dangers in cyberspace as well as elsewhere, but the threats to adolescents are significantly higher through the danger of family violence and abuse than of seduction by strangers on the Internet. And while there is a flourishing trade in pornography on the Internet, this material has become increasingly available in a variety of venues from the local video shop to the newspaper stand, so it seems unfair to demonize the Internet. Thus, attempts at Internet censorship are part of an attack on youth that would circumscribe their rights to obtain entertainment and information, and create their own subcultures.[32] Consequently, devices like the V-chip that would exclude sex and violence on television, or block computer access to objectionable material, is more an expression of adult hysteria and moral panic than genuine dangers to youth (which certainly exist, but much more strikingly in the real world than in the sphere of hyperreality).

New technologies are always demonized and in studying the kaleidoscopic array of discourses that characterize the new technologies, I am rather bemused by the extent to whether they reveal either a *technophilic* discourse that presents new technologies as our salvation, as a solution to all our problems, or a *technophobic* discourse that sees technology as our damnation, demonizing it as the major source of all our problems.[33] It appears that similarly one-sided and contrasting discourses greeted the introduction of other new technologies this century, such as film, radio, and television. Film, for instance, was celebrated by early theorists as providing a new documentary depiction of reality, even a redemption of reality, a new art form, new modes of mass education and entertainment— and it was demonized for promoting sexual promiscuity, juvenile delinquency, crime, violence, and copious other forms of immorality and evils. Its demonization led in the United States to a Production Code that rigorously regulated the content of Hollywood film from 1934 until the 1950s and 1960s—no open-mouthed kissing was permitted, crime could not pay, drug use or attacks on religion could not be portrayed, and a censorship office rigorously surveyed all films to make sure that no subversive or illicit content emerged. Similar extreme hopes and fears were projected onto radio and television.

It appears that whenever there are new technologies, people project their fantasies, fears, hopes, and dreams onto them, and I believe that this is now happening with computers and new multimedia technologies. A critical theory of technology, however, and a critical pedagogy, should avoid either demonizing or deifying the new technologies and should develop pedagogies that will help us to use the technologies to enhance education and life, and to criticize the limitations and false promises made on behalf of new technologies.

Certainly there is no doubt that the cyberspace of computer worlds contains as much banality and stupidity as real life and one can waste much time in useless activity. But compared to the bleak and violent urban worlds portrayed in rap music and youth films like Kids, the technological worlds are havens of information, entertainment, interaction, and connection where youth can gain valuable skills, knowledge, and power necessary to survive the postmodern adventure. Youth can create new, more multiple and flexible selves in cyberspace as well as new subcultures and communities. Indeed, it is exciting to cruise the Internet and to discover how many interesting web sites young people and others have established, often containing valuable educational material. There is, of course, the danger that corporate and commercial interests will come to colonize the Internet, but it is likely that there will continue to be spaces where individuals can empower themselves and create their own communities and identities. A main challenge for youth (and others) is to learn to use the Internet for positive cultural and political projects, rather than just entertainment and passive consumption.

Reflecting on the growing social importance of computers and new technologies makes it clear that it is of essential importance for youth today to gain various kinds of literacy to empower themselves for the emerging new cybersociety (this is true of teachers and adults as well). To survive in a postmodern world, individuals of all ages need to gain skills of media and computer literacy to be able to negotiate the overload of media images and spectacles. We all need to learn technological skills to use the new media and computer technologies to subsist in the new high-tech economy and to form our own cultures and communities; and youth especially need street smarts and survival skills, as well as new forms of multiple literacy, to cope with the drugs, violence, and uncertainty in today's predatory culture and volatile job market.[34]

It is therefore extremely important for the future of democracy to make sure that youth of all classes, races, genders, and regions gain access to new technology, receiving training in media and computer literacy skills in order to provide the opportunities to enter the high-tech job market and society of the future, and to prevent an exacerbation of class, gender, and race inequalities. And while multiple forms of new literacies will be necessary, traditional print literacy skills are all the more important in a cyberage of world-processing, information-gathering, and Internet communication. Moreover, what I am calling multiple literacy involves training in philosophy, ethics, value thinking, and the humanities, which I would argue is necessary now more than ever. In fact, how the Internet and new technologies will be used depends on the overall education of youth and the skills and interests they bring to the new technologies that can be used to access educational and valuable cultural material, or pornography and the banal wares of cybershopping malls.

Thus, the concept of multiple literacy and the postmodern pedagogy that I envisage would argue that it is not a question of either/or, that is, either print literacy or multimedia literacy, either the classical curriculum or a new curriculum, but it is rather a question of both/and that preserves the best from classical education, that enhances an emphasis on print literacy, but that also develops new literacies to engage the new technologies. Obviously, cyberlife is just one dimension of experience and one still needs to learn to interact in a "real world" of school, jobs, relationships, politics, and other people. Youth—indeed all of us—need to learn to interact in many dimensions of social reality and to gain a multiplicity of forms of literacy and skills that will enable us to create identities, relationships, and communities that will nurture and develop our full spectrum of potentialities and satisfy a wide array of needs. Our lives are more multidimensional than ever and part of the postmodern adventure is learning to live in a variety of social spaces and to adapt to intense change and transformation. Education too must meet these challenges and use new technologies to promote learning and to devise strategies in which new technologies can be deployed to create a more democratic and egalitarian multicultural society.

Notes

1. Diane Carson and Lester D. Friedman, *Shared Differences: Multicultural Media and Practical Pedagogy* (Urbana: University of Illinois Press, 1995) contains studies dealing with the use of media to deal with multicultural education. This book will be cited as *SD* in the text for all subsequent references. Examples of teaching media literacy that I draw on include Len Masterman, *Teaching the Media* (London: Routledge, 1989); James Schwoch, Mimi White, and Susan Reilly, *Media Knowledge* (Albany: SUNY Press, 1992); Dan Fleming, *Media Teaching* (Oxford: Basil Blackwell, 1993); Henry Giroux, *Disturbing Pleasures* (New York: Routledge, 1994); Henry Giroux, *Fugitive Cultures: Race, Violence, and Youth* (New York: Routledge, 1996); David Sholle and Stan Denski, *Media Education and the (Re)Production of Culture* (Westport, Conn.: Bergin and Garvey, 1994); Peter McLaren, Rhonda Hammer, David Sholle, and Susan Reilly, *Rethinking Media Literacy: A Critical Pedagogy of Representation* (New York: Peter Lang, 1995); Peter McLaren, *Critical Pedagogy and Predatory Culture* (London: Routledge, 1995); and Douglas Kellner, *Media Culture* (London: Routledge, 1995). See also the work of Barry Duncan and the Canadian Association for Media Literacy (website: http://www.nald.ca/province/que/litcent/media.htm).

2. This is the insight of Harold Innes, *The Bias of Communication* (Toronto: University of Toronto Press, 1951); Marshall McLuhan, *Understanding Media: The Extensions of Man* (New York: Signet Books, 1964); Neil Postman, *Amusing Ourselves to Death* (New York: Viking-Penguin, 1985); and others who argue that specific media have their own codes and biases. Such a call for more particularized media literacy puts in question more generalized models, though. As should be apparent, I

reject Postman's manichean celebration of print media and assault on imagistic "entertainment" media.

3. Kellner, *Media Culture* and Douglas Kellner, "Cultural Studies, Multiculturalism, and Media Culture," in *Gender, Race, and Class in Media,* ed. Gail Dines and Jean Humez (Thousand Oaks, Calif.: Sage, 1995), 5–17.

4. Kellner, *Media Culture.*

5. Kellner, "Reading Images Critically: Toward a Postmodern Pedagogy," *Journal of Education* 170, no. 3 (1989): 31–52 and Kellner, *Media Culture.*

6. Masterman, *Teaching the Media.*

7. Ibid., viii–ix.

8. Fleming, *Media Teaching* also provides a useful introduction providing theoretical and practical insights into how to teach the media, but his book is heavily oriented toward British media material and thus may also not transfer well to North American settings.

9. Carmen Luke and Allan Luke, "School Knowledge as Simulation: Curriculum in Postmodern Conditions," *Discourse* 10, no. 2 (April 1990): 75–91.

10. Carmen Luke, "Media and Cultural Studies," in *Constructing Critical Literacies,* ed. Peter Freebody, Alan Muspratt, and Allan Luke (Norwood, N.J.: Hampton Press) and Carmen Luke, *Technological Literacy* (Melbourne: National Languages and Literacy Institute, Adult Literacy Network, forthcoming).

11. Allan Luke, "Theory and Practice in Critical Discourse Analysis," in *International Encyclopedia of the Sociology of Education,* ed. Lawrence J. Saha (New York: Pergamon Press, forthcoming).

12. See Courtney Cazden, Bill Cope, Norman Fairclough, James Gee, Mary Kalantzis, Gunter Kress, Allan Luke, Carmen Luke, Sarah Michaels, and Martin Nakata," A Pedagogy of Multiliteracies: Designing Social Futures," *Harvard Educational Review* 66: 60–92, and Luke, *Technological Literacy,* 1997.

13. John Fiske, *Power Plays. Power Works* (New York: Verso, 1993) and John Fiske, *Media Matters* (Minneapolis: University of Minnesota Press, 1994).

14. Henry Giroux, *Border Crossing* (New York: Routledge, 1992); Henry Giroux, *Living Dangerously: Multiculturalism and the Politics of Difference* (New York: Peter Lang, 1993); Henry Giroux, *Disturbing Pleasures* (New York: Routledge, 1994); Henry Giroux, *Fugitive Cultures: Race, Violence, and Youth* (New York: Routledge, 1996); Henry Giroux, *Channel Surfing: Race Talk and the Destruction of Today's Youth* (New York: St. Martin's Press, 1997); Peter McLaren, *Critical Pedagogy and Predatory Culture* (London: Routledge, 1995); and Peter McLaren, *Revolutionary Multiculturalism* (London: Routledge, 1996).

15. Lawrence Grossberg, *We Gotta Get Out of this Place* (New York: Routledge, 1992); Douglas Kellner and Michael Ryan, *Camera Politica: The Politics and Ideology of Contemporary Hollywood Film* (Bloomington: Indiana University Press, 1988); Kellner, *Television and the Crisis of Democracy* (Boulder, Colo.: Westview 1990); Kellner, *The Persian Gulf TV War* (Boulder, Colo: Westview, 1992); and Kellner, "Intellectuals and New Technologies," *Media, Culture, and Society* 17 (1995): 201–17. See also Lawrence Grossberg, Cary Nelson, and Paula Treichler, eds., *Cultural Studies* (New York: Routledge, 1992); Henry Giroux and Peter McLaren, eds., *Between Borders: Pedagogy and the Politics of Cultural Studies* (New York: Routledge, 1994); and Dines and Humez, *Gender, Race, and Class in Media.*

16. Schwoch, White, and Reilly, *Media Knowledge.*

17. Sholle and Denski, *Media Education and the (Re)Production of Culture.*

18. McLaren, Hammer, Sholle, and Reilly, *Rethinking Media Literacy.*

19. Ibid., 225–35.

20. Searching the Internet for material devoted to media literacy and multiculturalism discloses a wealth of resources, including bibliographies, teaching material, and addresses of individuals and groups committed to these topics.

21. McLuhan, *Understanding Media.*

22. Postman, *Amusing Ourselves to Death* and Neil Postman, *Technopolis: The Surrender of Culture to Technology* (New York: Random House, 1992).

23. Kellner, *Media Culture* and Kellner, "Intellectuals and New Technologies."

24. Jon Lewis, "Practice What You Preach," *Afterimage* (Summer 1996): 26. Italics in original.

25. For my take on postmodern theory, see Douglas Kellner, ed., *Postmodernism/Jameson/Critique* (Washington, D.C.: Maisonneuve Press, 1989); Steven Best and Douglas Kellner, *The Postmodern Turn* (New York: Guilford Press, 1997); Steven Best and Douglas Kellner, *The Postmodern Adventure* (New York: Guilford Press, forthcoming); and my website: http://ccwf.cc.utexas.edu/-kellner/pm/pm.html. For an earlier sketch of postmodern pedagogy, see Kellner, "Reading Images Critically."

26. For other recent conceptions of multimedia literacy, see the discussions of literacies needed for reading hypertext in Nicholas C. Burbules and Thomas Callister, "Knowledge at the Crossroads: Some Alternative Futures of Hypertext Learning Environments," *Educational Theory* 46, no. 1 (Winter 1996): 23–50; the concept of multiliteracy in Cazden et al., "A Pedagogy of Multiliteracies" and Luke, *Technological Literacy,* and an expansion of the concept of hyperreading in Nicholas C. Burbules, "Rhetorics of the Web: Hyperriding and Critical Literacy," in *Page to Screen: Taking Literacy Into the Electronic Era,* ed. Ilana Snyder (New South Wales: Allen and Unwin, forthcoming).

27. Luke, *Technological Literacy,* 10.

28. Ibid.

29. Kellner, *Media Culture.*

30. E. D. Hirsch, *Cultural Literacy* (New York: Random House, 1987) and Henry Louis Gates, *Loose Canons* (New York: Oxford University Press, 1992).

31. *Wired* magazine is a good source for statistics and data concerning the growing computer and internet use among all sectors of youth and documents the vicissitudes of cyberculture. The main story in the business press during the mid-1990s is the consolidation of the information and entertainment industries, so the daily newspapers are also full of copious material on adventures in cyberspace which may be the locus of the next stage of the postmodern adventure (see Best and Kellner, *The Postmodern Adventure*).

32. On the attack on youth in contemporary society and culture, see Henry Giroux, *Fugitive Cultures: Race, Violence, and Youth;* Giroux, *Channel Surfing;* Mike A. Manes, *The Scapegoat Generation: America's War on Adolescents* (Monroe, Me: Common Course Press, 1996); and Best and Kellner, *The Postmodern Adventure.*

33. Douglas Kellner, "New Technologies, TechnoCities, and the Prospects for Democratization," in *New Technologies and TechnoCities,* ed. John Dowling (London: Sage Books, forthcoming).

34. McLaren, *Critical Pedagogy and Predatory Culture.*

FRAME
the
DEBATE

Form at end of book

A Longitudinal Study of Gender Differences in Young Children's Mathematical Thinking

Elizabeth Fennema,
Thomas P. Carpenter,
Victoria R. Jacobs,
Megan L. Franke,
and Linda W. Levi

Elizabeth Fennema is professor emerita and senior scientist at the Wisconsin Center for Educational Research, University of Wisconsin, Madison, 1025 West Johnson Street, Madison, WI 53706. Her specialties are mathematics teaching and learning and gender differences in mathematics.

Thomas P. Carpenter is a professor in the Department of Curriculum and Instruction at the University of Wisconsin, Madison, 225 North Mills Street, Madison, WI 53706. He specializes in mathematics education.

Victoria R. Jacobs is an assistant professor in the College of Education, California State University, San Marcos, San Marcos, CA 92096-0001. Her specialties are children's mathematical thinking and the professional development of teachers.

Megan L. Franke is an assistant professor at the University of California, Los Angeles, GSE&IS, 1029 Moore Hall, Los Angeles, CA 90095-1521. She specializes in teacher learning and development.

Linda W. Levi is an assistant researcher at the Wisconsin Center for Education Research, 1025 West Johnson Street, Madison, WI 53706. Her specialties are young children's mathematics learning and gender equity in mathematics education.

One area in which gender differences in mathematics have been studied minimally deals with strategies used to solve mathematical problems. The limited evidence available suggests that there may be some gender differences in problem-solving strategies. Differences have been found in grades 1–3, with girls tending to use observable strategies (such as counting) and boys tending to use mental strategies (Carr & Jessup, 1997). Gallagher and DeLisi (1994) studied high-ability secondary school students and reported that while there were no overall differences in the number of selected SAT items answered correctly, the females tended to use more conventional (commonly taught) strategies, while males tended to use more untaught strategies.

If the results from these limited studies can be generalized to a broader population, they give rise to two questions that are important for increasing understanding of gender differences in mathematics. Could differential strategy use presage the gender differences in learning complex mathematics that have been so well documented? Or do they just reflect different pathways to learning complex mathematics, and the pathway shown by females is reflective of

Questions

Why do you think that girls and boys in primary grades use different strategies to solve mathematical problems?

How might these differences influence the way girls and boys are taught mathematics?

Could differential strategy use presage the gender differences in learning complex mathematics that have been so well documented? Or do they just reflect different pathways to learning complex mathematics?

women's ways of knowing (Belenky, Clinchy, Goldberger, & Tarule, 1986)? If so, they may indicate that instruction for males and females should be different.

Research on Children's Strategy Use

Research has shown that the development of widely divergent groups of children's addition and subtraction concepts and skills can be characterized in terms of increasingly abstract strategies children invent to solve basic problems. (For summaries of this research, see Carpenter, 1985; DeCorte, Greer, & Verschaffel, 1996; Fuson, 1992; Gutstein & Romberg, 1995; Nunes, 1992.) This work suggests that most children first model problem situations with physical objects, progress to various counting strategies, and then move on to more abstract strategies such as derived facts[1] or invented algorithms.[2] This developmental path is seen in problems that involve small numbers, and it reappears as children invent ways to solve multidigit problems.

When solving multidigit problems, children first model the numbers with individual counters and then move on to more abstract solutions involving various materials representing groupings of 10. Operations with multidigit numbers are abstracted as children invent algorithms for adding and subtracting multidigit numbers, which enable them to solve problems without physical materials of any kind. In contrast to standard algorithms, which generally are learned by automatizing a series of specified procedures (VanLehn, 1986), invented algorithms usually are generated by children, either individually or in interactions with other students. The use of invented algorithms suggests understanding of number and place value that is not necessarily implied by the use of standard algorithms.

The following are three examples of invented algorithms for adding 38 and 26 that are frequently reported by children (Fuson et al, 1997):

Thirty and 20 is 50, and 8 makes 58. Then 6 more is 64.

Thirty and 20 is 50 and 8 and 6 is 14. The 10 from the 14 makes 60, so it's 64.

That's like 40 and 24, and that's 64.

There are fundamental differences between invented and standard algorithms. Standard algorithms have evolved over centuries for efficient calculation and are usually removed from their conceptual underpinnings. In contrast, invented algorithms are usually derived directly from the underlying multidigit concepts. In standard algorithms, numerals are aligned so that ones, tens, hundreds, and the like are in columns. When adding the columns, it is not necessary to know that the same units are being combined; one simply adds the numbers in a column. In most invented algorithms, the units being combined are specifically joined because they are the same units. Invented algorithms are invented by children. They are not just procedures that can be taught step by step but suggest conceptual understanding. There is evidence that encouraging children to invent them contributes to the development of understanding of more complex ideas (Carpenter, Franke, Jacobs, Fennema, & Empson, 1998).

Methods

The study investigated gender differences in problem solving and computational strategies used by 44 boys and 38 girls as they progressed from grades 1–3. The children were individually interviewed five times: in the winter of first grade and in the fall and spring of second and third grade. In each interview, they solved tasks involving basic number operations and their application to more complex problems.

Sample

The initial sample ($n = 132$) was 6 girls and 6 boys randomly selected from each of 11 first-grade classes in three schools. During the three years of the study, there was a boundary change that eliminated a fourth of the students for one school, and natural attrition eliminated others. The final sample consisted of 44 boys and 38 girls who participated in all five interviews. Eighty-nine percent of the students were White, and 11% received a free or reduced-price lunch.

Instruction

All students were in classes of teachers who were participating in a three-year professional development program designed to help teachers understand their students' intuitive mathematical ideas and to understand how those ideas could form the basis for the development of more formal ideas (Carpenter, Fennema, & Franke, 1996; Fennema et al., 1996). No curriculum materials or specific guidelines for instruction were provided, and there was variation in the instruction of different teachers. However, several features characterized the instruction. Children spent most of their instructional time solving problems utilizing both single and multidigit numbers. A variety of materials, including counters and base-10 blocks, were available. Students were given time to invent ways to solve problems using a variety of strategies, and alternative strategies were discussed with the whole class or in small groups. (See Fennema et al., 1996, for a complete description and assessment of these classrooms.) Although it was not emphasized, virtually all students had learned the standard algorithm by the end of the study (Carpenter et al., 1998).

Interview Problems

The interview tasks assessed students' strategies for generating number facts and solving addition and subtraction word problems and computation exercises, their ability to extend and use addition and subtraction procedures flexibly, and their ability to solve nonroutine problems. Numbers and contexts varied slightly between interviews for tasks that were used in multiple interviews. Items were selected so that they were not overtly gender biased, and their content and number size were chosen to be appropriate to the developing knowledge of the children. Examples of items are shown in Table 1.

Number facts. In the second through the fifth interviews, children's strategies for generating number facts were assessed. Each number fact was written horizontally on a card, and children were asked to explain how they figured out their answer. No paper and pencil or other materials were available. Answers were coded as correct or incorrect. Strategies were coded as counting, derived fact, or recall using protocols described in Carpenter and Moser (1984).

Addition and subtraction problems. Multidigit addition and subtraction word problems and computation were administered in each interview and involved joining, separating, or part-whole relations. Two-digit problems were administered in each interview, and three-digit problems were included in the third-grade interview. For most problems, children had a choice of materials including single counters, base-10 blocks, and paper and pencil. In order to increase the likelihood that children would use invented algorithms if they were capable, two addition and one subtraction word problems were administered with no materials or paper and pencil. Computation exercises were presented on cards with the digits aligned vertically. For each task, children's strategies were classified using a coding system described in Carpenter et al. (1998). Answers were coded as correct or incorrect, and strategies were coded as (a) modeling or counting, (b) invented algorithms, or (c) standard algorithms.

Nonroutine problems. In all but the fourth interview, children were asked to solve several nonroutine problems that involved multiple steps and required interpretation and analysis. Responses were coded as correct or incorrect.

Extension problems. The fourth and fifth interviews included two problems involving money and three-digit

Table 1	Examples of Tasks Used to Assess Thinking

Number facts (all grades)

    7 + 9   12 + 15

Addition/subtraction

Stasha had 28 Legos. Her brother gave her 35 more Legos for her birthday. How many Legos did Stasha have then? (grade 2)

Can you solve this problem for me? (Child is shown the following combination written on a card.) (grade 2)

64 − 27

248 boys and 168 girls came to the school picnic. How many children came to the school picnic? (grade 3)

Nonroutine

19 children are taking a mini-bus to the zoo. They will have to sit either 2 or 3 to a seat. The bus has 7 seats. How many children will have to sit 3 to a seat, and how many can sit 2 to a seat? (grade 1)

Janice has 5 bags with 4 candies in each bag. She also has 3 bags with 6 candies in each bag. How many bags can she make with 2 candies in each bag? (grade 3)

Extension (grade 3 only)

Ellen had 4 dollars. She spent 1 dollar and 86 cents for a toy. How much money did Ellen have left?

Gene has $398. How much more would Gene have to save to have $500?

numbers. (See Table 1.) No materials or paper and pencil were available to use. For both problems, children had to use their knowledge of place value and multidigit operations flexibly. Because they did not have paper and pencil, it was difficult to use the standard algorithm. The larger number in both problems included zeros, which afforded ways of thinking about the problem in terms of place value ideas and units of 10. Thus, these problems were not simply complex mental calculation exercises but were problems that potentially assessed children's understanding of number concepts as reflected in their ability to operate flexibly with large numbers.

Procedures

The grade 1 interview was conducted in January or February, both fall interviews were conducted in October or November, and both spring interviews were conducted in March or April. Each student was interviewed individually by a trained interviewer in a quiet place out of the classroom. Each interview was conducted over two days and lasted approximately an hour. Each task was read and reread as often as the child wanted, and the child was given as much time as necessary. Except as noted above, a variety of materials were available including individual counters, base-10 blocks, and paper and pencil. After an answer was given and if it was not obvious from observing, the child was questioned about his or her strategy. The interviewer continued probing until he or she understood the solution or it was clear that the child was not going to provide additional information. The interviewer recorded the answers and strategies in predetermined coding categories as well as tape recording the interviews.

Data Analyses

The analyses were done to identify patterns of gender differences across time and problem categories. At each time point, independent-sample t tests were used to compare the performance and strategy use of girls and boys on the four problem categories (number facts, addition/subtraction, nonroutine, and extension). The analyses can be thought of as nesting gender within time. Therefore, Type I error within each problem category was controlled using methods for nested analyses recommended by Marascuilo and Serlin (1988, pp. 524–527). A total alpha of .10 for all of the t tests conducted within a problem category was allotted. For each problem category, the .10 was divided evenly among the number of tests conducted. Because not all problem categories were administered at all time periods and some problem categories had more potential strategies than others, the number of tests within each problem category varied. Consequently, for the number fact tests, we used $\alpha = .006$; for the addition/subtraction problems, we used $\alpha = .005$; for the nonroutine problems, we used $\alpha = .025$; and for the extension problems, we used $\alpha = .05$. Interpretations focus mainly on consistent patterns of significant results and results for which effect sizes were substantial.

Results

Means and standard deviations for the number fact, addition/subtraction, nonroutine, and extension problems are reported by gender in Tables 2 and 3. Where significant differences between girls and boys were found, the larger of the means is starred (*) and effect sizes are reported.

There were no significant differences between girls and boys in the number of correct solutions during the three years for number facts, addition/subtraction, or nonroutine problems. In grade 3, boys solved significantly more extension problems than did the girls.

Gender differences in strategy use were completely different. Starting in grade 1 and persisting through grade 3, there were strong and consistent differences between the strategies used by girls and those used by boys to solve problems. Effect sizes of the differences ranged from 0.66 to 1.18. Girls tended to use more modeling or counting strategies, while boys tended to use more abstract strategies such as derived facts or invented algorithms. In the third-grade spring interview, the girls used significantly more standard algorithms than did the boys.

The cumulative percentages of girls and boys who used invented algorithms are reported in Table 4. Each percentage is calculated from the number of girls (or boys) who used an invented algorithm during the given interview or in a previous interview. At each interview, more boys than girls had used invented algorithms. By the last interview in grade 3, 95% of the boys had used an invented algorithm some time during the study as compared to 79% of the girls. The gender difference in the use of subtraction invented algorithms was more striking, with 80% of the boys and 45% of the girls reporting their use.

Invented Algorithms and Success in Solving Extension Problems

To investigate the relationship between the use of invented algorithms and success in solving extension problems, additional analyses were conducted. Two groups of students were identified based on their use of invented and standard algorithms. The *invented algorithm group* consisted of 53 students who had used invented algorithms by the fall of grade 2. The *standard algorithm group* consisted of 16 students who had moved directly from concrete modeling and counting strategies to using standard algorithms. Students in this group had not used invented algorithms by the grade 2 spring interview but had started using standard algorithms. These two groups represent divergent patterns of learning multidigit procedures. The invented algorithm group appeared to have first developed a conceptual understanding, which was reflected in their invented algorithms. In contrast, it appeared that the standard algorithm group started using standard algorithms before they demonstrated the conceptual understanding implied by the use of invented algorithms.

Of the 53 children in the invented algorithm group, 35 were boys and 18 were girls. Of the 16 students in the standard algorithm group, 14 were girls and 2 were boys. The results for these two groups on the extension problems are summarized in Table 5. In both grade 3 interviews, the invented algorithm group outperformed the

Table 2 · Number Fact and Addition/Subtraction Problems: Correctness and Strategies by Gender

Strategy	Grade 1		Grade 2 Fall		Grade 2 Spring		Grade 3 Fall		Grade 3 Spring	
Number Fact[1]										
Number of items		—	3		3		6		6	
Correct										
Girls	—		2.76	(.75)	2.84	(.50)	5.63	(.71)	5.76	(.63)
Boys	—		2.84	(.43)	2.86	(.55)	5.73	(.66)	5.89	(.62)
Counting										
Girls	—		2.29*	(.96)	1.63*	(1.08)	2.87*	(2.04)	2.11*	(1.91)
Boys	—		1.20	(1.17)	.77	(1.05)	1.34	(1.77)	.80	(1.64)
Effect size	—		1.01		.81		.80		.74	
Derived Fact										
Girls	—		.45	(.69)	1.03	(1.05)	2.18	(1.72)	2.87	(2.07)
Boys	—		1.48*	(1.21)	1.66	(1.14)	3.75*	(2.06)	4.00	(2.17)
Effect size	—		1.03				.82			
Recall										
Girls	—		.03	(.16)	.18	(.46)	.53	(1.03)	.76	(1.03)
Boys	—		.14	(.41)	.43	(.76)	.64	(1.20)	1.07	(1.61)
Addition/Subtraction										
Number of items	4		7		7		8		7	
Correct										
Girls	2.66	(1.28)	5.34	(1.76)	6.05	(1.39)	5.92	(1.73)	6.08	(1.48)
Boys	2.77	(1.26)	5.75	(1.50)	6.02	(1.64)	6.27	(1.80)	5.93	(1.49)
Modeling/counting										
Girls	2.34	(1.17)	3.53*	(2.20)	1.74*	(1.70)	1.50*	(1.31)	.58	(.92)
Boys	1.86	(1.31)	2.14	(2.03)	.73	(1.17)	.64	(1.10)	.34	(.65)
Effect size			.66		.70		.72			
Invented algorithm										
Girls	.32	(.70)	1.29	(1.56)	1.05	(.99)	1.21	(1.07)	1.63	(1.20)
Boys	.82	(1.08)	3.07*	(2.29)	2.77*	(1.89)	3.20*	(2.08)	2.66*	(1.51)
Effect size			.90		1.12		1.18		.75	
Standard algorithm										
Girls	.00	(.00)	.50	(1.16)	3.21	(2.23)	3.16	(1.82)	3.87*	(1.63)
Boys	.07	(.33)	.48	(1.17)	2.43	(1.81)	2.39	(1.87)	2.89	(1.24)
Effect size							.68			

Header note: *Mean Number of Responses (Standard Deviation)*

Note. N = 38 girls and 44 boys. Effect sizes of significant differences are based on pooled standard deviations. Problems differ across interview times due to increasing maturity of students.

*Two-tailed *t* test significant at .006 for the number facts and .005 for addition/subtraction.

[1]Not given in grade 1.

standard algorithm group on the extension problems. When we compared the number of extension problems solved correctly by the boys and the girls in the invented algorithm group, we found no gender differences. Also, those girls in the invented algorithm group solved significantly more extension problems than did girls in the standard algorithm group. These analyses suggest that using invented algorithms in the early grades seemed to provide a foundation for solving the extension problems in grade 3 for both boys and girls.

Table 3   Nonroutine and Extension Problems: Correctness by Gender

	Mean Number of Responses (Standard Deviation)				
	Grade 1	Grade 2		Grade 3	
Gender		Fall	Spring	Fall	Spring
Nonroutine[1]					
Number of items	2	2	3	—	3
Girls	1.26 (.89)	1.34 (.82)	1.89 (1.03)	—	1.63 (1.10)
Boys	1.36 (.84)	1.41 (.79)	2.07 (.97)	—	1.68 (.96)
Extension[2]					
Number of items				2	2
Girls				.50 (.76)	.82 (.83)
Boys				1.05* (.89)	1.23* (.83)
Effect size				.66	.49

Note. $N = 38$ girls and 44 boys. Effect sizes of significant differences are based on pooled standard deviations. Problems differ across interview times due to increasing maturity of students.

*Two-tailed *t* test significant at .05 level.

[1]Not given in fall grade 3.

[2]Given only in grade 3.

Table 4   Cumulative Percentages of Girls and Boys Who Use Invented Strategies

	Grade 1	Grade 2		Grade 3		
Gender		Fall	Spring	Fall	Spring	None
Addition						
Girls	18	47	58	66	79	21
Boys	41	80	89	95	95	5
Subtraction						
Girls	0	3	3	29	45	55
Boys	0	25	48	68	80	20

Note. The percentage of girls and boys using an addition or subtraction invented algorithm on problems that required regrouping during the given interview or in a previous interview.

$N = 38$ girls and 44 boys.

Conclusions

In summary, we found no gender differences in solving number fact, addition/subtraction, or nonroutine problems throughout the three years of the study. Each year, however, there were strong and consistent gender differences in the strategies used to solve problems, with girls tending to use more concrete strategies like modeling and counting and boys tending to use more abstract strategies that reflected conceptual understanding. At the end of the third grade, the girls used more standard algorithms than the boys. On the problems that required flexibility in extending one's procedures, boys were more successful than were girls. The ability to solve the extension problems in the third grade appears to be related to the use of invented algorithms in earlier grades, as both girls and boys who had used invented algorithms early were better able to solve the extension problems than those who had not.

Table 5 **Extension Problems: Correctness by Group**

Group	N	Mean Number Correct (Standard Deviation) Grade 3	
		Fall	Spring
Student group			
Invented algorithm group	53	1.13* (.86)	1.32* (.78)
Standard algorithm group	16	.19 (.54)	.44 (.73)
Effect size		1.19	1.15
Girls by student groups			
Invented algorithm group	18	.83* (.86)	1.17* (.79)
Standard algorithm group	14	.21 (.58)	.50 (.76)
Effect size		.83	.83
Invented algorithm group			
Girls	18	.83 (.86)	1.17 (.79)
Boys	35	1.29 (.83)	1.40 (.78)

Note. Based on two extension problems at each time period. Effect sizes of significant differences based on pooled standard deviations.

*Two-tailed *t* test significant at .05 level.

Notes

1. A derived-fact strategy requires relational knowledge about number facts. Children using derived facts use knowledge of a core of memorized facts to construct unknown facts. For example, a child might find 8 + 9 by saying that he or she knows that 8 + 8 = 16 and 8 + 9 is just 1 more or 17.

2. We use *invented algorithm* to identify strategies that involve place-value ideas. These invented algorithms are abstract procedures children construct to solve multidigit problems, and they generally lack the automatized quality that is associated with *algorithm*.

References

Belenky, M. F., Clinchy, B. M., Goldberger, N. R., & Tarule, J. M. (1986). *Women's ways of knowing.* New York: Basic Books.

Carpenter, T. P. (1985). Learning to add and subtract: An exercise in problem solving. In E. A. Silver (Ed.), *Teaching and learning mathematical problem solving: Multiple research perspectives* (pp. 17–40). Hillsdale, NJ: Erlbaum.

Carpenter, T. P., Fennema, E., & Franke. M. L. (1996). Cognitively guided instruction: A knowledge base for reform in primary mathematics instruction. *Elementary School Journal, 97,* 3–20.

Carpenter, T. P, Franke, M. L., Jacobs, V., Fennema, E., & Empson, S. B. (1998). A longitudinal study of invention and understanding in children's multidigit addition and subtraction. *Journal for Research in Mathematics Education, 29*(1), 3–20.

Carpenter, T. P., & Moser, J. M. (1984). The acquisition of addition and subtraction concepts in grades one through three. *Journal for Research in Mathematics Education, 15,* 179–202.

Carr, M., & Jessup, D. L. (1997). Gender differences in first grade mathematics strategy use: Social and metacognitive influences. *Journal of Educational Psychology, 98*(2), 318–328.

DeCorte, E., Greer, B., & Verschaffel, L. (1996). Mathematics teaching and learning. In D. C. Berliner & R. C. Calfee (Eds.), *Handbook of educational psychology* (pp. 491–549). New York: Macmillan.

Fennema, E., Carpenter, T. P., Franke, M. L., Levi, L., Jacobs, V. R., & Empson, S. B. (1996). A longitudinal study of learning to use children's thinking in mathematics instruction. *Journal for Research in Mathematics Education, 27*(4), 403–434.

Fuson, K. (1992). Research on whole number addition and subtraction. In D. Grouws (Ed.), *Handbook of research on mathematics teaching and learning* (pp. 243–275). New York: Macmillan.

Fuson, K. C., Wearne, D., Hiebert J., Human, P., Murray, H., Olivier, A., Carpenter, T. P., & Fennema, E. (1997). Children's conceptual structures for multidigit numbers and methods of multidigit addition and subtraction. *Journal for Research in Mathematics Education, 28*(2), 130–162.

Gallagher, A. M., & DeLisi, R. (1994). Gender differences in scholastic aptitude tests—Mathematics problem solving among high-ability students. *Journal of Educational Psychology, 86,* 204–211.

Gutstein, E., & Romberg, T. A. (1995). Teaching children to add and subtract. *Journal of Mathematical Behavior, 14,* 283–325.

Marascuilo, L. A., & Serlin, R. C. (1988). *Statistical methods for the social and behavioral sciences.* New York: W. H. Freeman and Company.

Nunes, T. (1992). Ethnomathematics and everyday cognition. In D. Grouws (Ed.), *Handbook of research on mathematics teaching and learning* (pp. 557–574). New York: Macmillan.

VanLehn, K. (1986). Arithmetic procedures are induced from examples. In J. Hiebert (Ed.), *Conceptual and procedural knowledge: The case of mathematics* (pp. 133–179). Hillsdale, NJ: Erlbaum.

FRAME the DEBATE

Form at end of book

WiseGuide Wrap-Up

The readings in this section focus on meeting students' needs. For the past quarter century, educators, parents, and other child advocates have argued about how best to educate students with special needs and have considered separate classes, partial inclusion as appropriate, and full inclusion.

Two other special needs populations—limited English proficiency students and gifted and talented students—are sometimes ignored as decisions are made about different categories of students.

The needs of female students are often overlooked as teachers try to provide all students with opportunities to learn. Equity and equality of opportunity are not the same.

R.E.A.L. Sites

This list provides a print preview of typical **Coursewise** R.E.A.L. sites. (There are over 100 such sites at the **Courselinks™** site.) The danger in printing URLs is that web sites can change overnight. As we went to press, these sites were functional using the URLs provided. If you come across one that isn't, please let us know via email to: webmaster@coursewise.com. Use your Passport to access the most current list of R.E.A.L. sites at the **Courselinks** site.

Site name: IDEA Partnership Projects

URL: http://www.ideapractices.org

Why is it R.E.A.L.? This web site, sponsored by the Council for Exceptional Children, includes the new regulations for implementing the Individuals with Disabilities Education Act (IDEA), as well as resources. Also included are constantly updated national satellite conferences and regional workshops. Links to related sites give answers to frequently asked questions; list books, videos, journals, and other resources; and provide accurate information and support for administrators implementing the IDEA regulations.

Key topics: IDEA regulations, IDEA resources

Try this: Click on "ideaquests." What questions are being asked related to minority students?

Site name: Renaissance Group

URL: http://www.uni.edu/coe/inclusion/index.html

Why is it R.E.A.L.? This site, asks and answers common questions about inclusion and gives basic guidelines for teaching in an inclusive classroom.

Key topic: inclusion

Try this: According to the site, what are some ways to prepare teachers for inclusion? How can students be prepared?

Site name: Special Education Inclusion

URL: http://www.weac.org/resource/june96/speced.htm

Why is it R.E.A.L.? This site, developed by the Wisconsin Education Association Council, asks and answers controversial questions about inclusion. It also provides definitions of such terms as *inclusion, full inclusion,* and the *regular education initiative*. The Individuals with Disabilities Education Act of 1990 (IDEA) and Section 504 of the Rehabilitation Act of 1973 are discussed.

Key topics: special education, inclusion, federal regulations

Try this: Provide a summary of recent legal action regarding inclusion. Do you anticipate there will be more court cases related to inclusion, or less? Why/why not?

Index

Note: Names and page numbers in **bold** type indicate authors and their articles; page numbers in *italics* indicate illustrations; page numbers followed by *t* indicate tables; page numbers followed by *n* indicate numbered notes.

H

habits, in character education, 72
Hagemann Elementary School, 50–51
Halford, Joan Montgomery, 98
Hammer, Rhonda, 239
Hansen, David, 90–97
Hardiman, Priscilla M., 54
Harris, William, 205, 207
health education standards, *137*
health services, in schools, 55, 57
high-stakes testing, 3, 131
Hill, Paul T., 3
hippocampus, 164
Hispanic students, school success of, 205, 209
history standards, *137*, 139
History Standards Project, 139
homosexuality, and character education, 84
honesty, educating for, 80–81
housing services, in schools, 55
human nature, negative views of, 67–68
human services. *See* social services
humor, 170, 171
hyper-general rubrics, 135

I

IDEA Partnership Projects web site, 253
Illinois, early bilingual education in, 207
immigrants, and bilingual education, 204–9
incentives, for teacher certification, 121
inclusion
    criticisms of, 200–202
    parent and school support for, 194–99
    web sites about, 253
Indiana University, teacher education reform at, 111–13
individualized education programs, 195, 198
individual needs. *See* special needs students; talents
Individuals with Disabilities Education Act, 253
indoctrination, 71
instruction
    accommodating brain research in, 166–67, 168–72
    accommodating multiple intelligences in, 176, 179–84
    culturally relevant, 225–33
    in morality (*see* character education)
    See also learning
instructional objectives, 134
instructional support teams, 194
integrated intelligence menus, 188–90
intelligence
    Gardner's definition of, 174 (*see also* multiple intelligences theory)
    traditional education's emphasis on, 162
    traditional view of, 175

interdisciplinary instruction, 180–81
Internet, 241, 242, 243
interpersonal intelligence, 177, 189
interpersonal learning style, 186, 187, 188, 189
intrapersonal intelligence, 177, 189
intrinsic motivation, 66–67
invented algorithms, 247, 249–50, 251*t*, 252*t*
IQ testing, 175, 204
Irwin-DeVitis, Linda, 90
Italian-born students, school success of, 204, 208

J

Jacobs, Victoria R., 246
James S. McDonnell Foundation web site, 191
Japan, education standards in, 129, 130, 138
Jefferson Center for Character Education, 67, 71
Jewish students, school success of, 204–5
job training, 55
journal writing, 171
Jung, Carl, 185–86
just communities, 15
justice, 79
juvenile probation services, 55

K

Kagan, Sharon L., 32
Kanze, Bruce, 92
Kellner, Douglas, 234
Kendall, John S., 136
Key School, 182
Kinder, Diane, 150
kinesthetic vocations, *188*
Kingston, Paul, 211
Kish, Cheryl K., 150
knowledge
    authentic assessment and, 159–60
    construction of, 166
Kohlberg, Lawrence, 73
Kohn, Alfie, 65
Kruse, Gary D., 164

L

Ladson-Billings, Gloria, 225–33
language
    and bilingual education, 203–9
    and cultural competence, 226
    foul, 79
    relation to values, 60
language arts standards, *137*, 139
laws
    about bilingual education, 206, 207
    about disabled students, 202, 253
    affecting school decentralization, 9

leadership groups, in character education, 82, 83
League of Value-Driven Schools, 83
learning
    biological basis for, 164–66
    brain research findings about, 162
    discussion and, 170
    reflective thinking and, 150–54
    role of emotions in, 169
    See also instruction
learning folios. *See* portfolios
learning styles
    overview of theory, 185–86
    relation to intelligences, 178, 187–90
leaving exams, 131
Lemoore High School web site, 253
lesson planning, 180
Levi, Linda W., 246
Levin, Benjamin, 13
Lewis, Jon, 240
Lewis, Karla C., 225
Lewis, Lionel, 211
licensing. *See* teacher certification and licensing
Lickona, Thomas, 78
Lieberman, Joyce M., 119
limbic system, 164
linguistic intelligence, 177, 188
literacy(ies)
    culturally relevant instruction in, 227–28
    multiple, 234–44
literature, teaching values from, 74
Lively, Kit, 101
logical-mathematical intelligence, 177, 188
Lombard, Thomas P., 194
Louisiana, early bilingual education in, 207
Luke, Allan, 238
Luke, Carmen, 238

M

Making Standards Matter, 1996, 140
Mandela, Nelson, 226
manners, 81
Marland Report, 211, 212
Marzano, Robert J., 136
master craft, 91
Masterman, Len, 238
mastery learning style, 186, 187, 188, 189
mathematics
    education in other countries, 129–30
    gender differences in thinking about, 246–52
    standards documents for, *137*, 138
McLaren, Peter, 238, 239
McREL, 141–43
media literacy
    defined, 234–35, 237
    in multicultural instruction, 235–41
    protectionist approach to, 239, 240

Frame the Debate
Review Form

Name _____ Date _____

Issue _____

1. Prior to reading about and discussing this issue, my personal beliefs were:

_____

_____

_____

_____

2. Describe the credentials and/or credibility of experts cited in each of the readings for this issue.

_____

_____

_____

_____

3. Summarize the main idea presented in each of the readings for this issue.

_____

_____

_____

_____

4. Summarize the facts that support each main idea.

_____

_____

_____

_____

5. Identify any opinions expressed.

_____

_____

_____

_____

_____

6. List any examples of bias or faulty reasoning.

_____

_____

_____

_____

_____

7. How does this issue correlate with material presented in class and/or in your textbook?

_____

_____

_____

_____

_____

8. Based on further consideration of this issue, my personal beliefs are now/still:

_____

_____

_____

_____

_____

COPY ME! Copy this form as needed. This form is also available at http://www.coursewise.com
Click on STAND!